BRADFORD
BORN AND BRED

Dedication

This book is dedicated to my late wife, Diana Mary Lister (1946–98)

BRADFORD
BORN AND BRED

Growing Up in the 1940s and '50s

Derek A.J. Lister

First published in the United Kingdom in 2008 by

Bank House Books

BIC House

1 Christopher Road

East Grinstead

West Sussex

RH19 3BT

British Library Cataloguing in Publication Data
A catalogue record for this book is available from the British Library

ISBN 9781904408413

Typesetting and origination by Bank House Books
Printed and bound by Lightning Source

Contents

Preface

Neither biography nor autobiography, this book is a catalogue of family events and observations taken from memory. My memories are simply recollections of life as seen through the eyes of a child, boy and teenager. I can remember wartime quite vividly and its immediate aftermath, although my clearest memories are of the late 1940s and '50s, a time when I lived with my mum, dad and brother in Listerhills, Bradford, and later in Wyke on the city outskirts.

The core of this book is autobiographical because most of the events I describe are as I saw them. But it is also a way of life experienced by many Bradford people born just before the Second World War, particularly those from a working-class background. I will show the highs and lows of family life, the sadness and sorrow, but also the happiness of having loving parents. Those children who lived through the 1940s and '50s will know what a remarkable experience it was, a time of not so long ago, but in many respects very different from today.

Although arranged in broad chronological order, this is not a story or continuous narrative, so the reader can pick any chapter at random.

In some of the early chapters my grandparents' mother, father, brother, family friends and childhood friends have small biographies, to help identify them all in later chapters.

As many of the mothers and fathers of our generation are no longer with us, I hope I reflect in some way what a lot they had to put up with! Most were children during the First World War, some losing fathers in that war and mothers in the flu epidemic of 1919. Most of our fathers went to war in the Second World War, or had other wartime occupations, and our mothers went through hardship, rationing and many other privations, and plainly just got on with it. We owe them a great debt.

The years covered are my first eighteen, 1938–56; from my schooldays, workplace and early rock 'n' roll years, to joining the army. Many names will be mentioned: people, places, streets, particularly from the area where I lived as a boy. Listerhills was just one of the many similar self-contained areas in and around Bradford.

I hope that this book will stimulate some thoughts in the minds of young parents and their children who are growing up in this very different world of the twenty-first century. Perhaps they have never known what enjoyment and enrichment can be found in a very simple family life. I hope, too, that it will stimulate memories and thoughts of the many people who lived through this era.

I have tried to avoid making statements that compare the past to the present, whether complimentary or not.

Memory is fallible, space is limited, and in the text I have referred to friends and acquaintances by name. If I have missed out anyone, spelt a name wrong or got a wrong date or time I apologise. It is very important that I point out that everything mentioned here is relevant to its time, and this includes words, thoughts and descriptions. Any offence is unintentional.

These are my memories. May they entertain!

Acknowledgements

To the many people who have contributed in some way to make this book possible: thank you all.

Sandra Parish, my partner and typist, who has given me her utmost support, with improving my original scripts and putting them in some semblance of the Queen's English creating, I hope, something readable. Special thanks for her patience throughout my trials and tribulations.

Bob Duckett, ex-Bradford Libraries senior librarian, for his support and enthusiasm, and his kindness in sub-editing each chapter throughout the last eighteen months. He is now known affectionately as 'the headmaster' for giving me days of worry and trepidation while I waited for the return of each chapter, each one given marks out of ten.

Reuben Davison deserves very special praise, and a huge sum of money, for his guidance and wealth of knowledge of the publishing industry, and for his invaluable help not only with the text but with the collation of the photographs. Many thanks to publishing consultant, great friend and part-time chauffeur. See Reuben's website: www.thewritechoice.org.uk.

My appreciation also to my publisher and editor Simon Fletcher for his constructive help and advice.

Graham Herrington ('the boy with the hoop') of Flat 3a, Oak Lane Studios, Manningham, Bradford, for additional local photographs.

Very special thanks to my good friend Margaret Wood, who was involved with the initial typing and organising of many of the original chapters. Without her support and patience this book would probably have been put on hold.

Harry Gration, television presenter. My special thanks to Harry for his kindness in writing the foreword to this book.

Richard Coatesworth for his kind help in making sure that my computer and printer was always up to standard.

Thanks to Ian Naylor for the photograph of his late father, the well-respected Detective Sergeant John Naylor, CID, Bradford City Police.

Darren Thomas: very special thanks for his help and kindness in supplying me with many outstanding quality photographs from the Kobal Collection Ltd. See www.picture-desk.com.

Sir Ken Morrison CBE for his help regarding the family history and kind permission to use photographs of Morrison's early shop premises.

Paul Hanson. Some of the photographs of the choir are from my own collection, but the late Paul Hanson took these photographs.

Colin Sutton, Bradford and Shipley cinemas historian, for his kind help and permission to use editorial from his archives of the New Victoria cinema and others on his website, www.kingsdr.demon.co.uk.

Colin (C.G.) Wilson and Mark Wilson of the West Yorkshire Road Car Online Reunion Website, www.wyrc.co.uk . My thanks for their permission to use the photograph of the Leeds bus at Chester Street bus station.

Councillor and ex-Lord Mayor of Bradford John Stanley King: special thanks for his help, thanks to his exceptional knowledge of the Bradford Transport system, and the use of photographs and postcards from his archives.

Graham Hall: my very special thanks to this gentleman for his kind permission to use postcards from his superb archives.

The staff at Bradford Reference Library for their help and support on my many visits for research, and also for the use of photographs from the archives. Very special thanks to Susan Caton, Carol Greenwood and all of the staff, for whom as usual nothing was too much trouble.

ACKNOWLEDGEMENTS

Perry Austin-Clarke, editor of the *Bradford Telegraph and Argus*. My special thanks for his kind permission to use photographs of the Bradford Floods of 1947, Bradford libraries and the Nignog Club logo.

John Hockney, my old friend, for supplying of a photograph of himself as a teenager when we worked together at the Kirkgate branch of Burton's in the 1950s.

Mrs B. Parry (wife of the late Bernard Parry): special thanks for her kind permission to use extracts from the book of the 150th anniversary of St Patrick's Church and School, Westgate, Bradford (1854–2004).

To the family of the late John Tindall, special thanks for their kindness in supplying me with a photograph of John, my St Luke's Hospital friend and companion in 1949.

Richard Foulke, BEM and his wife Pam for their very professional study of my family name, and for providing the interesting family tree.

Richard Clark, the well-known authority on capital punishment, for his kind permission to use extracts from his website, www.richard.clark32.btinternet. co.uk.

Zoe Barker of Wm Morrison's PR department for her kind help with research from the Wm Morrison archives.

Special thanks to my neighbour of yesteryear, John Nicholl, for supplying me with steam engine details from his excellent website about Low Moor Iron Works (http://www.ngfl.ac.uk/wards/lowmoorschool/history/lowmoor/Ironworks.html)

Mrs Irene Robinson (née Stewart). Special thanks to a lovely former Legrams Street neighbour for her kindness and enthusiasm shown to me when I was writing the early chapters of this book.

Mrs Kathleen Crow and Mrs Joyce Neill for their early letters of encouragement.

Miss Hilda Bolton, my former teacher at St Patrick's Infants' School (1943–45) for supplying me with a photograph that included some of my other former teachers, and filling in gaps of so long ago!

Nick Brook, son of the late Leo Brook, my former teacher at St Patrick's School, for supplying a photograph of his father, the pupils' favourite teacher.

W. Firth, J. Copland, Jack Booth, Robert F. Mack, Syd Dearnley, House of Fraser and the *Lancastria* Association for the use of their photographs.

Ben Coatesworth, aged five (my best mate and grandson) for calming me down on our long walks in the park.

Foreword
Harry Gration, Television Presenter

Reading Derek's book took me back instantly to my childhood in Bradford.

Born in St Luke's Hospital, I spent my early years in Southfield Lane, Kingsdale Crescent, Little Horton Lane and finally Toller Lane.

My grandad was a trolley bus driver and my dad was manager of Boots the Chemist in Darley Street. All of this in the '50s, so Derek's recollections have ignited my wonderful childhood memories.

The insight Derek gives us into the detail of Bradford's history in his first eighteen years is astonishing.

It is of course an affectionate ride through this great city's history, but the events that affected my parents and grandparents are not avoided. The Second World War and the effects it had on the social climate are brought to life.

I love Derek's 'no nonsense' style of narrative. It is to the point, all 137,000 words of it.

Read it. You will be transported back in time as I was.

Harry Gration

Chapter 1
My Family

Thomas Lister, my Grandfather (1878–1957)

On Father's Day I received a card from my grandson Ben, appropriately entitled 'Groovy Grandad'. This had me thinking about my grandad Tom, and the saying 'truth is stranger than fiction'.

It seems most grandads can, and do, exaggerate the past to their

Tom was involved in the Bradford tram accident at the bottom of Church Bank in 1907. His friend Matthew Hill, whom he was with, was injured and listed in the newspaper as a casualty. *(Author's collection)*

1

This photograph epitomised my grandfather, who I thought looked like the famous film star Sir C. Aubrey Smith. *(Author's collection)*

Buffalo Bill Cody, whom my grandfather met when his circus visited Bradford in 1903. (*Wikipedia*)

grandchildren, more out of love and affection than to mislead. My grandson (five years old) gives me a curious look when I tell him he should be working, and that when I was just a little older than him I was being pushed up chimneys to clean them!

Thomas Lister was born and lived at 252 Ripon Street off Otley Road, Bradford, in 1878. His parents were from Askrigg in North Yorkshire. Nothing much is known about his education, but on leaving school he took up painting and decorating like his father.

Later he joined the railways in Bradford and became a signalman at City Road Goods Depot. It was during my early days with him that he used to tell me stories of certain events in his life, particularly about his friend Buffalo Bill. I was always intrigued by this: was it true? At the house in Fenton Street, Princeville, where he and my grandmother lived, was a photograph that showed Buffalo Bill with his fringed buckskins, a smile on his face and gauntlet gloves in one hand, the other hand shaking Grandad's hand.

He retired from the railways in 1937 with a small pension. This he supplemented by bill posting for the Empress Picture House in Princeville, the cinema he used to take me to many times with his free pass in the 1940s and '50s. On Sundays I remember he always shaved with a cut-throat razor and dressed in a three-piece suit, winged collar and billycock hat. Then he was off to the service at Eastbrook Methodist Hall.

Other stories included the Bradford City cup win that he attended at Old Trafford in 1911, and the two days he spent in London to celebrate and watch Queen Victoria's Diamond Jubilee (1897) with his best pal Stanley Travis. Stanley was later to die of enteric fever while serving in the Boer War in South Africa. Grandad was also a passenger in the early morning Church Bank tramway crash in July 1907. He was uninjured, although a friend whom he was with, Matthew Hill, also from Ripon Street, was treated for shock, and his name shown on the list of the fourteen casualties in the *Bradford Telegraph*. Thomas married my grandmother, Lilian Thompson, the same year at St Andrew's Church, Listerhills.

Later in life he was the image of that famous English gentleman Hollywood actor, Sir C. Aubrey Smith. I can still smell the aroma of his pipe tobacco, Players Medium Navy Cut, a slice of which I once chewed. I had seen so many cowboys in films chew tobacco that I thought it would taste nice, like liquorice; it didn't!

Grandad Tom passed away in 1957. I missed the funeral as I was serving with the army in Aden at the time. On my return I visited my grandma, who had moved to Allerton, and asked her the story behind the Buffalo Bill photograph.

The Buffalo Bill Circus came to Bradford in 1903; the tent was pitched at Thornbury. However, there were severe storms on the Monday and the show on Tuesday had to be cancelled. The circus used three trains, which took a lot of organising, and it appears that Tom, although only twenty-five and without much experience, in his capacity as a young signalman worked out a delivery itinerary that helped the timings of the show. Buffalo Bill's attention was drawn to this, and he arranged for my grandad and his girlfriend (later my grandmother) to see the show. Later they were both introduced to the great man, and the photograph was taken. Two copies were later received in the post. So that was the story.

I miss my grandad, but I know for certain that I held the hand that shook the hand of Buffalo Bill.

Lilian Lister, my Grandmother (1888–1967)

My dad's mother was a kind of hypochondriac. The doctor made regular calls at the house, but Mum thought most of her illnesses were 'put on'. This meant that for many years my grandfather did most of the shopping and the chores with the help of their neighbour, Mr Buxton.

Sometimes, especially when Mum was ill or in hospital, I stayed overnight at my grandparents'. I slept in a small camp bed next to my grandmother, who slept in a very large bed. Her bedroom was heavily scented with lavender and face powder. Sometimes I rooted in the drawers, which were lined with old newspapers from the early 1900s, covered in powder and mixed up with many handkerchiefs and paste jewellery. Grandfather slept in the small bedroom. At times I sneaked into the large unused attic, which was always cold and miserable. This contained bits of old furniture, lino, and boxes of papers, envelopes and old bills. In one corner, behind a large Victorian dressing table, was an assortment of old framed oil paintings. These were of no particular interest to me, but years later I found out they had been painted by my great-grandfather, another Thomas Lister. Like the photograph of my grandfather with Buffalo Bill, the oil paintings have disappeared.

Staying overnight was fine in the summer, but in the winter it was creepy and I never looked forward to going to bed. At bedtime I was given a candleholder, which was lit with a long taper from the fire, and was ushered up the stone steps on my own. The candlelight flickered in the draught from under

My grandmother at Blackpool, her favourite holiday resort. *(Author's collection)*

the attic door, casting long shadows on the walls and the high ceiling. I prayed that the candle would not blow out and I used to think, as I climbed those stairs, of the film *The Four Feathers*, when a young Harry Faversham climbed a large wooden staircase. He also had a candle, but his flickered on old family portraits. The cold stone steps I climbed were just as eerie.

I was always well looked after on these overnight stays, although I used to think Grandmother was glad when I returned home and she could go back to being waited on by Grandfather.

Lilian was born the eldest of four children in Heap Street, Bradford, in 1888. Her father, Frederick Benjamin Thompson, was an outfitter's salesman, and her mother, Helena Kitchenman, was just seventeen when she married Frederick, aged twenty, in 1886. My grandmother married Thomas Lister in 1907, and they lived in Listerhills, and later in Princeville, for most of their lives. For a few years she worked at Sharps the Printers, on Bingley Road, as a proofreader. Being constantly ill, she retired from working in her thirties.

I only ever saw one photograph of Grandmother when she was young. This was kept in the top drawer of the sideboard. She was aged sixteen at the time, slim, and wearing a long white fitted Edwardian dress. Her long black hair was in ringlets, and she was the image of the silent film star Lillian Gish. I have never forgotten how beautiful she looked on that photograph, and when she was older she still looked the double of the then ageing Lillian Gish.

Like Listerhills, Princeville was mostly a conglomerate of back-to-back houses. Tucked in between Ireton and Lawrence Streets was 41 Fenton Street, the home of my grandparents. At the rear of the house was no. 37, where Jim Buxton lived. Like my grandfather, he was also retired as a signalman from the railway. His wife Eva, who died in 1934, had been a friend of my grandmother's. Over the years he spent lots of time with my grandparents helping out, almost like a lodger but still living in his house at the rear. He was a nice man, whose greeting of 'Hello, laddie' was a change to this young boy. As I've mentioned, Jim was therefore on hand to help look after my grandmother.

I hardly ever missed my Sunday visits to see Grandmother, and was given the princely sum of sixpence well into my teens. She always wore the same floral dresses with the fragrance of lavender water and mothballs. Around her neck she wore the same cut glass beaded necklace which always looked nice to me, not knowing at the time the differences between precious stones or glass. I believe that she loved me in her way, but she was never affectionate like my grandfather, and I do not remember many hugs or kisses, but nevertheless I loved her. When Grandfather died in 1957 she continued to cope quite well with the help of Mr Buxton, although by then he was in his late seventies.

It was quite a surprise when my grandmother and Jim Buxton married at the Bradford Register Office in 1960; it was a case of two could live as cheaply as one. After the marriage Mr Buxton sold his house at no. 37 and moved in with his new wife. Sadly, six years later he died, followed by my grandmother's death a year later in 1967. Eva Buxton, Jim Buxton and my grandparents share the same grave in Scholemore Cemetery in Lidget Green.

Harold Lister, my Father (1909–95)
My father was born on 30 October 1909 at the salubrious address of 184 Gashouse Row, Listerhills Road. An only child, he lived there with his parents Lilian and Thomas. The name Gashouse Row derived from the Bradford

Harold Lister (1909–95).
(Author's collection)

Corporation Gasworks that was situated in a large area at the rear of the houses.

The family later moved to Fieldhead Street where my dad attended both St Andrew's Infants' and Boys' Schools. He was quite good at maths and his beautiful hand-writing was exceptional. One incident at the school caused a medical problem. One day a boy threw an ink pen into the air, and when my dad looked up the pen penetrated his eyeball. It was touch and go if he would lose his sight, but his eye healed on its own. He always said he was in good company with his namesake King Harold, referring to the arrow in the king's eye at the battle of Hastings in 1066 – although he had a much happier ending than the king.

One of Harold's hobbies was playing football in the Bradford League, where it was noted that he had some skills that could be developed. He was also a drummer with the band of the local Boys' Brigade in Listerhills. He enjoyed Sundays after church service, when the band played and parade up and down Listerhills Road and Legrams Lane, winding through the local streets, my dad resplendent in his best suit, dark navy pillbox hat, white belt and shoulder strap, white gloves and polished side drum.

Harold left school aged fourteen and started work in the woollen mill of John Smith & Sons, Fieldhead Mills, Preston Street. His first job was that of a bobbin-ligger: it was usual to start at the very bottom of the ladder, and this was considered a menial task for boys starting work in the mills. When he was aged sixteen the management saw his potential and offered him a five year 'overlooker' apprenticeship. He accepted, and became a winding overlooker. The overlooker was in charge of a section, overlooking the transfer of yarn to the bobbins. This meant that over the next five years he spent some time learning this trade at Bradford Technical College.

Harold was still playing football when asked by an Accrington Stanley scout (the club was then in Division Three North) who had seen him playing in the Bradford League if he would like a trial. He was quite interested, although he didn't wish this to come between him and his career. At the same time he had been going out with my mum, who met him on Saturday teatimes in Bradford after he had played his match; he was always late! The showdown came one Saturday when my mum gave him an ultimatum – that it was either football or her! The answer was Sophia.

Harold was still living at home in 1930 with his parents, then at 56 Listerhills Road, when he finished his apprenticeship. Now a winding overlooker with job security, he asked my mum if she would marry him. On Boxing Day in 1930 they were married at St Patrick's Church, Westgate. He was twenty-one and she was eighteen.

Vida Lister, my Mother (1911–97)

My mother, Sophia Cooper, was born on 28 September 1911 in South Bank, Middlesbrough, and was always called Vida after an earlier Cooper who had died in infancy. She was the eldest of four brothers and four sisters in a Catholic family, all of whom attended St Peter's Roman Catholic School in South Bank.

Her mother's family, the Lenaghans, were from Crossmaglen in Northern Ireland, and they came to England in the 1880s. Her grandmother had six sons serving in the First World War, a fact recorded in the local newspaper, with the usual consequences. One, Thomas, was killed. Ironically he had been booked on the *Titanic* on its maiden voyage in 1912, and missed his rail connection to Southampton. Another son (Peter) lost an arm (he played professional football for Bristol City), and Michael was gassed.

Mum's father's family (the Coopers) came to Middlesbrough in 1882 from the lovely village of Barton Bendish in Norfolk.

Mum was brought up in a happy family with a life-long love for her brothers and sisters, although being the oldest was occasionally a problem in later life when family problems were brought to her to be sorted out.

Her constant worry was tuberculosis. Some of the older generation on her mother's side had died of this disease, and it was to be a blight again over the years when she lost her mother at the age of thirty-five, her brother John aged twenty, sister Roseanne at twenty-five (John and Roseanne were twins) and

Sophia ('Vida') Lister. *(Author's collection)*

brother George aged thirty. So the worry continued into my brother's and my young life, when we had our necks buttoned up, scarves on and made to wear a cap in all weathers. We never understood until much later in life the significance of our mother's actions.

Aged fourteen, she and her cousin Jessie arrived in Bradford to go into domestic service. The papers of the time show many positions like this on offer. Her first year was spent at a large house in Legrams Lane where she was supervised by the cook. Her many tasks included scrubbing floors and the stairs, sweeping carpets, cleaning out the fireplaces, lighting fires, bringing coal from the cellars and filling the coal scuttles. The Victorian era had just passed, but in this world nothing had changed. She was paid 15*s* a week, of which 12*s* 6*d* was sent home. She shared a room with the other girls.

Vida left this secure position. Why? Her employers left the odd sixpence under the carpet or on the stairs for it to be found and handed in. If not handed in, and surely it would be found in the cleaning, where was it? Who stole it? She didn't like this lack of trust; it was time to move on.

Next, in a house on City Road, her employer was an elderly man. She was paid 18*s* per week to work with a middle-aged housekeeper. She always said it was a beautiful house, all antiques, and the usual work as in her previous employment. The owner was a retired mill owner, the mill not being far from City Road. However, even as a fifteen year old she was not naïve, and she began to feel uncomfortable in her employer's company. Time to move again!

Nearly sixteen found her in a nice Victorian house in Cecil Avenue as part of a small staff to look after an old retired couple who treated her like a granddaughter. For once, in domestic service, she was happy, and also happy in the knowledge she was helping her parents with the money she was sending home. This lasted for twelve months, but when the old lady died her husband moved to Cornwall.

Now aged seventeen, a change in career was required, so my mum joined the many other girls of her age working in one of the mills in Bradford, namely John Smith's Textiles in Preston Street, in the weaving shed. While there she lodged with a lady called Ma Rouse in Marion Street at the rear of John Smith's. It was a knocked through back-to-back house with accommodation (three in each room) for six girls. She always spoke with affection of Ma Rouse and the girls, some of whom she was still in contact with in her seventies and eighties.

Ma Rouse's son had been in the 6th West Yorkshire Regiment in the First World War with Corporal Meekosha, the Victoria Cross winner. He often called, and everyone would go to the pictures or dancing.

It was at John Smith's Mill she met my dad.

Lawrence Lister, my Brother (1932–)

Lawrence was born on 2 June 1932 at 56 Listerhills Road, where earlier our dad had been living with his parents. He attended St Patrick's Infants' School, and when the family moved to Walden Drive on the Howarth Road estate he went to Howarth Road Infants' School. The family finally moved in 1939 back to Listerhills, this time to Legrams Street from where he returned to St Patrick's, this time to the boys' school.

Being the first grandchild of my mum's parents, he was a great favourite not only to them but to the many aunts and uncles in Middlesbrough. To my Auntie Cassie he was very special and she always referred to him as a 'little old man', he being quite independent with a shock of blonde hair, giving an almost saintly look; but at times he could be quite a handful.

Lawrence Lister. *(Author's collection)*

I don't know what his reaction was when I was born in 1938 as he was only six; but when the time came that he had to share a bed with me I don't think he was overjoyed, especially during the war years in a freezing bedroom.

At St Patrick's Boys' School most of the female teachers took a liking to him, especially Miss Veronica Worsley and Miss Nugent, and also the headmistress, Sister Christine. They always enquired about him after he had left school to study for the priesthood.

Lawrence's boyhood friends were quite an assortment of working-class boys with good family ties; however, he was wary of some! Among his friends were Roy Stewart (whose sister Irene was quite the bonniest girl in the area), Alan Creswell, Ernest Duckworth, Bill Tolley, Maurice Barber, Peter Ringrose and George Longbottom, most of whom lived in or around our street. Like most boys he sometimes fell out with his friends. One time he and I were cornered by five of those named in Lucy's front yard, our neighbour at the front. They let me go, and I was soon at our front door telling Mum that Lawrence was being bashed. He wasn't, but my mum soon scattered them with her favourite weapon, the yard brush. The next day they were all friends again.

I think he put up with me quite well, especially when I told tales on him or dawdled on the way to school. He even let me help him with his newspaper round, which he did for Craig's Newsagents on Legrams Terrace. That was until I started to put the papers through the wrong letter boxes (on purpose). As he said to our mother, 'He's messing'. Messing I was, so his 'help' was sacked.

One of Lawrence's favourite film stars was Dorothy Lamour, so much so that he somehow found an address in some magazine and wrote a letter to her. This was in wartime. In 1944 a letter duly arrived with an American postmark. Inside was a lovely photograph autographed by Dorothy Lamour.

He only took me to the pictures twice, once to see Laurel and Hardy at the Empress, and to the Tatler at the bottom of Thornton Road in the town centre, close to Town Hall Square. We went to the Tatler on the Tuesday; on the Wednesday it caught fire, closed, and never opened as a cinema again. Mum enquired (jokingly) if I had been 'messing', and looked sternly at me as the red glow of the fire could be seen above the houses.

In August 1945 Lawrence was the bringer of good tidings, running down the passage and shouting 'the Japs have surrendered'; and so they had. I was seven and he was thirteen. The next month, September 1945, he had left home, to become a pupil at Ushaw College, Durham, to train for the priesthood.

So it was actually only in my childhood years that I knew my brother, although I did get to visit him many times at the college; and there were the summer holidays when we went on holidays and daytrips together as a family. It was then that I appreciated it was nice having a brother again.

Lawrence was ordained as a Roman Catholic priest at St Anne's Cathedral, Leeds, on 19 July 1959. He served as a curate in Halifax (St Mary's), Beeston (St

Anthony's) and in Sheffield (St Theresa's). As the parish priest he served in Queensbury (St Theresa's), Leeds (St Urban's), Pontefract (St Joseph's) and finally back in Bradford (St Cuthbert's, Heaton). He retired in 2006.

The envelope sent from Beverley Hills to Legrams Street, in which Lawrence received a Dorothy Lamour glamour picture in 1944. *(Author's collection)*

Chapter 2
Back to Back

I was born at 116 Walden Drive off Haworth Road on 2 May 1938, delivered by a well-known midwife of the time, Nurse Bradbury. A few weeks later I was christened at First Martyrs (the round church) at Heaton. Why we moved I will never know, as we left a three-bedroomed house with a bathroom. Mum said some years later that it was to be near my dad's work, John Smith's textile mill in Preston Street. I was just over a year old when the move came. War had been declared, the phoney war was taking place, and a new family era dawned.

For the move Dad had borrowed a large handcart, and he made six journeys over two days to move all our belongings and household goods from Haworth Road to Listerhills, a walk of nearly 3 miles each way. Our new house had stone floors, no hot water, no bathroom, and was cold and draughty. I wasn't aware at the time of the culture shock to my parents. At my age I went along with the changes, unimpressed, but the sixteen years I lived there were some of the happiest days of my life.

Our New House
The new address was 30 Legrams Street, and it was a small back-to-back house built in about 1870 in an area known as Listerhills, 2 miles from the city centre. All the streets were cobbled around the rows and rows of back-to-back houses. The pavements were solid Yorkshire stone, all sizes, like gigantic jigsaw puzzles. Our house was down a passage at the rear. In the central area was a double midden, the middle section for dustbins, and two toilets each side for front and back residents. In front of the house was a small garden with, situated in the corner, a newly built red-brick and concrete roofed air-raid shelter. Overlooking all this, near the toilets, was a large gas lamp, which was no comfort for the six years of war as the gas was cut off, owing to black-out regulations.

The house consisted of four rooms, two up and two down. Downstairs was a small living room, on to which the front door gave directly, and an even smaller scullery with access to a cellar. When we moved out in 1955 the same bulb was being used in the cellar as in 1939. The two bedrooms upstairs were the same sizes as the scullery and living room, one larger than the other.

Our living room had a large double sash window, which was not level and dropped about 4 inches. The floor consisted of large slabs of uneven Yorkshire stone covered in lino. The fireplace was an original Yorkshire range, finished in black lead, consisting of a water boiler with a small tap, a large oven, and two pull-down ledges for placing kettles and pans over the fire grate. The height of Victorian luxury, *circa* 1870! It supplied the heating and the hot water for the house. The open fire was the centre of the household, the focal point around which we would gather. We watched with fascination as the flames danced and flickered, emitting gases that hissed out like a Bunsen burner. As we contemplated the glowing coals we could see among them many familiar faces or scenery. We held out our hands to welcome the warmth and comfort it radiated, while the front of women's bare legs became mottled from the heat.

After the war the very latest brown and cream fireplace, purchased from Mollett's, took the place of our wonderful Yorkshire range. When the range was taken out it made the room appear larger, but less at the expense of lots of character. The tiled fireplace industry was at its height at this time, and it was a time when antique shops and knockers did well with large assortments of brass candlesticks, ornaments and other items: they were bought cheaply as there was no room to display them on the new fireplaces.

We filled the tin bath for our Friday bath-night ritual from the range's hot water boiler. The galvanised tin-bath, about 6 feet long, was taken from the small scullery where it hung from a small hook on the wall and was placed in front of the fire. When the water cooled, pans of water which had been boiled on the oven rings, and occasionally from the copper boiler in the scullery, were added. In those days before central heating, or any other source of warmth, and with the lino-covered floor, you could be right next to the coal fire in the tin bath and be hot on one side and freezing on the other.

At the right-hand side of the fireplace were the original built-in cupboards and, below, six large drawers.

Only Lawrence and I were bathed on Friday nights. My parents, I presume, used the bath at more discreet times; I never asked. Mum only ever used our range for the bathwater, while its oven was useful to warm our pyjamas before bedtime. For baking and cooking she used an old-fashioned gas oven in the scullery: its four gas rings and oven always seemed to be lit for some purpose or other. This oven would even serve as a heater in the cold weather. The scullery was really quite small and was painted green and cream, as was the kitchen cabinet we bought later; this was fitted at the front with wire mesh for ventilation to help preserve food. Nobody I knew had a fridge.

Gas was paid for through a penny slot gas meter, a permanent fixture at the top of the cellar-head, with the electricity meter by its side. It was always wise to have spare shillings on hand for this latter: a sudden plunge into darkness brought forth cries of dismay until relief came and the meter was replenished. One of the many jobs delegated to me was to keep an eye on the electric meter clock, which clicked and spun, so as to be aware of an imminent black-out. The only appliances other than the lights for which electricity was used were the wireless, electric kettle, my mum's iron and an old pre-war Belling Empire bar-type fire. With a cast-iron body, this was mainly used upstairs when someone was ill in bed: I always found its warm glow a comfort during illness and cold winter nights. A few years later a gas-miser (water heater) was placed over the sink. It was as if the wheel had been discovered in the Lister household.

Our main source of fuel was coal, and the coalman Mr North visited with his horse and cart once a fortnight. Each delivery was two sacks. Mr North lifted each dirty sack on to his back, carried it through the passage to the cellar grate in the wall, stooped over the grate and let the coal pour out from over his shoulder. Mum was generally on hand to check the bags, to see that not too much slack was included. The best type of coal was 'shiny cobs', and it was my job to separate these from the slack in the cellar. Slack was basically coaldust, which I shovelled into a separate heap so we could use it later, mixed with water, to bank up the fire at night if we went out. One poke when we returned home and the fire erupted into flames. I never liked being down in the cellar as it was cold, damp and smelt of whitewash. There were also grey webs in the dark corners, where monstrous spiders lived. I never lingered when sorting out the coal and always checked the electricity meter beforehand. No way did I want to be in the cellar when the light went out. The only item apart from coal stored here was a cobbler's last, which my dad used to put metal 'segs' in our shoes so they lasted longer; we used to kick the ground with them to make sparks.

The living room furniture was plain and simple with a small polished drop-leaf table with four chairs to match, and a 1930s-style two-seater settee with two matching chairs. All these fitted snugly into the small room. The wallpaper was always bright, generally with floral designs to make the room light and cheerful. This was changed every two years because the gases from the fire and soot from the chimney soon discoloured it. Wallpaper was always purchased at Willey's, the popular wallpaper shop in Bradford. A large square of 'lincruster' was on the wall by the door; this was a precaution in case people's wet clothes rubbed the wall when they entered the house. Around the walls were family photographs and holy pictures, and on the mantelpiece a clock and two brass candlesticks. A chrome biscuit barrel, won in a cycle race by my dad some years earlier, was on the centre of the table under the window that was next to the wireless perched on a stand. Mum kept the house spotless. I loved it. It was home!

Ruling the Roost

With regard to discipline at 30 Legrams Street and beyond, the person who ruled the roost was my mum. It has to be said that she was quick tempered and didn't suffer fools gladly. These fools included my dad, Lawrence, me, all our relations, neighbours, and any stranger who happened to be in the wrong place at the wrong time, or give her a funny look. She was a feisty lady, but fair. Throughout my formative years I was never frightened of her, only wary, having had many confrontations with her. Although I got the odd smack on the behind, or legs, it was her look that hypnotised me into abject obedience. Her shout could be sharp and loud, and she controlled me with a single word, or a threat. One that always succeeded was threatening to send me to Linton Camp. This was a place near Grassington where orphans or children from poor families were sent for a holiday. I was under the impression that it was similar to Pleasure Island from the film *Pinocchio*, the island where naughty children were sent. Children thought that going to Pleasure Island was a reward for being naughty – that is, until their ears grew into donkey's ears and they developed a donkey's face. Then a tail grew, and the naughty child was transformed into a donkey. One day, aged five, I had been threatened with Linton Camp; I don't remember why, but it must have been serious. Ten minutes after the threat I was standing on my own outside in the passage, fully dressed, my raincoat buttoned up, a scarf around my neck and a cap on my head. It was raining, and I held a small suitcase containing my clothes. Large tears rolled down my cheeks as I waited for my mum to take me on the journey to the dreaded Pleasure Island. Then, down the passage came my Auntie Margaret. 'What's the matter?' she asked. 'I'm off to Pleasure Island,' I replied, gulping and crying. She took me by the hand and into the house where my mum was also crying. She picked me up and cuddled me; I think she may have thought she had gone a little too far. Five minutes later my case unpacked and I was playing with my toys. It was the only time I got close to that visit to Pleasure Island, although the threat was still administered from time to time. I always said it was my Auntie Margaret who saved me that day, and it was a subject of conversation for many years.

It was my dad who used to take the brunt of Mum's temper. Even with an impeccable war record he was quite placid and saw the good in everyone. After seeing the film *Les Miserables* he began to quote a line, 'It is better to give than receive', but Vida soon put that rebellion down.

My dad was no handyman but even the most menial tasks, repairs or maintenance had to be paid for. One time he leaded the outside windows of our back-to-back house in Legrams Street, and didn't make a bad job of them. But the accolade given to him by my mum for his work was withdrawn when he put the large wooden ladders he had been using through the front room windows. I disappeared!

One Saturday morning Dad was moving the upright piano in the front room for some reason, without first moving the two large holy statues placed on top of it on either side. There was a loud crash as the statues, one of the Sacred Heart and the other of Our Lady, fell to the stone floor in a thousand pieces. I was in bed at the time, heard the crash, put the earphones of my crystal set on, and pulled the sheets over my head. I had quite a long lie-in that Saturday morning.

My dad never shouted or smacked either Lawrence or me, although once he came close to it with dire consequences for him. One Wednesday evening, aged about ten, I was lying on the settee reading a comic. It being Wednesday, my mum had gone to the Union of Catholic Mothers meeting. The kitchen buffet leg had been loose for some time, so my dad decided to repair it with glue. He knelt on the rug close to the fireplace and partially covered the nice white tabbed rug with a small newspaper. All of a sudden the glue was knocked over, missed the newspaper and spilled on to the rug. I laughed, and it was the first and only time I saw his temper. 'Dash it, and you would laugh,' he said, followed by a very small tap on my leg. 'I'll tell my mum when she comes home that you've hit me,' I shouted. 'Tell her,' he replied. At nine o'clock my mum arrived home and before she had time to take her coat off I said, 'Dad spilled glue on the rug and hit me.' 'Don't you hit him,' she said. 'If there's any hitting to do I will do it.' I could still hear her as I slipped quietly up to bed, away from the one-sided altercation taking place below. It wasn't that I was a spoiled child; I only told on him because what had occurred was unique.

Dad never drank or smoked, and I never heard any bad language from him. His popular utterances were 'dash it' and 'like Billy-o'. If I asked where my mum was one of his favourite responses was, 'She's run off with a black man.' He called anyone who was at fault for anything 'a flat-cake'. He was a lovely father.

One thing about my mum, she would always back us if we were within our rights. It was like having Caesar's Praetorian Guard in reserve. There was a good example of this when my dad was having problems with his manager, Cleonard Gould, at his place of work. They had never really got on – and my dad used to say that Gould had never forgiven him for catching him out when he was batting in a cricket match for John Smith's at Bingley Road cricket field. My dad was a good overlooker, always well liked with his workers – and my mum said perhaps it was because he was so popular that things had come to a head. I was home from school one lunchtime, and Dad and Mum were discussing Gould's latest confrontation. After a while my mum just said one word. 'Chuck.' I saw the look of relief on his face, as if that was what he had been wishing for; but like most fathers at that time he had a responsibility to his wife and children to keep his employment. The next day Dad gave notice. Gould was shocked, and asked him to stay. But my mum had helped make the decision and there was no going back. Cleonard Gould gave him a good reference, but what else could he do after twenty-six years' loyal service. A few days later my dad was working for Stroud, Riley Co. Ltd, Worsted Spinners, at Oswin Mills, Bolton Woods. There was no pressure with this company and he had a little more money, but most of all he was happy.

Through a whim, word, or look, Vida defended herself and her family to the end. It was she who kept us disciplined, well mannered and eager to please. Above all she was loved, and we would not have wished for her to be any different.

Chores

At the beginning of the week, dressed in the housewife's attire of a turban and pinny, my mum prepared for her daily chores. Monday was always washing day, for which she used an electric copper boiler in the scullery. This was a round metal container with a wooden top. There was nothing much available in the way of detergents so my mum used soapflakes made by Lux, which were chippings of bars of soap designed to hand-wash clothes. Also on the shelf in the scullery were soda crystals (washing soda), which could be used for washing

A typical Bradford Monday washday, 1940s. *(Graham Hall)*

delicates as well as cleaning around the kitchen. Among other soapflakes and powders available were Dolly Blue, Compo, Rinso, Coalman's Starch, Boralic Soap and thick bars of smelly carbolic soap. Into the copper boiler went the dirty clothes, which were poked down with a wooden pole; then, placing the wooden lid on top, Mum let the clothes boil. From time to time she pounded the clothes with a large posser, which resembled a medieval battering ram; its weight alone was enough to smash out the dirt. After the boiling time was up the steaming clothes were taken out of the boiler with wooden tongs, to be rinsed in cold water and then placed in the tin bath. An iron-framed mangle with two large wooden rollers could be fixed on to the boiler and the clothes were put through this to squeeze out any surplus water. This was hard work as the mangle was turned by a large cast iron handle. The clothes were then pegged out on the line in the yard between the house and our air-raid shelter to flutter and dry in the breeze, propped up by a long wooden prop. In the spring and summer everything went outside to dry, while in the winter washing was draped on the clothes-horse in front of the fire, causing a slight mist and I'm sure on some occasions a rainbow! This washday scene was re-enacted in most of the houses at the front of the street, the only difference being that long clotheslines were hung from one side of the street to the other, displaying a colourful array of everything from large bedsheets to ladies' bloomers.

Every Tuesday my mum cleaned the house from top to bottom, which included a whole range of jobs, from buffing the lino and polishing the furniture to shaking rugs and mats. She took quite some time blackleading the range, and polished it with Zebo grate polish until it looked as pristine as the day it was installed in the house some seventy years earlier. For a few hours after he had made our house look like a showhome my dad, brother and I had to tread carefully, but it soon acquired its lived-in status again.

On Fridays, in preparation for the weekend and any visitors, my mum 'did the doorstones' with a donkey stone (a scouring stone); she always used the same colour, brown with a white border. This chore was a work of art, passed down with pride as an important ritual to be carried out with dedication. Not only the front steps but also the window sills were treated with the same colours and finish. The outside toilet steps were completed last, still with the same matching colours. The toilet itself was always clean and smelt of Jeyes fluid and bleach. The walls were whitewashed with a snow-white finish, and on the back door was a nail for small newspaper squares. (Glossy magazines, when available, were not much use!) It was said that these newspaper squares were reading material, being a form of education to people as they sat contemplating on the toilet. Each toilet appeared to have its own library: ours was the *Telegraph and Argus*, and my grandparents' squares were the *News of the World*. On visits to people's houses you soon became aware of the family choice of reading material. After the war Izal medicated toilet rolls became available at an affordable price, and they were soon to be found in workplace toilets. White Izal sheets weren't popular with everybody as there were small and slippy – and it was a while before the softness of newspapers was displaced from the lavatory reading rooms of the nation.

Finally on a Friday the yard was swilled out with buckets of soapy water, in between which my mum pushed the water to the grate with a large stiff broom. A bucket of clean water was then thrown on the stone flags, then another, leaving a pristine surface.

Despite this immense workload, my mum also found time to work as a burler and mender for some time, first at Banisters and later at Edie's Mills, both in Listerhills – but when she became ill in the late 1940s she had to retire.

Dustbins were emptied weekly by the local council and the service was impeccable. The dustbin men were always ready with a joke and a cheery smile. They swung the large bins on their backs, walked up the passage and emptied all the smelly contents into a special wagon. The bin was then replaced. Perhaps on an odd occasion they left a thin line of cinder dust behind them, or eggshells, but these were soon swept up without any complaints.

Our outside windows were cleaned once a fortnight by a jovial windowcleaner called Willie Wellock, a small character who wore a flat cap and a boiler suit, and a go-between among local housewives. If there was some news or a little scandal then Willie could always confirm or deny it. His bucket always contained a plentiful supply of hot water, supplied by the housewives during his and their gossiping.

When the house was clean, with windows glistening, doorstones an array of colour and the yard swept, there was no country house or castle I would have rather been at than 30 Legrams Street.

Money Matters

In practically every home money was a constant worry. People would talk of 'making it last', 'making ends meet', 'stretching it out' or 'not wasting it'. Poverty, which many grandparents had known, seemed always to be waiting around the corner. A cup of tea never solved the problem, but did give some respite, together with the words 'we'll get along somehow' or 'I'll expect we'll manage', and the two that answered any problem, 'never mind'.

There were many times when I knew my parents were short of money, but Lawrence and I never did without. My mother always paid her way. Every week from my dad's pay-packet she put away all the week's payments: food, rent, coal, gas, electricity, hire purchase and other items like clothing. Anything left over was put on one side for treats or the annual holiday. The age of general affluence was still beyond the horizon and out of sight. We searched pockets and clothing to find forgotten or misplaced money, and took bottles back for refunds of coppers. Lawrence and I were lucky to have a mother who could handle money well and a father who worked hard. As

Mr Micawber said, 'Something will turn up' – and it usually did.

My parents took out those wonderful 'penny policies' with the Royal Liver Assurance. These paid out a small amount on reaching a certain age or upon death, in most cases just enough to pay for the burial. If there was enough change left over it was spent on tea and boiled ham sandwiches at Collinson's for the bereaved family and friends. Our insurance man was Mr Brownrigg, a large man who wore a homburg hat and a double-breasted waistcoat: his size always seemed to overwhelm me, but he was a nice man. He called on us with a loud knock on the door and a resounding 'Hello' every Friday evening at seven o'clock to collect the premium. The assurance book was placed on the table, and if Mr Brownrigg had any of the old silver threepenny pieces in his change he swapped them for pennies out of my money box. After taking the money and marking the assurance book, he sat by the table and regaled my parents and me with tales of his life in the army during the Boer War.

Most of our furniture was purchased from a Mr Lyle, who had a shop in Leeds Road. The furniture was paid for in instalments, direct to Mr Lyle on his Saturday morning rounds. Most of the houses in the street, including ours, were owned by Mr Wilson. He was another large man who wore a large hat and an expensive overcoat, and looked like Al Capone, the American gangster. He paid one of the tenants to collect the rents, thus avoiding confrontations with the housewives. Mum was 'on to him' on several occasions, especially when the plaster of the ceiling in the passage came down in lumps. He pointed out the football marks on the ceiling!

Personal bank accounts were far from common and families like ours kept small amounts in Post Office Savings. The money in my moneybox didn't warrant this, as I required cash at a minute's notice. Using a flat-bladed table knife, I could empty it with a clatter of coins in seconds. I sometimes gave demonstrations to visitors and my mum's friends, and they inevitably found some loose change in their pockets to add to the coins I was putting back. Before my demonstration I used to take out any silver I had so as not to appear too rich. It worked most times.

My mum was the manager and my dad the provider. As well as his job as an overlooker he thought nothing of taking on part-time jobs for extra money for quality-of-life items and for emergencies. Sometimes on Saturday mornings he worked at the Scenic Display, whose premises were at the corner of Listerhills and Norfolk Street. It was heavy work, lifting and moving theatrical props and scenery, for which he was paid 10s. Occasionally he was employed as the commissionaire at the Empress cinema in Listerhills for a couple of evenings a week. One time he applied to the GPO for the position of postman, but was not selected, which was a disappointment to him.

Later, when we lived in Wyke, Dad travelled to work at Stroud, Riley in Frizinghall, working from 7.30am until 4.30pm. Then he went, using my old bicycle, to Newbould's Bakery on Sticker Lane, to work the evening shift from 5.30pm to 10pm. This was repeated each working day. For a time he was employed at Low Moor Steel Alloy as a fireman on the small railway engine named *Henry Woodcock*, which was used to transport pig iron within the works. My mother put an end to this job after he was caught between the buffers when coupling two railway trucks one day, and suffered a badly bruised ribcage. He was lucky. On finding out that he was not seriously injured, or worse, my mum said 'Trust your dad', which was relief rather than sarcasm.

Chapter 3
Listerhills

Listerhills was one of the many self-contained districts that abounded in Bradford. A large area, it was first shown on the Bradford Ordnance Survey maps in the mid-nineteenth century, and was probably named after the Bradford wool baron Samuel Cunliffe Lister.

Listerhills came under Bradford Central Division. It encompassed an area from Thornton Road south to Brownroyd near Girlington, west to Shearbridge and Great Horton Road, then north and back to Thornton Road. In the area around Legrams Lane, where I lived, most of the houses were back-to-backs dating from the 1870s, as indeed were most houses in Listerhills. Around St Andrew's Villas, St Andrew's Place, Lady Lane and Selby Place were large Victorian houses built at the same time for larger middle-class families.

The main source of employment in Listerhills was the woollen mills, of which there were many. The largest was Ira Ickringill & Co. Ltd (Worsted Yarn Spinners), a large prominent Victorian building with twin towers in Legrams Lane; there were also John Smith's in Preston Street, Eady's on Richmond Road, where my mum worked for some time in the burling and mending department, and Banister's Mill in Longside Lane.

Many other smaller industries and businesses were in the back streets, including Joseph Stott Joiners on Talbot Street, the Standard Rug Company on Great Russell Street, H.C. Slingsby's Ltd manufacturers of industrial equipment in Preston Street, and the small foundry in Handel Street, Howarth and Walter Ltd. By our bus stop at the junction of Archibald Street and Legrams Lane was Holdsworth and Burrill's (later to become part of British Road Services).

Listerhills was served by trolleybuses, which started in the city centre at the bottom of Thornton Road between the New Victoria cinema and the New Inn

Archibald Street, Listerhills, looking up to Legrams Lane. On the left is Fanny Hardaker's shop. The next street is Legrams Terrace; on the corner is Joe North's off licence and general grocer. *(Author's collection)*

public house. No. 36 to the Lidget Green terminus, no. 37 to the Pasture lane terminus and the Clayton terminus bus, no. 38, all provided a very good service.

Streets and Shops
In Legrams Lane, dominating the area, was the parish church of St Andrew's (1859–1963), with its tall spire and clock that chimed the half-hour and the hour. Close by was the infants' school. From Norcroft Street along Legrams Lane to Ira Ickringill's mill was an assortment of shops selling goods of all descriptions, all with their own particular smells.

One of the better known-shops on Listerhills Road was Fred Drake's gents' outfitters, which had a display frontage of three large windows. Fred had started the business in 1912 and built a good clientele until his retirement in 1947.

The hub of this area, opposite the church, was Herbert J. Whitworth's newsagent and St Andrew's post office. The postmaster, George W. Whitworth, was a quiet, unassuming man who had been decorated with the Military Medal for Bravery in Burma during the Second World War. Nearby was Nicholson's, an old-fashioned chemist shop where most medicine bottles given out had a cork top, and ointments and pills were in small round cardboard containers. The poison book was signed before poison was dispensed, and you had to be known by the chemist before such transactions took place. Behind the counter were

St Andrew's Church (1859–1963) dominated the Listerhills area. My grandparents were married there and my dad attended the school on the right. *(Graham Hall)*

large mahogany cabinets each containing rows of drawers. Each drawer was painted in gold leaf with the name in Latin of the contents. On top of these cabinets were large glass minaret-shaped jars containing coloured water in vivid colours, which gave an overall display of brightness to the shop. Mr Nicholson, the chemist, was a very tall kindly man who was noted for his help and advice to both young and old. I saw him a few times when I had something in my eye. He sat me on a stool and, using what looked like a toy paintbrush, removed the foreign object. A smile, a dab of the eye with lint, and there was no charge.

Next to the chemist was H.L. Hudson's stationers and newsagents, and across the street in St Andrew's Villas was the small Number 10 branch of the Bradford Co-operative Society, a wallpaper shop and Lambert's Wines off-licence. Along the front of Legrams Lane was an array of shops all the way up to Edwin Jowett's grocers at the corner of Archibald Street. Next door to Jowett's was the confectioner's shop run by Misses Edith and Alice Priestley, two spinster sisters who specialised in cakes, and had a large selection of biscuits in tins with glass tops for viewing.

Locally this was called the 'bun shop'. There were Palmer's, the well-established grocers, Harold Fearnside pork butchers, Tom Blamire's, the largest greengrocer in the area, who had other shops in other districts. At William Firth's fish and chip shop it was essential that at lunchtime you arrived early, otherwise you could be held up by young bobbin liggers with a list of fish and chip orders for the workers at the local mills. Other shops

The trolley-bus served Listerhills well. We had three to choose from: no. 36 to Lidget Green, no. 37 to Pasture Lane, and no. 38, the Clayton bus. This picture shows the Clayton trolley-bus at the Thornton Road departure point in the town centre.
(Robert F. Mack)

included Clegg the grocer, George Merrick's electrical, auto shop and cycle dealer, William Wood's shoe shop, Townend the draper, F.G. Rowe the optician and Greenwood's outfitters, one of the many premises of this well-established West Riding clothier.

The very popular Congress store, set in the middle of the Legrams Road shops, was more of a meeting place for housewives than a place to purchase groceries. But the housewives' charm was wasted on the friendly manager Mr Shepherd (Shep), who could more than hold his own at his store in the 1940s and '50s, with the gossiping housewives and their caustic comments and loud banter. I should know as I spent lots of time in their company, as I helped carry the groceries home. It wasn't a place for the faint hearted, but was wonderful for the housewives.

The many corner shops around my street catered for the immediate needs of the locals, and in most cases provided a reasonable living for their owners. In Great Russell Street was Garthwaite's, a nice family grocer's shop. Legrams Street (my street) had four shops: Mosley's, a general store that had, or so it seemed, everything for sale including bread (with no wrapping – so you could enjoy biting the corners off on the way home), lumps of yellow and white stone (donkey stone) for cleaning the doorstones, and small bundles of firewood at *2d* a bundle. There was always a strong smell of firelighters, paraffin, carbolic and white Windsor soaps. Jean, the daughter, was a lovely girl who had a hair-lip; she always served with a smile and was loved by all.

Fanny Hardaker's sweets and cigarettes was not exactly the top shop in the neighbourhood, but she catered for items like sherbet-dips, liquorice sticks, gobstoppers and the strange sounding beano bubble dabs. She sold cigarettes and oddments like vinegar from a barrel, to fill our small bottle, from which I would sip all the way home, ignoring the rumours that it dried up your blood. Dyes of many colours with strange names, including vermilion, indigo, nigger brown, bottle green and pillar box red, were all contained in small cotton bags on her shelves, not forgetting, for whites, the famous 'dolly blue'.

Bessie Durran's was a confectioner's where there was always a queue at 9am on Saturday mornings for hot currant teacakes, and then there was Barber's, the fish and chip shop just around the corner from my house. Here too you often had to queue for ages, especially on Fridays, when the bobbin liggers arrived with their orders for John Smith's Mill in Preston Street.

On Legrams Terrace there was North's off-licence and general store with its hand-pulled ale pumps, popular with the old ladies in their shawls with a jug discreetly hidden underneath; and at the other end of the street was Archibald Craig's, a small newsagent's with the best choice of fireworks for November. Fieldhead Street had only the one shop, George Dibb's the greengrocer, again very popular. During the war in the windows were displayed two bunches of pottery Fyffe bananas (the real thing was unavailable throughout the war). I 'ate' those bananas many times! Edinburgh Street had a barber's shop where I was scalped by a new barber, and next door was Hurley Ellison's, the butcher who was a member of St Patrick's choir and wasn't averse to giving us choirboys a clip on the head (there was always a reason) during the singing of High Mass. At the bottom of Edinburgh Street, no. 64 was William Hilton's, the popular ice cream business that had been established in the 1920s. It was from Hilton's that we all bought our first ice-lolly after the war: it was peppermint and cost ½d.

It was surprising with all these local shops that during the week there never seemed to be men shopping, pushing prams or carrying bags. It certainly was the women's domain.

Facing Ickringill's Mill was a large Victorian house set in its own grounds and surrounded by a high wall. It was originally built for the mill owner, Ira Ickringill, who lived there for a short time before moving to York, but was later used as accommodation for the mill managers and their families. At the rear of the house were tennis courts and over the wall behind them was a field known to everyone as John Willie North's field, named after a well-known local figure. Also known as 'the field', its entrance was at the end of Legrams Street close to the warehouse that belonged to John Roberts (Wool) Waste Merchants Ltd. This field was desolate and unkempt, and went all the way down to the railway lines of the City Road goods yard depot to an area we called 'the Coaly' – full of weeds, and in the summer a colourful assortment of dandelions, docks, nettles, willowherb, bindweed and cow parsley. On one side of the field was the city greyhound dog track and below that an old Victorian rubbish tip where there were to be found Victorian pot lids, stone jars and bottles. On the other side were the gable-end houses of Archibald Street that went all the way down to Talbot Street. Back on Legrams Lane, to the right of the Victorian house, were some allotments that ran parallel to the city dog track. Across from the allotments was the Empress Picture House. In between the entrance and the exit to Holdsworth and Burrill's were four small seventeenth-century cottages, which were later demolished to improve access. The cottages had been inhabited right up until demolition.

This was my part of Listerhills, with its chimneys belching smoke among the back-to back houses with cobbled streets, warrens, ginnells, snickets, alleyways and passages. There were always the distant whistle of a train and the clang of goods wagons in the shunting yard at the City Road depot. Then there was the rhythmical sound of clog-irons and hobnailed boots on the flagstones and cobbles as workers made their way to the mills and other industries through the backstreets. The air was rent with the mill whistles' piercing screams, and when the sound of footfalls and whistles had faded a kind of silence prevailed.

Chapter 4
Bradford in the 1940s and '50s

During the 1940s and '50s hardly anything had changed in Bradford's centre since before the war. It still had many fine Victorian buildings and, although smut-laden, they still showed quality and pride. Overlooking all were the beautiful parish church, Town Hall, St George's Hall, Mechanics' Institute, Swan Arcade, the Wool Exchange, the Alhambra, and the New Victoria cinema.

Shopping

Three large department stores dominated the town. Brown, Muff's was on Market Street. On Manningham Lane there was the fine art-deco building of Busbys, looking more like a glamorous ocean liner than a department store. This unusually styled building looked magnificent when lit up on winter evenings, especially at Christmas. The third big store was the Sunbridge Road Emporium (later to become Sunwin House). It was a nice, open, clean store that had its own clientele and attractions, one being its escalator – the first in Bradford. Incidentally my mate Vincent Davey (my best mate – of whom more later) and I were asked to leave the Emporium for messing about on the escalator, and were sheepishly escorted out of the building. We were asked at least three times over a period to remove ourselves from Busby's as well, for shouting across the shop floors and once for accidentally knocking some toys off a display stand in the basement toy department.

Among these stores was a variety of large and small shops, most established for many years and household names to generations of Bradfordians. For the ladies the town centre bristled with fashion shops. Lady of Fashion, Novello's, Clayden's, Marshall and Snellgrove, and the furriers Peter Brunskill and Kino's were very popular. Gentlemen's outfitters were prominent; after all, Bradford was

Manningham Lane, with the Regent cinema on the left, late 1940s. Further along on the same side is the fine art-deco building of Busby's department store, popular for Santa's grotto at Christmas. *(Graham Hall)*

still the world centre of the woollen industry. Montague Burton's had three large shops, two in Tyrrell Street and one in Kirkgate. Other tailors of equal standing were Made to Measure, Alexandre's, Weaver to Wearer, John Collier and O.S. Wain, the shop that for years had the monopoly in the hire of dinner suits. Around the corner on Bridge Street was Snowden's Outfitters, popularly known as 'Snowdens Corner'. Dunne's, in Ivegate, was popular for its hats and caps, and Hope Brothers was a much respected gents' outfitters in Lower Kirkgate next to the Talbot Hotel (which was famous for the statue of a hound above the door). If a rambler required special attire for walks on the moors, then Millets offered a whole range of clothing and accessories. Colletts the gents' outfitters in Swan Arcade, catered for an upmarket clientele, and Starkies' Outfitters adjoining the Ritz cinema was very popular. With the advent of rock 'n' roll in the mid-1950s, Hargreave's in Sunbridge Road offered a nice selection of frilled fronted shirts, string ties and the popular luminous socks, which brought a shake of the head and a frown from elderly people. I had a pair that were lime green! Wallis's, at the bottom of Manchester Road, also had an assortment of rock 'n' roll wear.

Remembered by most Bradfordians is Lingard's, not because the original building was destroyed by fire in 1940 or for its merchandise, but for the thrill of seeing the overhead cash containers at work. When you gave your money to the assistant he or she placed this in a brass overhead container, which ran along wires to a colleague seated in a booth overlooking the counters. When a lever was pulled the container swooshed along the track, and shot back with your change and receipt.

In Busby's Santa's grotto a young Pauline Matthews (Kiki Dee) is slightly hesitant with Father Christmas, as her elder sister Betty looks on. *(Author's collection)*

Shoe shops for both men and women seemed to congregate around the Darley Street area; they included Timpson's, Barrett's, Stead and Simpson, Saxone, Dolcis, Freeman Hardy and Willis, Cable Shoes and Dr Scholl.

The High Street chemists Timothy White and Taylor and Boots were well established. Among the other chemists were Rimmington's, and on Sunbridge Road Parkinson and Clark. Shops with a speciality were everywhere. Kendal's sold rainwear and umbrellas, Chadwick's for leather goods, Taylor and Parsons for ironmongery and furnishings, while Bryer's in Forster Square were the leaders for the sale of fabrics. Mollett's was a must for that new tiled fire-place when the Yorkshire range had to go. For the cyclist there was Baines in Lower Piccadilly, and two Halfords shops which also catered for cycles and motor accessories. There was even a Catholic repository shop at the bottom of Sunbridge Road which sold religious items for Catholics, from missals to rosaries.

For jewellery, Fattorini's were prominent in Tyrrell Street, although Mappin and Webb, Arensberg's, Minoah Rhodes and Fowler and Oldfield were very competitive. Choice ceramics, china and glassware were sold at Jackson's in Darley Street, and Timms and Dyason provided the same quality goods from its own arcade in Town Hall Square. It was in this arcade that I stood to view the Queen and Prince Philip's visit in 1954. Dalby's Antiques was perhaps the only large antique establishment in the city centre; this was situated on the corner of Town Hall Square, facing the 'Crystal Palace' (toilets). Dalby's windows were always displayed with all kinds of china, jewellery, fine art and furniture.

The beautiful façade of Kirkgate Market with Kino's prominent sign. Also on the corner is Alexanders, gents' tailors. *(Jack Booth)*

Christopher Pratt's on North Parade had been established on the same site for many years and was very popular for its high quality furniture.

As well as a Marks and Spencer, there was a Woolworth's store in Darley Street. It had individual counters with its own assistants and a wonderful central staircase with handrails of solid brass.

From ping-pong balls to a pair of football boots, sporting enthusiasts had many shops to choose from. Among the popular ones were Sports and Pastimes in Market Street, Nutton's close to Forster Square, Carter's, and Len Hutton (the Yorkshire and England cricketer) had a shop in Bridge Street for a short time. I purchased a set of darts from the great man for 1s 9d. He even wrapped them up for me and shook my hand. This was a great moment in my life.

Probably Bradford's best-known small shop, renowned for its marvellous meat pies and sandwiches, was Philip Smith and Son in Ivegate. It was advertised as the oldest pork shop in Yorkshire. Pre-Christmas queues formed from early morning down Ivegate days before the event. A special favourite was a stand pie for Boxing Day. If the juice from the meat pies happened to mark your clothes, then the dry cleaners Crockatt's, Martin's, Smith's and Mercury, all in the town centre, were on hand with a two hour cleaning service!

Looking up Darley Street, 1940s. Barrett's and many other shoe shops were prominent here. The Central Library, which had a beautiful Victorian interior, was close to Kirkgate Market. *(Graham Hall)*

There were many cafés and snack bars in the town centre, especially in the large indoor Kirkgate Market. In Darley Street there were also the quality shops of Silvio's and Betty's café. On Tyrrell Street were two well-known establishments. One was Collinson's Café, a coffee and grocer's shop. Its coffee roaster sent an aromatic smell wafting over the pavement into Tyrrell Street, and the restaurant was famed for its three piece orchestra. Next door was the Farmer Giles Milk Bar, which my parents always advised me not to visit as it had a reputation; for what they didn't say. It was surprising how many other people used to say the same thing – also giving no further reasons. In 1937 it had a juke box installed: perhaps that was it!

Regarding reputations, the New Inn on the corner of Town Hall Square and Thornton Road, an old coaching house, was well known as a den of iniquity. Similar notoriety was attached to the Old Crown and The Grosvenor in Ivegate, and the old Back Empress on Tyrrell Street. Other places of leisure in the centre that didn't have this problem were The County, frequented by woolmen from all corners of the world who were visiting the Wool Exchange, and Spinks' bar and restaurant. The Talbot Hotel, which I was to frequent, had a 'Gentlemen's bar'.

One of the most enjoyable and interesting areas, away from the shops,

Ivegate, 1950. This street had a mixture of pubs, amongst which were the Old Crown, Unicorn and the Grosvenor. The well-known meat pie shop Philip Smith and Son was also in Ivegate. *(Graham Hall)*

**A busy afternoon in Bradford's Victoria Square showing many modes of transport –
including cars, trams, trolley-buses, motor buses and even a motor-cycle.** *(Graham Hall)*

was John Street Market. Built in 1931 on the site of Copper Quarry, the
market was surrounded by John Street, Westgate and Rawson Road. The
roofed stalls sold a wide range of items, from pigeons to plates. The crockery
salesmen entertained the crowd by flinging tea services, dishes and plates in
the air and catching them with lots of clattering and drama. To watch this
was a treat for young and old alike.

Perhaps one of Bradford's premier grocery stalls was that of William
Morrison. It was William and Hilda Morrison who in 1899 started this
empire, with stalls in Bradford and Dewsbury markets. As a boy their son
Ken, youngest of six children, helped out at the stalls in Rawson Market and
John Street Market in the 1940s. Later, while he was serving in Germany as
a National Serviceman in the RAOC, his father William became ill. Ken was
asked by his mother if he wished to keep the family business going. He
decided to give it a try and returned from National Service to run the
grocery stall in Rawson Market. In 1952, at the age of twenty, he took over
the business. The rest is history.

Much time could be spent wandering round the market, and for
refreshments there were lots of cafés and snack bars around the perimeter.
My favourite was the pea and pie stall that sold a plate of peas and a glass of

Tyrrell Street, including the famous Farmer Giles Milk Bar and Collinsons café, whose coffee roaster wafted an aromatic smell over the pavement. Next door was the Back Empress pub, and next door to that was the second of the three Bradford Burton's.
(Graham Hall)

Tizer for 3*d*.

In 1951 Bradford markets celebrated seven hundred years of their Royal Markets Charter, granted by Henry III in 1251. Stalls were decked with bunting and flags, with special counter displays, and two Bradford trolleybuses were painted with royal livery and the dates 1251 and 1951 to celebrate the event.

Bradford had its own 'speakers' corner', the large open car park next to the Ritz cinema on Broadway. On Sunday evenings crowds gathered to listen to individuals, each standing on a box and exploiting to the full the Englishman's privilege of free speech without fear of arrest. Communists proclaimed the doctrines of Marx, Lenin and Trotsky, and insults and jeers were inevitably hurled at them – the usual comment being, 'If it's so good in Russia why don't you go and live there?' Religions also came in for insults as the speakers for Catholics, Methodists, Church of England and other denominations did their utmost to convince the onlookers of their faith. I saw Frank Scully, my teacher from St Patrick's School, many times on his box, and he was always very strong and eloquent in his defence of Catholicism. While some of the discussions turned into arguments, I don't remember any threats or scuffles; in fact, lots of laughter was always part of Speakers' Corner. Most spectators turned away with laughter or a smile on their faces as they dispersed. Well, it was something to talk about at work the next day.

Transport

Bradford had always had a good transport system with trams, trolleybuses and West Yorkshire buses offering good cheap services. For most local and far-away destinations the town was provided with an excellent train service from both Forster Square and Exchange station. Both of these stations could connect you with any part of the country.

As most transport services finished at about 11pm, people could be seen scurrying around Bradford centre every evening as the Town Hall geared itself up to give us its eleven o'clock chimes. From many shop and warehouse doorways courting couples emerged to catch that last bus. Many lads had to walk home after seeing their girlfriends to their bus stop, especially if their last bus was the other side of Bradford. This was the accepted thing. If you were lucky and had some spare cash you could visit the taxi rank in Town Hall Square, but otherwise it was the long walk home. Women as well as men took these walks after missing buses, either in groups or singles, and hardly any trouble occurred. The most that people had to contend with was the occasional drunk; just crossing over the road was all that was usually needed to avoid confrontation. After eleven o'clock Bradford took on the look of a ghost town. Traffic diminished and everything came to a standstill.

Employment

Most of the woollen mills were still fully operational at this time, so there were plenty of jobs for men and women alike, in office work or in the mills themselves as liggers, doffers, combers, spinners and woolsorters. Plenty of office work was also available in other companies. Apprenticeships were served by mechanics, engineers and electricians; large companies such as the English Electric and Croft Engineering were prominent. There was also a huge amount of shop work available. Jobs could be changed frequently. Someone could leave a job in the morning, look through the situations vacant in the lunchtime edition of the *Telegraph and Argus*, and be working elsewhere in the afternoon.

Law and Order

The old Bradford City Police force (1848–1974) was mostly made up of local men who knew the area and the local villains. The police were still respected, and in most cases a word was sufficient to stop any trouble. Of course there were occasions when people were rebellious, so there were times when actions spoke louder than words. The birch could still be used until the late 1940s, the Riot Act could still be read, and capital punishment was still, in some cases, the penalty for murder. The police force had its headquarters, complete with cells, in

The well-respected and popular CID Sergeant John Naylor of the Bradford City Police, at the scene of the Garnett Street murder off Leeds Road, 1955. *(Ian Naylor)*

Always worth a visit in John Street Market was the pie and pea stall. My favourite was a saucer of peas with vinegar and a glass of Tizer – wonderful! *(Picture House Ltd)*

the Town Hall. At the rear, on Norfolk Street, was a building that housed the fingerprint department. On a visit from school in 1950 I found it a dingy place, but its expertise was much sought after by other police authorities. Bradford City Police was one of the forerunners in fingerprint detection as early as 1903.

The policemen always looked resplendent in their uniforms, some wearing medal ribbons from both world wars. The police whistle was still in use and its sound carried for over a mile. Three short blasts became a recognised signal that assistance was required. The policeman's wooden truncheon was easily drawn through the trouser pocket, and was used to threaten or subdue any violent character. I used to like seeing a policeman in his cape with its linked fastener in the shape of a lion's head. One evening Vincent and I saw one of them on Goit Stock Back Lane on Thornton Road, standing under a gas lamp; there was a mist and it was raining. With his figure silhouetted against the light, which enhanced his cape and helmet, the scene was practically Victorian. As we passed he said, 'Goodnight, lads' and, not looking up, we replied 'Goodnight'. A few yards further on we looked round, and he had disappeared. We ran the rest of the way home!

I don't think there was a lot of crime just after the war, as everyone wanted to get back on their feet and there was a strong atmosphere of pulling together. It was a time when you could go out and leave the doors unlocked without fear of being burgled. Having said that, the door of our Legrams Street house was locked and we were all in bed when we were burgled one night in 1949. The thieves, having pulled themselves up to the scullery windowsill, climbed through the window on to the kitchen sink and down to the floor. On going downstairs in the morning Dad shouted up to my mum that we had been burgled. I was downstairs in a flash, to find that all the drawers and cupboards were open; other than that, everything was in order. A chocolate bar (not ours) was lying half-eaten on the fireplace, close to our mission box (used to collect loose change for the Catholic missions in Africa). The box was due to be emptied, but although it had been moved it was unopened. Nothing had been stolen. My mother came to the conclusion that the perpetrator was a Catholic, and nothing would convince her otherwise. She repeated her theory many times to the police when they arrived. After the fingerprint detective had finished his task, he showed me the many fingerprints around the windows, and I was very impressed, especially when he let me dab his brush, full of white powder, over the area. The other policeman was a CID detective: he did most of the talking and wore a large trilby and the standard gabardine coat. I could hear my mum repeating 'mission box' and 'Catholic', trying to convince him – and probably succeeding. Perhaps the mission box had pricked the burglar's conscience. We were not the only ones to have been broken into that night, as items had been stolen in six other similar incidents that had taken place in the surrounding streets. No one was ever caught.

One mysterious case reported in the local paper (for which serious crime was always front page news – including graphic photographs, with dotted lines showing the direction in which criminals escaped or where the body was found) was the disappearance of Father Henryk Borynski, who vanished after leaving his lodgings in Little Horton Lane on the evening of 13 July 1953. He was chaplain to the 1,500-strong Polish community in Bradford. He had 10s in his pocket when he disappeared. He left behind £250 in savings and all his possessions, including his prayer books. No trace of him has ever been found.

During my early life Bradford had its share of murders. In September 1944 a Bradford taxi driver named Harrison Graham, aged fifty-eight, was found dead in his taxi on Rooley Lane in the early hours of the morning. He had been killed by a blow to the back of the head with a blunt instrument. As a six year old my interest in this murder was cultivated because the father of a young friend of mine was taken in by Bradford City Police for questioning. After twenty-four hours he was released without charge. The murderer was never found and the case is still unsolved.

A murder that shocked the city and the nation was that of sixty-seven-year-old Mrs Frances Hodgson, a widow who was stabbed to death in her small shop in Garnett Street off Leeds Road on Thursday 31 March 1955. She was found lying on her shop floor in a pool of blood, with stab wounds from which she died the following day. A full-scale murder hunt took place, the like of which Bradford had not seen for many years. Over a thousand people were interviewed and around five thousand handbills appealing for more information were distributed to shops, factories, mills, workplaces and clubs throughout the city. Vincent and I visited the scene on the Saturday, as everyone was talking about it. The area was predominantly working-class, and consisted of many back-to-back houses similar to our houses in Listerhills, while the shop was double-fronted with adverts for Turf cigarettes and Robin starch on the windows; in fact, it was a replica of many hundreds of others in Bradford. There wasn't really much to see as we joined the small crowd of sightseers other than a lone policeman standing outside the shop door. From time to time a police car arrived and burly plain clothes policemen of the CID emerged and entered the premises. When they left we noticed that they observed the crowd for a while as if looking for someone. As this happened a few times while we were there we thought it best to leave. A thin man appears to have been the main suspect, but the clues dried up and the case was left unsolved.

Bradford's Football Teams

When Britain declared war on Germany in 1939 football came to an abrupt end. Large crowds were banned, stadiums were given over to military use and most players joined up. However, football acquired a new status over the next six years, and the game became hugely important to Britain. For the average supporters watching their local club, though, it was football with a marked difference. Games now included guest players from other clubs, as well as amateurs pulled from the crowd to play alongside household names. Matches were interrupted by air-raids, leagues were decided on numbers of goals scored, and cup games could go on for hours because replays were not allowed.

My dad had always supported Bradford City, and I saw some of their wartime games; even my mum attended some matches. We always stood at the Kop End. Being very young, I sat on one of the leaning spectators' bars directly behind the goals. It appeared to me that most of those attending were young children, teenagers and old people, as so many of our young men were away in the forces. The ground was hemmed in by hundreds of terrace and back-to-back houses, while the terraces and pitch were dominated by the large cooling towers on Midland Road: the air was always thick with fumes from the local chemical works. It was always a dark and austere occasion, with most of the fans dressed in gabardine raincoats and flat caps or trilbies. I don't ever remember the sun shining.

The players had long shorts down to their knees and wore large leather football boots with enormous toe-caps. All the players had the same hairstyle, short back and sides, and their skin was sallow as they hadn't been out in the sun. The only colour was in the players' shirts of claret and amber. The wartime team members I remember are the forward George (Spud) Murphy, half-back Joe Harvey and central defender George Hinsley. After the war new faces came to City, which was now in the Third Division Northern League; they included inside forward Derek Hawksworth, and wing half-back Andy McGill and Wheelan (Polly) Ward, a small inside forward and a great favourite with the crowd. From Liverpool came the inside forward Abe Rosenthal and the Bradford-born defender Dick Conroy. It was always pleasant to watch the local band, Hammonds Sauce Brass Band, playing tunes and military marches before the match and at half-time. At half-time two men carried a large canvas sheet between two poles around the perimeter of the pitch, collecting money for charity. Many of the coins that were thrown missed and hit the carriers!

Bradford Park Avenue's football ground was adjacent to Horton Park, and attached to the Yorkshire County Cricket ground. This was a perfect setting and, unlike at City games, the sun was always shining. I didn't support Park Avenue but attended the very rare derby matches. These drew crowds of over twenty thousand people, and City and Avenue fans mixed together in an atmosphere of banter and jovial disputes. These games were generally controlled by around a dozen City policemen who also enjoyed the match as generally no trouble occurred.

Two Bradford Park Avenue players I remember seeing in the mid-1940s were Len Shackleton and the goalkeeper Chic Farr. Len Shackleton had played for Park Avenue before the war and continued playing in the wartime seasons while serving his country as a Bevin Boy. (These were young men recruited from 1943 until the end of the Second World War – 10 per cent of male conscripts aged between eighteen and twenty-five. They were chosen by ballot to serve in the mining industry rather than the armed forces and were named after the Rt Hon. Ernest Bevin, wartime minister of labour.) Such was the football leagues fiasco during the early part of the war that Len Shackleton played two away matches on Christmas Day 1940, one for each Bradford club: in the morning he turned out for Park Avenue at Leeds; in the afternoon he scored while playing for City at Huddersfield. The eccentric Chic Farr was an old-fashioned goalkeeper who wore a large cloth cap and regarded the 6 yard box as his private domain. He was a player who was always respected by both sets of local supporters.

After the war both teams were up and down in the newly formed Third and Fourth Divisions. While City ambled on, never gaining much in promotion, Park Avenue was nearly always close to relegation. In fact, the directors decided after the dreadful 1955–56 campaign that no Avenue team would again disgrace the old red, amber and black colours, and new colours of green and white were issued for the new season.

Rugby League

Bradford Northern reigned supreme in the late 1940s. At the beginning of the war, like City and Park Avenue, rugby league was thrown into a state of confusion. As the war dragged on more and more players were away with the armed services, so players were allowed to play for whatever club they wished. With return to peacetime rugby, Northern was soon in the forefront of rugby league. My pal Vincent and I supported Northern, but we only attended a few home games as we had so many other interests, sports and adventures that took up our time. The games we saw were exciting, once we had conquered the rudiments of the game. We soon knew the names of all the players including Trevor Foster, Ernest Ward, Eric Batten and Frank Whitcombe (known to all the youngsters as Fatty Whitcombe). He wasn't really fat, but with an 18 stone frame he looked to us to be an enormous man. Another regular player was George Carmichael, who was married at St Patrick's Church: most of Bradford Northern attended. I was the altar boy for his Nuptial Mass, together with John Walsh. After the service he gave us £1 each, which was a fortune to us.

We could slap our favourite players on the back, as the dressing rooms were in a building at the top of the stadium. Players and officials had a long walk down cindered steps to the pitch, which was some 300 yards away. On returning at the end of a match the players and officials had to run the gauntlet of the public back

An Odsal tram stands at the terminus in Halifax Road. It was these trams that whizzed us down from Odsal to the town centre, which was a wonderful, exhilarating feeling when sitting on the open top deck. (*J. Copland*)

44

up to the top of the stadium. If the crowd had been upset by a player (home or opposition), he was booed and hassled all the way. And God help the referee!

The late 1940s were a good time for Bradford Northern as they won many honours, including the Challenge Cup in 1947 and 1949. Getting to the ground at Odsal Top was no problem, as it was on a tram route. Returning to town could be difficult, however, as hundreds of people queued to leave the ground at the same time. The trams lined up on Halifax Road, and each one then trundled down the tracks to the tram stop to fill up. It was the best ride ever, especially if we could get on the open front on the top deck. The trams went at breakneck speed down Manchester Road. It was a wonderful and exhilarating feeling as the wind blew through our hair, with the smell of Jeyes Fluid and heated metal, and the sound of whining machinery and clanging bells. Red faced, with eyes watering, we alighted from the tram at journey's end. 'What a night,' we would say to each other.

In the early 1950s we drifted away from Northern: the trams had gone, and there was no more pounding in the 'boneshakers' down Manchester Road; they had been superseded by diesel buses and trolleybuses. The trolleybuses didn't have the presence or the noise of the trams, but were undeniably more comfortable and good for jumping off. The club, although still a major force, went into decline. It had been good while it lasted and was an experience for both Vincent and me. I think Vincent was really more of a fan than I as he bought a rugby ball. While I could catch it, I didn't care too much for the tackling or falling about, so I knew I would never play for Bradford Northern.

Yorkshire County Cricket

For all Yorkshire schoolboys with an interest in cricket, going to see a Yorkshire county match at Bradford Park Avenue cricket ground, which was adjacent to the football ground and close to Horton Park, was a very special thrill. We watched our heroes' techniques, and then tried to emulate them. It was often said that a strong Yorkshire team meant a strong England team, as so many of our county players were capped to play for their country.

Thus it was in the 1940s and '50s that our gang, not yet in its teens, made its way to the county ground. We had packed lunches, or whatever we could afford, be it spam or bread and jam. These and a bottle of pop, Tizer or American cream soda were welcome on hot days.. There were certain areas in the ground where we were able to sit, so it was an early start to try and secure the front seats. On those hot summer days we watched the likes of the world-renowned batsman Len Hutton, all-rounder Vic Wilson, batsman Norman Yardley, slow left-hand bowler Johnny Wardle and others showing their prowess on the pitch.

In 1950 Yorkshire played the West Indies at Park Avenue. The West Indies team consisted of players who were to become legends, including Worrell, Weekes, Wallett, Ramadhin and Valentine. After the match we youngsters mingled among these great players, who were very chatty, and gave us their

Our favourite Odsal Speedway ace, Joe Abbott, who was tragically killed on 1 July 1949. Vincent and I saw the tragedy and never returned to Odsal Speedway. *(Graham Hall)*

autographs. In the test trial of 1950, also at Park Avenue, we saw Bradford-born Jim Laker take 8 wickets for 2 runs. I could only marvel and, like many supporters at the time, be saddened that Yorkshire had let him go to Surrey in 1946. After his performance that day I changed my bowling style from medium pace to Jim Laker's off spin. It didn't work during my trials at the Rec with the gang. I got slogged everywhere, so I returned to my original medium pace.

During the lunch and tea intervals at these county matches, bats and balls were produced and all around the perimeter of the ground hundreds of budding Len Huttons and Vic Wilsons showed their skills – much to the amusement of the older Yorkshire patrons. For days afterwards when we were playing, in the street or at the Rec, someone would say 'I'm Len Hutton' or 'I'm Jim Laker', and would act out a scene that they had seen at Bradford Park Avenue.

Odsal Speedway

In 1945 the National League for Speedway was formed and speedway came to Odsal. From the beginning it was a success and crowds of 20,000 were not uncommon at the cinder track that ran around the perimeter of Bradford Northern's rugby football ground.

I was aged ten in 1948 when I started going to the speedway; as usual, Vincent was my companion. Those Saturday nights were exciting, with loud tannoy announcements and noisy klaxons reverberating around the stadium. Competitive teams came from what were to me faraway places, like Wembley, West Ham, Newcross, Harringay, Lancashire Belle Vue and fifteen other towns that made up the league. We soon got to know the names of our team, among whom were Eric Langton, Syd Littlewood, Oliver Hart, Arthur Forrest, Ernie Price, Eddie Rigg and our hero Joe Abbott.

The team could sometimes be badly weakened with accidents, which were almost a weekly occurrence. On one occasion Eddie Rigg had a broken collarbone, but was back to the track and riding in two weeks. Joe Abbott, the veteran Odsal rider, was rushed to hospital, believed to be suffering from a fractured skull; it turned out he had only broken his nose. Speedway riding was not for the faint-hearted! Vincent and I would always try to get close to the pits, where the riders assembled with their mechanics. The smell of racing oil always wafted through the air, lingering up noses and in hair and clothes. We leaned over the pit wall to talk to the team, most of whom would talk to us and the other supporters who were milling around. Joe Abbott always bantered with the crowds, and once, when Vincent and I were at the front, he grinningly left a prominent thumbprint on our cheeks. That evening when I returned home my mum made me wash it off, much to my despair – but I couldn't really go to school the next week with a large oily mark on my face. When I met Vincent on Monday morning I was annoyed to find he still had his oily mark *in situ*. Within five minutes of our arrival Sister Christine had made him wash it off. Was I glad!

Odsal Speedway was so successful that enamelled badges were issued in the form of gold wings with a white star in the centre of a red triangle, and the words 'Odsal Speedway'. Every year a small enamelled boomerang-shaped piece was issued, to add to the bottom of the badge. These were very popular, but neither Vincent nor I ever had one, for reasons that will be made clear later.

During the 1949 season the injury jinx began again. In June Jack Biggs injured his leg in an accident at Harringay and the following night at Bradford Dick Seers and Joe Abbott were involved in a three-rider pile-up. Seers went into hospital with fractured ribs, a broken shoulder and a smashed wrist. Joe Abbott quickly recovered and was riding again before racing ended that night. All this was overshadowed when Joe Abbott was killed in a pit-bend crash at Odsal on 1 July 1949. At the pits-bend he sped into the corner with a wide-open throttle.

His bike slid and Joe made frantic attempts to regain control, but the front wheel locked and he was pitched over the right side of the machine. He fell head first. A doctor was quickly on the scene and certified Joe as dead, the cause being multiple injuries including a fractured spine near the neck. News of Joe's death wasn't given to the crowd, just that he had been taken to hospital suffering from serious injuries. Vincent and I witnessed the whole scene from the pits, and saw his inert body with people bending over him. Within minutes he had been carried away on a stretcher. It was not until the next day that the newspapers gave the news that he had died at the scene, and a gloom fell over Bradford. This episode made such an impression on both Vincent and me that we never went to watch the speedway again. From that day on I never had the desire for any type of motor-cycle.

Changing Bradford

New housing estates were planned and built in the mid-1950s, designed to take people from the back-to-back and old terrace housing, which was now deteriorating – some into slums. New estates like Buttershaw, Holmewood, Delph Hill and Woodside offered a paradise of open spaces, gardens and modern houses. At first most of these estates had no shops, no schools, no church or pub. There were excellent bus services so people could escape to their old familiar areas, but nothing for them where they lived. Even so, for the great majority who moved to these estates it was a dream come true. People who had never had a garden now took a pride in their lawns, flowerbeds and hedges, and while the children were small they enjoyed the freedom of the grassed areas. My parents and I, who moved to Delph Hill in 1955, found all this true, but missed the community spirit that had existed in those tiny streets which we had left behind.

Chapter 5
Bradford Characters

Characters of all kinds have been part of life in Bradford for ever. Most leave an indelible mark on the memory, either with affection or because of incidents that should have been avoided.

Corduroy Joe

This was the name we gave to Mr Robert Torpey, who lived on Legrams Street close to the entrance of John Willie North's field. His wife was a member of the Sunbridge Road Mission. Mr Torpey had only one leg and used a crutch to get about. All his clothes were of corduroy material: his flat cap, jacket, waistcoat, trousers, and even the pad support on his crutch. We affectionately called him Corduroy Joe. If he saw you wearing any corduroy item of clothing, such as a lumber jacket, which was popular at the time, a discussion took place with him about its quality.

We never knew if Joe was one of the many First World War veterans who lived in our streets, and if so if he had lost his leg in service. We never asked. He was a nice man with a cheery smile.

Gordon Wilkinson

In Marion Street at the rear of Great Russell Street the houses were back-to-back on one side, and on the other side was the rear of John Smith's woollen mill and Slingsby's, famous for making wooden ladders and containers (the sound of their sawmill could be heard in most of the surrounding streets). Gordon Wilkinson lived here.

Gordon was a few years older than us and his popularity was thanks to his capacity to supply goldfish and carp. These he procured from the many mill dams around our area, the most famous being Holden's dam at Sir Isaac

Holden's Mill between Princeville Road and Duncombe Street. It was well known that the mill pond was well stocked with goldfish and carp, which had been there some years and had grown quite large. The outer walls were over 12 feet high, and it took some courage not only to scale the walls but also to avoid any staff. Security was tight, as almost every summer children drowned in the dams when they were tempted to go for a swim to cool off. Many trespassers were prosecuted as a warning in order to avoid these tragedies. How Gordon avoided the security over the years no one really knew. All summer he sold his fish from a large container at *3d* or *6d* dependent on the size. This must have been quite lucrative. I, like many other lads, wouldn't go anywhere near the dams, and we used to wonder how he climbed that wall! He was a loner and we never found out.

Richard Russell Ackernley

At the crossroad traffic lights of Ingelby Road and Legrams Lane, on the corner at 132 Legrams Lane, lived an eccentric recluse named Richard Russell Ackernley, or to us 'Old Man Ackernley'. The house was a large detached Victorian building set back in its own small grounds, now Longfield House. He stood at the gate of the house with his ferocious dog called Peggy, and while he insulted adults and children his dog snarled and snapped. He was taken to court many times for the dog's behaviour but, as he commented many times in the *Telegraph and Argus*, that money was no obstacle to keeping the dog at liberty. This led him to pay fines of nearly £300 to prevent the dog being destroyed.

We children had to pass him when we left the Arcadian cinema. Word would pass along that Ackernley was out at his gate, so to avoid any confrontation we crossed the road at the lights to the other side of the road, walked along until we were past, then crossed back to our side of the road.

Educated at Bradford Grammar School, Mr Ackernley studied wool sorting in Bradford and then ran the family business of A.J. Collins and Co. He was said to be one of the most smartly dressed men in the city. It appears that a tragic illness necessitated a brain operation in 1945, and this completely changed his character. From being an able and much respected man, he became the eccentric we knew in the latter part of his life. He died at his home in 1953, aged seventy-one, leaving over £59,000 in his will to his sister and the National Trust.

The Legionnaire

We didn't know his name, only that he had been in the French Foreign Legion some years before the Second World War. It was suggested that he was a foreigner, but which country he was from no one seemed to know. He had a weather-beaten face that could have seen service in foreign climes, and a large black drooping moustache, the sort that villains had in the old Charlie Chaplin films. He was a large and well-built man, and wore hobnail boots, scruffy trousers and an old railway jacket, which was covered by a huge leather apron fastened from his neck. A dirty flat cap completed the outfit.

The legionnaire had a large horse and cart, and carried bales of wool for the local wool firms: he was often seen around our cobbled streets. On dark rainy days when he wore a cape he looked very scary to us young ones. Sometimes his horse and cart were left outside a house in the streets – and my mum used to say he was a lady's man, which I didn't understand. We knew he had lady friends, as we'd seen him with them down in the Coaly, at the bottom of John Willie North's field near the City railway goods yard depot. If word got round that someone had seen him in the Coaly with a lady friend, we went to seek him out among the shale and weeds. Why? I think we were growing up and just curious. I don't think anyone knew what to expect or what we might stumble on. Sometimes, as we got close to the secluded spot, his head rose from the weeds and he bellowed 'Bugger off!' in a Yorkshire accent; so much, we said, for him being a foreigner. Off we would run to the top of the field through the allotments and on to Legrams Street with red faces and hearts pounding. We had escaped the legionnaire.

When we saw French Foreign Legion pictures at the cinema we thought of him. In our boyish way we admired him and were proud to know him, albeit from a distance.

The Matchbox Man
For many years at the top Godwin Street entrance of Bradford's Kirkgate Market, at the top of the steps leading down into the market, stood a man who had one leg and supported himself with crutches. Around his neck was a coloured band that supported a tray, which carried boxes of matches that he sold for 2d each. I never knew his name, or if he was one of the many casualties of the First World War, or the victim of some accident. From when I first went into town with my mum until well into my teens, he was always there in the same place.

When I was a child my mum had instilled in me to put 2d in his tin, but not take any matches. The people of Bradford have always been generous with any charities, and I know I was not the only one to do this: I would be surprised if he had to replenish his stock very often.

Kate Kennedy
As much a part of Bradford as the Wool Exchange (now Waterstones), Kate Kennedy's liking for liquor was what led her into trouble; she appeared in court as often as the prosecuting solicitor. She was one of those people who invariably attract a crowd. If she led the law a dance, then at least she provided passers-by with comic relief.

I had two confrontations with Kate. The first was when I was about ten years old and had gone with my mum to St Patrick's Church one winter's evening for a visiting missionaries service. My mother always sat at the back of the church close to the entrance, and that particular night we were close to the font. The service was halfway through when the large door opened and the wind and cold blew in, followed by Kate singing and dancing – having been ejected from the Beehive pub on Westgate. One of the church doormen tried to calm her down, and asked her to leave, but she spotted the font and made for it. Cupping her hands, she proceeded to scoop up the holy water and throw it all around the congregation. Needless to say my mum and I were in the front line and received most of her blessing! It was one of the few times in my life that my mum didn't retaliate – as we were in church. As quickly as she had started, with a flurry and a few choice words, Kate was gone. The service carried on throughout the fracas but was talked about for many years, especially by my mum.

My own big confrontation with Kate came when I was seventeen and going home for lunch from Burton's. I was waiting for the Wyke bus outside the Odeon cinema at the bottom of Manchester Road, when suddenly around the corner she came into view, probably to visit one of the many pubs up Manchester Road. As usual she was singing and dancing. She made an obscene gesture and shouted some profane remark into Lawson's Fisheries, which was full of customers, lifted her skirt in the air, showing her knickers, and then proceeded towards me standing alone at the bus stop. I tried to look away but was caught, for with a sudden move she linked her arm to mine and pulled me around to dance. People stopped, stared and laughed, in relief that they were not the intended victim. Faces appeared at the windows of the shops and offices in the Odeon precinct and joined in the laughter. I was still at that age where embarrassment came easy, and I knew my face was crimson. How I wished that bus would come, or that she would latch on to someone else. Just when I accepted that this was going to be one of the worst moments of my life, I was saved when two of our wonderful Bradford City policemen, on a tip-off that there was trouble at the bottom of Manchester Road, came running round the corner and up to the dancers. Both policemen were laughing as they gently pulled her away, but asked if I was all right. I said 'Yes' with relief. They turned away and proceeded down Manchester Road towards the Town Hall. Suddenly Kate was away from the policemen and back to me, grabbing me and giving me a large drunken kiss on my lips. Still laughing, the policemen pulled her away again, this time holding her more securely, and disappeared around the corner. The large crowd began to break up, and the Wyke bus came round the corner – late. I boarded, went upstairs and sunk down on the back seat. When I got home my mum said, 'You're late', sniffed and asked if I'd been drinking. I shook my head and said nothing.

Kate Kennedy, born in 1886, passed away in May 1959 at the Park Nursing Home, Bradford. She had made 255 court appearances for being drunk and disorderly and was imprisoned a few times from the 1920s to the mid-1950s.

John Street Market, 1954. The large shop in the centre is one of the early Wm Morrison shops. *(Wm Morrison archives)*

'Big Anna'

'Big Anna', or 'Russian Anna', real name Anela Torbai, was born in Poland in about 1909. She had been well known in Bradford since arriving in England as a displaced person in 1948, and she worked for some time at the Bradford Combing Company in Fairweather Green. She was well over 6 feet tall and had a large muscular body. Her face was large and rather distorted, and her size, looks and physique gave her an overpowering, almost scary presence, which people tended to avoid. She was always dressed the same, wearing a well-worn dress, a man's jacket adorned with badges, cardigan and old fur-lined boots. Her hair was cut short and sometimes covered by a large head scarf or her trademark woollen hat. It was said that she had been a prisoner in the infamous Dachau Concentration Camp during the Second World War, where her experiences had affected her mind – but she was actually quite clever, and multi-lingual.

For many years Anna worked around the Bradford markets, especially the old John Street Market in Westgate. She helped many of the traders, talking loudly to the stallholders and their customers, and often breaking into powerful, piercing, startling song. Sometimes the stallholders paid her to go away and bother the customers on somebody else's stall. Her hands were so large that she could balance four tins of large peas on them. This was particularly useful when she was helping the stallholders to hand out goods to the customers. She also assisted 'Burma' Johnny, who ran a stall selling all manner of goods in the open air market; her job was to collect the cash from his customers, with no doubt 100 per cent success. I saw her many times when I was in the choir at St Patrick's Church as she attended mass there. She wandered round the church and then came down to the altar rails when communion was being dispensed.

The only time that I came into direct contact with her was in the John Street Market. I was about fourteen years old and looking at the stalls with my mate Vincent when a lady walking by with arms full of shopping fell in front of us. We ran forward and picked her up, and as we did so a large shadow enveloped us. It was Big Anna who had come over to help. She smiled at us, said nothing and ruffled our hair with a massive hand.

We shall never know the trials and tribulations of her early life. Suffice it to say that when Bradford adopted her it gained a citizen who contributed in some small way to the life and character of the city. This showed through in the letters of condolence in the papers, especially from the local traders, when she passed away in 1985, aged seventy-six.

Chapter 6
What Did You Do in the War, Daddy?

Joining Up

My dad was thirty years old when war was declared in September 1939. He had been working at John Smith & Sons for fifteen years since leaving school aged fourteen. A winding overlooker, his position was a reserved occupation, meaning that he wouldn't be conscripted for the armed services. So, married with a boy aged six and a baby just over twelve months old, he had a well-paid and secure position that would see him through the war.

One of Dad's workers in the winding shed was a Mrs Johnson. One morning a policeman came down to the mill to convey the sad news that her husband had been killed in action in North Africa. On hearing this Mrs Johnson fainted. It was some time before she came round and was taken home. It was some comfort that she had two children, Rhona and Robert (Bobby), who was to become one of my childhood pals. Although this was just one of many similar situations that took place every day during the war, it had quite an effect on my dad. On the same day he came home from work and told Mum that he wished to join up! There was to be no crying or argument. If that is what he wanted, he had her blessing.

So it was that on 1 October 1942 my dad was accepted for the army as 14304328 Sapper H. Lister, Royal Engineers, aged thirty-three. At his medical he was downgraded to Grade II (a) (Vision) because of the accident at school that had caused damage to one eye. His AB 64 Part II Soldiers Service Book shows his height as 5 feet 6 inches, weight 117 lbs, and chest 33 inches, eyes blue, hair brown, complexion sallow and two scars, on his right elbow and under his chin. These were the result of a cycle accident in 1935, when he had an altercation with the tramlines on Market Street, which resulted in concussion

The new recruit in 1942, 14304328 Sapper H. Lister, Royal Engineers.
(Author's collection)

and two days in the Bradford Royal Infirmary. The accident was worthy of five lines in the *Bradford Telegraph and Argus*.

Dad's initial training took place at Fullwood Barracks, Preston, well into February 1943. From his many letters home it appears he was happy there, and still believed he had made the right decision although he missed his wife and two boys, or his 'little buds' as he always affectionately wrote. But if he had been unhappy he would never have said so, as he was never a moaner. One thing was sure, he missed us as we missed him! All his letters concentrated on how we were, and he never said anything to worry us.

In June 1943 he was transferred to Elgin in Scotland, where he spent time on courses about pontoon bridges, then on mine-laying and securing (not for the faint hearted). At the end of the year he was transferred to Kirkby Lonsdale in Cumbria for more courses and training. During this time he came home on spells of leave, the longest being ten days, with occasional forty-eight hour passes. He always seemed to return in the middle of the night. Lawrence and I always looked forward to this and we tried to stay awake. The nights seemed still with no noise, and then far away we heard the sound of army boots, the studs making the noise of a soldier's identifiable march. It got louder, until coming down the passage the sound reverberated along the street; probably by now the whole street was awake. The front door opened, a few whispered words, then up the stairs he came. The bedroom door opened and a beam of light from the landing lit up the room against the secure black-out blinds. Most houses had a chamber pot, so we placed ours by the door so he would kick it. He always did. This was just part of our fun to welcome him home. This was followed by 'Have you bought us anything?' There was always some small present. My brother often wrote to him and I included a drawing. One time Lawrence said, 'Don't forget to bring your rifle and your bayonet home,' and he granted our wish. It stood in the corner by the bottom of the stairs, and I remember it was very heavy.

Mum received a letter from him one day to say that he had been promoted to L/Cpl (Lance-Corporal). My dad wrote very neatly but she misinterpreted the L/Cpl as Lt /Col (Lieutenant-Colonel). For the next few days all our friends and neighbours thought his promotion to Lieutenant-Colonel was wonderful!

While Dad was at Kirkby Lonsdale we visited him a few times, staying at a large house owned by a doctor. I was almost six at the time and remember vividly the doctor's elderly father. He was ninety-eight, and sat at a large rolled top writing desk and fed me with mint imperials as he wrote with a quill pen. The room smelled of mothballs, mint and the old furniture's odour of beeswax and turpentine. I walked round the garden with him holding his hand. He told me about the different plants and their names, which I didn't understand. He was a kindly old man and I didn't really appreciate his age until much later. He told me that when he was my age he had been to London with his father to visit the Great Exhibition of 1851.

During one of our visits Dad took us to his camp, which was really off limits. A mistake! Parked in a compound was a row of bren gun carriers and I wanted to go in one. So he lifted me in and there I was, six years old, in my own bren gun carrier. There were repercussions: when we had left he was put on a charge by the company sergeant major for putting me in a military vehicle. This sergeant major was one of the first of their company to be killed, two days after the Normandy landings.

To Normandy and Beyond

Dad landed in Normandy D-Day plus six, 12 June 1944. It was the end of July before we had any news by way of a field service card; all he could say by way of ticks on the card was that he was all right, and he gave an address to write to. Not long after arriving in France he was able to receive letters from home. His letters home were all love and kisses for us, because he could never say where he was, where he had been or where he was going.

The crossing had been rough and Dad was seasick all the way to Arromanches, their landing point. They were lucky: they were taken off the ship by landing craft to the beach, which was crowded with men and equipment. Six days previously the area had seen fierce fighting but it was secure now, with most of the infantry moving inland. It was still dangerous, though, and most of the men got a soaking leaving the landing craft – as it was in fairly deep water and they had heavy equipment to carry. Dad didn't like this, as he couldn't swim.

Although the area was secure there were many mines, which caused casualties every day. It was down to the officers and men of my dad's company to clear these, a dangerous task. It takes a lot of courage to secure a mine if one only has the use of a bayonet to prod the earth at an angle. Metal detectors helped to find the mines, but taking them out of the earth was still done with the bayonet.

Moving slowly inland took some weeks. There were only three casualties, one of whom was a pal of my dad's: a lad from Derby called Bill: they had been together since training. The field in which they were working had been secured, but a mine suddenly exploded: it was probably booby trapped. Bill was blinded. My dad went to see him after the war at St Dunstan's Home for blind servicemen; it upset him so much that he never visited again.

It was the small events that stuck in Dad's mind, like watching a German plane shot down above them. The pilot managed to bail out but his parachute didn't open. He fell to the ground a few hundred yards away, and when they reached him he was half his original height because of the force with which he had hit the ground. Dad and another soldier buried him. Going through his pockets for the War Graves Commission, for identification purposes, was almost too much. There were family photographs, one probably showing his wife and two children. My dad said he looked a fine young man, and although he was one of the enemy they shared similar families – a wife and two boys.

Daddy's gone to war, 1942. *(Author's collection)*

One time near Nijmegen Dad was slightly wounded. He was with a party of sappers who had just got into their vehicle when a German 88 opened up. Before they could get out a shell landed quite close, killing both the driver and the officer in front. Only one person was wounded in the rear, Lance-Corporal Lister. He shouted he had been hit as blood began to soak his tunic above the breast. He was pulled from the vehicle and dragged along to the nearest cover, behind a wall. A large piece of shrapnel protruded from his top tunic pocket, soaked in blood. It was then revealed that the shrapnel had pierced the bible in that pocket. It had taken the full force, so the shrapnel had only slightly penetrated his skin and caused a flesh wound. A temporary large plaster drew the skin together to stop the bleeding, and when they got back to the billet the MO took the plaster off; the worst part, Dad said. He was back on duty the next morning, feeling rather bruised. After the war this shrapnel had pride of place on our mantelpiece.

My dad's religion was Church of England, but he always went to St Patrick's Catholic Church with us. In his first letter home he said that he had been received into the Catholic Church before leaving for France. He had been taking religious instruction at Kirkby Lonsdale.

A few weeks later Dad had another near miss. His guardian angel was certainly with him on this occasion! He and twenty other men had just clambered into a large TCV (troop-carrying vehicle) after removing mines from a country lane when all hell was let loose. Mortar shells came over, fired from woods about 2 miles away. No one waited to be told to get out of the vehicle, and in a minute they had all jumped into a ditch that ran parallel along the road. They kept their heads down to keep away from the white-hot shrapnel flying through the air. The firing suddenly stopped and all was quiet again when suddenly a voice shouted, 'Don't anybody move. The ditch is alive with shoe-mines.' These were small but devastating mines that could kill or maim. They were all linked to one another along the ditch so if one went off they all went off. Amazingly, twenty men had jumped into the long ditch at all angles and no one had tripped a mine!

It took an hour for the men to extricate themselves from the ditch, each knowing that a single slip would set off the mines. One of the men had suggested that they should try to disarm the mines while still in the trench, but small tools that could be used for this were in the vehicle, still standing on the road with not a mark on it. It was found later that the mines were also booby-trapped, and would have gone off if anyone had attempted to disarm them. So dangerous was the trench that the infantry came along later with a Piat (projector infantry anti-tank) gun, and with a couple of rounds set the lot off.

This was a German ploy that the Allies were just catching on to. The Germans mined a ditch and waited for transport to come along. When they opened fire the soldiers in the vehicles made for the ditch. Deadly! The soldier in my dad's group who had first seen the problem and warned the others received a

The telegram sent to my mum on the day Dad sailed for Normandy, D Day plus six, 12 June 1944. *(Author's collection)*

Mention in Dispatches; he was from Leeds and a good cricket player. Two weeks later he was killed while clearing a house of booby traps.

My dad told me many things about booby traps later in life. He said the worst mines were those shoe mines. The enemy logic was that it was far better to blow off arms and legs, as soldiers then had to escort the casualties behind the lines, thus reducing the front line troops.

The places chosen for booby traps in houses and other buildings were ingenious, and deadly. One such was the picture on the wall that was left at a crooked angle. Human nature is always to straighten it, and when touch it you set off a small charge behind the picture, resulting in a lost arm or fingers, or even blindness. Other places included toilet seats, toilet chains or handles, drawers left partly open with a valuable item showing, and the same with cupboards. Chairs were dangerous too: you're tired and have a lapse in concentration, and sit down. Stairs were a favourite location: as my dad said, 'there's always one on the stairs'. The Germans knew we would find it, so they often added another one two or three steps above, hoping that the novice who has found the first one would think the stairs were clear.

Most of the information passed down to my dad and the others was the result of casualties, similar in a smaller way to bomb disposal officers. I'm so glad my mum didn't know what he was doing.

In 1945 Dad was on the Dutch border. The only scare his company had was when they were surrounded for a short time by the Germans during their last great push in December 1944. By this time he had started coming home on the odd leave, with his kit bag always full of presents. How he managed to carry some of the gifts was a wonder, as everything was always intact with no damage. He didn't drink or smoke, so he used his issue of cigarettes to barter with other soldiers and even with civilians. Among the items he brought home were two very large cased piano accordions, a large xylophone (also in its case), two Philips dynamo-operated torches (the envy of my schoolmates), exotic perfumes and stockings for my mum, and some beautiful monogrammed tablecloths (still in use) from a castle in Germany.

Just before the end of the war Dad was moved again, this time to the outskirts of Hamburg, which was occupied but devastated thanks to the recent bombings. Later, when he had returned home, if I left part of my meal he told me of the starving German children (all around my age) whom he had seen, and how they looked for food scraps in the bins and generally hung about begging. Fraternising was still not allowed but, as he said, they were just kids, so sometimes he made sure they got more than scraps. The downside of this was that word got round, and soon hundreds of children arrived all wanting food.

In May 1945 the war in Europe was at an end, but not for my dad. He was now part of the occupation forces, in Hamburg until the following December when he was posted back home, to Elgin again, and then back to Kirkby

Dad returned to John Smith's in 1946. With him on this photograph is another overlooker, Charlie Trigg. Both he and Dad had volunteered for the forces in 1942 although they were both exempt from war service in their capacity as overlookers.
(Author's collection)

Lonsdale. This was not, as we all thought, for his demobilisation, but so he could serve as an instructor. His leave home was frequent, and we often went to Kirkby Lonsdale, staying at the doctor's house again. Sadly the doctor's father had passed away just two months before his one hundredth birthday.

It was July 1946 when my dad was finally released from the army. His record had been good, and conduct on his release service book was described as exemplary. So on midsummer's day he returned home with his demob suit, which consisted of brown suit, shirt, tie, shoes, socks and a hat. Within a week he was back at work, a winding overlooker at John Smith's. He had been missed, as the female workforce in his section constantly told my mum throughout his time away.

Dad's Return Home

When my dad returned from the forces after the war he soon readjusted. I had missed him and he had missed Lawrence and me. With Lawrence now at Ushaw College we were really a family of three, except when he came home for holidays.

It was in the late 1940s that my dad took me on walks on many Sundays. A favourite was catching the trolleybus to Clayton and then walking along the country lanes to Queensbury. Even if it was raining or there was one of the appalling snowfalls we experienced at this time we headed off for the day. This was when he told me of his time in the army, and I would join him in singing 'Praise the Lord and pass the ammunition'. On these walks we saw a good number of German POW work gangs, who were working under strict control on the railways and the roads. Without their helmets they looked like everybody else, although surly and unhappy – unlike the Italian POWs who passed us in army trucks and always waved and laughed, although their waves were generally directed at young women!

Some Saturday mornings Dad took me to the mill with him, when from time to time he had to oil the looms – a laborious job with a small oilcan. It was another world among the silent looms, with the overpowering odour of scoured wool and wooden floors ingrained with oil. He frequently came home with a plaster on his head, having hit his head on the steel frame when changing belts underneath a loom. My mother usually said, 'You'd think after all these years he'd have learned.'

After the war Dad took me to Bradford City's football ground. Before the match started, and at half-time, the crowd was entertained by the local Hammond's Sauce band. On most occasions they played the regimental march of the Royal Engineers. Dad always became very emotional. Memories!

Chapter 7
Home Life in Wartime

Although I was born in 1938 and was perhaps too young to understand what the Second World War was about, I do have surprisingly strong memories of the time. Wartime in our household was accepted as it was in many other families: we just had to get on and make the best of it. With the coming of the war in September 1939, the government believed that an identity card scheme was essential for security, and that it would also help with the introduction of rationing. People were obliged to carry them at all times, each card including name, age, occupation and address. The card did not include a photograph in the vast majority of cases. I never carried mine, as I was so young; my mum always carried it together with my brother's.

As the war progressed our familiar streets began to change. For example, all the iron railings were cut down for salvage: we were told they were going to make tanks and weapons. This was a nuisance for householders, as children could easily get over their walls. Static water tanks began to appear. Usually brick built, these held over 1000 gallons of water for fire-fighting purposes. I always kept well away from these as they were known to be dangerous to children.

Gasmasks

Everyone was supplied with a gasmask, except for small babies like me who had a gas helmet. Mum had to place me in it, and pump continuously so I could breathe. She wasn't happy with this, and apparently neither was I. This device was later replaced with a brightly coloured Mickey Mouse gasmask – which I thought was a toy. I remember difficulty in breathing when I practised putting it on, and the smell of rubber and the tight straps tugging my hair. When I started school I took my gasmask with me each day, carrying the obligatory cardboard

64

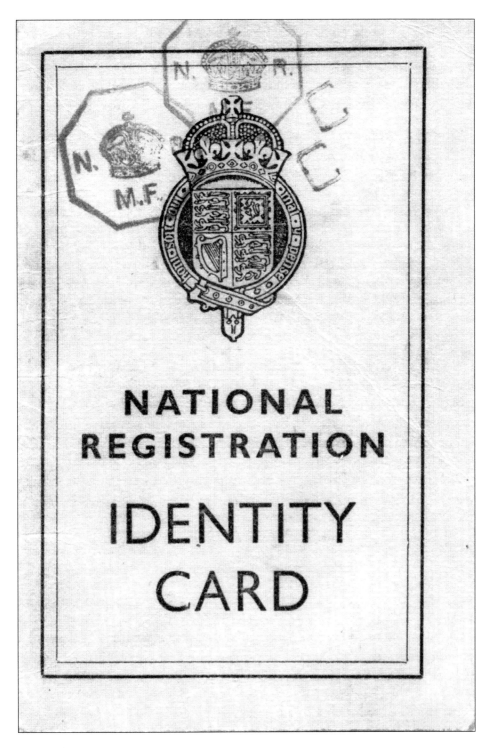

**My identity card, 1940. As I was only aged two, Mum carried this with her identity
card.** *(Author's collection)*

box around my neck – on which we had to have our names printed, so our gasmasks didn't get lost among the many others piled high in the cloakroom. Gradually more and more adults and children stopped taking their gasmasks about with them – and later my mum wore hers in the kitchen to peel onions. I found the look of this scary, but it was a brilliant idea!

Rationing and Shortages

I was nearly two when food rationing started in January 1940. I, like other children of my age, could still enjoy the small luxuries of orange juice, cod liver oil, more milk, or eggs, if available. Most children hated cod liver oil, but I liked it, and also the orange juice issued in small glass bottles. By May 1940 considerable restrictions were in place and more and more rationed goods were being added to the list.

Each member of the family had a ration book. Ours were the most common type, the buff-coloured ones. These were taken to the butchers and grocers of your choice, where you had registered for your provisions. Each book contained tokens that could be used or saved up at the owner's discretion. Shopkeepers removed the tokens before they issued the goods. We registered with Ellison's Butchers in Edinburgh Street and the well-known Congress Stores in Legrams Lane. The amounts allocated to each person were very small, and our mothers had to be geniuses to cope with the shortages and provide a relatively substantial meal for us each day.

Not everything was rationed, but most things were in very short supply. If you heard of a shop having a delivery of everyday items you hurried to join the queue in the hope of purchasing something. Queues were always long, and on many occasions my mum left me in one, holding her place, while she did other shopping. As supplies became short some items became impossible to obtain, especially imported goods such as tea, bananas, oranges and grapes: it was six or seven years before those fruits were seen again. Butter, lard, sweets, cakes, flour, eggs and sugar also became hard to get, followed by meat and fish. With these small weekly allowances of foodstuffs, the nation was fitter and slimmer than at any other time in its history. Hence my Auntie Cassie's nickname for me, Gandhi!

In addition to the rigid rationing of food, clothes were also rationed and controlled by the issue of clothing coupons from 1 June 1941. Every individual was allocated a maximum of just sixty-six coupons per annum, which equated to one complete outfit a year! Much was done to encourage women to repair old family clothes. In our house my mum unravelled the wool of old unwanted jumpers and then re-knitted it into other garments. She was especially good at producing cable-stitch pullovers for my brother and me, all the rage at the time. She wound the unpicked wool round the back of a chair and made it into skeins of wool; when she washed it in clear warm water, all the crinkles fell out. I know this because I had to help her. Mum said many times that she would have liked to have had a daughter, so she taught me to knit. I became quite proficient, but still dropped stitches. I wasn't too good at jumpers but was quite good at scarves, although as I didn't know when to stop they could be quite long! Then one day she wanted her knitting needles back. I thought it was because I was getting better at knitting, but no: 'You should be out playing football,' she said. I never knitted again from the age of eight!

There was a shortage of ladies' stockings and many times I watched my mum as she used a type of liquid make-up on her legs (Silktona) and, with an eyebrow pencil, drew a seam up the back of her legs. She usually asked me if it was straight and, not having much idea, I always said yes. At times Nancy, my mum's friend, would spend hours, or so it seemed, with my mum making up each others legs. I suppose it was a case of needs must. Their final comment was always the same: 'I hope it doesn't rain'!

The rationing and shortages gave rise to a small and stylised bald-headed cartoon figure looking over a wall, commenting on the lack of things. 'Wot no Cigs?' and similar appeared everywhere, and the name of Chad was born.

The Blackout

Our house changed somewhat because of the blackout regulations. We had all the windows taped to strengthen them and prevent glass splintering from any bomb blast. We also had blackout material, which my mum sewed on to the curtains; it was an offence to show even a chink of light. ARP (Air Raid Protection) wardens were appointed, usually ex-soldiers or non-combatants. Their only identification was a tin helmet with 'Warden' printed across it, and an armband with the initials 'ARP'. These initials were also painted in white on the outside of their homes. Two were appointed in Legrams Street, Our belief as kids was that they did nothing but shout 'Put that light out!', but I know now they did sterling work throughout the war.

In the blackout all buses and cars had shields fitted over their headlamps that allowed just three small strips of light to penetrate the total blackness before them. Accidents were common. Street lamps were turned off and people often bumped into one another. Kerbstones were painted white and white bands were painted around lampposts. My clearest memory of the blackout is when I found half a crown in Princeville Road as I returned home with my mum from my grandparents' house. This event went down in the Lister annals: not only was it a large sum of money, but how did I find it in the blackout?

Toys

Toys were scarce in wartime – with those available generally being made out of cardboard and paper rather than wood or tin. Supply lines were cut, meaning that no toys could be imported from Japan and the Far East, let alone Germany. Most of the toys sold were in some way war-related, for example jigsaws of

Spitfires or wooden tommy-guns with a round magazine, which made a 'rat-a-tat-tat' when you turned a small handle. Our reading matter was war-related too, with plane-spotter books or stories recounting the bravery of the RAF. There was usually some neighbour, probably a retired resourceful joiner, who produced wonderful wooden toys, mostly cars and planes. Aged four I received a large Lancaster bomber with a 2 foot wingspan, beautifully finished in a gloss paint camouflage finish. On all the gun turrets were small nails to represent the weapons. I became so obsessed with it that it accompanied me to bed, much to the annoyance of Lawrence – as we shared the same bed.

Lots of toys were exchanged with friends and family and I obtained a small amount of Meccano this way. As with most toys of the time, many pieces were missing. A shortage of nuts, bolts and metal strips meant the models I made were rather limited, especially compared with the size of Meccano kits that belonged to other children.

Lawrence had a pre-war clockwork Hornby '00'-scale train set. The engine was a blue Pacific named *Sir Nigel Gresley*, and there were two coaches. Being young I wasn't allowed to play with this, but my brother allowed me to join in when the track was set up. Even this became boring, and after only a few minutes it was returned to its display box and put away in the top cupboard.

Frog model plane kits were among my favourite toys. From an early age I put together these balsa wood kits from a plan, cutting out all the pieces with a razor blade and fixing them together with strong-smelling glue that had an aroma of pear drops. When this was completed I strengthened everything with strong adhesive cellulose 'dope'. There was nothing more thrilling than to wind up the tough rubber inside the fuselage fixed to a propeller and launch the model into the air. John Willie North's field was my airport. Sometimes the planes flew, occasionally quite well; but more often they didn't fly at all. Somehow they never seemed to emulate the feats illustrated on the box, and sooner or later they crashed with disastrous consequences. It was good fun, even when I had to rebuild them – if enough parts were still available.

Air Raids

My memories of the air raids are vague; although some occasions I can remember in detail, even though I was very young at the time. We had a newly built solid brick and concrete air-raid shelter in the garden which gave us 99 per cent protection. We would have known nothing about the other 1 per cent – which would have been a direct hit!

In the centre of most of the streets were long purpose-built shelters. These were for the residents who lived on the front of the streets; we, being at the back through the passage, had our own. Inside our shelter was one large steel double bunk bed that as time went on began to rust in the damp atmosphere. There was no door, just an open space across which we placed a large blanket secured at the

**Kirkgate Chapel, at the rear of Burtons and adjacent to Kirkgate Market, was
completely destroyed on 31 August 1940.** *(Bradford Libraries)*

top with two nails. Mum and Dad sat on two buffets while Lawrence and I had the bunks.

A raid could take place at any time, though mostly during the night. When the siren sounded we were both scooped up and taken to the shelter wrapped in blankets until the all-clear sounded. I remember my mum sending my dad into the house many times (5 yards away) to find, and collect, the many items forgotten in haste. These were mostly mine: dummy, cuddly donkey and, my favourite, my Mickey Mouse gasmask.

Bradford experienced four raids between 22 August 1940 and 14 March 1941. While our raids were nothing like the blitz of other cities, the siren still wailed at odd times throughout the war. Even though we may not have been the intended target, the German raiders' flight paths passed close on their way to the industrial cities of Manchester and Liverpool, which prompted alerts. Mum became an expert on the sound of the German bombers, even identifying the type of aircraft. The only one I managed to recognise was the Dornier with its undulating drone, but I think everyone knew that one.

My mother's good friend Margaret, who was my godmother, worked at the Rawson Hotel, and every Saturday afternoon my mum called to see her, taking me along (Margaret wanted to adopt me!). On one occasion, Saturday 31 August 1940, Margaret bought me a Dinky army truck – my only Dinky toy. Good toys cost a king's ransom and even at two and a half I recognised what a gift this was. But while playing with it at the hotel I pushed it down the side of a settee so far that neither Margaret nor my mum could retrieve it. Margaret said she would find someone to get it out later as it required someone with a small hand.

That evening and the following morning the Germans launched their third raid on the city, causing considerable damage in and around the city centre and over a broad area beyond. One woman died and 111 other people were treated for injuries. Lingard's departmental store was gutted, as well as the adjoining Kirkgate Chapel; only the courage and skill of the firemen saved Kirkgate Market. A bomb also tore through the roof of the Odeon cinema and landed in the stalls. The fruit section of Rawson Market was also devastated, as was part of the meat market, and the Rawson Hotel, where we had been in the afternoon, was itself damaged. The raid started at 11.13pm and ended at 2.40am, during which time 116 bombs were dropped. Tyrrell Street, Aldermanbury, Sunbridge Road, Upper Millergate, Northgate, Otley Road, Wapping Road and Laisterdyke were all damaged. Everywhere windows were smashed, blown out or cracked. Overhead tramway wires were down in places as were telephone lines. Smouldering rubble and the lingering acrid smell of smoke were still there the following day when my parents took me into town to join the crowds of people surveying the damage. As I looked at the Rawson Hotel I knew that I had lost my new Dinky toy.

Rawson Market was badly damaged in the same raid. This was also the raid that
destroyed my new Dinky toy at the Rawson Hotel.
(BHRU; Bradford Libraries)

The bombers returned at 8.46pm on 14 March 1941. The raid that March night seems to have been the heaviest in Bradford in terms of the number of bombs dropped. However, the damage appears to have been slight: two houses demolished, eight others damaged. Casualties were light. Nearly two months later a German bomber on fire crashed in Idle and burnt out; three people were killed and five seriously injured, while two cottages were demolished and two more were badly damaged. The crew bailed out and the pilot, who landed close to Bradford, was captured. The three remaining crew members were captured in another part of the West Riding.

As time went on we ceased to go into the air-raid shelter as it had become very damp, and the white fungus associated with bricks was showing. Mum had scrubbed, swept, even bleached the shelter continually, to no avail. So when the siren wailed, which it still did from time to time, we all sat indoors on the stairs. It was warmer there, and at least we could have the wireless on, which was some comfort over the noise of the planes passing overhead.

All Mum's brothers and sisters lived in Grangetown, Middlesbrough. Being the eldest, I suppose she felt herself responsible for them and had to check from time to time that everyone was all right. Sometimes Lawrence went with her, or just me, leaving my dad and brother at home – as Lawrence had to attend school and Dad worked. She just kept me off school and away we would go. I still remember the *2s 6d* return fare and taking no notice of the large posters that said 'Is your journey really necessary'? In Mum's case, it was!

Although the raids in Bradford were comparatively light, this was not so in Grangetown. Throughout the war my mum, brother and I spent holidays and weekends there, staying with my mum's sister Auntie Cassie, Uncle Stan and my cousin Kathleen, who was my age, at their house in St David's Road. They had an Anderson shelter, which was more comfortable than ours. It was in this that we spent many nights listening to the booming of the Ack-Ack guns and the drone of Dorniers, Junkers 88s and other planes bombing the Cargo Fleet Ironworks and the large shipbuilding facilities and docks along the River Tees.

So, from the relative quiet of home, we went to a whole new world of barrage balloons, noise and dark nights, lit up with the criss-cross of searchlights and the incessant shower of shrapnel that fell to earth with a clatter on the roofs and streets. The next day was spent collecting it. Sometimes I actually heard the whistling sound of bombs falling close by, and one night one of them hit a house at the bottom of the road. The family, in their Anderson shelter, were completely buried by debris from the house but were dug out unharmed.

There was a consolation; we could go to Redcar twenty minutes away. It was nice. The beach was partly mined and covered with barbed wire, but it was a change from the atmosphere of war, and to a child it was still the seaside.

In some small way I had been involved in air raids during the Second World War, both at home and away. I was too young to really know of the dangers, but even so the memories were impressed on my young mind. I and my family were lucky; many others were not.

The End of the War

On 7 May 1945 the war was over, and the next day was proclaimed a holiday: VE Day. A spontaneous street party occurred as if by magic. From somewhere came an upright piano, which was placed on the pavement outside no. 17 where the Padgetts lived. Trestle tables were found, and tablecloths laid. Food, although sparse in quantity, was produced for all the girls and boys on Legrams Street. Michael Farrell, my pal who lived in Handel Street, lived in the only house in that street, so he and his mother were invited to our street party. By way of thanks his mother brought along a 2lb bag of sugar, scarce because it was still on ration. After the party there was an enormous bonfire, around which everyone danced and sang until well after dark – which, with Double British Summer Time, was quite late. Some people found it hard to rejoice when their loved ones were still fighting the war in the Far East.

One day in August 1945 I was reading a comic when the wireless newsreader gave out the news that the atomic bomb had been dropped on Hiroshima in Japan. I wasn't at all clear what an atomic bomb was, but it was obviously something bigger than anything that had been previously used. Following the second bomb on Nagasaki the Japanese surrendered. VJ Day was 15 August, the excuse for another spontaneous street party. A second bonfire was lit on the cobbled site of the VE one. Eventually a more formal street party with tables, funny hats and jellies was held, but this was not nearly as much fun as the VE day celebration.

My final memories of the war were the Nuremberg Trials and various other war crime trials that took place in 1945 and subsequent years. When these were over and rationing had finished, the war really was over. Soon strangers in uniform were coming down our street, picking children up and hugging them. A schoolgirl friend of mine, Sandra Anstey, went to the Exchange station with her mother to meet her father, arriving home after being a prisoner of war in Germany. She didn't recognise the strange man who picked her up and said, 'Hello love.' Sandra, whose bicycle had broken the day before, innocently replied, 'Can you mend bikes, Mister?' Just one poignant event of the time!

**A poignant moment in 1945 was when a young Sandra Anstey
asked her father, on his return home after being a POW in
Germany, 'Can you mend bikes, Mister?'** *(Author's collection)*

Getting Back to Normal

Normality began to return to the streets. The rag and bone men were back with
an assortment of goods not seen since before the war, to be purchased or
exchanged for rags and weighed on a scale at the rear of their cart. These
itinerant vendors had their own particular call, the words nearly always
indistinguishable, which could be heard from many streets away. The knife
sharpener was back as well. He turned the pedals on his upturned cycle,

while small fixed oval sandstones spun and sharpened knives to a razor-sharp finish.

May Day was celebrated with more enthusiasm than during the war with girls prams, boys' and girls' cycles, wheelbarrows and scooters cleaned up and trimmed with assorted coloured papers. The many shire horses that hauled carts carrying everything from bales of wool to bags of coal were also decorated, with harness brasses gleaming, chains jangling, and the horses' tails and manes plaited with an array of coloured materials. These colours contrasted starkly with the drab, soot-stained surroundings, and the constant clatter of horses' hooves on cobblestones and the crunch of iron-bound cartwheels brought sheer joy to all of us.

Immediately after the war coal-fired gas tar boilers appeared in the streets, to repair the cobblestones. Lumps of bitumen were melted down in the boiler, and then a black stream of tar was run off into buckets to be poured in between the cobble sets. It was good for the chest (we were told), but whether it was or not it certainly had a hypnotic effect on us. When the workforce had gone we picked out the still soft tar and moulded it into various shapes. The result was arms, legs and clothes all being covered with tar, resulting in mothers dispensing a clip around the ear – but that wonderful smell was well worth the punishment. Precious margarine or lard had to be used to remove the tar.

Clothes were now off ration, but clothing in general was still drab. Many men still wore old army battle-dress blouses and greatcoats for work; in fact coloured clothing was almost non-existent. I still wore my brother's 'hand-me-downs', including a cap, raincoat, jacket, trousers, shoes and socks. Each item had a white label sewn on it, with the number 160 printed on. This was Lawrence's clothing identification number at Ushaw College, and so for many years it was my 'identification number' as well!

In 1949 sweets came off the ration, but the demand meant they were soon rationed again – until 1953, the same year I started work.

My mother never liked pets, but we did have a budgie. Peter was his name and he was sky-blue in colour. Our budgie was no different from others: everyone with a budgie told you of the great feats they are capable of. Most could recite nursery rhymes and their names and addresses, some with bad language thrown in. Ours was the same, but without the bad language. As my dad said, 'It can do anything except bring the coal up from the cellar.' Peter was a trusting little pet, who never bit, and how I loved him. When I was returning from school he had an uncanny habit of jumping from perch to perch and squawking when I was a few hundred yards from the house, only stopping chirping when he was on my hand. It was a wonderful feeling to have this loveable character tucked into my shoulder chattering away as I sat reading a book or comic. Peter was with us for around four years, into the early 1950s. One morning we found him lying dead at the bottom of his cage. A teenager now, I was heartbroken. Dad wanted to take him to work to put in the mill furnace, but I decided to bury him in our small garden along with the goldfish, minnows, and frogs that I had buried over the years. I wrapped him in a cloth, placed him in a tin box so the cats wouldn't dig him up, and buried him on a cold winter's morning within the shadow of the air-raid shelter. I was upset for some time and the house was suddenly very quiet. His cage and effects were given away, as nothing could replace our Peter – who could do everything but bring the coal up from the cellar.

Short Back and Sides

This was the phrase used by our fathers and grandfathers when requesting a haircut. It was passed down to us – as there were no alternative styles until much later. I had my first haircuts at home, generally with a normal pair of scissors and a small basin placed on my head. It was my dad who suggested he took me to his barber after my mum accidentally cut into my ear with the scissors; I was two at the time.

My dad's barber was Terry's, at the end of Westgate near City Road. A box was placed on the chair for small ones like me to sit on. Terry's daughter always cut my hair. I believe it was quite unusual for female hairdressers to work in a barber's at this time. Her haircutting was fine, even with the old-fashioned hand clippers; it was later I didn't like! Because she brushed me with a brush already full of hair from earlier patrons, I went home with ears, nose, eyes, neck, shirt and body covered in hairs. 'Stop scratching!' Mum would say days after the haircut.

One of the main topics of conversation in the barber's was how the war was going, but this was nearly always overshadowed by how Bradford City was going on. Strange priorities! On reflection, perhaps I was being shielded from grown-up talk.

By the time I was about five I didn't need the box any more, and I then went to Charlie's barber's shop, down Preston Street near Slingsby's and John Smith Textiles. There were two chairs facing a large mirror, adverts for Brilliantine, Gillette razors and in the centre a large portrait of Denis Compton (the England cricketer) advertising Brylcreem; this earned him the nickname 'The Brylcreem Boy'. Charlie was a tallish, fresh-skinned, slim man with thinning sleek black hair plastered back with brilliantine, and a thin moustache, the type we used to associate with 'spivs'. He wore a long white coat with scissors protruding from his left pocket. Charlie was no spiv, but probably one of the many ex-servicemen settling back into civilian life after the war. We all liked him, and he did a good short back and sides. He always left plenty on the top, which pleased my mum because she could put a quiff in the front, with finger, comb and water. After the haircut he rubbed in hair cream, his own brand: it looked like the gloy we used at school for sticking paper together, and was sticky. If it was sunny when you left Charlie's, in two minutes your hair became hard like a crust. My mother soon had it sorted with the quiff! Charlie was cheap at 1s.

Only once did Vincent and I not support Charlie. When a new barber opened at the top of Edinburgh Street (next door to Ellison's, a popular butcher), with electric clippers, an innovation to us, we had to give it a try! Our new man was a DP, the abbreviation used for 'displaced person' or refugee. These were mostly Poles, Ukrainians and Latvians who came to Bradford from Eastern Europe after the war. They were invariably bilingual and modest, and very soon integrated into our way of life, contributing much to the post-war future. The barber's English was limited, but he appeared to know 'short back and sides'. We had gone in for the usual, and came out almost bald: not only had he given us a short back and sides, but the entire top had gone. Both our mothers were angry and said we looked like refugees; my dad added, 'More like fugitives from a chain gang.' Our biggest embarrassment, however, was being suspected of having nits: shaving the head was one of the remedies for hair lice. This happened to girls more than boys, so Vincent and I were a novelty, especially at school, where most of our classmates gave us a wide berth. It took a week or two before our hair grew back to any extent, and during this time going to the cinema and most other pursuits were curtailed. We didn't go back to our DP friend, although he became established and was there for some years – minus two original customers.

So it was back to Charlie's for the next few years. I still had my quiff when I worked at Brown, Muff's, from 1953 to 1955. By then I was shaving, although my bristles were just the fuzz of a peach. I could have many shaves with the same razor blade, thanks to my dad's (army) method of sliding the flat of the blade around the inside of a glass to keep it sharp. It always worked!

It was in 1955, when I was working at Burton's Westgate, that I walked into a barber's in James Street and said, 'New style please.' Half an hour later I was back at Burton's to display my DA (duck's arse) and Tony Curtis haircut! The quiff had gone! This was the 'Teddy boy' era when new styles from across the Atlantic were in vogue. Short back and sides was on its way out and a new hairdresser had opened in Forster Square, called Mario's. Although expensive, it was the place to be styled. I soon became a regular customer. Mario had been an Italian POW, had stayed after the war and married Mary, a local girl. The business is still flourishing today in Westgate.

What goes around comes around. After eighteen years of basin cuts, short back and sides, quiffs, head shaves, Tony Curtises and others, I returned to very short back and sides in the army in 1956.

Christmas
Excitement mounted in the days before Christmas Day for us boys and girls, who enquired of each other endlessly, 'What are you getting for Christmas?'

Many ridiculous answers were given: a tank (a real one!) and a real rifle and hand grenade (in a letter to a friend's father in the Forces!), while girls talked of real babies, and we all wanted bananas, oranges and tons and tons of sweets and chocolate. Well, we all dreamt.

Busby's department store on Manningham Lane was very popular with children at Christmas, with its wonderful 'Santa's Grotto'; a visit cost 1s. This was my first introduction to Father Christmas, in 1941. I remember, aged three, not being as enchanted as I was told I should have been, because the present I received was a small tin tank. Being wartime I suppose it was thought to be patriotic, but on my next two visits to see Santa I also received a tank! A hat trick of tanks over three Christmases must be a record of some kind. I didn't go to see him the following year as I had become a non-believer. What with infant school gossip and my wondering how this over-sized man (who smelt of mothballs) could climb down our very small back-to-back chimney and never leave a mess made me sceptical.

As Christmas Day approached Vincent and I went carol singing in the evening around the dark streets. Most people were generous and invited us into their homes, where we sang our carols in a nice warm atmosphere – far better than standing on a windswept doorstep accompanied by rain or snow.

Our repertoire was short and kept simple by only singing the first verses. We could sing 'O Come All Ye Faithful' in English or Latin, having learnt 'Adeste Fideles' with the church choir. Other favourites included 'We Three Kings', 'Silent Night', 'Good King Wenceslas', and the carol we finished with:

> We knock at the door, we ring the bell
> We see what we get for singing so well
> If you haven't a penny, a half penny will do
> If you haven't a halfpenny, then God bless you.

When we were in St Luke's Hospital in 1949 John Tindall told me that his gang, the Canterbury Warriors, had a different version of the last line: 'If you haven't a halfpenny we'll put your window through!'

We steered clear of some houses; others let you sing all the carols, then shouted 'Not tonight' through the door. Other more unsavoury characters shouted 'Bugger off!' Shrugging our shoulders, we would move on to the next house. There were not many coppers in our collection, and the half crowns, two bob pieces and shillings mounted up, so at the end of each evening we could have as much as a pound each. Sometimes we were given chocolates and sweets as well as money, so the rewards were well worth the rain, snow and the odd rebuff – especially as Christmas Day was just around the corner. It could be a very lucrative time for us.

The celebration of Christmas in the Lister household was a religious one: the day always began with nine o'clock morning Mass at St Patrick's Church, leaving any unopened presents until we returned home. As I got older, we all attended Midnight Mass, which was also well attended by non-Catholics. The problem was that, together with other children of my age, I found it hard to keep my eyes open and stay awake during the service. Getting to bed late didn't stop baggy-eyed children, sleepless with excitement, being awake even earlier than normal to open their Christmas presents.

Lawrence and I always had a pillowcase on the rail at the bottom of the bed to hold our presents, although I don't remember this being filled to the top. Being eight years older than I was, Laurence had proper 'big boy's toys', games and books, while I had more childish presents. An apple, some nuts (if available) and sweets were often at the bottom of my pillowcase, which always gave off a pleasant aroma when I opened it. When I was young I often wondered where Father Christmas had got his sweet coupons from. My reading was good from a very early age, so Christmas annuals like the *Beano*, *Dandy*, *Knockout* and *Funnies* were always included. My mum had taught me how to model plasticine, especially 'puffer trains', and every year a packet was included, with its own peculiar smell. Once I got a tin Tommy Talker (a kazoo), but because of the noise that I had made on this instrument it had strangely disappeared by Boxing Day.

One present that I always enjoyed was a John Bull printing outfit. I spent hours cutting out the small rubber letters, placing them in a wooden block and pressing this block on the inkpad. Your editorial was then printed on paper for all to see, including your fingerprints from the inkpad! Drawing books were popular and came with wax coloured crayons, five to a packet. I used to be very careful not to snap them, and tried to make each crayon last until it was down to a stub. On one occasion I received my very own torch; they were scarce, as were batteries. I was often told off by my mum for wasting it, especially when I put it under my chin in the dark and pulled a face to frighten people. My dad added that I didn't need the torch!

We always had the same old pre-war Christmas tree, which was 3 feet high with wire branches covered with imitation greenery. Most of the decorations were the same age, with animals, fairies, stars, 'Wesley bobs' and other odd-shaped items. Some still had Edison-screw bulb holders for the lights, although these had long since become obsolete. The tree was always placed on top of the wireless in the corner of the room, and looked resplendent with tinsel and strips of colourful paper. This paper was also used to make paper chains, which were hung across the ceiling and around the walls. They were held together with water paste but mostly disintegrated when the paste dried, falling silently to the floor. During the war we tried to save Christmas decorations because new ones were almost impossible to buy. If an ornament was broken it was a serious loss. Even the tinsel on the tree was unravelled and put away.

We always had a few pieces of holly, strategically placed on the top of photographs. On the ceiling by the front door, for the unwary, was a sprig of mistletoe. The mere thought of it brought a twinkle to the eyes of everyone between the ages of nine and ninety. As a boy I thought 'Ugh' and 'It's sloppy' when I saw adults kissing under the mistletoe – but years later I found it was an excellent excuse to kiss some girl I fancied; if rebuffed, I could blame it on the mistletoe, Christmas or even a drink.

Our Christmas Day dinner was always very appetising and filling, although I don't remember chicken or turkey on the menu until well after the war. Vegetables were plentiful and piled high on the plates, or in my case low on the plate as I was still not a big eater. We always had a Christmas pudding, which was stuffed with the old silver threepenny bits. I often wondered, when biting into one of these, just how many revellers choked to death on a coin in a Christmas pudding. When dinner was over we listened attentively to the King's speech on the wireless. Our impression of him was that he was a shy man with a stammer, and every year my mum would say 'I wish he would have a good cough.' The King's speech was followed by a special 'forces favourites', which relayed messages and music chosen by relatives of those who were serving in the forces.

Our dinner was hardly digested before another assortment of food came out, mainly sandwiches and my mum's cakes. I always liked to watch her bake, and was fascinated as she gathered the pastry, rolled it in her hands, and sprinkled flour on the board before rolling the pastry out thinly. Apple pies were her speciality: years of experience made it all look so easy. I was given the uncooked pastry scraps for my speciality, jam tarts, which always turned out the same – crispy with rubbery jam. The highlight was scraping out the mixing bowl with my fingers. My jam tarts were the highlight of our Christmas Day tea! Friends and neighbours came and went all evening, adding to the excitement. We played board games before Lawrence and I wandered off to bed.

Boxing Day was always spent at my grandparents' (the Listers), at 41 Fenton Street, Princeville. It was from one back-to-back house to another, the only difference being they had no electricity, only gas. We arrived before lunch, which was always timed to start at one o'clock. My grandmother was always on time, even though everything was cooked on her Yorkshire range. Bubbling and steaming pans were taken off the fire with precision timing: it was a work of art, and the food was always wonderful! Every year there was a chicken or a turkey; where these were obtained during the war years we never asked. The pudding speciality on Boxing Day was a rice pudding, which was baked on the grill of the Yorkshire range until it had a light brown covering, again timed to perfection.

Gifts had already been exchanged: mine was usually 2s 6d, which was more than the sixpence I was given on my usual Sunday visits. Lawrence got 5s, and my parents received some small gift. My grandfather always sneaked me an extra

2s 6d, but I was instructed to say nothing and never did, not even to my parents. Jim Buxton, the neighbour who spent lots of time at the house, was always there on this family occasion. After the delightful meal I played with games or toys, or read an annual that I had brought with me. My mother and grandmother sat and dozed while my grandfather, dad and Mr Buxton played cards. My grandfather and Mr Buxton both smoked pipes so the air was full of rich pipe tobacco smoke, while cards were dealt to the sound of the chink of coins changing hands.

As darkness fell in the late afternoon the two gas mantles above the table were lit, with a hiss and a pop, to throw a dull blue glow around the room. It was old fashioned but it gave a wonderful atmosphere of warmth and good feeling, something that a bright electric light couldn't emulate. Boiled ham was produced at teatime for sandwiches, which were filled with raw cut onions tasting of vinegar and sugar. These had been prepared a few days before, and were dark brown in colour: they were delicious. Grandmother always produced a homemade trifle, made from ingredients that in the 1940s were always difficult to obtain. Half a bottle of sherry and a small amount of rum were always included. It was little wonder that I always got daft after Grandmother's trifles, especially when my grandfather taught me to pour hot tea into a saucer and drink it with a slurping noise. After much giggling and spilt tea I became quite skilled at this, but my mum was never amused.

To finish off, a bottle of liqueur would go a round or two with the adults, followed by a nice cup of tea. This was made on the sole gas ring at the top of the cellar steps: there was no scullery or kitchen in the house – just a pot sink in the cellar. After tea, trips were made to the outside toilet, through the dark passage at the rear of the house. A small kerosene lamp was placed by the door to light our way. Every time I returned from the toilet people would exclaim 'My, that was quick', and it always was: no way was I hanging about in that dark passage or the toilet on my own.

Once everyone had settled down we played the card game Newmarket for money. I played with my own money, and when I lost I didn't expect or receive my losses back – quite a learning experience for a young boy. When everyone had either won or lost, out came the Lotto. The small wooden numbers were shaken up in a large bag and the numbers were called out to fill the player's cards. I enjoyed this game immensely, until the sherry and rum trifle took its final toll. Off I drifted into a deep sleep, in a chair with my knees curled up under me, interrupted only by the sound of adults laughing and talking until I heard my mum saying, 'Look, he's asleep, we'll have to be going soon.'

In a dream I was lifted up, my shoes were placed on my feet and my coat, scarf and cap were put on. Then a door opened and I was awake. It was the front door, and the cold night air was sweeping across my face. It wasn't a dream. Out into the cold night air we went, with me half-asleep again and mumbling yes or no to the conversation going on. Oh, how I wished I was home in my warm bed!

BRADFORD BORN AND BRED

Upon reaching home I was brought back to life when the room light was switched on. The dull-looking fire packed with slack and tea leaves was raked with the poker, and as if by magic it burst into flames and began to warm the room.

Christmas hardly changed as I became older. Sometimes I spent time with mates or girlfriends on Christmas Day and Boxing Day, with parties and more of a teenage scene – but it is the Christmases with my brother, parents and grandparents that I remember most clearly. In fact, as time went by the only thing that really changed for me in relation to home life as a whole was the impact of this teenage scene, of which more later. The apron strings were cut, and it was accepted that there would be a slow transition from the bonds of family life. Even so, I still felt a deep love for these times, and for my parents and brother.

Chapter 8
Family Friends and Neighbours

Our family had many friends and neighbours, but there are a few whom we always recall with fondness, remembering times spent together in our homes and on outings. These memories are tinged with love, affection, sadness, tears and laughter.

The Cunliffes

Among my parents' special friends were Bill and Margaret Cunliffe. Margaret came from Wicklow in Eire. She was born in 1900, so was a little older than my mum. In 1916, while working in Dublin, she received slight shrapnel wounds to her leg while sheltering near the General Post Office in O'Connell Street, during the artillery bombardment of that building in the Easter Rising of 1916. Her name was shown in the civilian casualty lists. It was in the 1920s that she came to Bradford and found work at John Smiths Mill, where she later met my mum. They became good friends when they lodged at Ma Rouse's in Marion Street, close to the mill. She later married Bill Cunliffe, and it was with Margaret and Bill that my parents spent much of their leisure time. Margaret and Bill had two daughters who were well into their teens when I came along in 1938. My brother Lawrence had always been fussed over by Bill, Margaret and the girls, and Bill cuddled and entertained me while visiting our home or at their house in Bolton Road. They became my godparents when I was baptised.

My dad and Bill were close friends, and at one time had talked about volunteering for service in the Spanish Civil War (on whose side I never discovered); my mum and Margaret talked them out of it. When war was declared in 1939 Bill, aged thirty-six, was one of the first to join up – as 4850010 Pioneer William Edward Cunliffe in the Pioneer Corps. After a short time he was promoted to sergeant, serving with 50 Company Militia Auxiliary,

The sinking of the *Lancastria* at Dunkirk, 17 June 1940. The ship is shown on its back. My godfather, Bill Cunliffe of the Pioneer Corps, was last seen in the water near the propellers. RIP. *(By kind permission of the Lancastria Association)*

and was one of the many men on the beaches of the retreating British Expeditionary Force in 1940. Bill was not one of the lucky ones who returned from Dunkirk, as he was one of the many casualties on the ill-fated *Lancastria*.

The *Lancastria*, formerly a Cunard liner, was bombed and sunk by Junkers 88 bombers in the estuary of the River Loire on Monday 17 June 1940, while attempting to rescue troops at Dunkirk. Four hits, including a bomb straight down her single funnel, caused the ship to list, roll over and sink within twenty minutes. She was crammed with approximately 6,000 troops, RAF personnel, civilians and crew, of whom over 4,000 lost their lives. This incident remains Britain's worst-ever maritime disaster, but like many other shipping disasters of the Second World War it remains little known today. After the war Margaret was visited by one of Bill's friends, a fellow sergeant who had been on the *Lancastria*. He told her that when the ship had turned over he had seen Bill by the ship's up-turned propellers.

Although she was no relation, I always called Margaret 'Auntie'. She always said that she and Bill had wanted to adopt me.

Nancy Byrnes

Nancy Byrnes, another Irish girl from Wicklow, also worked at John Smiths Mill and was friends with my mum and Margaret. She lodged on Great Russell Street with an old lady who was well into her nineties called Mrs Pullen. Nancy was a lovely lady, and beautiful, with brown eyes, pale face and dark hair. That wonderful expression 'she had a face like the map of Ireland' was made for her. A cuddle from Nancy was always welcome, although with her Irish wit she once made me blush bright red. I was aged about twelve, and Nancy was sitting chatting and laughing with my mum on the settee. I had been reading and decided to go to bed, when I felt something on my chin. Going to Nancy, I said, 'What's this on my chin?' Nancy pulled me close, and proclaimed, 'It's a whisker'. I said, 'Do you think I will have to start shaving soon?' My mum laughed and said, 'No, don't be daft!' As I turned to go upstairs Nancy shouted, 'That's nothing. You'll soon have hairs where you daren't tell your mother!' I ran upstairs blushing, followed by the sound of laughter. Nancy never married, but there were always rumours that there had been someone in her life long ago.

Jessie Mee

Mrs Jessie Mee lived on Talbot Street with her brother Tom, an ex-Bradford Pal soldier who had been taken prisoner on the Somme in 1916. Jessie, born in the 1890s, had had another brother who had died in Egypt during the First World War. In the living room there was a photograph of him, a typical 'British Tommy' on a camel with the sphinx and pyramids in the background. This photograph had been taken not long before he died. Mrs Mee could read tea leaves, and her predictions were uncanny. She told me that during the First World War, while her brother was in Egypt, she awoke one night to feel someone was holding her hand, and a voice said, 'Don't worry, Jessie, I'm all right.' Two days later she received a telegram telling her that her brother had died of typhoid at the time she had experienced the hand and voice. Jessie was a nice old lady and a good friend to our family, particularly to my brother when he was studying for the priesthood.

The Farrells

The Farrell family lived at Handel Cottage, Handel Street, next to the foundry of Howarth and Walter Ltd. Tom and Kathleen were Michael and David's parents. Michael was my school friend, and teenage friend, for many years. The Farrells' old grandmother lived with them, as well as Patsy the dog, one of those dogs that forever jumps up and down, covering everyone with dog hairs. Their house had a small living room and a small kitchen – as well as a bathroom, which they invited us to use as an alternative to our tin bath and Windsor slipper baths. Tom had a printing press in the cellar: the small window was always open, so the noise of the press could be heard along the street. He printed leaflets, cards and posters,

Our family friends the Farrells lived in the only cottage in Handel Street.
(Author's collection)

mostly for St Patrick's Church. This was his hobby, as he worked for the Bradford Dyers Association on Water Lane, looking after their transport. My parents had a lot of time for Tom Farrell. I always remember the times he passed my mum some money in an envelope to help with clothes and other items for Lawrence at college. Tom's big disappointment was that he had not been in the army during the war, but he more than made up for this with his generosity and kindness to us when my dad was away with the army in Germany.

The Duckworths
The Duckworths, Bernard and Agnes, had three boys, Bernard, Kevin and Brendan (all younger than I), and lived on Springfield Street, off Whetley Hill. Agnes, like my mum, was a stalwart member of St Patrick's Union of Catholic Mothers. She and her jovial husband Bernard were very good to Lawrence during his time at Ushaw College. Agnes also invited me to their house at school dinnertimes, especially when my mum was ill. When I was in my early teens they told me to call them Agnes and Bernard, at a time when it was really disrespectful to call adults by their Christian names. I did as they asked, but was never really comfortable: I still thought I should be addressing them as Mr and Mrs.

The Holdsworths
Albert and Annie Holdsworth lived in a semi-detached house on Brooksbank Avenue, at Lidget Green. They had two boys Arthur and Roy, and a younger girl, Sandra. Lidget Green was where my mum had wanted to live for many years. On the way home she often said, 'I wish we lived up here.' Sometimes I replied, 'When I'm big and working I shall buy you a house up here.' A squeeze on my hand said it all.

The Tylers
Mr and Mrs Tyler and their son Colin lived in a back-to-back house near Exmouth Place, Bolton Road. At the end of their street was a wartime static water tank. Colin and I were told to keep away from this, as during the war children had been drowned in similar tanks. Mr Tyler and my dad used to reminisce about their service in the war, with a backdrop of a souvenir German helmet hanging from a hook on a wall. Mrs Tyler and my mum updated each other with news, some of which made Mrs Tyler laugh. She had a wonderful laugh, which always gave me a nice warm feeling as I played with Colin and his toys. Mrs Tyler died in the early 1950s of breast cancer. Janet was a lovely lady and was sadly missed by my parents, especially my mum.

Mrs Wainwright
A friend of my mum's called Mrs Wainwright lived on Arncliffe Terrace,

Legrams Lane. Our visits were limited to about two or three times a year, and the evenings only. As my dad never accompanied my mum there, I was always my mum's escort. On arrival she gave me some comics to read, a glass of pop, and I sat on a large soft sofa in front of a lovely blazing fire. The scene was always the same. My mother asked if I was all right and then disappeared into the parlour with Mrs Wainwright. As I was interested in comics I was soon lost in a world of adventure, being only disturbed from time to time with the sound of indistinct conversation. Some time later my mum emerged and I was made ready for the trip home. With goodnight pleasantries we were off, me with no idea what these outings were all about. It wasn't until I was a little older that I found out the reason for these evening visits. Mrs Wainwright was a corsetière, one of those wonderful ladies who worked privately from home, making corsets for our mothers and others. Every area in Bradford had one such woman. Her husband worked nights, so ladies could only visit in the evenings for measuring and fitting.

The Glossops and the Newells

While we had many close neighbours, perhaps the best were the Glossops and the Newells. Living next door to us were Nellie and Arthur Glossop, and Jean their daughter. The Glossops had moved into no. 32 at about the same time as us in 1939. My mum and Nellie spent time in each other's houses almost every other day, to gossip and to have the odd Woodbine. A knock would sound on our door, and Nellie would say, 'It's only me, Vida'. There were no 'tuts'; it was just accepted that our neighbour was calling. If the door was open when I came home from school, and Mum wasn't around, I knew where she was.

Mr Glossop was called up and joined the newly formed Parachute Regiment. He took part in the regiment's air-drop on the Rhine in March 1945.

Our other neighbours were the Delaneys, who lived at the back of our house on the front of the street, but moved in 1940; they later became well-known scrap merchants on Shearbridge Road. Our new neighbours at no. 28 at the front were Lucy Newell and brothers Frank and Arthur, all unmarried. Arthur had a full-time job, but in his spare time had joined an amateur theatrical group that always performed musicals. He loved dancing, especially tap, and practised on a large tin tray in his front room. We could hear him through the wall, but became accustomed to his constant taps and shuffles. We were never perturbed, or objected; it was Arthur's hobby and, after all, he had been in the thick of the fighting with the Durham Light Infantry at Monte Cassino in Italy in 1944. My dad would look up from reading and say 'Arthur's at it again', smile and return to the newspaper. To get away from Arthur, Lucy sometimes popped in to spend ten minutes with my mum 'catching up'.

Frank was the eldest brother, who had been too old for the war. He was a quiet man who didn't say much, but he always smiled and enquired how we were.

Brother and sister Arthur and Lucy Newell, our long-time neighbours on Legrams Street. Arthur's tap dancing could be heard through the stone wall into our home, as he practised on a large tin tray. *(Author's collection)*

His sudden death in 1950 left a void in his brother's and sister's lives, as, indeed, it did for us.

If I had something new to wear at Whitsuntide my mum always sent me round to show Lucy. With a freshly washed face, combed hair, clean socks and shoes I was on show for a few minutes at their house, being asked to parade and turn round to many acclamations of 'Show us your shoes', 'What a lovely jacket' and 'You're a smart lad', until something was dropped into the top pocket of my jacket. It was an unwritten law that I didn't look into the pocket until I was outside. I never came away with less than £1! A similar act was carried out for Nancy, Margaret, Mrs Mee, Mr and Mrs Glossop and the Farrells. I always looked forward to Whitsuntide.

Lucy and her brothers were members of the Longside Lane Working Men's Club. Every year the club had a trip to the seaside for the members' children. Lucy always asked me if I wanted to go and I often did. The trip was full of our arch-enemies, the Longside Lane Gang, whose members ran into three figures. There was always a truce on these trips, however, and I would mix and pal up with them, and generally have a good time. What a treat it was to go by coach or train for a day at the coast, usually Blackpool. We were all given a book of tickets for free rides at the pleasure beach, half a crown to spend and a packet of sandwiches. The day finished with a fish and chip tea at one of Blackpool's large fish restaurants. All the children had a very large blue label attached to our lapels, with our names on and in large letters the words 'If I am lost', and what to do if this occurred.

The Newells' toilet was next to ours at one side of the midden. We had a code for the dark winter nights, as it could be quite scary in the dark toilet with a torch – and sometimes not even that: it could be unnerving to hear footsteps coming down the passage as someone approached the toilet. A voice would say, 'It's only Lucy', or Frank or Arthur. This went on for many years, and was comforting especially if I had just been listening to Valentine Dyall's 'The Man in Black' on the wireless! Sometimes goodnights were exchanged.

Other Neighbours

Just over the wall to our right were the Broadbents and next to them was a quiet well-dressed lady, Marjorie Cockcroft, who always kept to herself but would pass pleasantries. Others on our street like the Stewarts, Padgetts, Hodgsons, Richardsons, Creswells, Wardens, Ogdens, Harrisons and Wilfords were also missed when we parted in 1955, and things were never the same with our new neighbours. All these people and others added a certain feeling of well-being. They were all 'good neighbours' who were unpretentious and hard-working, with their family values endorsed by love and affection. I missed them all.

Chapter 9
School Life

Princeville Nursery

Having been a poorly child and still being susceptible to ailments, I was very close to my mum, but when I turned three it was proposed (by whom I never found out) that I should start my education and attend a local nursery. The aim was to wean me away from Mum's apron strings, although she was reluctant to let me go.

A place was found for me at Princeville Nursery on Ireton Street, close to the Princeville Boys' and Girls' School. On one side of the nursery was Willowfield Street with adjacent rows of back-to-back houses, one of which was Fenton Street where my grandparents lived. On the other side was Brownroyd Street; the top end of the street by the nursery was unmade, and halfway down was the entrance to the city greyhound track.

It is remarkable how many people remember their first day at school so clearly, and I am no exception. There was something very different that day, especially when I was given a new pair of sandals to wear, which I didn't understand as I had been used to wearing a small pair of clogs. I had liked these as I could make quite a noise stamping on the flagstones in our passage, but they were not acceptable for a three year old running around classrooms and playgrounds!

On my first day my mum was crying. I didn't really know why she was upset, but her tears upset me, so we cuddled each other. I had my breakfast and, never having a big appetite, was content with my Puffed Wheat and a glass of milk. It was September, and the long hot summer of 1941 was beginning to cool down. I was attired as if going to the North Pole, with a balaclava on my head, scarf, coat, small jacket, pullover, short trousers, new stockings and sandals; and, secreted in a pocket, a dummy.

Two other items I had to take with me were my small donkey soft toy, and my blue Mickey Mouse gas-mask, both of which I slept with. I was now ready for the journey, but I wasn't sure where I was going!

The nursery hours were from 9am until 11.30am and 1pm until 3pm. There were no facilities for meals at lunchtime, so it was two journeys there and back for mothers. The journey from our house in Legrams Street was a fifteen-minute walk, up Legrams Lane past Holdsworth and Burrell's (Transport) and a large Victorian detached house, past the allotments over the railway bridge, which was the main line to the City Road goods depot, then left into Brownroyd Street to the nursery.

The journey was quick, and there seemed to be other mothers with children of my age, tugging, pulling and crying, coming from other roads, streets and snickets, all going to the same destination. Mum had told me I was going to school, which I had seemed to accept but I didn't really understand or know that I would be left there. I was in for a surprise.

On arrival I suddenly realised all was not well, as some of the other children were screaming and crying. As we went through the door my mum was greeted by a lady who seemed to be expecting me. Mum took my coat and scarf off and pulled off my balaclava, and someone said, 'It's a boy'. No one could blame them for their surprise because, with my piercing blue eyes, I was mistaken for a girl many times. (I think my mum wanted a girl: she was going to call her Moira.)

I was now beginning to be aware of the terror of being parted from my mum and taken away by strangers. Through all the noise and bedlam a nursery teacher asked all the mothers to leave. My mum burst into tears, which set me off. I clung to her and wouldn't let go. She gently pushed me away and said 'You'll be all right', and was off sobbing through the door and out of the school gate, leaving me shocked and crying that she'd left me.

I didn't know at the time, but she didn't go back home. She waited the two and half hours round the corner, peeping from time to time to see if she could see me. I cried until she came for me, and then stopped when I saw her face; but we both started crying again when we trotted home for dinner. When we arrived home I had some sago with raspberry vinegar, and what our landlord said was the staff of life, bread and jam. I was soon dressed again in the coat and balaclava ready for the afternoon session.

I knew where I was going this time so was more obstructive on the journey, pulling away and crying. This went on for two weeks. I believe I played with some of the other children on a climbing frame and in a large children's toy house, but I didn't like it. All I really remember is that I cried a lot.

Came the time when my mum had had enough. Dad said it was making her ill, so I was withdrawn and everything was nice again. Mum smiled and I was happy once more, playing with my toys and wearing my gasmask and clogs.

Some of the teachers who taught me at St Patrick's. Top left: Bernard Moore, Miss McAndrew, Miss E. Wheelan. Standing on the far right: Miss E. O'Brien. Kneeling at front left: Miss H. Bolton.

St Patrick's Infant School

It was over a year after the Princeville nursery débâcle that I was told to say goodbye to my gasmask and clogs, put the sandals on and go to school. It was impressed on me that my new school was for big boys, and it was also mentioned that most of my young friends were already attending school. I seemed to accept the fact and, indeed, looked forward to this big adventure.

St Patrick's Church on Westgate was where we, as a family, attended Mass every Sunday. This was therefore the church school that I would attend. My brother Lawrence was already at the school in Standard Three, which he liked; and he was doing well.

I spent a few weeks in the nursery school to become accustomed to school ways. It wasn't a bit like Princeville Nursery and I remember enjoying it. This nursery was a pre-fabricated building opposite the Rington's Tea offices, between St Thomas's Road and Wigan Street.

I seemed to settle in well, and it wasn't long before I had moved to the infants' school on the adjacent Paradise and Dyson Streets. This school had been built in 1892. As well as having the infants' section, which was two classrooms on the ground floor, it housed the girls' school on the floors above and to the rear.

Also incorporated into the building was a small playground in the basement, with an entrance along a dark sloping passage. In this area there was also a hall used for functions and school dinners. Down Paradise Street was an entrance into the same building, which on the first floor housed St Michael's church hall. This was used for many years as a parish concert room and rehearsal room for the Bradford Catholic Players. Below this entrance were the club and billiard rooms of the CYMS (Catholic Young Men's Society). Somewhere among all this was my classroom!

There were only three of us at home now, since Dad had joined the army and was in Scotland, but life went on. For the first few months Mum diligently took me to school down Preston Street, Handel Street, Thornton Road and up Westgrove Street. Fifteen minutes and we were there, and this time neither of us ended up crying. I didn't take my gasmask, and my clogs had long gone. I was happy enough and liked school.

Our ground-floor classroom had large windows covered in masking tape to protect against flying glass during air raids. It overlooked Rebecca Street and the school's small playground at the rear of the Beehive pub. The classroom itself was quite large and at one end was an upright piano. There were no desks, only mats and very small chairs to sit on, and a few tables to use as worktops for over forty children in each class.

Of the school's teachers, who seemed to work intermittently between the infants' classrooms, were Miss Hilda Bolton and Miss Peggy Casey. The head of the infants' section was Sister Cassian. The girls' school headmistress was Sister Cuthbert, and for the boys' school Sister Christine. All were nuns of the order of Sisters of Charity of St Paul, who lived in the convent in the same building as St Patrick's Church.

Vincent Davey, my future best mate, followed me not long after, as did a new friend, Michael Farrell, who lived in the only house in Handel Street. Mum had asked Lawrence to start taking me to school, which he did for about a week, but I put him in turmoil by being awkward and making him late. A solution was found as Eileen, Vincent's older sister, who also attended the school and was taking Vincent, agreed for me to join them. I already had a good friend in Michael and made other friends quickly. Vincent was in the other class.

The infants were mixed boys and girls. This was a new venture for me, as I hadn't had much to do with girls before this. I had only been there a few weeks when I was attracted to a girl called Teresa Doherty who was then the same age as me, about five! What the attraction was at that age I don't suppose I knew, although I did know she was nice looking and Michael Farrell thought the same; so, aged five, I had competition.

We could stop for school dinners, which was advised, as afterwards we could play out in the school playground for half an hour and then go back to the classroom to have a sleep. One particular day, as usual, we were each given a mat; these were placed on the wooden floors in neat rows, girls and boys mixed together. We took our shoes off and lay down to sleep. A large black sheet, which also served as a blackout blind, was lowered over the windows. It went dark and everyone was soon off to sleep in a few minutes, except for the odd chatterbox who was told to be quiet by Miss Bolton (who was sitting at her desk in the far corner of the room). Except me. Why? Because next to me was Teresa Doherty! When it was all quiet I decided to try and kiss her. With no hesitation I knelt, leaned across and kissed her on the cheek. She didn't move as she was fast asleep. I turned to go back, but before I could reach the safety of my mat a voice rang out. 'Derek Lister!' Miss Bolton jumped up, as did forty-plus children. Framed in the classroom doorway was Sister Cassian.

She came across to me rather slowly and asked me to stand up. She then told the class to go back to sleep. All went quiet as I was ushered to the staffroom. Miss Casey was there and asked what was wrong. Sister Cassian whispered in her ear. A smile crossed Miss Casey's face, and I was sure I could also see Sister Cassian smiling. Then Sister Cassian turned to me with a stern face and told me in no uncertain terms that I had come to the school to learn, and not to go about kissing girls. She then told me to stay in the staffroom with Miss Casey and to go back to my classroom when the children had woken up.

I had not known what to expect. Perhaps it was the few tears I shed on the way to the staffroom that had melted hearts. It taught me a lesson, though, and I didn't venture down that path again; well, not for a year or two! I told my mum what had happened, as it was all round the school and, knowing her, she would have got to know. She shouted for a while but that was all. Later, when my mum was in the Union of Catholic Mothers, she and Sister Cassian laughed at this episode. Because of my venture a change was made to the sleeping arrangements of the lunchtime naps. In future the boys were to lie one side and the girls on the other, with a 6 foot aisle between them. Miss Casey, whom I later knew for several years, said the teachers always called the gap the 'Derek Lister Demarcation Line', and apparently even Sister Cassian referred to it as that.

I enjoyed being with other children. As we were all going through the same process of learning there was really no competition at this stage between us. The teaching style was formal, with an emphasis on the three Rs: reading, writing and arithmetic. Every morning started with religious instruction, followed with spelling or tables tests before we began working with our slate or textbooks. Teaching aids were few, and Miss Bolton used seashells in old milk tins to help with our early counting and sums. Although aged just five we already knew the basics of reading, as the ABC and times tables were instilled into us by repetition. Good clear letters of the alphabet were required, and neat printing was practised with chalk on a slate, or with a pencil on a ruled exercise book if they were available.

We learned many things, such as multiplication tables and lists of weights and measures, by repeating them out loud as a class. We were soon familiar with these everyday facts. Our two teachers were good, loved and respected. They made everyday things and ordinary items interesting. They were, of course, giving us a good grounding of knowledge that would be knocked into shape when we reached the age of seven. Then we would go to Standard One in the boys' school across the road.

As we didn't have individual desks we sat at small tables for painting and drawing, which we did on thick grey paper, both back and front – to save paper. 'Remember there's a war on,' someone kept saying! We used old coloured pencils and crayons, as pens were not available to us at this stage, and took the drawings home for our parents to admire. If our pictures were particularly good they were displayed on the classroom walls to encourage us.

In winter, particularly in the early mornings, the classrooms were freezing and we were allowed to keep our overcoats and scarves on. I always remember that some of the boys and girls were without thick coats, and some even wore pumps, or wellingtons with no stockings. I felt sorry for them.

We were allowed to use the outside playground in the summer and began to learn games like Tiggy, also known as 'You have it'. In this game you tapped someone, then that person chased everybody, tapped someone, and then repeated with that person being 'it'. There was no time limit, and the game could go on for ever or until boredom or injury occurred; but what physical exercise! At times the whole playground was covered in chalk-drawn hopscotch squares.

Sometimes we had a ball that we used as a football. One kick, and twenty or more small bodies followed it like a swarm of bees. Our game always resulted in cuts and bruises from falls on the rough playing surface. The girls played their own games, which were usually skipping or whip and top. But when the whistle sounded we formed up in twos, held hands and marched into school in complete silence. Discipline was strict.

There were many thin and frail bodies at the school, both boys and girls, as it was still an austere time, and everything was rationed. There were no fat children at St Patrick's Infants'. We were continually reminded that the war was still on. Some children were off school for a few days if the family received news that their father, uncle or brother had been killed or wounded in action.

Christmas was always a special time. Towards the end of the year our work was focused on the nativity and Christmas celebrations. We made paper chains from coloured strips of paper, gluing each link with thick white paste applied with a paint brush. The windows were covered in cotton wool snow, and cardboard boxes were decorated to become snowmen. In the afternoons we painted Christmas cards for our parents.

On the last day before the holiday we had a party where we played games, sang carols, enjoyed a Christmas tea and performed our nativity play. In my first play I was given the part of Herod; some would say typecasting! Mum was somewhat annoyed, probably wanting me to have the part of infant Jesus, but I liked being Herod and played it with relish – in a scene that lasted about ten seconds. I only spoke two words.

The party, which was well attended, was held in our classroom, decorated with a large Christmas tree with presents. These had been provided by Alderman Kathleen Chambers, who the following year, 1945, would be the first female Lord Mayor of Bradford. There was a present for all of us, distributed by a jovial Father Christmas. I was given a packet of plasticine: at least it was something I wanted.

One of the teachers played the piano and we, the mothers and teachers joined in to sing our Catholic hymn 'Hail, glorious St Patrick'. We finished with a resounding 'God save the King'. There were quite a few tears from most of the mothers, as they remembered their loved ones at war. We were only children, but we all seemed to understand.

I liked Miss Bolton the best, and used to push everybody to get close to her. She had not only introduced me to the joys of learning but had also became the most important women in my life after my mum, Auntie Cassie, Auntie Margaret and Teresa Doherty. Indeed Mum regularly told how I frequently informed Miss Bolton that I intended to marry her when I grew up.

I was nearly seven and would soon be going to the boys' school. I had been in the infants' school for over two years and had enjoyed every minute. I had a host of new friends, both boys and girls, and Teresa Doherty was actually talking to me. The girls and the boys would soon be parting, each to go to their segregated school.

Nothing much happened in my final year. All of a sudden we had grown up, if only a little. In my time at the infants' I do not remember having any arguments with my schoolfriends, and I didn't give Sister Cassian cause to scold me again. We had sadness, though. St Patrick's lost three of its boys: Denis Conroy and Josh Ramsden drowned while swimming in a nearby local dam one Sunday afternoon, and Ernest Hetherington, a pal, was running down Westgrove Street into Sunbridge Road when he was hit by a car, dying instantly.

St Patrick's Boys' School

It was late 1945. My dad was in the army in Germany and Lawrence, aged thirteen, was going to Durham to study for the priesthood. We saw him off from outside the Ritz cinema on Broadway; Mum, as ever, was tearful. There with us was the Scully family, who lived on Rebecca Street and were also members of St Patrick's congregation. Their son Peter, who went to school with Lawrence, was going to the same college for priest training. When the coach left we joined the Scullys and went to the Ritz cinema to see *The Wizard of Oz*. I had not seen the film before and enjoyed it, as did most people around me, although my mum was quiet. After saying goodbye to the Scullys we caught our trolleybus home. On reaching our house Mum opened the door, and again burst into tears, sat down, hugged me and said, 'We're on our own now, and have to look after each other.' For once I didn't respond by crying, just gave her a kiss and said 'OK'. I

St Patrick's Boys' School entrance (centre) on Sedgefield Terrace. To the right are the convent and the church. *(Author's collection)*

don't really know what I thought other than at last I could have a bed of my own. I'm sure Lawrence must have thought the same about having a bed of his own at college. I have to admit, though, we always got on, although I used to cause him trouble on many an occasion and he was no doubt glad for the break!

I had begun to grow up. Aged seven, I was going to the boy's school in two weeks' time: Standard One. Mum said I was now the man of the house. This was a big responsibility for one so small although, even at my age, I knew it was in name only.

St Patrick's Roman Catholic Boys' School, situated off Westgate, was a fine two-storey building that had been opened in 1872. The school, affectionately known as White Abbey College, was adjacent to the church and at the beginning had been used both as a junior and senior mixed school, but in 1915 the girls transferred to the Scruton school building in Paradise Street. Our boys' school was situated at the corner of Sedgefield Terrace and Rebecca Street. In my times Sister Christine, of the Sisters of Charity, was the popular and much-loved headmistress.

Classrooms and Playground

The school had three classrooms on the ground floor: Standards One, Two and Three. A corridor ran adjacent to these classrooms, with glass panel windows to the ceiling from which the classes could be observed by Sister Christine and the other teachers. At one end of this corridor, close to the Sedgefield Terrace entrance, was the headmistress's office; at the other end of this corridor was the Vaughan Street entrance and Form One.

Both entrances had staircases to the first floor, and the Vaughan Street staircase led to a small room that was Form Three. Form Two and Form Four were situated in the main part on the first floor, and were divided by a large curtain. At the wall end of Form Four was a large crucifix depicting Jesus dying on the cross.

There was just one very small playground within the building, sandwiched between the rear of the school and the convent. The old toilets had names of pupils from the late nineteenth century and dates carved into the lead pipes; in fact the toilets had remained unchanged since 1872. The playground was used by Standard One only; the other playgrounds were outside in Vaughan Street and Rebecca Street. As the school had no playing fields the opportunities to develop sporting skills were poor, although once a week each class walked in pairs to the old recreation ground at the top of St Michael's Road. This was a cinder-covered playing area surrounded by back-to-back houses and a mill wall; needless to say casualties of all ages were always high, with cuts, bruises and the fearful grazes that cinders produce. Across from St Patrick's Church was an area that would have made a wonderful playground and recreation area for our school, the old Bradford Infirmary site, but the idea was turned down because Westgate Road ran between the field and the church and school. Surrounded by a small wall and not grassed, it was just a muddy field with four long red-brick air-raid shelters (built for the school) in one corner. In the late 1940s these had become waterlogged and rat-infested, with the usual foul smell from within. Round about this time one of the school pupils, while messing around, had dislodged a stone and discovered a large wad of the old white £5 notes to the value of over £700. Being poor and a good Catholic he handed it to the police, and nothing further was heard!

Leaving the nursery and infants behind I could now go on my own to school, although for the next few years I joined up en route with Michael Farrell living in Handel Street, Terence Moran from Bright Street and George Stockley who lived at Foster Street, all Listerhills lads. I grew up with them in the classes at the school and spent most of my early life with them. We met at the bottom of Norcroft Street and the four of us would dawdle, laughing and shouting all the way, until the school came in view at the top of Westgrove Street. As I was older Vincent and I were never in the same class. Over the next eight years I was in some classes for one term, others for two terms, as everything took some time to level out, what with male teachers returning from the war and female teachers retiring.

Standard One

Although I was with most of the other boys from the infants, in Standard One there were no girls. There were usually around thirty pupils, each of us sitting at a double desk. These were old, and the inside and outside had ink stains from the ceramic inkwell ingrained into the wood – along with many signatures and rude comments by previous occupants. A very large fixed blackboard ran across the room's end wall, and in front of it our teacher, Miss McAndrew, had her desk. Miss McAndrew was new to the school and I liked her from the start, although she could use the cane. To me and all the class this was quite different to the punishment that had been meted out in the infants' school. But we were boys aged seven, and could be quite a handful.

As it was a Catholic school, the first priority was the teachings of the Church. The infants' school had given us a basic grounding in prayers, hymns and the commandments, but now we were seven, at an age to be reasoned with, to be taught and understand the teachings of Christ. This culminated in confession and our first communion.

The catechism was at the heart of the teaching. This was read out by the teacher, copied by us and then read out in parrot fashion. Miss McAndrews' church and religious teaching were supplemented by the priest, who popped in and asked questions about the catechism. A booklet containing the catechisms could be bought for sixpence. My family could afford one, but being a poor school in a poor area there were many families who could not. The church paid for theirs.

Standard One was the class that brought us into line, not only with our religion but with our academic progress, namely the three Rs. Our writing (joined up) improved, as did our reading; but in my case arithmetic was not popular, as my school reports showed over the years. As with most schools of the time positions of esteem were given to pupils for good behaviour, for being good at lessons, or for just being good. Needless to say I never achieved this accolade. One such was the ink monitor who filled our ceramic inkwells from a large bottle of Stephens's ink. In fact the teachers had no need to leave their desks because of the many jobs they could delegate, even down to cleaning the blackboard.

I think Miss McAndrew was a good and fair teacher, but she occasionally lost her temper and gave the odd clout or slap on the legs. She had a cane, which she hardly ever used because she had a get-out ploy – which was to send the unruly child to Sister Christine, who would cane him. I only received the cane once from Sister Christine, together with a few clouts from Miss McAndrew. Discipline was strict: just another learning experience after the tranquillity of the infants'!

'Fold your arms' or 'Put your arms behind your back' were both forms of discipline that brought the class back on course after it had been rowdy. We also had a dunce cap, a large pointed hat with a large D printed on. Again, I had the privilege of wearing it on quite a few occasions, but as all of the class at some time got to wear it nobody really felt inferior; in fact, it got to be that we felt privileged in wearing the dunce cap and inferior if we didn't! The cap was quite a conversation point for my parents: my dad, still in Germany, laughed when he received the letter telling him about it.

Another form of punishment was keeping the whole class in after school, sometimes for as much as an hour, even in winter months. Irate parents descended on the school looking for their offspring while Mr Durkin, the school caretaker, waited to clean the classroom with sawdust and a strong-smelling disinfectant.

There was quite an assortment of lads in my class, most of whom I would be with until I left school for good. They were from all walks of life. It was a poor area, so some of the children were dressed in old torn pullovers, ripped short trousers, no stockings and old boots or pumps that were too big and had probably been handed down. Even in summer some children wore wellington boots. With thirty-plus boys in a classroom the smell of dirty clothes and unwashed bodies hung in the air. I was thin, but some of the others were very thin, and looked as though they had not eaten for days. While it is always said that children can be cruel, I don't remember this being so in our class; we all mixed, fought, cried and played together. The country was still austere, with sweets on ration and fruit such as bananas and oranges almost unobtainable, so we had to stick together.

Around this time the school began to take in Catholic displaced persons, most of whom spoke no English. But even at their early age, like most of their parents, they soon had a good knowledge of St Patrick's English language with more than a hint of the Yorkshire dialect and all the bad habits that accompanied the language and the class. As an example, we often used the phrase 'it's a bramah' – meaning that something was particularly excellent. This word came from Joseph Bramah, a Yorkshire locksmith who was renowned for his quality and reliability.

It was during my first year in Class One that my mum made more than one of her many visits to the boys' school. I usually walked home with Michael, Terry and George, but on one particular day was on my own. The next day at school Sister Christine sent for me. With her was a woman who lived down Lower Westgrove Street, who accused me of drawing with chalk on the pavement outside her house. I vehemently denied this, so much so that I started crying. I knew Sister Christine didn't believe her, but she had to go through the motions as headmistress.

When the woman left, Sister Christine asked me to take a bucket of water and wash the chalk off, which I did, but with a feeling of resentment. On my return Sister Christine told me to go back to class and to forget about it, which I did. It was not until a few days later that I learnt Michael Farrell had told his mother what had happened, and she had then told my mum. Mum was soon down at the school, saw Sister Christine and enquired who this woman was. Sister Christine would not divulge her name, and in the end it was I who told my mum where she lived. I was with her when she knocked heavily on the woman's door, and by the time the door opened I was over 100 yards away down by the bobbin mill! Fifteen minutes later Mum joined me. I didn't say a word and neither did she, but I knew justice had been done. In a way I felt much better.

Within a short time we started preparation for our confession and first communion. My first practice confession was to Father Patrick Sreenan. It was Father Sreenan who had also helped and proposed my brother to the priesthood. My first communion took place on the Feast of Corpus Christi, with most of my class.

Standard Two

After a good year and decent school report from Miss McAndrew, most of the class moved up to Standard Two. Thanks to birthday dates some of our number stayed on in Standard One, so we lost some friends, but found others who had had to stay back in Standard Two.

Miss Elizabeth Wheelan was our new teacher. She was a small plump dark-haired lady who wore dresses with coloured flower patterns and with a pleasant aroma of perfume, always the same one. Her bark was worse than her bite, but she could be loud, her voice penetrating the surrounding classes. At times she used the cane, but only as a last resort. The odd smack was also dished out, and she was quite a good shot with the wooden chalk eraser that was used to clean the blackboard. A big disappointment to us was that the dunce cap was no longer evident; it was rumoured that the nit nurse had banned it on medical grounds.

The arrival of the nit nurse to inspect our hair was dreaded by every one of us. She was a short lady wearing a snow white coat, and her hair was black with a fringe, not unlike Mo of the Three Stooges. She lined us up in the corridor to see her one by one, and used the headmistress's room, leaving the door open for all to see. It was plain when our friends had a problem, for they came out clutching a card, which told them they had signs of nits, to take home to their parents.

Miss Wheelan's handwriting was in a copperplate style. She made the blackboard look like a beautiful document when she had written details of English, composition and spelling, and I tried to emulate her beautiful script. I was later admonished by other teachers who said I was trying to be too fancy. I persevered, though, and later in life people asked where I had learned the art of copperplate writing, and which art college I had attended. The answer was always the same: Miss Wheelan, St Patrick's School, Standard Two.

Miss Wheelan's nickname was Lizzie, a name we would not have thought of using within her earshot, only in secluded areas of the school. One time while she was out of the classroom someone wrote 'Lizzie is fat' on the blackboard. On returning she looked at the offensive words, rubbed them out with a duster, turned around and called out 'Taylor'. Billy Taylor it was. He had forgotten that Miss Wheelan knew all the class's handwriting or printing. He was sent to Sister Christine, and returned later holding his hands under his armpits and trying not to cry. Billy was a hero for a few days, although I think Miss Wheelan saw the funny side of this indiscretion. We were all aware of the consequences of our failings and misdemeanours.

Every year each class in the school collected money for the Bishop's Fund. This was for Catholic Missionaries in Africa, and children collected and brought in their halfpennies and pennies, or whatever could be afforded by working-class families. As the pennies poured in the teacher marked in a book the total given by each child. Whoever contributed most made a visit to the bishop at St Anne's Cathedral in Leeds, where he gave his thanks and a signed photograph.

Time passed quickly with Miss Wheelan, although with government changes in education I spent nearly two years in her class. My school reports had not been too bad and I was generally in the middle group, my best subjects being history, geography, writing and religious instruction. More male teachers were now returning from the war and were taking the place of the women, and soon St Patrick's had a male-dominated teaching staff.

Standard Three

Meantime I moved into Standard Three, where I spent nearly two years with Miss O'Brien and failed my scholarship.

Miss Elizabeth O'Brien was born in the 1880s and was from Southern Ireland. She was a staunch Catholic, an Irish patriot, and what a good teacher she was! Thin and frail, with a look of Old Mother Riley, Miss O'Brien was a strict disciplinarian who would stamp her feet in temper and desperation, sometimes breaking into tears. This was not because of the problems we caused, but from her frustration at trying to penetrate our brains. She was, of all the female teachers at the boys' school, the one I liked the best. Although she was an Irish patriot, I learned more from Miss O'Brien about English history than anyone else. Being Irish, she taught us about the Irish famine. This was expected as most Irish families in the area were descendants from the potato famine immigrants of that time (1846–50).

We were given a detailed knowledge of history from the Roman invasion to the Norman Conquest and all the monarchs up to our George VI. Aged ten, I knew the history of the Magna Carta and the many battles, of Hastings, Crécy, Agincourt, Crimea, Trafalgar, Waterloo and the Boer War, in which she told us her brother had fought – with the Dublin Fusiliers at Ladysmith in 1900. She also told us about many inventions and discoveries such as radium (Madame Curie), penicillin (Sir Alexander Fleming), television (Logie Baird) antiseptics (Lister), telephones (Alexander Graham Bell) and many others.

Another of Miss O'Brien's fortes was general knowledge. This could be anything from the capital of Tibet (Lhasa) to how an amoeba reproduces. Years later I could always answer questions like this, on television quiz programmes and so on, thanks to Miss O'Brien.

In arithmetic, which I still didn't like, she impressed on us the need to know the basics, and I did manage to increase my mathematical knowledge in the time I spent with her. My writing was good, thanks to Miss Wheelan, a fact recognised when Miss O'Brien said to me one day that 'Your writing looks as if you are following in the footsteps of Miss Wheelan', a remark that brought a glow to my face.

In 1946 the National Health Service introduced free milk for schools. This came in third-of-a-pint bottles sealed at the neck by a waxed disc, which could be extracted by popping the centre. You took out the wax disc to discover cream had formed on the back; tongues were applied and the cream disappeared. Later in the 1950s our milk was delivered in narrower topped bottles with a thin metallic top, which we spun with our fingers, thereby creating a small flying saucer. Straws were issued by the straw monitor, another of those esteemed positions that I never experienced! The milk was delivered at the entrance to Vaughan Street, and milk monitors were delegated from each class to pick up the crates and take them to their classrooms.

One afternoon Sister Christine sent for me. I wondered what for, as generally a call to her study meant that some misdemeanour was to be investigated. But she had a request for me. Would I take Albert — of Standard One to the boot and shoe shop on Westgate, and buy him a pair of boots and socks. It was January, it was snowing, and Albert had arrived at school for the last two days with no socks and wearing pumps with no toes in. I held his hand as I took him to the shop; it was still snowing, with a brisk cold wind. Soon we were both very wet and cold; I had my overcoat on while Albert wore a large overcoat and balaclava supplied by Sister Christine. I couldn't really see him as we walked along, but could feel his small hand in mine and could see two thin legs and his pumps pushing through the snow.

The shop was empty when we arrived. The owner was a middle-aged man who looked like Dickens's character Mr Pickwick, who came forward with a smile as if he was approaching two escapees from the local workhouse. Mr Pickwick looked aghast when he saw my small friend's condition and said in a cheery voice, 'We'll soon have you fit up, young lad.' The pumps were discarded in a bin, Mr Pickwick brought a small towel from the rear to dry Albert's feet, and within a few minutes Albert was wearing a new pair of stockings and a shiny new pair of black lace-up boots.

Albert's face lit up, and so did mine. The boots were 17s 6d and the socks were 1s, but our Mr Pickwick would not accept the £1 note that Sister Christine had given me. Instead he wrapped up a spare pair of stockings and put them in Albert's pocket. Back at school Sister Christine was pleased, as was I; above all, so was Albert. I was to find out much later that Albert's father had been killed in the war, his mother had 'run off with someone', and Albert was being taken care of by his grandmother, who was an invalid.

This sort of poverty was not too common at our school, but school photographs of the period show an assortment of thin knobbly-kneed children clothed in frayed misfitting pullovers, jackets and over-sized wellingtons, although there's a smile on every face. Those, like me, who were better dressed, mingled and played with the rest, poor or otherwise. In general we were not under-nourished, as wartime rationing had given us enough calories to get by on. There were no fat children in our class or, indeed, the school. The only boy to whom we gave the title was 'Fatty' Colclough. Peter was not really fat, just bigger than the rest of us.

I never liked school dinners, with their strong and distinctive smell. They bore little resemblance to my mum's cooking, and I always took the opportunity to go home at lunchtime if possible. I was a fussy eater who didn't like most of the food on offer. To me brussels sprouts, turnips and cabbage (if available) were awful, but potatoes, meat (no fat) and peas were all right, especially when finished off with puddings and custard. Dad used to say 'Wait until he gets in the army' with regard to my fussy eating. He was right.

If families were considered to be poor then their school dinners were free, although the children who benefited from this always seemed to be stigmatised, and children could be cruel. Dinners were served in the basement hall of the infants' school, after which many children of all ages played in the streets surrounding the school. Until 1.45 pm no one was allowed back into the classroom unless it was raining, but when it was snowing no-one wished to return to class! For over an hour snowballs of all were thrown in all directions, and some of the older lads from the top forms threw them like small cannon balls. Inevitably injuries occurred, mostly facial, especially swollen eyes where the snowball had made contact. On our return to the classroom the air was full of a damp fusty smell, which only this sort of children's behaviour could produce.

It was while in Miss O'Brien's class in 1949 that I was top of the class for giving my pennies to the Bishop's Fund. A few weeks later I was taken to meet the bishop in Leeds. Miss Winnie Casey (sister of Peggy Casey of my infant days) took me, although why we had to set off at 7am I never knew, as our meeting with the bishop was at 9.30. However, we were held up in Armley by the police and a large crowd; the reason, I found out later, was that a hanging (Dennis Neville for the murder of Marian Poskitt) was to take place at Armley jail that morning. In a strange coincidence, the bishop at this time was Henry John Poskitt, sharing the murder victim's surname!

It was almost 8.45 before we arrived at the cathedral. The bishop shook my hand while Miss Casey told him that I was the brother of Lawrence Lister, who was studying for the priesthood at Ushaw College. He acknowledged this by patting me on the head and giving me a signed photograph of himself. I think the sum I collected was around 4s 6d, quite a sum in 1949.

Being thin, and showing my ribs, I was a very good runner. Sometimes I ran all the way home, which was a mile and a quarter, in five or six minutes. I was aware of the time because running up Preston Street I could see St Andrew's church clock at the top in Legrams Lane. I was probably the fastest runner in the school aged eleven. The only other person as fast was Peter Doherty, and the only way we could compete was to race from the girls' school, along Rebecca Street and along Vaughan Street. We were both fast; sometimes he won and sometimes I did. As we had no playing field, the hard tarmac road was the only way to prove the point.

The Archaeologist Who Never Was
I was always in the top three in history, especially Roman history. From an early age I knew all the Latin names of a Roman soldier's dress, armaments, equipment and siege machines. I also found it easy to draw Roman soldiers, while my classmates always drew British Second World War soldiers and sailors. My scenes were always dominated by a Roman soldier or sometimes a centurion, because his helmet was different – with a plume set into it. Other than Roman

The Leeds bus leaves Chester Street bus station on our journey to York via Leeds.
(Colin and Mark Wilson)

history I found it easy to memorise historical dates, events, kings and queens, inventors and inventions, all of which was taught by the good and dedicated female teachers from standard one to standard four at St Patrick's school. But above all Roman history was my favourite subject. There was only one other person in my class who had the same interest and that was Donald Swaine (Swanny). Donald was my age and lived in a back-to-back house in Hollings Street off Thornton Road with his parents, sister Veronica and younger brother Kenneth. We always got on well together. He had a sense of humour not unlike mine, but was quieter and unassuming. Swanny and I discussed things we had read or seen at the cinema about life in Roman Britain, and especially what had happened to the Roman Ninth Legion. Theories from professors, scholars, and archaeologists had been rife for years with regard to Legio VIIII Hispana (the name means the Ninth Spanish Legion), which had apparently vanished beyond Hadrian's Wall in AD 119, seemingly in fulfilment of Boudicca's curse after the legion had put down her revolt in AD 60. Donald and I agreed that we would become archaeologists and find out what really happened to the Ninth Legion. So we both knew what we wanted to be – but first we had to pass the eleven plus.

Aged ten, I had never been to York – although I had read and heard so much about this Roman city (Eboracum) with its wall, minster and museums. It was only 30 miles away, but to us it was a daytrip and difficult to get to. One day during the school holidays my mum said she would take me as well as Vincent and Donald, who likewise had never visited York. On the day Donald made his way up to our house for an 8am start, as the journey was long and entailed the use of three buses. My mother had packed some sandwiches and a flask of tea, and for us a large bottle of American cream soda. The journey began with our trolleybus ride to Bradford town centre, then a walk up to Chester Street bus station to catch the West Yorkshire bus to Leeds. Arriving in Leeds, we made our way to Wellington Street bus station, which catered for services to the east coast. It was a very small station, and the queues for all destinations were large. However, we were soon away on the Malton double-decker bus, which would drop us in York.

It was noon when we finally arrived. All three of us were excited to be there at last. We had been craning our necks on the way, remarking on the obvious contrast with our dark cobbled streets. Everything looked old but clean, and the racecourse was so green. How we would have loved to play football on it. My astute mother said we should eat first, knowing that once we had been enveloped in all the wonders of York we wouldn't bother to eat. It was a warm and sunny day so we made our way to the river bank, where we had our sandwiches, my mum drank the tea and we indulged in the American cream soda – which was taking over from Tizer, if only for a while. After what appeared to be only a few minutes we ambled along towards Clifford's Tower, which we ran up. Close by were the law courts and York Castle Museum, where we visited the condemned cell where Dick Turpin was reputed to have spent his last night before being hanged at Knavesmire on 7 April 1739. Then we had a short walk to the minster. My mother could see that we wanted to go to the Roman museum, so she said she would go round the shops and probably visit the minster – and off we went on our own. Her last words were to meet her back at the minster at 4pm, not to speak to strangers, and if there were any problems to look for a policeman. So, with a wave, two ten year olds and a nine year old headed off to the Roman museum, situated across the road from Lendal.

The museum was a large Georgian building, set in gardens that had Roman columns, obelisks and other artefacts dotted around them. It was free to enter, and lived up to all our expectations. The rooms were large and contained many display cases, each showing something different – coins, brooches, bone needles and combs, for example. One case had over two hundred combs and I noted, as I fingered the steel comb in my pocket, how little this object had changed in over two thousand years. As Donald pointed out, some did indeed look like the infamous nit comb. The coin cases were full of gold, silver and bronze coins, each scrupulously labelled and dated, and indicating if the coin had been donated, and where it had been found. Why wouldn't someone donate one to me, I wondered? They had hundreds!

Two hours later we made our way back towards the minster, still discussing what we had seen, with Donald and me yet more resolved to be archaeologists. Vincent, while interested, was really not as enthralled as us. For many years my mum told of her memory of three young boys walking towards her, like three brothers; all dressed alike in open neck shirts, short trousers held up with the popular snake belt, socks round our ankles and all wearing black pumps, with cheeky grins on our faces. Somewhere a church clock was chiming four.

It was time to go, so we made our way to the bus station passing Micklegate Bar, which had access up the steps to the Roman wall. My mother gave us a few minutes to have a walk along the wall, just to say we had been on it. We three agreed that one day we would walk all the way around the wall.

We were delayed in the city on the way home because it was near teatime and the rush hour, and thousands of people were leaving their workplaces on bicycles. We finally arrived back in Bradford at about 8.30pm, and as it was late my mum decided to make sure Donald got home. We all got the Thornton trolleybus and walked him to his house, where Mrs Swaine and my mum had a little chat, Mrs Swaine asking Donald, as mothers did, 'Have you thanked Mrs Lister?' 'Yes,' said Donald; and we were on our way up Preston Street to Listerhills, and home.

Eleven-Plus
When some of the class took the eleven-plus exam I didn't; I missed it by a few weeks because of my birthday. Among my friends who passed were Paul McKee (his father was a prominent Bradford councillor) and Elmer Blauminous. Elmer, who was from Latvia, was not only intelligent but, like most of the immigrants, could speak English far better than most of us. He was a wonderful artist who had made many friends and was well liked. Elmer went on to Carlton Grammar School, where he improved his artistic flair. Bernard Woodward, who came all the way to school from Ireton Street in Princeville, also passed his scholarship. Bernard, another prolific artist like Elmar, also went on to Carlton. Of the class of thirty-two only six passed. Some then moved up to Form One and Form Two, but I had to stay down with Terry, George and Michael.

In the last few months in Miss O'Brien's class before taking our eleven-plus exam, as much as possible was crammed into our heads, When we took a mock exam most of us passed. Looking back, I think this was probably a psychological move to give us all confidence. In my case, and most of the class, it didn't work. That trip to York had made me determined to pass the exam and become an archaeologist more than ever, but it was not to be! The following year I failed. Only five passed in our class, including Donald and my equally good running partner Peter Doherty. I was terribly disappointed as were my parents, although there were no recriminations as they knew I had done my best. Terry and George failed, as did John Walsh. John lived with his family in Sedgefield Terrace; his father was a funeral director. Michael Farrell took the eleven-plus later; he passed and went on to St Bede's.

My aspiration to become an archaeologist had gone. In those days archaeologists graduated from universities, and as I would not go to a grammar school I couldn't have taken the next step to university; my City and Guilds certificates, taken some years later, didn't have the same influence. Donald went to St Bede's and we kept in touch. Later he joined me and Vincent at the Bradford Archaeology Group walks, and our famous hitchhiking Sundays.

As a sad postscript, Donald, a teacher, was battered to death in Bradford as he walked home in the early hours of Christmas Day in 1986. He had been celebrating with his colleagues from the Bradford branch of the Youth Hostels Association. His killer, a former Rampton patient, was jailed for life in November 1987.

Form Two

In 1950 some of us missed Form One and moved up to Form Two in the first-floor classroom. Our teacher was Frank Scully, an ex-Royal Marine Commando who walked with his head to one side and his hands, showing his palms, swaying

St Patrick's Boys' School, Form Two, 1950. Back row, left to right: -?- , Peter Speight, Peter Moran, -?-, Peter Courtney, -?- , -?-. Second row: Bernard Woodward, Douglas Hird, George Stockley, Albert Holmes, Peter Colclough, Edgar Walsh, Terence Midgley. Front row: Danny Webster, -?- , Freddy Vicars, Bernard Williams, John Walsh, Kevin McCusker, Tommy McCue, Derek Lister, Billy Taylor. Note the array of boots, shoes, pumps and sandals – and the knobbly knees. *(Author's collection)*

with the walk. He was the strictest disciplinarian in that school and was not afraid to dish out punishment with both hand and cane. For the slightest misdemeanour he would come down hard, so after being with Miss O'Brien he was a shock to our young lives. After many months he slowed down a little, having instilled such discipline in us that parents came to thank him for changing their children's behaviour. Mr Scully had used the old army training adage of him against us, and it had worked. We respected him and he respected us.

I don't think we ever had a full day out on our visits to the recreation ground on St Michael's Road. Carrying an old Gradidge bat and the only two pads the school possessed, sometimes we were no sooner be in the street marching along in twos than, because of some misdemeanour on the way, we were turned around and sent back to class to sit with our hands on our head. You could hear a pin drop. One time Mr Scully kept the class back until well after 5pm. The rest of the school had gone home and it was very quiet when all of a sudden, there was a loud knocking at the class-room door. It was one of the boy's fathers, who had been drinking, demanding to know what was happening. He couldn't get into his house as his son had the key; the boy was supposed to be at home with his father's tea ready. After a few words the father tried to hit our teacher, who ducked and then hit the father on the nose. It was like a ripe tomato being burst, with blood on the wall, floor, steps and Frank's sports jacket. Frank shouted to the boy to take his father home. All this had gone on while we all sat in silence, watching the fracas with our hands on our heads. It was well known that the boy's father was a bully, as the boy often came to school with injuries caused by his father's brutality, so this behaviour was not unexpected. Both the boy and all the class thought that Frank Scully was great. Frank visited the father, we thought to apologise, but after his visit the brutality ceased.

Frank once sorted out a problem for me and a few others who had trouble with a certain pupil, a big tough lad called Harry. He was strong, and even aged twelve he looked to be one of the many dopes who used to take up the advert at the back of magazines – the Charles Atlas advert, where on paying some money you were sent details of how to develop your chest and muscles. Most of our class was sure that Harry was into this, and also that he had been watching too many American gangster films. I generally kept out of his way at playtime, but sometimes he confronted me, producing from his pocket a small leather bag. Inside the bag was sand, tied tightly at the top and shaped like a cosh. He called it 'little Joey'. It was blackmail. If I didn't bring him some comics then 'little Joey' would sort me out, so I did from time to time bring him some comics. This blackmail was happening to others in the school as well as me. I knew I only had to mention it to Mum and she would be down at the school; however, most children had a problem with telling tales, in that there could be repercussions from the villain.

Just a minute, I thought, these are my comics bought with my money. I was right: one word and Mum was down at school next day, standing on the landing talking to Frank while I sheepishly looked out of the window. 'Don't worry, Mrs Lister, I'll sort this out,' said Frank. I was so relieved, but as he turned to go my mum said, 'And another thing, Mr Scully. There's a boy in the class who's been grabbing Derek's private parts.' With a final flourish she added, 'That's not nice for a Catholic school.' Frank blushed, and my intention at this point was to jump over the balcony. I had mentioned this to her some time ago, and she'd replied, 'Boys can be silly.' Silly or not, she had remembered. In the end Frank sorted out both problems, and there were no recriminations. Harry's blackmail threats came to an end, although to be fair I had never seen him hit anyone with 'little Joey'. The lad who had been grabbing my 'private parts' died six months later from a brain tumour aged fifteen – and it is because of that, rather than the other, that I have never forgotten his name.

The so-called 'cock of the school' was Albert Holmes, taller and tougher than anyone else. In the early 1950s he looked just like the tearaways in the film of a few years later, *The Blackboard Jungle*. Austin Regan, who was in Albert's cohort, was equally tough. It could be said that most of the lads in the school were tough, as many were from large families and had to fend for themselves. However, there was always a good few like me who were good runners and could leave their assailants miles behind. What was it about living to fight another day?

Harry Hodgson was a well-liked school friend with a mop of ginger hair, softly spoken, whom you would never see angry, upset or using bad language. Freddy Vickers and Danny Webster were two friends who were both very frail. Maurice Leven was of French parents and, although brought up in England, he had a slight French accent and answered to the name of 'Frenchie'. In the 1950s, still being a French National, he received his call-up papers for the French army. He stayed in the UK, with a life-long threat that if he set foot on French soil he would be arrested. Paul Baines was another nice lad, who we thought looked like Sondar out of the *Eagle* comic. Sondar was a deserter from the invading Treens who sided with Dan Dare, so Paul was stuck with the name. About this time I had the nickname 'Lizzie' given to me; it stuck for a year or two, then disappeared.

Barney Williams, Peter Cairns, Harry Mcavan, Douglas Hird, Leo Hennigan, Alan Sugden, Tommy McCue, Kevin McCusker, Danny Mazurke, Peter Colclough, Peter Speight, Billy Taylor, Harry Taylor, Dennis Sharpe and many others in our class were all characters of one kind and another. Ours was a mixture of mostly Irish, English and others, all from hard-working families living in the areas of White Abbey Road, Whetley Hill and Manningham Lane. Fighting was very rare. Although there were many fallings-out, these were short lived with no one seeking revenge.

Most of my time in Frank Scully's class I sat next to John Walsh. John and I were firm friends and it was John who had taught me to serve Mass and become

Leo Brook, a much loved and respected teacher who thanks to his war experiences with the Eighth Army taught us many German songs, which resounded through the corridors of the school.
(Nick Brook)

an altar boy. We were also members of St Patrick's choir. John and I used to call ourselves twins as we both had the same birthday, 2 May 1938. John was older by two hours: he been born at 6.30am and I at 8.30am. It was a wonder that John never passed his scholarship as he was the more intelligent of the two of us. However, when we were in Form Two he left to attend a Catholic college in Aberystwyth.

The male teachers were now taking over from the female staff, and one of the new Form One teachers was everyone's favourite. Leo Brook, we called him Leo behind his back, was a small man with chubby cheeks, fresh complexion and a mop of well-groomed, dark and wavy hair with just a tint of ginger. His class and his speciality was music. Everyone attended Leo's music class at least once or twice a week. He had been in the Eighth Army (Desert Rats) during the war, and taught us patriotic songs including 'I vow to thee, my country', 'Jerusalem' and the traditional music of 'Hey-ho come to the fair'. Old hymns and themes such as 'The vicar of Bray' were always sung with gusto, although at times the unusual could be heard resounding down the corridor from Form One, for example 'Lili Marlene' and a sprinkling of other German songs. Leo made music not only interesting, but enjoyable. It was he who introduced us to classical music, as he took our class to morning music recitals held in the theatre at the Bradford Mechanics Institute; everyone seemed to enjoy them. I never saw him use his cane as he always had full control over the class, and we were hypnotised by his charm and good humour. He was not averse to giving someone a clip over the head, but not often. I, like the rest of our class, learnt and sang songs I would otherwise have never known, and it was all thanks to our beloved Leo Brook.

Form Three

In Form Three, a room on the first floor, the teacher was Vincent Muff, brother of Leo Muff, who was our choirmaster. His forte was chemistry and we attended his class once a week. I didn't learn much with him. It was a case of two opposites: I didn't like him, and he didn't like me.

On Friday mornings we were taught woodwork at Green Lane School, which was half a mile away, off Whetley Hill. The teacher was John Bolland. He had a slow, drawling, nasal voice, which was a gift for comedy impressionists like Terry Moran and me. He could be quite abrasive. Sometimes Terry and I, as altar boys, were asked to go to the church and serve old Canon Curran's nine o'clock Mass. We did this a few times on a Friday, which made us late for our woodwork class. As soon as we entered Mr Bolland said, 'Lister, Moran, late again,' and proceeded to cane us, oblivious to our excuses, until eventually we had Sister Christine protest about his unfairness. Thankfully he took notice.

I believe Mr Bolland realised I would never be any good at woodwork, which I accepted. The only item that I was ever proud of was a four-legged high stool that I had made, with coloured raffia work for the seat. Well, it started off as a high stool but finished as a footstool. My problem was that I had difficulty making the legs even, so I took too much off each of them in turn.

Things were certainly improving at St Patrick's School, as swimming lessons were now provided for pupils of the top forms, which included us. These lessons took place at Carlton Street School. But I was not particularly interested, and my mum had a fear of me getting my hair wet and catching cold, so although I

City of Bradford Education Committee

St Patrick's School *Boys* Dept.

Scholar's Report *for Term ended* *Feb* 195*1*

Name *Derek Lister*   Std. or Class *III*

Subject	Marks Possible	Marks Gained	
Reading	50	48	Vg
Recitation	50	40	g
Composition	100	83	Vg.
Dictation and Spelling	50 / 12	} 52	G.
Writing	50	48	Vg
Arithmetic	100	30	Poor.
History Social Studies Geography	100	60	Fls.
Science	100	80	G
Drawing Relig: Duties	11	10	Exc
Needlework			
Singing			
GRAMMAR	100	33	Poor.
GEOMETRY	100	53	F.

Times absent *Good.*   Position in Class *7*

Times late *Good*   Number in Class *32*

Conduct *Good*

Progress F *Good.*

Teacher's Initials

S. C.   Head Teacher

Parents are requested to read carefully the above Report with a view to encouraging the children in their work at School, and to sign the following statement—
TO THE HEAD TEACHER—
I have read the foregoing Report on the work and conduct of my son/daughter.

Mr H. Lister   PARENT.

L.S. & Co.

My school report from Form Three, 1951. I was above average, but arithmetic was never a strong subject.
(Author's collection)

attended I never took part. Mum provided me with a note each week saying that I had a weak chest. It was again because my poor mother's family had been victims of tuberculosis. So I hung about in the changing rooms and made sure nobody's clothes were stolen: at least I was some use!

It was at about this time that Mum decided I should be wearing long trousers. For over twelve years I had felt the cold on my legs in those dreadful winters, the only protection being from stockings that were pulled up and held in place by a hidden elastic garter that was always either too slack or too tight. As my kneecaps were always exposed they showed many scars of different shapes and sizes, warlike trophies to compare with other boys. Then there was always the draught to contend with, from the cold winds that blasted the nether regions through the short trouser bottoms. I was also on the fringe of puberty and beginning to feel that long trousers were essential.

My first pair of long trousers was purchased from Marks and Spencer's in Darley Street for 22s 6d. Flannel trousers they were called, and that's just what they were, flannel with really no cut or flare, and grey in colour. I didn't complain, realising that for the first time in a decade my kneecaps were protected and warm, but the trouser bottoms were 24 inches wide which gave me a look of a sailor from HMS *Vanguard*. In Form Two only a few of the bigger lads had long trousers, but soon they spread throughout the class; after all, who wanted to be the last one wearing short trousers?

Form Four

After nearly two years it was finally time to move out of Frank Scully's class into Form Four. The teacher was Bernard Moore, a wartime army captain who had been a Japanese prisoner of war. Mr Moore was every inch an officer and a gentleman, with the looks and bearing of a film star. What he thought of his new motley crew I will never know. We all looked up to him with schoolboy admiration. Only once did he speak of his confinement under the Japanese. In the newspapers at the time were many complaints that we didn't have enough food and clothing, and this prompted Mr Moore to tell us of some of his deprivations. There was no hint of self pity, and he seemed more to be speaking out of sadness for his friends who never returned home.

We liked Mr Moore, but after a year he left us for a teaching post in Southampton; we were shocked at his sudden departure. When he told our class that he was leaving there was a brief silence, and then Maurice Malloy stood up and said, 'Well, sir, I know we have had our differences, but we all think that you are a great teacher and we all wish you the best of luck.' With these off-the-cuff remarks fourteen year-old Maurice covered it so well. Mr Moore was touched. Was this St Patrick's School or some private school in Oxford?

During my years at school we still celebrated Empire Day on 24 May each year. Geography lessons were given over to looking at a map of the world and learning all about the widespread British Empire, with its patchwork of red. In those days the quotation that 'the sun never sets on the British Empire' was true. It was also a half-day holiday for children throughout England, as many schools held pageants.

Bernard Brown took over from our Mr Moore. Bernard was much younger and in his late twenties. He sported a beard, which was an innovation for us and the school. About this time our beloved Sister Christine retired and a headmaster called Jim Brown arrived from Durham. Jim had a real North-East accent, which was a new dialect for St Patrick's. Like Mr Bolland's voice, Jim's accent was easy to imitate, and most of the budding impressionists like me had a field day. Jim looked a rough diamond, but above all he was a good and fair headmaster. He was well liked and respected by all the school.

Bernard Brown, our teacher, settled in and we all got on well together. Bernard's nickname was 'Soap', which was down to Danny Mazurk. Danny had said it once in his presence and Bernard had smiled, so it stuck. He was something of an opera singer and had appeared in local shows and, later, with the well-known Catholic Players. He had even sung at the world-famous La Scala Opera House in Milan. Although this was not our scene, during some frivolity in the classroom one day he asked each of us to sing our favourite song. It went without saying that there were no operatic performers among us, which I think disappointed him. The star was Maurice Malloy singing all the verses of Guy Mitchell's hit song of the time 'She wore red feathers and a hooley hooley skirt'; he sounded like Guy Mitchell too. It must have been good, because even Frank Scully's head appeared round the curtain dividing our classroom from his, and he looked on with approval.

Soon most of the class would be leaving, I among them. We now concentrated what was termed as 'letter writing' – for jobs. These jobs were quite surprising. I remember among them were surgeons, stationmaster, plumbers, electricians, the inevitable train driver and even one beautifully written application to be Bradford's chief constable. It was really all tongue in cheek and make believe, but as time went on the applications became more sensible and maybe attainable.

There was now more time in the classroom, and a sense of winding down before we left the school. Our teacher Bernard and other teachers of the boys' school, including female teachers from the girls' school and even from the infants', decided to take to us, some 600 children in all, to Sunny Vale Pleasure Gardens near Hipperholme to celebrate St Patrick's Church centennial. Bradford city centre almost came to a standstill as a large column of children wound its way down Westgate to the Exchange station where a special train had been laid on. It was a lovely day and Bernard really opened up to us, now beginning to call some of us by our Christian names. He was also cavorting with a young and beautiful teacher from the girls' school named Miss Patricia Holt, so he had to put up with a lot of stick from these budding adults – and his nickname was used incessantly. Mr Brown and Miss Holt had a good time, and so did we! The teachers didn't bother to keep the older girls and boys apart so there was lots of fraternisation, with kissing, holding hands and other things. Cigarettes were also lit, out of the teachers' view as there were plenty of hideaways to disappear to. How I wish my first love, Teresa Doherty, had been there, but she had passed her scholarship and gone to St Joseph's College. It was a lovely day out for us, as it must have been for Bernard and Miss Holt – who were later to marry.

I have three poignant memories of our time with Bernard Brown. The two minutes' silence on the death of George VI and standing to attention beside our desks. The news that Barney Williams's older brother Peter was missing while serving with the Duke of Wellington's regiment in the Korean War and the class saying prayers for him; later he was reported to have been captured and become a prisoner of war. Receiving the news that Alan Sugden's brother had been killed in a motor vehicle accident while serving with the army in Germany.

Leaving School

I finally left St Patrick's School in July 1953, and while I was excited about my new life and prospects I was also sad. I had been at that school for eleven years, during the war and later in the austere years of deprivation and uncertainty of the future. St Patrick's, to me, was a wonderful school with dedicated teachers who did their best for all of us, although at times it must have seemed like a hopeless situation to them. The school never let me down. Over the following years, when commentating on my life's progress, my mum said, 'Well, look how well our Derek's doing, despite the fact that he didn't pass his scholarship.'

My school days were one of the happiest times of my life. So it was a sad day when I walked away from the school for the last time, down Westgrove Street, clutching my gift from Bradford City Council for the Queen's Coronation, a round tin of toffees.

Chapter 10
Illness and Remedies

'There's always something wrong with you!' This was my mum's usual cry right up until I went into the army. She was right: Mum had had many sleepless nights and much worry ever since I had been a baby. I was always a frail and peaky child and if the wind blew on me I inevitably caught cold. My ribcage resembled that of Gandhi, a name that my loveable Auntie Cassie affectionately gave me. Many ailments were still life-threatening; for example, diphtheria, scarlet fever, nephritis (kidney problems), polio, typhoid, tuberculosis, rheumatic fever, meningitis and whooping cough. Less serious were mumps, chickenpox, measles, croup, yellow jaundice, tonsillitis, rickets, impetigo, mastoids, dermatitis, ringworms, worms and lice. Inevitably I caught some of these.

Colitis
Not long after I was born I became very ill with a violent form of colitis. I wasn't able to hold down my mum's milk, or milk of any kind – as its richness made me violently sick. Therefore I had no form of nourishment, and my weight plummeted to just a few pounds. I looked forlorn, with sunken eyes and emaciated body. We had just moved from Heaton to Legrams Street, so we had to find another doctor. My parents were distraught, as the outlook of my recovery was looking bleak. Our new neighbour, Lucy Newell, told Mum to try a new doctor, Joseph Henry, who had just set up practice at 110 Preston Street. An appointment was made, and after a thorough examination Dr Henry told my mum to feed me bananas and sherry mixed into a paste. After a few days my stomach began to accept this unusual remedy, which gave a lining to the stomach. A couple of weeks later I began to take milk and other nourishment. My

mother always said it was Dr Henry who had saved my life, and I have never forgotten his name.

Before the NHS

People didn't trouble GPs without good cause, as most had to pay for the doctor and medicines. There might be 5*s* on the mantelpiece for the fee, or 3*s* 6*d* if the family were not so well off. It was not until 1947 that Sir William Beveridge's dream of the National Health Service came to fruition. The professional attitude to working-class patients was frequently robust, and this was accepted with tolerance; in middle-class families greater courtesies were paid. Medical diagnosis was often of academic rather than practical importance.

By December 1941 the Government had introduced the Vitamin Welfare Scheme, where all children under the age of two years old received free supplies of cod liver oil compound and blackcurrant juice, and orange juice when available.

Tonsillitis

Until the age of five I had many sore throats. My mother took me to see a lady doctor, Dr Waller on Shearbridge Road. (Dr Henry was in the army, and been taken a POW in Crete.) Dr Waller shone a large torch down my throat and exclaimed that they had to come out, as they were the size of golf balls and beetroot red: surely an exaggeration! Within a week I was in the Bradford Eye and Ear Hospital on Hallfield Road, which also admitted patients with tonsillitis. Once my mum had left I cried a lot. The next morning victims of both sexes were bathed and clothed in nightshirts. Together with the other crying children I was put in a large cot at one end of the room. One by one we were taken to a large well-lit room with shiny dishes and what I though were lots of knives and forks. My last memory was of a large awful-smelling rubber mask being placed over my nose and mouth. After that I don't recall much other, except that when I woke up in a metal-framed bed the pillow and sheets were red with blood from my mouth. My dad came home on leave to visit me, although they wouldn't allow him or my mum into the ward: they could only wave to me through the small round window of the ward door. I waved back, sobbing, with blood running down my chin. The next day I felt a little better, but my throat was still very sore and I could still taste blood. I was given plenty of drinks, but no food until lunchtime, when I had some ice-cream which tasted so cool and smooth in my throat. The doctors and the nurses kept visiting my bed, asking me to open my mouth for inspection, and sounding my chest. I was almost the last to leave the ward; most of my friends from the large cot departed before me.

My dad had returned to camp not having been able to cuddle me. From what my mum said he had been quite upset. I always remember when Mum came to take me home: she wrapped me up like an Eskimo, with a large scarf over my mouth to keep the cold out – leaving just enough space for my eyes to peer out. An hour and two buses later, I was on the settee at home reading my comics. Life was almost back to normal – and I still had many sore throats.

Scarlet Fever

It was summer 1944. I was six and my brother was twelve. For a few days Lawrence had not been feeling well. He was sweating and red spots had developed on his body. Mum called in Mrs Booth, who lived at no. 10, as she was experienced in childhood ailments. (She was the comedian Ernie Wise's aunt, and he spent many hours at her house in Legrams Street.) One look and she said, 'He's got scarlet fever.' She advised my mum to ring for an ambulance, which she did from Miss Gallimore's on Great Russell Street: she was one of the few people in our area with a private phone.

The Bradford ambulance fleet had two special ambulances for infectious diseases, one for scarlet fever and one for diphtheria; they were commonly known as the fever vans. The ambulance duly arrived and Lawrence was wrapped in a large red blanket and taken away to the Bradford Fever Hospital at Penny Oaks, off Leeds Road.

There was no charge for treatment at the hospital or for the ambulance. If the patient wanted to stay at home but the facilities for isolation were inadequate, then he or she could be compulsorily removed to hospital. Such was the concern of Bradford Health Authority about this and other diseases that the fever hospital treated diseases in separate wards, with one each for typhus, scarlet fever and typhoid. Bradford had been at the forefront in the treatment of such diseases from the late nineteenth century. In 1848 there had been many deaths from cholera, and in the decade after 1861 there were 1,798 deaths from diarrhoea, 63 per cent of which were children aged under one year. In the 1870s there was a particularly virulent outbreak of typhoid, attributed to milk contamination, which affected over 6,000 people. In the summer of 1893 smallpox, of which Bradford had suffered epidemics in the 1840s and 1850s, returned: 995 cases were confirmed, and 113 people died. This was followed immediately by an epidemic of almost 1500 cases of scarlet fever, caused by an infected milk supply at Bolton Woods. In the 1940s there were still many Bradfordians alive who had lived through many of these and other earlier epidemics, so the city took any form of these diseases very seriously.

As Mrs Booth had diagnosed, Lawrence had scarlet fever. My mum wasn't allowed to go to the hospital with him, or to visit him. A nurse came to the house the next day to confirm his illness and gave my mum a number. This was used to give medical reports in a nightly column in the *Telegraph and Argus*. Under each heading, dangerously ill, very poorly, poorly, better and much better, a list of numbers appeared. It was said that if a number wasn't there the patient was probably dead.

The nurse informed Mum that the house had to be stoved and sealed the next day. Stoving was the disinfecting of a house where disease was prevalent. But when she saw me, felt my brow and took a look at my body, she said, 'He's got it!' An hour later the ambulance that had taken Lawrence away the previous day arrived. I was wrapped up in the red blanket (was it the same one? surely not) and off I went, with all the neighbours standing around at a discreet distance muttering and watching. It was rumoured that we had caught the fever by playing near the drains in the street, but the doctors eventually concluded that I had definitely caught it from my brother. There were no further cases in the area that week.

The next day the house was stoved and sealed and, as my dad was away in the army, my mum went to stay with my grandparents in Fenton Street. She visited the hospital a few times: when I say 'visit', I mean she was able to look up at the window of our ward on the second floor. On arrival she would go to the reception, and they would inform our ward nurse that our mother was outside – together with many other mothers, all waving and crying. I don't think we realised how ill we were, but both our hospital numbers were initially in the 'dangerously ill' column in the *Telegraph and Argus*. We slowly moved down to 'much better', but it was a slow process of quite a few weeks, with no comics to read or toys to play with (because the disease was so contagious).

My dad came home on compassionate leave from Kirkby Lonsdale; he was in Normandy a few weeks later. I believe that seeing us through the second-floor windows and not being able to have a kiss and a cuddle or say goodbye must have affected him. Mum wrote to him every day about our condition and recovery.

Across from our beds in the mixed ward was a girl aged about six. We could talk with each other during our isolation and illness but it wasn't a particularly good time to play or communicate. She had blonde curly hair and spoke with a lisp, and when I was not counting spots I was talking to her. She was a Catholic and went to St Mary's Infants' School; she was looking forward to attending the big girls' school that year. One night there was a lot of activity around her bed, and the next morning the bed was made up but empty. Some of the older children asked where she had gone, and the nurses replied that she had gone home. I was only six so I accepted this, although I wished she had said goodbye to me. Some weeks later, back home, I mentioned the blonde girl who had suddenly gone home to my mum. She drew me close and told me the girl had died that night, and it was better that I knew what had really happened. I broke down and cried. For a long time afterwards I mentioned 'the little girl with the blonde hair' when I said my prayers.

Chickenpox, Measles and Mumps
Chickenpox was common, and parents let their children play with children who had the disease, so they would catch it and get it over with. I also had measles. One of the cures for this was to go to bed, shut the curtains and not let any light in, and to rest and recover in the darkened room. I missed out on whooping cough, luckily. Some cases of this disease left sufferers with problems like deformities of the rib cage in later life.

I also had mumps, with time off school again, when I sat about the house with a scarf around my neck. Jean Glossop, the girl next door, had mumps at the same time. Silly jokes went round family and friends: had we been kissing? I wasn't amused: it wasn't funny having a continuous headache and difficulty in swallowing. It wasn't made any easier when the rent man said that I looked like a hamster with food in its cheeks.

Sunray Treatment
I had my share of colds but never influenza or bronchitis, which was something to compensate for the many ailments I had. When I was still thin and frail after scarlet fever, Dr Waller suggested a course of sunray treatment.

The venue for this was the former Congregationalist chapel at the bottom of Little Horton Lane. The treatment room was small and dark, with six sunlamps set at strategic positions. In another room we had to take all our clothes off, and it was mixed. I was six, at an age when I was beginning to start feeling embarrassed. My mother persuaded me to undress and go to stand in the sunray room with the other boys and girls. After applying a large pair of goggles to my eyes I reluctantly joined them. At least my group of children were all the same age, so after the girls had looked to see what the boys had, and the boys had looked at the girls to see what they hadn't, we were all brought forward in line with the sunlamps.

When the machines were switched on there was a large crackling sound and, with a flash, a white warm light enveloped us. The only thing I remember is that it was nice and warm, but even so I was pleased when my mum said after a few sessions that we wouldn't be going again. At the end of all this I still looked frail and peaky.

Stomach Trouble
After the war I began to have lots of stomach pains, which were treated with all kinds of remedies, some old, some new. Many old ladies who lived locally were asked their opinion of any sicknesses, and for remedies for the many illnesses that prevailed. Mrs Booth, who had diagnosed Lawrence as having scarlet fever, often peered at me as I lay on the settee with my stomach pains. Sometimes I had as many as four or five old ladies looking, prodding and suggesting remedies to my mum. Our milk lady, Lily, always suggested (and indeed made up) a Kaline

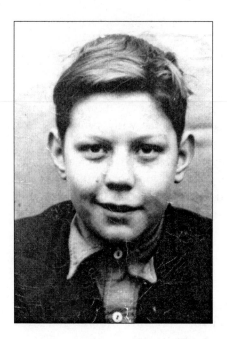

John Tindall, a pal I never forgot, and me. At the time we were both in St Luke's Hospital for observation. *(John Tindall's family and Author's collection)*

poultice; not for the faint hearted. Mrs Booth was also of the opinion that a poultice could clear up most bodily ailments. She made up an assortment of these and laid them on my stomach. Other ladies suggested a 'worm cake', or thought I might have a tapeworm, and suggested the best cure for this was a large dose of syrup of figs.

Miss Martin, an old lady well into her eighties who lived in nearby Edinburgh Street, advised the use of her favourite remedy, that of bloodletting with leeches. My mother was shocked, although the other ladies said she had had lots of success with this remedy. The only leeches I had seen were in films: large fat slimy things like slugs filled with blood, on their victims' bodies, arms and legs after they had waded through a swamp or tracked through the jungle.

I don't believe any of these old ladies' remedies had any success in diagnosing or curing me. I was sure that at least one of them would have been burnt at the stake some two hundred years before. Miss Martin resembled an old witch. She was small, thin and bent, and wore a long black dress that hung disconsolately to a point a few inches above the insteps of her tightly laced old-fashioned high black leather boots. The only thing missing was the pointed hat.

My stomach pains always returned. The local soothsayers and witches hadn't found a cure – but at least I hadn't turned into a frog. In 1949 Dr Jack Howard of Horton Grange Road, who was my grandparents' doctor before and after the war, and went on to look after four generations of Listers from 1947 until 1988, had me admitted to the children's ward at St Luke's Hospital with the intention of getting to the bottom of the problem. I was in the first-floor ward among a group of similar aged boys and girls, with the girls on the one side of the ward and the boys the other side. Next to me was a boy the same age called John Tindall. He would be quite an influence on me. On the other side was David Gamwell, a prolific comic-swapping friend who lived on the next street to ours, Great Russell Street.

We weren't in a surgical ward, as we were in for observation only. It smelt of a cocktail of antiseptic, ether, chloroform, anaesthetic, disinfectant and carbolic soap, which left a lasting impression on me. The floors were of polished wood, and were polished and dry-mopped twice or more daily. There were eight beds either side of the room, each with a locker, and in the centre was a long oak table with a desk at the end. This was for a night nurse or ward sister, who was on call for any of the sixteen boys and girls during the long nights.

John Tindall was a smashing lad, and very streetwise about the big wide world. He was a member of the well-known Canterbury Warriors of Canterbury Estate, situated a few hundred yards away from the hospital. His attitude towards girls was an eye-opener, and it was he who filled in many blank spaces about them! My only response to his teachings was 'Why?' He must have thought 'We've got a right one here' – but he didn't laugh or patronise me, and I was grateful to him for helping me put together the jigsaw pieces of life.

I told John that our gang had had minor run-ins with the Warriors, but he didn't seem to have heard of us, which shows how mediocre we were. He respected the Longside Lane and Princeville gangs, and told me about the many skirmishes that had taken place between them. On many occasions he sang the Canterbury Warriors anthem, which started 'We are the Canterbury Warriors'. I thought was great. Our gang in Listerhills had nothing like that, although in truth it could have started with the line 'We are the Listerhills Dopes'.

Observation in hospital meant just that. Every morning a specialist accompanied by matron and two nurses arrived at my bedside. They removed my pyjama top and felt and prodded my stomach. 'Does this hurt?' I was asked, as well as the inevitable 'Have your bowels moved?' I went for X-rays after having an enema, when a large rubber tube was inserted into my bottom and a large jug of what could only have been soapy water was poured down a funnel into me: I didn't like it one bit! This was the only thing I didn't like in the hospital, so much so that every time a nurse came to my bedside I said, 'You're not going to do that thing with the rubber tube, are you?' not knowing the medical term for this intrusion.

Most of the nurses were nice; one in particular I fell in love with, especially when she tucked me in at night. I never knew her Christian name, as all staff were referred to by their surnames. There was, though, one awful nurse who had me in tears a few times as she was very abrupt, hardly smiled; just plain nasty. It wasn't just me; she was also awful to John, who told her a few times to 'f—off', which meant the matron came and chastised him, but he never seemed to get upset.

Visiting times were one hour per day, 2pm to 3pm, with no evening visits. My mother visited alone on weekdays as my dad was working, then they both visited at the weekend. Typically for my loving parents, on some evenings they stood outside and looked up and waved at my window. This always seemed so very special.

There were always plenty of comics and books to read, while across on the girls' side dolls of all shapes and sizes appeared, so it started to look like a maternity ward. Once we had a singing competition, when each boy and girl had to sing a song or, if you couldn't sing, recite some poetry. I sang 'Buttons and Bows' and John sang the 'Woody Woodpecker' song. It was a young girl with a lisp who won the competition, singing the alphabetical love song 'A, You're Adorable', a popular song of the time. She sang it beautifully that I fell in love with her as well.

After nearly two weeks a few of the children, including me and John, were allowed home. Our results were 'observation negative', in other words no organic problem had been detected. I said 'so long' to my good pal John and we said we would keep in touch. I was so glad I had met him.

After this time in hospital my stomach pains seemed to disappear. I thought the problem had been wearing a belt, especially my snake belt, which I had never found comfortable. My mother said it was probably growing pains, which seems to cover most juvenile complaints. Whatever the cause, it troubled me no more.

My Mother's Hysterectomy

In 1947 my mum had to go into hospital shortly after we returned from a wonderful holiday in Eire. Aged nine, I didn't know what 'hysterectomy' meant; I only knew that when she came out of hospital she was ill for many months. Dr Henry had returned from the war and was back at his old practice in Preston Street, but during his absence my mum had been seeing Dr Howard. It was he who had my mum hospitalised, where she was under the well-known Bradford specialist obstetrician and gynaecologist at St Luke's Hospital, Geoffrey Theobold.

My mother suffered terribly, especially with her nerves, after the operation. It was the help of Dr Howard and a new drug called phenobarbitone that, after a long time, she overcame the illness. Meanwhile, as Lawrence was away at college and my dad was working, I learnt to clean the house, do a small amount of cooking and do the shopping. Sometimes we borrowed a single bed for my mum so that she could sleep downstairs, which helped her when the weather was cold. I sat and read to her, her library books about cowboys. She was never demanding, and I enjoyed looking after her – but I was pleased when she recovered enough to run the household again. It was nice when she was back to normal, shouting and bawling; I'd missed it and so had my dad. Even so, she was troubled with her nerves for many years.

Nits and Squints

Nits could be quite prevalent, and once a week mother would get out the 'nit comb' and proceed to comb through my hair as I bent over a newspaper. There were always sighs of relief from her when nothing moved on the paper. She never discovered any nits on me, thank goodness. If really infected with nits, the hair would have to be cut off, and everyone would know the reason why. My mother always said 'that I had strong hair' but, when it was cut I lost my strength. One look at my face and body would undermine her statement, that I was more like 'Gandhi' than 'Samson'. Children could be cruel to other children when having had their hair cut off, remarks were made especially to girls, for if the cause had been impetigo, the scalp was shaved. A purple substance, gentian violet, was applied to the head, which was used as an antiseptic.

Some children had squints, or one eye out of alignment, and remarks like 'he's got one eye and a butterball' were made to the unfortunate child. Many children had to wear glasses with a patch over one eye to correct visual problems from the age of three onwards. In the 1940s and '50s school group photographs often show at least one child wearing glasses and with a patch over one eye. The 'catch 'em young' approach made little difference, as a study later found that in lots of cases this method was totally unnecessary.

Fleas

It's really no wonder we caught many ailments as we played out days and nights, with marbles in the gutters by the grates, spending lots of our time in John Willie North's field, and paddling in the 'mucky beck'. Sometimes I would come home with a 'passenger' and wake up the next morning with flea bites. As our house was spotless, with an aroma of Lanry and carbolic in every room, my mum hated fleas: she stripped the bed to find the culprit and then proceeded to cover the sheets with DDT. In the mornings I woke up with a white face.

Cleanliness and Cures

Although many children were victims of illness and disease, Bradford Corporation and the newly formed NHS, contributed to a vast reduction in and sometimes eradication of particular ailments with new antibiotics. A clean environment must have helped too. The streets in both town and districts were kept spotlessly clean by the many street cleaners, with their cream trolleys adorned with two large brushes and a shovel. These workers brushed even the most uneven cobbled streets, the men taking a great pride in their job.

Every month our streets were visited by the corporation grate-cleaning van, which had a large rubber funnel fixed to its top. When the grate tops were pulled away the funnel was lowered, to drain all the silt and rubble that had accumulated. When the grate was replaced the drain was flushed with disinfectant. We always watched at a safe distance, as we still thought we could get fever from the grates. This street cleaning was supplemented by many housewives who cleaned and whitened or yellowed their doorstones, sweeping outside to the causeway edge.

Bradford city centre, although dull, always appeared clean. Litter signs and notices abounded, for example 'Spitting prohibited £5 fine', and wastepaper and rubbish bins were used by both children and adults as second nature. Public toilets were looked after with pride by the cleansing department. All districts had two or three of these, most of which were gents' urinals and the town itself had many placed conveniently. The jewel in the crown was the large public convenience in Town Hall Square, known popularly as the Crystal Palace. There was another rather rude title as well: the House of Lords . . . where all the big nobs hang out. . . . These toilets were looked after for many years by a member of St Patrick's Choir, namely Jim Carroll, and were known for their cleanliness: it was said that a banquet could be held there. White tiles covered all, and the large and ornate urinals had the name 'Shanks' positioned at eye level. As there was nothing else to look at it was a marvellous form of advertising! On the walls high above were signs placed to make you aware of VD (venereal disease), making the reader aware that 'early treatment was essential' and including a telephone number for St Luke's Hospital. The toilet cubicles were made of mahogany and oak with beautiful solid heavy doors and a highly polished large brass coin (1*d*) lock. I had used these toilets from an early age, sometimes on my own, and had never felt uncomfortable.

There was always something special about having an attendant present. I know Jim Carroll was fed up with the old joke that he could have his holidays at his own convenience!

Alongside the preoccupation with cleanliness, age-old remedies were still in vogue. The one I never liked was Fennings' fever cure, which seemed to burn the enamel off my teeth and required a sweet to remove the horrible taste. Syrup of figs was a must for small constipated boys: it tasted nice but resulted in many visits to the toilet. For coughs, my mum would send me for a bottle of Mr Knight's cough medicine to Harrison-Parkinson, the chemist at the bottom of Sunbridge Road close to Newby's, the fishmonger. The medicine was their own make, it cost 2*s* 6*d*, and whatever was in it it seemed to work. Another pick-me-up my mum swore by was malt Robeline. The jar carried a picture of Tarzan on the label, but after many months of taking it I still looked like Gandhi. Other pick-me-ups like Delrosa and Rose Hip Syrup helped, as did Lucozade in its distinctive cellophane-covered bottle – which was considered a very special treat.

Polio and TB

Polio was a common childhood disease in the UK, and hundreds of polio victims were confined to iron lungs in the 1940s and '50s. Summer after summer polio epidemics would break out, and parents lived in fear that their children might contact the disease and be left crippled, paralysed or confined to an iron lung for the rest of their lives. Polio symptoms were fever, fatigue and a headache – so just a slight fever caused panic in the household.

TB (tuberculosis) was still prevalent. The TB sanatorium at Grassington with its 200 beds was nearly always full with adults and children from all over the north of England. All these patients were sent in the hope that the pure Dales air would help them recover from this dreadful disease. I was fourteen when my Uncle George died at the sanatorium at Middleton St George in County Durham. He was the fourth member of my mum's family to succumb to TB. Spitting by anyone was seen as abhorrent, as it helped to spread this dreadful disease.

One hazard that didn't help anyone with a chest or lung complaint was fog. Almost every winter this descended as a result of the smoke from mill chimneys and house coal fires. I was caught out many times by this horrible damp stuff that darkened your hair, face and clothes with black soot. It was usual to hold a handkerchief over your mouth; failure to do so resulted in breathing in the soot. Journeys home through the fog could be long and hazardous. Accidents were numerous, from collisions with vehicles, walking into objects or falling over unseen obstacles. The phrase that 'you could hardly see your hand in front of your face' really was true. Later the word smog was used to describe smoke-intensified fog.

Teeth

Teeth were generally not looked after, especially by the working class. Most old people had an array of black and brown teeth set at assorted angles, almost like tombstones in a neglected cemetery. During the war toothpaste was virtually a luxury, with Kolynos, Solidox, Odal and Colgate the most popular, and some people turned to old-fashioned methods. One such was Mr Wainwright, an retired mill worker in his eighties who had a lovely set of white teeth. He told my dad that for over seventy years he had used soot and ash from the fire range, rubbed on with his forefinger. When young I had a small toothbrush, and mainly used Kolynos toothpaste when available. After the war more toothpaste was available, such as tins of hard pink block Gibbs Dentifrice, which tasted much better than my Kolynos.

For extraction of my milk teeth our standard method was to tie the tooth to a piece of string on a door knob. Slamming the door shut was generally sufficient to leave the tooth swinging on the string, without any pain. Later, for the removal of molars, I was sent to the school's dentist in Manor Row. Entry was through a large and ornate door, along a marble floor to a very large staircase, at the top of which along the wall was a long Victorian horsehair seat. There was hardly any lighting, it was cold and gloomy, and I sat here, legs dangling, listening to the tick of a large clock in the corner. To make matters worse I could hear the patients' cries; be it boy or girl, the screams were always the same. There was not much in the way of a bedside manner. A man with a mask over his mouth looked for the rogue tooth, and when he found it he slapped a mask over my face. I could taste a similar gas to the one I was given when I had my tonsils out as a five year old. I don't remember fighting against it, but some cries of fear must have escaped me, as they did other victims. When I revived I was sent out to the bench again, to wait until someone said I could go back to school. I returned there spitting blood and protecting my mouth with a bloody hanky.

My dad had false teeth quite early in life, my mum a few years later. After seeing what could happen I began to take care of my teeth. I certainly didn't want the 'tombstone teeth' look.

Spots

It seemed, as I became a teenager, that I had had most of what was common in the way of diseases, and had really been quite lucky. As a teenager my biggest worry was spots and how to get rid of them. Some of us were really unlucky and had acne, and even though I didn't have many spots in comparison with them, when I got one it always seemed to be on the end of my nose. No doubt it was really quite small, but to me it was like Vesuvius. My mum's usual comment was, 'Don't squeeze it, it'll make it worse,' and it did! I couldn't bear to see this thing on my nose, probably with a yellow head, and I tried not to make eye contact with anyone, especially girls. There was always a tactless dope who would say 'What's that on your nose?' or 'Do you know you've got a spot on your nose?'

To make matters worse spots always seemed to appear when you were going somewhere special, like a party or dance. If you were meeting someone for the first time they would always remember not where you met or the time, just that you had a large ugly spot on the end of your nose. My grandmother said that in her younger days (in the nineteenth century) a remedy was to wash your face in your own urine: she said the secret was in the acid content, and that it worked. My grandfather came up with a much easier and less unpleasant suggestion, which was to use normal Fairy household soap, and I found this successful. In John Street Market there was a stall that sold herbs and soaps, including a soap for spots called Sloamans, which smelt of wool fat and probably was. This and the Fairy soap seemed to keep the spots at bay, so I was one of the lucky ones.

Building Me Up

After I left school I had no other serious complaints, just the common cold. My mum took Sanatogen to help her recover from her serious operation in 1947, and was still taking in the 1950s. I began to take it as well, to help build me up – as my mum kept saying. I was still thin, with a 35 inch chest and 22 inch waist, and my weight was 10 stones. But I had begun to grow: when I started at Brown, Muff's I had the nickname of 'Pinocchio'; this was later replaced by 'Longshanks', after the tall Edward I. With the judicious use of Sanatogen and new tablets called Pro-Plus (a pick-me-up), I became quite fit.

How fit was a question that was to be answered in the not too distant future when I attended a medical for my National Service.

Chapter 11
Extreme Weather

The Flood of 1946

After many days of exceptionally heavy rain Bradford woke up on Friday 20 September 1946 to find the city, and most of the West Riding, inundated with some of the worst floods in living memory. Roads, railway lines, houses, factories and shop premises in most towns in the area were badly affected. Bradford's misery had been added to when the Bradford Beck, unable to take the full volume of water, had burst and overflowed at the bottom of Preston Street, sending torrents of water rushing down Thornton road to the city centre. With gullies choked with debris and grates overflowing, the water ran down into Canal Road and soon the centre of Bradford resembled a lake, with many parts of the city being flooded to a depth of 4 feet. Thousands of pounds-worth of damage was caused to goods stocked in premises below street level. Broadway and Town Hall Square were a foot deep in water, while office workers in the Swan Arcade were marooned and crowds of workpeople made extensive detours round the flooded streets. Buses were stranded, and in some places passengers could only alight by taking the plunge to the pavement.

The stalls of the Ritz cinema on Broadway were flooded with many seats and carpets ruined, and the large Compton organ was destroyed beyond repair. Water reached the stalls and the organ of the New Victoria cinema, but unlike the Ritz organ, the cinema's mighty Wurlitzer was saved. Bradford's Mechanics' Institute, situated in the centre of the city, was also flooded to a depth of over a foot. Many of the city centre shopkeepers quickly moved goods from basements to higher rooms. Trams and buses could only run in the outer areas to which the flooding had not spread, although some maintained a partial service by running through the floods where the water was at a lower level. Scenes of chaos were all

A view from the Town Hall that shows the extent of the flooding in the centre of Bradford. The toilets ('Crystal Palace') and the New Inn at the corner of Thornton Road both suffered damage as the water had gushed from the Beck down Thornton Road (top right into the centre).
(By kind permission of the Bradford Telegraph and Argus)

around the city, but after a while people made light of the situation, and everyone helped each other to resolve the many problems. The war had been over for only a year, so the common will of many Bradfordians soon overcame any difficulties.

I had gone to school that morning, so I was in class when the news came that the Beck had burst at Preston Street. Going to school earlier that morning had been no problem, and Thornton Road had only had water overflowing from blocked grates. We could not have known that in a short while this would change to a torrent of water rushing down to the city centre. Teachers were not concerned at this point, but a few of us, including George Stockley, Terence Moran, Michael Farrell and me, had to cross the river of Thornton Road to return home. The teachers tried to reassure us by saying that the water had to go down sometime, but it was still raining. A suggestion was made by our teacher Miss Wheelan that we could miss Preston Street and Thornton Road out by

A photograph taken from the Town Hall showing the Mechanics' Institute on the left. In the centre is Carter's sports shop, which like most establishments in this area had its basement flooded. *(By kind permission of the Bradford Telegraph and Argus)*

walking along City Road to Girlington and over the top to Listerhills; and the best time to go was now, at lunchtime. Just before we were due to set off a large open Bedford wagon belonging to the BDA (Bradford Dyers Association) pulled up outside the school in Rebecca Street. It was Michael Farrell's father, who worked in the BDA transport shed in Water Lane. This appropriately named road was flooded, being close to Thornton Road, but he had managed to move the wagon out and had driven his way through the raging waters up Lower Westgrove Street to our school. No questions were asked: we all climbed up the tailboard on to the back of the wagon, and off we went – back the way he had come. We thought it was a big adventure, and had no thought of danger as he slowly drove at an angle across the surging waters. We were soon on the higher ground of Norfolk Street, where we all disembarked and made our way home.

I told my mum why I was home so early; she had heard that the city was flooded, but not that the Beck had overflowed. She had a great fear of water, and was perturbed to hear that I had come across a river of water in an open wagon, but calmed down when I told her it was Mr Farrell's BDA wagon. When Dad had not arrived home from the mill for his lunch at 12.15pm, Mum wondered if

Tyrrell Street. The position of the vehicle gives a good impression of the difficulties and damage sustained during the floods.
(By kind permission of the Bradford Telegraph and Argus)

it was because of the floods – and it was. The mill was in Preston Street and only 100 yards from where the Beck had burst; the lower part had taken in much water and some areas were badly flooded. The management had asked for volunteers to bring a swimming costume so they could help to pull the skeps and bobbins from the flooded areas, and my dad, having no costume, borrowed one from our neighbour, Arthur Newell, who lived at the front house. This costume was an all in one, in yellow and black hoops, like a bee, and if that was not bad enough, it was made of wool – more appropriate for a Charlie Chaplin film than wading about in water under the glare of the many people who had turned up to watch the event.

I went down to watch. It was still raining and the skies were overcast; being September it was getting quite chilly. As my dad had been out of the army for only a short time he was quite fit, but still skinny, with a 28 inch waist. I was eight, and felt rather proud of my dad on that day, watching him come and go with some of the other volunteers, not swimming but wading in the cold, dirty water, pushing the skeps to dry land, and fishing hundreds of bobbins out of the water and stacking them on the dry pavements at the top of Preston Street. All the time the woollen costume sagged and got larger and larger, out of proportion to his skinny frame.

I suppose that, as he was an overlooker, it was expected of my dad to volunteer with no extra remuneration; but in his next wage packet (and in those of the others who took part) there was an extra £1 note. There was a special treat for my dad when he arrived home looking tired, wet and forlorn: this being Friday night, he was first in the tin bath.

My Saturday morning club at the New Victoria wasn't spoiled, but my friends and I had to sit in the back stalls for a few weeks until all the front stalls had dried out. There were many adventures in the floods, although much damage had been done and many of thousands of pounds were lost to industry and shopkeepers. Worse was to come in the new year of 1947, with a severe winter that would last for over three months!

The Severe Winter of 1947
Coming soon after the floods, from late January to mid-March, and into April 1947 Bradford (and most of Britain) was to face yet another test, this time from snow and freezing temperatures. The city had thirty-six days of snow, and fifty-seven days and fifty-nine nights of temperatures below freezing, and the newspapers proclaimed it was 'Colder in Britain than in Iceland!'

A constant topic of conversation for the English, if there is nothing else to talk about, is the weather, and for well over three months weather was the constant topic. The amount of snow that fell during this time was a record, with snowdrifts of between 15 and 20 feet deep being reported. Perhaps worst of all to bear for Bradfordians, considering the lack of fuel and the shortage of food, were the low temperatures. From 18 January to 16 March the night temperatures were below freezing, and it was not until 19 March that the relentless cold began to ease. It had been a national disaster: 1947 was a winter to remember.

I had never been as cold before, and have never been so cold since, although like most schoolboys I thought it was a children's paradise when the snow first started to fall; we wished it would last forever. From day one there were many snowball fights, and sledging was in full flight down Archibald Street. Alas, it was too much of a good thing as the snow soon began to blanket the streets. Day after day the snow piled up, creating a white maze of passages of tightly packed snow, in places 10 feet high, dwarfing my 4 foot 6 inches. At night the empty streets seemed filled with an eerie silence.

Friends, neighbours and even my playmates disappeared from time to time as we could get lost, or injured by slipping on the tightly packed ice, or even buried by falls of snow from overburdened house roofs. Although main roads were passable, soon all transport became non-existent. There were fuel and food shortages, and power cuts – so mills began to work three or four days a week. This resulted in many workers, including my dad, being put on short time.

Coal became scarce, though domestic deliveries did get through under atrocious conditions, mainly by horse and cart. The poor horses were always a sorry sight as they pulled the heavy loads. Our coal merchant was devastated when his shire horse slipped and broke a leg. It was sad to see the horse in pain, especially as it was some time before the local vet arrived. He gave it an injection to put it to sleep, and a few hours later a Bradford Corporation wagon arrived with lifting gear to take it away. This was a difficult job, and help was given by some Polish soldiers and Italian prisoners of war who were in the area clearing snow from the roads. Some bystanders asked if the horse could be cut up for public consumption, as horse meat was part of the national diet at this time thanks to the shortage of other meats. We young ones were not amused.

With the snow continuing unabated, very few children were able to go to school. I went with other children and parents, mostly for safety, as making our way through snow passages on to the main roads and to school could be dangerous. Mr Durkin, the caretaker, managed to keep the coke boilers going and was lucky to have quite a stockpile of fuel so the school was able to keep open. Even so, most days it was freezing in school, even with the radiators at full blast, so we had to sit with our overcoats on during the lessons – and the school's ancient toilets, outside in the small playground, were frozen. I hardly missed any classes.

Life at home was not much better, with stone floors, no double glazing and the only form of heating being the old Yorkshire Range fire. Heat from the small coal fire reached out about 2 feet and then dissipated into the cold house, so we were constantly sitting almost on top of the fire to keep warm. There were reductions in gas supplies, but whenever it was available my mum switched the gas oven on and leave the oven door open. This helped, even though the oven was in the scullery. In the mornings there was always a heavy frost, even on the inside of the windows, both upstairs and downstairs. Jack Frost certainly painted some lovely pictures and designs on my window. These I viewed every morning with wonder, until my warm hand created a gap so I could see that, as usual, it was still snowing.

With my dad on short time, I sometimes joined him on a journey through the many snow passages and then with great difficulty over the mounds of snow into John Willie North's field. In the field the snow was in large drifts, not unlike sand dunes. There were always tracks heading down to the 'Coaly' as most local people were of the same mind, and wanted to get hold of some coal. Down by the railway tracks, close to the goods yard, were piles of coke and slack left by engine tenders; and we also dug into the hard ground next to the tracks, where coal had accumulated over many years and was covered by soil, weeds and thick ice and snow. I say 'we' dug, but it was my dad who did all the digging while I collected the loose coal and slack. Once again I thought he was great as he dug away into the hard frost to secure warmth for us, just as, a few months ago during the floods, I had admired him when he was wearing that funny swimming costume and moving debris from the mill. Each time we returned with a wet sack half full of fuel. We always saw many neighbours and friends down in the 'coaly', all on the same mission. There was never any trouble, problems or resentments.

It was still blizzard conditions, and in Bradford all able-bodied men were put to clearing the snow. Among them were many ex-soldiers who were thankful to have kept their army greatcoats, waterproof capes and substantial boots, all of which were a boon in the severe weather. The mail was getting through but the poor postmen had to dig postboxes out to reach the mail. Many farms were cut off and the animals were suffering from food shortages. Old prams and sledges were put to use, collecting fuel of any kind. In the shops potatoes were put on ration and schools were warned that unless the weather improved school milk would be stopped. Forty-one thousand people in Bradford had now signed on for unemployment benefit. Many were given a 'snow-card', which meant that they had to report to Harris Street Depot (the main city Cleansing Department's depot) to help with clearing the streets.

At home we were still very cold but at least we were a young family. Every day an elderly person in the surrounding streets passed away from pneumonia or hypothermia brought on by the intense cold. Vincent Davey and I borrowed a large pick from our neighbour Lucy and, armed with this and two spades, we cleared the snow from outside old people's houses after school and at weekends. For Vincent and me, aged eight and nine, it was hard work in such freezing temperatures. We dug and hacked away with the pick at solid blocks of ice covered by thick snow, and each time we cleared an area we knew that it would be covered with even more snow the next day, and that the ice would be as tightly packed again. Most of the time we worked in the dark on these freezing winter evenings, two forlorn figures wearing balaclavas, jackets, overcoats, woollen gloves with no fingers and wellingtons with two pairs of socks – all of which were wet through within a few minutes. Of course we still wore our short trousers, which inevitably led to our kneecaps being chapped. It was one way to keep warm, although on entering the house my face, hands and legs ached straight away because of the change from freezing cold to the semi-heat of the house. We broke our pick one night, which made our task much harder, but we carried on with our two spades, our hands being jarred by the spade's impact on thick ice. We always knew that the elderly were really grateful, especially when we had cleaned the most important path – to the outside toilet. In most cases the toilet pipes were frozen or, at worst, had burst, causing large areas of solid ice to be formed, thus making it very dangerous under foot. Inside the toilet, even if the pipes were wrapped in old sacking, the water cistern would be a solid block of ice and the toilet chain immoveable. The only way to unblock the pan was by pouring boiling water down it. This usually had to be repeated many times before the ice could be flushed away, and inevitably it returned in a few hours. Small oil lamps were sold in their thousands, to be placed on top of the cistern to keep it from freezing. In a normal winter they may have worked, but in these exceptional conditions they didn't. During these three months the days of the toilet being used to 'make out a will' or catch up with the news on the newspaper squares hanging on a nail were gone, and the toilet was quickly used for the purpose intended!

By now gutters were falling down at an alarming rate and roofs were collapsing under the weight of snow. Every day news came in that somebody's gutter was hanging off, which was a danger not only to householders but also to passers-by. The snow and ice hung over the gutters in large folds and the larger these became the more pressure was put on gutters. We threw snowballs at the gutters to help bring the snow down, thus relieving the pressure, but we had to be careful not to hit upstairs windows. It was perhaps the only time we could throw snowballs at houses without fear of reprisal. It worked, although missed shots with the snowballs did result in the occasional window being broken.

With electricity cuts in the morning and afternoon, offices and shops in Bradford, normally ablaze with light, carried on trading with only oil lamps and candles. There was no electricity for domestic users between 8.30am and 11.30am, and 1.30pm and 3.30pm. Funerals were held up, and many people in outlying districts were trapped in their houses. Emergency services were given priority, just about managing to keep up with demand – although with great difficulty. There were still serious delays on the motor bus and trolleybus routes and many railway lines were still blocked. Street lighting was reduced still further and the gas lamps were cut by 50 per cent, being confined to the central areas and bus routes only. Some of our meals were eaten by candlelight, that was until the supply of candles ran out, and on the odd occasion when we had no fire in the grate we all went to bed early.

Theatres and cinemas cut their performances to fit in with the power reductions. Sometimes it was just as cold inside the cinema as outside in the snow. Our only other form of entertainment was the wireless, but sometimes it was hard to smile at the programmes while wrapped up against the cold. Even so, we managed to listen to our favourite programme, *Dick Barton Special Agent*, at 6.45 every evening. The snow was now piled up above our downstairs window sills and paths had to be cleared every day. The night sky was clear almost every night bringing with it freezing temperatures.

Vincent, Jean Glossop and I decided to build a large igloo in the back yard, by forming the snow and ice into blocks. It was really quite easy, for when they were in place they just froze together. Igloos were being built all around, both small and large, and ours was quite a size and height: we could just about stand up in it. There was a hole in the top, just like a real igloo, and to be honest it was colder inside than outside; how Eskimos could live in them was a marvel to us.

139

Jean wanted to play at being Eskimos, with the igloo as our house. I had played games of house with Jean before, so I politely declined.

One night Vincent and I (being the original dopes) thought we would sit in the igloo to see how long we could stand the cold. It was a clear night and the temperature was well below freezing. Our adventure lasted just half an hour. After both our coats had frozen to the ground and icicles had formed on our hair and balaclavas, we found we couldn't raise ourselves from the floor, so I had to shout for my dad to rescue us. Vincent and I were lifted up like two stiff dummies by my dad, helped by our neighbour, Jean's father Arthur. Mum sat us both in the scullery on buffets inches from the oven which was on at full blast, and soon the scullery floor had small puddles everywhere as the heat from the oven melted our clothes. She went on and on in the background while my dad called us a couple of flat-cakes. I agreed it was a stupid thing to do, as people of all ages were dying when they were caught out in these freezing conditions. Vincent and I were definitely not 'Nanooks of the North'!

After this ridiculous experience we decided to play safe and built in our small garden a massive snowman complete with one of my grandfather's pipes. It was over 6 feet tall and was there for many weeks, as the unusual conditions preserved it. He was given the name Tom, after my grandfather, and in a way it was a comfort knowing that he was outside and would still be there in the morning when I peeped through my icy bedroom window.

February came around and we were still truly gripped by the big freeze. Sometimes, when it seemed that a thaw may be on the way, we were hit by another wave of blizzards that made the drifts even more mountainous. Roads were dug out three or four times as more snow fell and freezing wind drifted it back over the cleared roads. Some of the drifts reached 22 feet in sheltered spots. However, all was not doom and gloom as people began to skate on the frozen lake in Lister Park. On 23 February records were broken for the longest cold spell since records were kept in Bradford, and on 27 February the city had its fortieth night of frost.

Keeping warm at home was always the priority. Each night, before going to bed, pans were boiled and hot water bottles were filled and placed in the beds. It was wise to go to bed before these were cold, and to snuggle down covered by many blankets, eiderdowns and overcoats. This worked if you stopped in bed, but if you had to get up to use the chamber pot you returned to a very cold bed; it was even worse if you had to use the outside toilet. Being young, I was exhausted each evening, and woke up in almost the same position as I had gone to sleep.

Something that people had improvised was a type of bedwarmer. A lamp socket was fixed in the centre of a small wooden greengrocer's crate, complete with a bulb. This was placed upside down on the bed, and the sheets and bedding placed over it. The bulb was switched on, and in this confined space the light of the bulb heated the sheets. We had one, and it worked, although like most people using it we never really contemplated the risk of fire or injury from this Heath-Robinson invention.

It was now 2 March and only once in the last forty years had there been a colder night in Bradford, but things were now a little easier as the fuel crisis was beginning to end. The newspaper headlines predicted 'The Big Frost's Last Fling', as warm air from the Azores was on its way. This thaw didn't come, however, and more heavy snow fell. More roads and railway lines were blocked. It was not until 16 March that the long-awaited thaw set in, helped by a terrific hurricane that swept the British Isles during the night.

Bradford's warmest day for sixty days was 18 March: at last the long cold spell began to recede, and Bradford began a clear-up operation reminiscent of the floods six months earlier. I knew it was the end when I woke up one morning and saw that my snowman was just a small mound of snow and slush, on the top of which lay Grandfather's briar pipe.

Agricultural losses such as sheep, corn and potatoes were enormous, and it took three years for agriculture to recover fully from the ravages of the winter. The hard winter together with the floods showed how much Bradfordians could take in such adverse conditions, as everybody 'mucked in'.

The harshest winter of my life drew to a close. At the time I didn't realise that of all my family it was my mum who had been affected the most. I don't know how she coped. For so long she had been doing the washing and drying, not only of dirty clothes but also wet clothes, day in and day out in a confined scullery. Clothes were dried over the oven door and on the large clothes horse placed in front of the fire – where the wet clothes made the cold room damp. There was always a nice meal on the table and she never forgot bread and jam for my supper, all while strict rationing was being observed.

Spring was late that year, and during the Easter holidays in early April there were even more snow falls. The weather was so cold and rainy that the newspapers reported that spring was 'a wash-out'. However, weather predictions for 1947 promised a warm summer and a good harvest – and they were right. Somehow Mother Nature always restores the balance.

Chapter 12
My Upbringing as a Roman Catholic

Family

I was brought up as a Roman Catholic thanks to my mum's mother, Catherine Lenaghan. She had come over as a young girl with her family from Crossmaglen, Northern Ireland, to Middlesbrough in the 1880s. Catherine married Arthur Cooper who came from a staunch Methodist family, making an unusual religious pairing in the early 1900s. All their children, including my mum, were brought up as Catholics. When my mum married my dad in 1930 it was a mixed marriage: my dad was Church of England. But Lawrence and I were brought up as Catholics and my dad always encouraged us to go to Mass on Sundays. It was in 1944 that he became a Catholic, as previously mentioned. My mum, being a staunch Catholic, was to guide both me and my brother in the religion at St Patrick's Church in Westgate, Bradford.

Following the 1845 potato blight that spread throughout Ireland, causing famine and death to millions, several thousand Catholic emigrants settled in the Bradford area. A new Catholic church was built for them. The land chosen was situated at the top of Cropper Lane (now Rebecca Street and Westgrove Street), which had been built up some five years earlier. Most of the rest of the land in the area was open fields and hedgerows, extending down to the beck at Goitside near Thornton Road. On the other side was White Abbey Road, a narrow thoroughfare that was part of the coach road to the north. The Lower Globe public house was the last place where the coach took on passengers. Directly opposite was the Bradford Hospital, later to be called Bradford Infirmary, at the junction of Lumb Lane and White Abbey Road. Later, when this was demolished, during our school days, it became a recreational ground known as the Old Infirmary. The area around the church was divided into streets that still exist today: Vaughan Street, Wynne Street and William Street (later changed to Sedgefield Terrace). The

In my first Communion outfit ready for the big day at St Patrick's Church in May 1945, aged seven. *(Author's collection)*

St Patrick's Church, Westgate, showing the priest's house incorporated into the church.
(Bernard Parry)

laying of the foundation stone took place on 17 March 1852, and with the opening of the church in April 1855 St Patrick's became an independent parish. It was at this church that we as a family worshipped from the early 1940s.

I was taught from a very early age to say my prayers. Before I went to bed I knelt by the bedside and said a 'Hail Mary', 'Our Father' and a 'Good Act of Contrition'. During the war I always asked to 'keep my daddy safe' and that he would come home soon. Sometimes I included, 'If I should die before I wake, I pray the Lord my soul to take.' There is candour in this little prayer that makes you shudder: it always seems strange to hear little children pray these words when they have only just begun to live. I finished my prayers by naming many friends and relations, asking God to bless them. By this time I was almost asleep. On cold winter nights I said my prayers in bed, usually praying myself to sleep.

In 1944 my mum joined St Patrick's Union of Catholic Mothers, which had a strong membership that worked hard to raise funds for the parish and provide help whenever necessary in parochial matters. The Union also took part in many social activities, including dinners, dances and trips to the seaside. In the late 1940s they formed an Old Tyme dancing club, which met in the basement hall of St Patrick's Girls' School on Rebecca Street. The music played on these

The Rt Rev. Canon J. Curran, the well-loved parish priest of St Patrick's Church. As an altar boy I served at his Mass many times. *(Author's collection)*

occasions was provided by an old gramophone, and it was here that I was introduced to the Military Two Step, the Gay Gordons and other 'old tyme' dances. Being only twelve I was quite embarrassed, especially when dancing with my mum. The club was attended mostly by mothers, with daughters and other women, both friends and relations; male dancers were thin on the ground. I was much sought-after to partner big-bosomed ladies who smelled of lavender water and cavorted around the room with me, exclaiming 'What a nice-looking boy you are!' Well, it made my mum happy, as I was her escort on cold winter evenings along the dark and dismal streets of Water Lane and Thornton Road. My dad attended a couple of times, but Mum and I thought it better that he stayed at home: he was the proverbial dancer with two left feet! We were relieved when he decided not to return, and so was he.

The Union of Catholic Mothers made many daytrips to the seaside, as well as pilgrimages to Walsingham in North Norfolk, to the shrine of Our Lady. This had been a place of pilgrimage and worship since medieval times. It was always the same array of nice ladies on these trips, and photographs taken before these journeys show smiling faces from twenty-year-olds to old ladies in their eighties.

Aged seven, I made my first communion – which also involved my first confession. Making a personal confession to a priest in a confessional box sitting on the other side of a grill alarmed me initially, but I soon became used to it. As I got older, and sinned more, I became more reluctant to go along to confession. I had been taught that if I missed out any of my sins, be they venial or mortal, it was regarded as not making a good confession. When the priest came out of the

St Patrick's Union of Catholic Mothers about to set off on a pilgrimage. Everyone knew to meet outside the Swan Arcade. My mum is in the centre, thirteenth from the left. *(Author's collection)*

sacristy and along to his confessional box many confessors waiting in the pews hid their faces, so as not to be identified – but there was little point, as the priests recognised most of their parishioners. I know, because as I left the confessional one Saturday evening, Father Sreenan asked, 'Derek, have you any idea how Bradford City's gone on?' At the end of confession the priest gave absolution and a penance in the form of a prayer. My penance always seemed to be the same five Hail Marys and one Our Father, which I repeated at the lady chapel altar. I remember once telling the priest in confession that some non-Catholic lads had called me a cat-lick and left-footer, and I had replied that they were proddy dogs. He was still laughing when I left the confessional box.

Holy communion, on the other hand, was quite straightforward, although at the time very strict. From midnight you had to fast, with neither food nor drink being allowed. It was not unusual for young and old parishioners to faint during the morning service. We always knelt for holy communion and received the host (the sacrament) on the tongue only. At this time only the priest administered holy communion, and we had been taught by the priest and nuns that it was sacrilegious for anyone but the priest to touch the sacred host. Going to Mass and receiving the sacraments was something we looked forward to.
Serving at Mass

St Patrick's Church altar
(St Patrick's Church 150th Anniversary brochure)

During my time at St Patrick's Church, the Rt Rev. Canon J. Curran was the parish priest. He was ably assisted by the likes of Father Sreenan, Father Burns, Father O'Flynn, Father Ryan and Father Delaney, quite an assortment of Irish names. When I was ten years old my twin of the same birthday, John Walsh, taught me how to serve at Mass. Two servers were required to assist the priest. The right server attended to the wine and water and rung the handbell for the exposition of the blessed sacrament. The left server, who was not as important, assisted the right server in small acts to help the service run smoothly. There were many responses that had to be made to the priest, all spoken in Latin. At first I was at a loss to respond, but gradually with the help of a missal I could follow the Mass in Latin. The missal showed Latin and an English translation on each page.

On the wall of the sacristy there was a list of servers for all the Masses of the week. Most of my duties were on weekdays; if I were at school and serving nine o'clock Mass, I missed the beginning of my lessons. I had my own black cassock and white surplice, kept in a cupboard in the choir changing room.

While serving Mass was serious, there were times when there was frivolity and occasions when accidents happened. One morning John fell over the bell on the altar and rolled down the carpeted steps. I bit my lip until it bled, otherwise I would have had convulsions. Father Burns, who was saying the Mass, carried on reading the altar missal with his back to the congregation, but there was a smile on his face. On another occasion John and I were sitting in an alcove by the altar while a sermon was being given by one of his curates. We were either side of the elderly Canon Curran, who fell asleep and started to snore. Luckily I could sit back in the alcove without being seen by the congregation, so I could laugh; I could also hear John laughing in his hideaway. When the curate finished his sermon I had to wake the canon, who smiled and politely said, 'I must have dozed off.' Both John and I loved the canon, so we put it down to the curate's sermon.

From time to time the canon was unwell, and on more than one occasion John and I, dressed in our cassock and surplices and carrying holy water and the thurible (incense container) had to accompany one of the priests up to the canon's bedroom so the priest could administer the last rites. He always seemed to recover.

All the clergy were special and loved by the parishioners. Father Sreenan was a lovely man; it was he who had interviewed Lawrence with regard to his wish to study for the priesthood, and concluded that my brother had a vocation. It was he who some time later came to see me at home as I also wished to become a priest – because I was an avid reader of stories of public schools that always had midnight feasts in the dorm, secret passages, and exclamations of 'You're a brick'; I thought college life would be similar. Father Sreenan's visit lasted two minutes. He told my mum 'No chance', and off he went with a smile on his face. I don't think Mum was disappointed as one son at college was enough, but she did give me the opportunity. Five minutes after Father Sreenan's visit I was out playing, the whole incident forgotten.

Father Burns was rather slow when he said Mass, so we knew we would have the full hour, but Father O'Flynn was much faster. We timed him on the large sacristy clock. One morning Mass took place in sixteen minutes, inclusive of the administration of communion. The record was still standing when I finished my time as an altar boy, and I don't think it was ever broken.

When Requiem Mass and a funeral took place, we altar boys were required not just for the Mass but also for the funeral at the cemetery. Generally two servers were enough – one to take charge of the holy water and the other the thurible. These journeys to the cemetery were not without mishap. The thurible was an ornate container on a chain, which was swung to keep the charcoal inside hot and glowing while the incense on the charcoal gave out that sweet smell associated with churches. In a small room adjacent to the sacristy was a small portable gas ring on the stone floor, with the gas supplied by a rubber tube from a gas point in the wall. A round piece of charcoal was placed on a spoon that was then placed on the gas ring; once it was glowing it was placed in the thurible. All very Heath Robinson, but I don't know of any accidents!

The perks for going to the cemetery were that one of the mourners would give us never less than *2s 6d* when the service was over, and that we were taken there in style in the back of a Rolls-Royce, while the priest sat in front with the driver. One time on the way to Scholemore Cemetery I accidentally kicked over the thurible which was placed on the floor. Out popped the glowing charcoal ember on to the plush thick carpet where it continued to smoulder and burn. A smell of incense and burning carpet prevailed, while at the same time a thick cloud of smoke filled our half of the vehicle: a glass window divided us from the driver and Father Burns in the front. Father Burns turned around and saw the smoke. Not thinking, he slid the window back, letting the smoke into the front compartment. He and the driver were overwhelmed with the smell of smoke and incense, and the Rolls-Royce skidded to a halt close to the post office on City Road. John and I opened the door and jumped out; Father Burns and the driver did likewise. The priest's Irish accent came over loud and clear: 'Oh boys, what have you done?' Meanwhile the driver was now in the back seat using a small fire extinguisher on the smouldering carpet, exclaiming, 'What the f— were you doing? Sorry, Father!'

By this time neither John nor I could see anything because of our running eyes. A telephone call was made from the post office to Hey and Sons, the funeral directors, for another vehicle, which arrived some twenty minutes later. The holy water container had spilled in the mêlée, so we had to go back to the church for a refill. Father Burns, another driver, John and I, with new holy water but minus the thurible, arrived at the cemetery an hour late.

Family and friends were all sitting in a convoy of vehicles close to the open grave, and the coffin was already in place in the grave. Word soon got around to the mourners of why we had been delayed. I got the impression the relatives thought the Rolls-Royce had been burnt out, because John and I later received a 10s note each from a bereaved relative. We both wondered if we could do this again, as it had been quite a lucrative day. During our return journey to the church Father Burns told us to be more careful in future and that was the last we heard of the matter. Three years later when working at Brown, Muff's in the gents tailoring department, I sold Father Burns a raincoat. I asked him if he remembered the Rolls-Royce incident. He said he always had a chuckle when remembering the 'Rolls-Royce fire', which made me wonder how much he embellished the tale when repeating it.

It was a horrible winter's day when John and I attended a funeral at Undercliffe Cemetery with Father Delaney in our capacity as altar servers, aged thirteen. This time I was in charge of the holy water and John the thurible. When Father Delaney had finished the service at the graveside I offered him the holy water vessel, inside which was a large brush dispenser used to disperse the holy water on to the coffin, and then offered it to the mourners. Halfway round the graveside I stumbled over lumps of wet brown clay as I passed them the brush, lost my balance and slipped down into the hole, with a resounding crash on to the coffin. The holy water container followed and hit me on the back. I gradually stood up on the coffin, looked up and saw a sea of faces staring down at me. It was ten minutes before I could get out, as I couldn't grip the grave's slippery wet sides. No one seemed to have arms long enough to reach me, and no one wanted to lie down in the mud in his suit to rescue me. It was left to one of the large burly undertaker's assistants to jump in, lift me up and push me into waiting arms. He couldn't get out until someone brought a wooden ladder from the cemetery lodge. I was wet through, covered in soil and feeling utterly dejected. By now everyone seemed to be more concerned about the coffin. 'Is the wood cracked?' 'Yes, I can see a crack,' said some wise dope. 'It looks dirty,' said another, as if it was going on display in Cartwright Hall. 'It's going to be covered in bloody soil,' shouted someone from the back. I looked on in despair and wished everyone else would fall in the hole. John and I wandered back to the car and Father Delaney followed, now showing some concern and asking if I had broken anything. 'The best thing we can do is to take you home to rest.'

The Rolls-Royce pulled up in our street; by now it had started to snow and John looked as sad as me. I nodded to him, and wandered down the passage with Father Delaney to my house. I must have looked a forlorn sight, dressed in a cassock and surplice and covered in mud. Father Delaney explained the situation, gave me a pat on my muddy head and left. Twenty minutes later I was in the tin bath filled with hot soapy water in front of a roaring fire. I soon got over this mishap, but was annoyed and disappointed when John told me later the mourners had left no money for us. I often wondered why!

Throughout those years I mostly attended nine o'clock Mass, even if not serving at Mass on Sunday mornings. Later, when I joined the choir, I also attended High Mass at 11am and Compline and Benediction at 6pm.

When a missionary visited the church there was usually an evening service in which he gave a sermon about his life out in Africa, India and one of the other countries where Catholicism was being taught. He always concluded by asking for funds to help him and his mission to bring the word of God to the country in which he worked. These services were always well attended even though they were mostly in the winter. Again I was my mum's escort on many of these occasions. We sat huddled together for warmth on the back seat near the entrance, where it was always freezing – but my mum always sat at the back as she found it too claustrophobic at the front, even though it was probably warmer there. The church radiators never fully heated the vast interior on a cold winter's night. Other lads from my school and some from my class, Freddy Vickers, Harry Hodgson, John Walsh, Terry Moran and many others, attended with their mothers, and sat in pairs dotted around the church. When the plate came round for the pennies, threepenny bits, sixpences and shillings they all added up to a few pounds for the missionary's flock.

Since birth I had had two small aluminium religious medals pinned to my vest – one of the Sacred Heart and the other Our Lady's Miraculous Medal. Both were pinned over my heart. My mum had a great affiliation to Our Lady, the Mother of God. Sometimes as a family at home in the evenings we knelt around Our Lady's statue and recited the rosary. The light was turned out and a small candle was lit in front of the small statue; the fire gave off a warm glow and the candle flickered. I didn't think it was eerie, but rather comforting.

A debt was owed by St Patrick's to the Sisters of Charity of St Paul and the Sisters of the Cross and Passion, because of the many years of teaching and spiritual guidance they gave to us children and also their work among the poor and those in need. The Sisters of Charity of St Paul, although working in the parish for some time, had originally taken up official residence in 1859 at a house in Drewton Street. They later moved to a house in Sedgefield Terrace near to the church, and then to the convent building adjacent to the church. Among the sisters in residence while I was at school were the boys' school headmistress, Sister Christine, the girls' school headmistress, Sister Cuthbert, and Sister Cassian who looked after the infants' school.

Special Catholic feast days with church processions, like the Feast of Our Lady and Christ the King, were always celebrated with considerable splendour at St Patrick's. Particularly notable were the May and October processions that involved the young schoolgirls; especially the one in October, when the crowded congregation watched in awe the ceremonial crowning of the statue of Our Lady of the Rosary. Processions at Easter and on the Feast of Christ the King were dominated by small boys in white satin suits and red sashes. They were called 'strewers', their job being to strew flower petals in front of the monstrance that held the blessed sacrament as it was carried round the church in a processional fog of incense, amid the scuffling feet of the altar servers. On two occasions I was one of these strewers, and although young I looked on it as an honour to be chosen to celebrate this holy event.

The Choir

In 1948 I decided to join St Patrick's Choir. This was in the days of packed pews, smiling boys in white surplices and choral music that made the church rafters ring. After the end of the war the choirmen returned to take up their duties with the choir. They gradually rebuilt it into one of the premier choirs in the city, under the direction of organist and choirmaster Edward Hanlon, assisted by precentors Eric Armstrong and Leo Muff.

At St Patrick's we were fortunate to have a team of young men who acted as servers at the ceremonies. These consisted of the acolytes (candle-bearers), thurifer and the crucifix-bearer, all ably led by the MC (Master of Ceremonies) Joe Gallagher – the top job, the senior posting of the serving fraternity. The choir and servers took part in Solemn High Mass on Sundays as well as an

St Patrick's Choir in its full glory at High Mass. I am sixth from the left in the second row. *(Paul Hanson)*.

evening service of Compline, sermon and Benediction. The mixture of fine music and impressive ritual attracted large congregations from the parish and beyond.

In 1948 I joined this popular choir, and during the next five years I made lots of new friends – enjoying the social life as well as the spiritual side. Vincent, who was also interested in becoming a member, came along with me for the vocal test one Wednesday evening. Choir practice took place in Form Two classrooms on the second floor of St Patrick's Boys' School. I stood by the piano while the choirmaster played scales, which I had to sing to the best of my ability. I must have been good, for with no formal practice I passed. Vincent, who looked on, said that I looked a dope, opening and closing my mouth like a goldfish. When it came to his turn I understood his remark, as he also looked like a goldfish – and also passed the test. All this took place with the other choir members looking on; it was a real confidence booster, especially if you didn't feel confident!

Edward Hanlon, the choirmaster, was a gentleman. He was a prolific smoker, and this might have contributed to his early death not many years later. His fine musical direction instilled into the choir polished performances of many fine Latin masses. Leo Muff, one of the two precentors, had more than a passing resemblance to Peter Brough's ventriloquist's dummy, and we used to call him Archie Andrews (not to his face). He was a hard taskmaster at choir practice: his attitude was of a strict teacher and he wasn't averse to giving you a clip round the ears. He had his favourites, and I was not one of them – but this was no popularity competition: we were there to sing, and sing we did. The other precentor was Eric Armstrong, a rotund, genial man, not long out of the Air Force, who

St Patrick's Choir appearing at the Bradford Alhambra Theatre as street urchins in the Carl Rosa Opera Company's production of Bizet's *Carmen*, November 1950. Back row, left to right: Paul McKee, Terence Moran. Third row: -?-, -?-, Michael Murtagh, Derek Lister. Second row: Gerard Doherty, Philip Howden, -?-. Front row: Peter Doherty, David Briggs, Tony Smith. Miss Theresa O'Hare, the lead singer, looks on; we all had a crush on her. (*Author's collection*)

always had a smile on his face and a good word to say to me. I liked him from the beginning.

Older members of the choir comprised men of all ages who sang tenor, alto and bass. One of the basses had been in the choir for over fifty years, since 1895. He was a nice old man, although rumour had it that he mimed. There were as many as thirty boys, aged between eight and fifteen. Some were from my school, and others were from the local area and St Bede's Grammar School. Most were existing friends, like John Walsh, who taught me to serve mass. John's brother Leo was also a junior member. Malcolm McAllister, who lived at Arthington Street, was the same age as me and it was said that we looked alike. Peter Doherty was the boy who sometimes outran me in races at our school. There was the very tall and amiable Paul McKee, and the 'Listerhills Lot', Michael Farrell, Terence Moran and Martin Monaghan. Dennis Towers was known to us all as 'Fatty Towers', and there was also the small and dynamic Tony Smith of Westgrove Street. Among the rest with whom I formed new friendships were Peter Child (Rusty) and his cousin Michael Murtagh, Antony Freschini (whose father was the head waiter at the Midland Hotel and arranged for me to meet Laurel and Hardy), David Briggs, Gerard Doherty, Tony Wildman, Philip Hanson (brother of Paul Hanson, assistant organist), Donald O'Hara and Richard Quinlan. A little older than us were Joe Clark, Jimmy McGuinness and Terry Midgley.

Choir practice was held on Tuesday evenings between seven and eight o'clock. Summer and winter Terry, Michael, Martin and I met midway down Norcroft Street. We then meandered down Water Lane at the rear of BDA Transport, across Thornton Road, and up into Lower and Upper Westgrove Street to the school. On summer evenings the journey was pleasant but on winter nights it could be scary, with an odd gas lamp only illuminating a small area. Our footsteps and laughter echoed along the streets and warehouses.

They say that practice makes perfect, and after a few weeks we were good enough to take part in the services. We had to be there at least half an hour before the service, and congregated in the changing area – a very small room with old large oak lockers around the walls for our cassocks and surplices. We all had our own hook, but lads being lads our garments often got mixed up, much to the consternation of Willie Lever – sometimes the MC in charge of the choir. He was well into his seventies and had been involved in the parish for many years; his family was the well-known W. Lever undertakers in Bradford. He was a little fussy but a nice man.

Changing into our cassock and surplices became more of a problem later when celluloid collars were introduced. In the centre of the collar a bowtie was fixed, and the mass tying of these in a confined space was a sight to behold. The men also changed in the same area, minus the collar and the bowtie.

We all assembled in the sacristy and paired off in twos, with the men at the rear followed by the priest. Joe Gallagher, the MC, knocked on the door of the steps leading to the organ loft, and at this signal the organist began to play some resounding music. At the same time the doors swung open and we proceeded into the church led by the cross bearer, acolytes, and thurible to the altar.

The boys had the first two rows of benches on the left of the altar. Behind us were the tenors, some of whom were not averse to clipping the backs of our heads for any misdemeanours during the service; they also noisily unwrapped sweet papers and crunched sweets. On the opposite side of the altar were the bass and alto choristers, and at the front of the choir was the conductor – usually Leo Muff.

Soloists were chosen from among the trebles, and included Malcolm McAllister, Martin Monaghan, John Walsh and Jimmy McGuinness. I never received this accolade; I knew that I was not good enough. It required much confidence to be on show at the end of the bench to a packed congregation. The soloists were always very good, and I was always proud to be part of the 'backing group' when we sang 'Ave Maria' or another hymn that required an angelic voice. It was little wonder that High Mass or a feast day celebration was such an occasion. It was this that filled the pews with people from all walks of life, not only Catholics but others, who came to hear the wonderful singing of St Patrick's choir.

At Christmas we were always on call, and spent many evenings before Christmas Day singing carols in the locality. Off we went, without cassocks and surplices, around the streets of Lumb Lane, White Abbey and other such salubrious areas. It was just a crowd of young boys, minus the choirmen, as they knew better not to be out on the bitter cold winter nights. Sometimes it rained and sometimes it snowed; ours was not to reason why. However, it made the people happy, especially the older members of the church – many of whom lived in the area.

On special feast days like the Feast of Our Lady, Easter Sunday and Christ the King we wore scarlet cassocks, which I always preferred to the sombre black cassocks. We also wore these scarlet cassocks when we sang at a choir member's marriage, which seemed to me quite often. All this was free of charge. 'Not bad,' I used to say. 'Fancy having the best choir in Bradford sing at your wedding for nothing!' It must have made the bride and bridegroom very happy.

In November 1950, for a week, we choir boys took part in the Carl Rosa Opera Company's production of Bizet's *Carmen* at the Alhambra Theatre. We were dressed as street urchins (in character!), and in Act One sang the chorus of the street boys. At the end of this scene, when we were chased away, Tony Smith had to steal some bananas from a fruit seller's barrow and follow us off stage. It was all very funny and enjoyable, and for a twelve year old a great experience.

The choir introduced me to other pleasures, such as days out and local trips. A traditional event was the Good Friday walk. After the Mass of the Presanctified on Good Friday morning, the men and boys hastened to Saltaire. Then, via the Glen Railway and Dick Hudson's inn at Eldwick, we set off across Ilkley Moor, come rain or shine, to arrive at Middleton Lodge in time for the three o'clock open air Stations of the Cross service held in the monastery grounds. Afterwards we left for home, via Ilkley, and returned to Bradford by train.

Among the lighter moments were walks for the boys in Goitstock Wood in Bingley. Some of the more energetic brought their swimming trunks and splashed about in the river. These and other events were organised by Leo Muff and Paul Hanson, as were some Saturday afternoon visits to Drummond Road Baths in the summer. I went along a couple of times.

Choirboys' Holidays

My favourite social occasion with the choir was the annual choirboys' holiday, which I first went on in 1949 – a trip that introduced me to Yorkshire's jewel in the crown, Staithes. Our time was well spent over the seven days of these holidays: we were active from dawn to dusk, and it was always hot and sunny. In charge of us were Leo Muff, Eric Armstrong and Terry Parry. The price of the holiday was £2 10s, and my pocket money was 7s 6d. We met at Bradford Exchange station, and travelled via York and Scarborough to the wonderful coastal line to Staithes. We generally had a few pre-booked carriages to ourselves,

The first holiday in Staithes, 1949. Back row, left to right: Eric Armstrong (assistant choirmaster), -?-, Paul McKee, -?-, Joe Clark, Leo Muff (assistant choirmaster). Second row: Paul Holmes, Tony Wildman, Michael Verity, Michael Farrell, Peter Child, James McGuinness, Dennis Towers, Michael Murtagh. Front row: Vincent Davy, Bernard Woodward, Derek Lister, Malcolm McAllister, David Briggs, D. Morgan, John Walsh, Anthony Frescini. *(Paul Hanson)*

with stickers on the windows reading 'Reserved for St Patrick's Church Party'. Most of us had our mothers to see us off, with plenty of advice and instructions to send a card to let them know we had arrived. I was always surprised how many mothers, including mine, would pull out a hanky, spit on it and wipe some dirt from our face! The journey was fun, with much laughter, pushing, shoving and changing of seats. There was also much crowding around the windows, and inevitably the protruding faces returned saying 'I've got some muck in my eye', from the smoke and soot of the engine. The scenery on the coastal line from Scarborough to Staithes was beautiful; the train hugged the cliff tops, through tunnels and over steep gradients. This line was not loved by the enginemen: in the summer it could be an idyllic ride, but in the winter it was extremely exposed, and engines were prone to stalling and slipping on the wet or icy rails.

Staithes railway station was small, and typical of the country railway stations of the time, being full of milk churns, fish boxes, pigeon baskets, luggage and the odd passenger. A little further north on the line, just 200 yards away, was the high railway viaduct that spanned the valley. The station was close to Cliff Road, about half a mile from the village. A few hundred yards down Staithes Road towards the village, on the right, was a small camp of huts, our billets for the week. Each hut contained some fifteen beds, so we were allocated two huts. Each bed was 2 foot by 6 foot, with two blankets, two sheets and a pillow. The toilets and basic washing facilities were some 20 yards away. We were all advised that we had to sweep out our huts, keep things tidy and pick up any litter outside. Being mere lads, we didn't care about our accommodation, as we had come to enjoy ourselves.

At the camp there was a small tuck shop for necessities. Sweets were on sale but as rationing was still in operation there was not much choice; but there was always ice cream. An adjacent large building was the dining room. The meals were basic but quite nourishing, using produce that didn't require a ration book. Meat was scarce, and it was said that the little we had was horse meat. But there were plenty of potatoes and vegetables, followed mainly by rice or custard tart. I always enjoyed the breakfasts, with vast dollops of salty porridge, plenty of eggs and large slices of freshly baked bread with strawberry jam. In the 1940s we were all used to odd variations in food because of rationing, and I don't remember any complaints from us.

Discipline in the choir was strong on these holidays. If anyone got out of hand (and this was rare), the punishment metered out was 'the pump', smacking with a shoe that Leo Muff administered on the backside. This was accepted by everyone and was not really as bad as school discipline. Leo held our spending money, and if you wanted to buy something you had to ask for the money required; this could be refused. I didn't mind so much when I was younger, but as I got older I began to resent my money being withheld; in time I rebelled against this.

After a brief look round the camp and its facilities some of us were soon down the hill, past the wild cliffs with soaring and shrieking gulls and into the village, with its quaint ancient streets and alleyways mingled with red-tiled cottages and houses overlooking the ancient harbour. Nets and lobster pots were festooned over railings, as fishermen waited for the next tide, some smoking old clay pipes. The women still wore their Victorian bonnets, fussing around, mending nets and salting the fish. I was only eleven when this wonderful sight greeted me on my first visit.

Sports were organised by Leo Muff and his fellow guards. The other huts were occupied by youngsters like ourselves from schools and clubs, and we played cricket and football against them on the large field at the rear of the camp. Most of the holiday was organised, with walking excursions or trips out, but we had a few half days when we could spend time on our own. During this free time some of us always made our way down to the village and on to the small jetty. We had bought hooks and line for 1s 9d from the shop at the camp, and with our legs dangling over the end of the jetty we sat for hours 'crabbing'. We all hoped to catch one of the large red crabs as seen in the shops, but the ones we caught were always very small and we threw them back into the sea. When the tide was out we sauntered around the very small sandy and pebbly beach, collecting the pebbles. They were all shapes and sizes, and had been moulded by

Cullercoats: the last photograph taken of me as a choir member. On returning home it was time to move on! Left to right: Philip Doherty, Michael Murtagh, Terence Moran, Derek Lister, John Walsh, Paul McKee, Peter Child and David Briggs (of the dart in the head episode). *(Paul Hanson)*

the sea as had the pieces of pottery and ceramics that we found close to the shore. These were mostly from the ruins of the pub called the Cod and Lobster, which on numerous occasions had been damaged by the sea and rebuilt.

When we weren't running about we sat by the fishing boats and listened to tales of the sea from the old fishermen, who were glad to have such a young and appreciative audience. It was also enjoyable to sit by Captain Cook's cottage and cast my mind back two hundred years to when he was an apprentice living at the cottage and working in a shop. Around the cliffs close to the beach were a series of shale and sandy beds that contained a profusion of fossils. It was exciting to find the shape of a fossilised fish, millions of years old, which came to light when we broke up the rocks and shale. The most commonly found fossils were ammonites and belemnites. The former are the ridged and coiled shells that spiral like a catherine wheel. We organised competitions to see who had discovered the best fossil, such was their abundance.

We had long walks, carrying our packed lunches, on occasion past the potash mine close to Boulby Cliff, sometimes referred to as the highest cliff in

England. We walked inland to the picturesque village of Hinderwell and then down to the fishing village of Runswick Bay. Traffic was almost non-existent, so we walked on the roads with no fear of being run down.

Another highlight was the hire of a bus for the day. It was always one of those delightful single-decker buses with a sliding door at the front and a double seat next to the driver, which we all fought to sit on. We all clambered on board and set off, again with our packed lunches. Negotiating Sleights Bank at Sandsend was always exciting, as the bus's brakes squeaked and shuddered on the downward hill. Later, the bus crawled very slowly back up on the return journey. Whether our visits were to Scarborough, Whitby or Saltburn, each one was an adventure. They always culminated with about thirty tired boys singing songs on the way back to the camp, as the sun set and the small bus chugged its way along the coast roads, passing the large steel viaducts on which ran the coastal trains:

Ten green bottles hanging on the wall
Ten green bottles hanging on the wall
And if one green bottle should accidentally fall
There'd be nine green bottles hanging on the wall.

On and on we went, down to 'No green bottles hanging on the wall'.

My first holiday at Staithes was a wonderful experience, and in 1950 we went back again: same boys, same adults and the same enjoyment. This time one of the fishermen's boats was hired to take us down to Whitby and back – which I found less happy. The sea was rough, and although I wasn't sick my knuckles were white with gripping the side of the boat throughout the hour-long journey. I didn't enjoy our time in Whitby, as I was worried about the boat trip back. I was definitely not to going to follow in the steps of Captain Cook!

In 1951, by way of a change, we went to Keswick in the Lake District. Keswick had its mountains, hills and rain, and even though the same crowd of boys went on this holiday it was not the same as our holidays in Staithes. My best memory is of Leo Muff and Eric Armstrong playing a piano duet, Christian Sinding's classic *The Rustle of Spring*. It was wonderful, and showed their talent as musicians. The following year, 1952, we were back at Staithes for another wonderful holiday. This was the last time I went to Staithes with the choir.

My last holiday with the same group was to Cullercoats in August 1953. Now aged fifteen, I had just started work at Brown, Muff's. Cullercoats, a small holiday resort sandwiched between Whitley Bay and Tynemouth was a first for most of us choirboys. My usual friends were with me on this holiday, and for the first time our choirmaster Mr Hanlon came, accompanied by Leo Muff and Paul Hanson. Our home for the week was a large red-bricked Victorian house in a road adjacent to the beach. The house catered for groups like us, with lots of bedrooms with a few beds in each. Downstairs was a dining room and in the cellar a large games room. As usual, on arrival we had to give our spending money to Leo Muff, something I never really accepted, as my parents had always trusted me with money, but now especially, aged fifteen and working, it rankled more than ever. So I told him I wasn't handing it over and that as I was now working I should be responsible for my own money. Leo didn't like this, or my attitude, but had to accept my decision.

Most days were spent on the beach around an old rusted tanker that had been washed ashore some years before. We also played cricket matches in a nearby sports field and went on walks into Tynemouth and Whitley Bay. This resort had a very large funfair called Spanish City, but the powers that be didn't encourage us to visit this. Somehow we were invited to visit a luxury schooner from Sweden that was moored on the Tyne. Food had been laid out for us, and we had never seen anything like it. It was like something out of a movie, with chocolate and cream cakes of all sizes, oozing cream, and lots of cool drinks. As rationing was still being enforced, this was a truly pleasurable experience.

On the Friday before returning home some of us were down in the games room playing darts. It was my turn to throw the dart, and as I did so David Briggs, a good pal of mine, crossed in front of the dartboard, ducking underneath it. My dart struck David on the top of the head. He let out a scream, and Leo Muff, who was coming down the steps to the cellar, asked what the noise was about. Someone said, 'Derek Lister's just stuck a dart in David Briggs's head.' Leo erupted and said I would be punished, even though David said it was an accident. In the evening, after tea, I was made to bend over a bed in one of the bedrooms in front of everyone and received the pump six times. I felt really degraded: here was a fifteen-year-old worker being physically punished for an accident!

The following day, when I returned home, I told my mum what had happened. She was livid, and wanted to go and see Leo Muff to give him the pump. I told her not to bother as I had finished with the choir, and from that day I never returned. I had been in it for seven years. It wasn't a vocation or a remunerative position; I just liked singing and messing around with my pals. My choirboy days were over thanks to this humiliating experience. Most other memories of this time, though, I look back on affectionately.

Choir Pantomimes
In addition to Sunday's ecclesiastical duties and these holidays, the choir also put on pantomimes, with a full cast of principals, chorus and dancers, and with the valuable help and assistance of parents. The pantomimes were played to full houses in St Michael's Hall, Paradise Street, and each was more successful than the last. They were scripted and produced by Leo Muff. Each script was both fluent and funny, and he always included local names and people. Most of the stories stuck to the original theme, and the choreographed chorus dance

The choir production of *Ali Baba*, 1951. Playing Escudo (Cassim's wife) was my first major role. Back row: James McGuinness (Ali Baba), Malcolm McAllister (Merina Ali's wife). Front row: Kevin Clough (Wassy, Ali's daughter), Derek Lister (Escudo, Cassim's wife), Tony Smith (Folly, Cassim's son), Philip Hanson (Fussy, Cassim's daughter), Michael Farrell (Cassim Baba), David Briggs (Wally, Ali's son). I never realised that I had a son and a daughter! *(Paul Hanson)*

sequences were hilarious. The musical director was our choirmaster, Mr Hanlon. The orchestra consisted of Basil Walsh on the piano, Philip Buckley, Jack Byrne and Ernest McGoldrick playing violins, and Joseph Brennan playing the drums. The programmes for the event were professionally printed by Michael Farrell's father, cost 3*d*, and included all the cast names, patrons and clergy. The pantomimes generally took place in March or April for four nights, starting on Wednesday and finishing on Saturday.

The first production, in 1950, was *Cinderella*. Rehearsals were held in St Patrick's Boys' School for two months before the opening night. Everyone enjoyed taking part, and there was always a hushed silence on the first night of rehearsal when the cast was chosen. John Walsh was chosen to play Cinderella, and in his wig we all fancied him! He was that good. Jimmy McGuinness was Prince Charming, Tony Smith Buttons, Dennis Towers, Martin Monaghan and

The programme for another choir pantomime, *Puss in Boots*.
(Author's collection)

Robin Hood, our pantomime in 1953. It was during the fencing scene at the end that I nearly changed history by causing injuries and near death to Robin Hood. The picture shows John O'Hara as my Squire, me as the Sheriff of Nottingham, and Michael Farrell on the right playing the Lord of Esholt. *(Bernard Parry)*

Paul McKee the Ugly Sisters, while Peter Child was a very fetching Good Fairy. Vincent and I were in the chorus. The show was a tremendous success, and plans were immediately set in motion for another pantomime the next year.

Ali Baba was chosen as our next production. I played Escudo (Cassim's wife), Ali Baba was played by Jimmy McGuinness and Cassim Baba (my husband) was played by Michael Farrell. Like me, Malcolm McAllister played a female role, that of Merina (Ali's wife). Anthony Frescini, the coachman in our last pantomime, was the robber chief, Abu Hasan. Peter Child played Aroma (Ali's servant), David Briggs was Wally (Ali's son), while Kevin Clough was Wassy (Ali's daughter). Other members of the choir were brought into the chorus to play an assortment of sunbeams, robbers, barmen, waitresses and ladies of the harem. The Forty Thieves were represented by ten of the extras, who marched round and round the scenery to give the impression of forty thieves as they sang 'We are the Robbers of the Woods'. Again the show was a great success, and my mum said that as Escudo I looked like the daughter she had always wanted. My bottom was pinched many times and I was asked for a date twice, so successful were the make-up and wig. Perhaps the highlight of the pantomime was the Sunbeams, with a hilarious dance sequence performed by a 'corps de ballet' of choirboys wearing tutus and football boots.

In March 1952 the third choir pantomime was *Puss in Boots*. I thought I had played Escudo very well and was looking for a leading part, but others thought differently. I was relegated to the chorus as a citizen, in other words an extra in a crowd scene. So much for my star profile! Others held their lead parts, with Peter Child playing the king, the princess played by Malcolm McAllister and the innkeeper by Michael Farrell, Terence Moran came in for a lead part, the

Marquis of Carabas, while John Fitzpatrick, previously of the chorus, had the title role. I was disappointed as even Vincent had a small speaking part, the ogre. I suppose it was fair to give opportunities to each of us, so I accepted my role as 'citizen' with grace. The pantomime was once again successful, with generous applause and many nice comments to the cast.

During 1953 I would leave school, start work and set myself on the road to adulthood. The pantomine chosen was *Robin Hood*. On the night when the cast was chosen I assumed I'd be in the chorus again. Malcolm McAllister was again picked for a lead part, this time the title role, while Terence Moran was Maid Marian. Names and parts were delegated thick and fast, and then I heard that Derek Lister was to play the Sheriff of Nottingham! I could hardly believe my ears. I put everything I had into learning my lines at home, with my mum reading the other parts, while I sang and acted as ruthlessly as possible.

In the final scene of the pantomime I had a sword fight with Robin Hood. We practised many times with swords made of wood; the choreography of the fight was well thought out and looked as realistic as a 'real' swordfight could be. During the rehearsals I was told many times to desist from emulating the likes of Errol Flynn, Basil Rathbone, Stewart Granger and other swashbucklers of the silver screen. 'It's the choir pantomime,' shouted Leo Muff, 'not MGM Studios!'

The night of the dress rehearsal went well and we all looked resplendent in our finery. I was wearing a dark green velvet bodice, velvet green pantaloons, and my legs were stained with 'strained' tea. On my feet I wore Terry's mother's fur-lined boots and on my head I wore a smart green velvet hat with a large feather trailing at the back. The make-up to my eyebrows and the addition of crow's feet to my eyes gave me an awesome appearance of doom. I loved it.

The first night was packed, mainly with young people as it was half price admission for them on the Wednesday evening. Older people of the parish waited until the performances were more polished towards the end of the week. The scenery and the set were very realistic, being supplied by Scenic Displays who also provided all the Alhambra's scenery. All started well, and when I made my first stage entrance I was booed – much to my delight, as the booing of a villain was applause to me. My speaking parts were mostly with my squire, played by Donald O'Hara, and another rogue like me, the Lord of Esholt, played with gusto by my friend Michael Farrell. The only song that I had to sing was a duet with Michael: we strutted about the stage giving an admirable rendition of 'The Bold Gendarmes'. In the final scene I imprisoned Maid Marian in a tower on the battlements; Robin came along to rescue her, and that's when the swordplay commenced. On the first night our wooden swords had been replaced with real theatrical steel broadswords, which were lightweight, sharp and with a point on the end. Big mistake – even though there was no problem in holding the steel sword or fencing with it. At the end of our fight I was to position myself with my back to the battlements, and as Robin lunged at me I had to fall backwards over the battlements to my death. Behind the scenery I would be caught by two men and fall on to a mattress. My only problem was when to end the fight.

The first night was a disaster! I got carried away, as everything I had ever seen of swordplay at the cinema came back to me. Poor Malcolm was on the receiving end. First I slashed and cut his wrist, then his arm, this time with the point of the sword; then he received a third wound, a large gash under the left eye. I didn't hear the mumbled shouts from behind the battlements for me to move back and fall over, and I carried on slashing and stabbing. Malcolm, by this time more in anger than acting, physically pushed me over the battlements, and with blood running down his face and wrists rescued Marian and sang his love song to her. During the finale I was booed all the way to the front of the stage.

Malcolm was not pleased with his wounds and we nearly had a real backstage fight, but he calmed down and I said I was sorry. Leo Muff then had his say. Why I had not kept to the script? Was I trying to change history, with Robin being killed by the Sheriff of Nottingham? 'If I could replace you I would!' Again I apologised and said it wouldn't happen again, and it didn't. For the rest of the week I kept to the script, although it was not easy when one night Malcolm's sword had a near miss to my head and I wondered if he was trying to get his own back. At the end of all the performances I was booed and even asked for my autograph. What more could I ask for? I must have been good – but I knew I could never improve that first night's 'bloody' performance!

Catholic Young Men's Society

In 1953, and now working, I joined St Patrick's Catholic Young Men's Society of Great Britain (founded in 1854), along with George Stockley, Terence Moran, Martin Monaghan and Michael Farrell. For nearly a century the men of the parish had been noted for their Catholic action and had helped clergy and parishioners when required. The club was religious, but also held social activities and was run by older long-time members. The CYMS club room was down Paradise Street at the rear of St Mary's hall. The inside had not changed for years, and all the furniture and lighting was old fashioned, but it had atmosphere. In the small meeting room inside the entrance was a display of large and small silver cups, plaques and salvers for billiards, snooker and table tennis tournaments of bygone years. On the ground floor were three billiard tables and a table tennis table. Arranged around the wall by the billiard tables was padded seating, set high so spectators could view matches in progress. Above the seats were framed photographs of former and existing members in First World War uniforms. In the far corner by the windows were a small bar and a few tables for card playing. Here on Sunday lunchtimes my friends and I relaxed and played snooker. Most of the members, although they appeared to be old men to us, were kind and good hearted and we could have a laugh with them. Old Joe Cross, then in his late seventies, who could give as much as he took, was a favourite among us. However, some could be officious especially if our noise and laughter disturbed them when they were playing cards. But generally the atmosphere was light hearted, and the club was run efficiently by the then-president Ernest Mackinder.

As well as attending religious retreats, sometimes at Myddelton Lodge in Ilkley, we had daytrips, usually to Blackpool. The coach boot was always well stocked with beverages. On one trip to Blackpool we had the coach back seat with Joe Cross in the middle. Poor Joe: I don't think he ever forgot it to his dying day, and he would reminisce to anyone who would listen of the day out 'with my lads'. On another occasion we, being good Catholic lads, went to see the X-rated wax works called 'Anatomy of Life' at Madame Tussauds. After an hour or so of 'shall we or shan't we' we decided to give it a go. No one questioned our admittance although we were only sixteen and, like X-rated films, eighteen was the age limit for entry. The wax works consisted of models of human organs, especially male and female genitals. Many showed the effects in great detail of sexually transmitted diseases. We were all very quiet, and no jokes or clever remarks were made as we slowly wandered around, gawping at each display. Once outside again, in the bustle of Blackpool with clattering trams and noisy people, we came out of our trance – but nothing was said, no discussions; it was as if we had never visited the 'Anatomy of Life'. We were all deep in our own thoughts, and I know I felt sick. For once we were very quiet on the way back home to Bradford. I made a vow I would never get married and instead become a monk in Tibet, but this resolution was short lived.

One thing about the CYMS was that it introduced me to the sight of dead bodies. When older members passed away we were invited to their homes to kneel and say prayers around the open coffin. This was generally placed, ironically enough, in the living room. I always seemed to be at the front on these occasions, just a few inches away from the corpse. I always noticed the abundance of nasal hair and the sweet-scented aroma that came from the coffin. It did feel strange, but there was nothing to worry about, and as someone said at the time it was the living you had to watch out for!

On 23 May 1954 St Patrick's branch celebrated the CYMS centenary celebrations. Mass and holy communion were celebrated at the church by Bishop Heenan of Leeds and breakfast followed at the Victoria Hotel. A photograph of all the CYMS members and the clergy who attended was taken outside the girls' school in Rebecca Street to commemorate the event. Terry, Michael, Martin, George and I were there with our fathers, who were also members.

The CYMS was indeed an integral part of my life and I was always grateful to belong: it was really quite spiritual and the daytrips were an added bonus. Moving to Wyke in 1955, though, pulled me away from St Patrick's Church and the CYMS. My new church was St Winifred's on St Paul's Road, which at that time was just a hut. The parish priest was Father Herbert Backhouse, a softly spoken man well loved by his parishioners. If you were late for Mass and it was already in progress he would break off and ask you to come and sit at the front of the church. This was a problem if you were shy, but you would not be late again. My dad helped at the church on Sundays by taking the collection plate around the congregation. He was also part of the bingo staff and a pools promoter, collecting the subscriptions for the football pools on Friday evenings, in all weathers.

Young Christian Workers

I used to walk to church every Sunday from Wyke to St Winifred's mostly with my mum. Aged seventeen, I was almost as tall as her by now, and sunshine or rain we wound our way down Woodside Road through old Low Moor, still a village with an abundance of snickets, cobbled streets and back-to-back houses, then up into St Paul's Road where we spent the next hour attending Mass. I loved that journey with my mum as it always brought back so many memories.

I was still seeing my mate Vincent, but with the distance between us, Wyke to Listerhills, and working during the week, it was mostly at weekends that we met. Just going to church on Sundays seemed so very different from the halcyon days at St Patrick's Church followed by the CYMS. I was missing the friendship of groups – but I soon found a replacement for the CYMS, the Young Christian Workers of St Joseph's Roman Catholic Church in Pakington Street. From time to time I had attended Sunday Mass at St Joseph's, where the parish priest was the Rev. M.J. Dunleavy. This magnificent church had been built in 1887, in size on a par with both St Patrick's and St Mary's. It was surrounded of hundreds of back-to-back houses with a backdrop of St Luke's Hospital. On my visits there was always a full congregation at each Mass and evening Benediction. It was one morning at the Sunday Mass that someone suggested I should join the Young Christian Workers. I mentioned this to Vincent, who agreed that we should both join.

In 1955 the YCW had been at the church since 1940. There was also a girls' section, which was a bonus to us but not the reason for joining. The boys met in St Joseph's crypt, which was not for the faint-hearted especially on cold, dark winter evenings when I couldn't concentrate at the meeting, being worried in case I was the last out of the crypt. The girls met in the more impressive club room in Clayton Lane. Sometimes we attended meetings at Stella Maris, 12 Melbourne Place. This was a large old Victorian house with many rooms, passages and a cellar with an old upright piano, where budding pianists showed their musical ability by playing 'Chopsticks'. The spiritual side of YCW consisted of group prayer meetings and retreats to spiritual places, while we also had discussions about everyday life and its problems. For example, if a grate was missing in some street or road and was potentially a danger to the public, then we gave full details of where the problem was and we sent a letter to the

Some members of St Joseph's Young Christian Workers after a football match. It's a real 'Goon Show' line-up with an array of different outfits. Back row, third left, is Bob Hunter, with the author on his left. Front row, centre, is the arch-Goon, laugh-a-minute Ken Taylor, and on his left is Tony Walker. At the far right is my mate Vincent.
(Author's collection)

appropriate council department. This sort of thing wasn't really exciting, but it made us think and act responsibly.

It was here at the YCW that Vincent and I found a host of new pals who made the next eighteen months of our lives very happy ones – until National Service came along and broke up friendships. Our closest new friends were Tony Walker, full of humour and frivolity, his mimicry of the Goons second to none, so much so that I couldn't sit next to him in church; Bob Dooley, small in stature but with a big heart; Bob Hunter, tall, good looking and astute, but sometimes very quiet; Bob Kelly, suave, an Irish lad with a smile, but sometimes abrupt; and many others. In charge of this motley crew was Gerald Grace, then in his early twenties, ex-army, with film star looks. On hand to help out was Ken Taylor, again in his early twenties, ex-RAF, chubby, full of life and later a wonderful Catholic priest. With his impressions of the Goons, it could be said that Ken was the Ned Seagoon of the North. To sit in the company of Ken Taylor was a joy, and my mum often asked afterwards if I had been crying. 'Yes,' I replied, 'crying with laughter. I've been with Ken Taylor.' No matter where we went, if Ken was with us we always had a laugh: it was hard sometimes to concentrate on the serious and spiritual side of the YCW in his company. He was genuinely funny, a good leader and above all a good friend. Ken (1933–2006) was ordained into the priesthood in 1967. He was appointed to many parishes, including St William's in Bradford and Sacred Heart, Bingley.

When a YCW trip to York was arranged, to visit a Catholic church and listen to some hymn singing, it turned out to be a disaster. Halfway through the organ stopped. 'Could some of you young men', asked a nun, 'help pump the organ?' It appeared that the electricity supply to the organ had failed. Four of us, including Ken, volunteered, and were taken along to an organ loft. The nun pointed to two large handles, one each side of the organ, which pumped the bellows. It all started well, and the organ came to life again. However, Ken started with his Goon impressions, and within five minutes the two other volunteers and I were almost helpless with laughter. Suddenly there was a resounding crack: Ken's handle broke in two and the organ stopped playing, the choir stopped singing and the service, for more than 300 people, was over. 'No one is to blame. It's an act of God,' said the nun. More like an act of Ken.

As the service took place at 11am and finished at 11.25 the day was still young, so we looked for somewhere to eat. We found a small café close to the Minster and Ken, Tony, Vincent and I sat at a table and looked at the menu. After a while a waiter with a napkin over his arm came to the table and said 'Right, young men, are you ready to order?' in a very effeminate voice. That's all it needed. I dared not look at Ken, and was soon biting my lip so much I could taste blood. To no avail. When my eyes made contact with Ken's I let out a scream like a maniac, ran to the door and out into the street laughing, followed by Vincent and Tony equally convulsed with laughter. A minute later Ken calmly walked out of the café with no smile, just a blank face. It was not until we rounded a corner that he started laughing. Walking along Lendal we bought some sandwiches and Tizer and made our way to the river, where we sat on the grass, quenched our thirst and hunger and laughed for the rest of the afternoon. This was the Young Christian Workers! When I arrived back home my mum took one look, smiled and said, 'You've been with Ken Taylor.' I said 'Yes' and started laughing again.

There were also Sunday dances in Clayton Lane Hall on Sundays after

Benediction. These were always well attended, mostly by members of the YCW of both sexes. It was a chance for us to meet and maybe date some of the girls. It was the rock 'n' roll era, but as we had no gramophone to play our favourite tunes the dance music came from two elderly gentlemen, on piano and drums. Actually they were quite good, although we could only dance quick steps, waltzes, or foxtrots, all fairly new to me and the others – but the girls seemed to help move the boys about in these grown-up dances. There were some nice girls, many of whom I fancied, but as at my rock 'n' roll nights at the Kings and Queens in Idle, I was still quite shy. Many YCW lads met their future wives at these dances.

Sometimes we got a football team together to play against some church choir or club. With an assortment of kit we turned out and did quite well, if Ken forgot the Goons for a minute.

Through my parents I had a good religious upbringing in the Catholic tradition, of which I was always proud.

Chapter 13
Theatre and Cinema

Pantomimes

The first time I went to a theatre was in 1943. This was to the Alhambra with my mum, to see the pantomime *Cinderella*. I don't remember much about it although it was pleasant enough, with the singing and dancing. Our seats were in the 'Gods' (the balcony). They cost 2*s* 6*d* for my mum and 1*s* 6*d* for me.

Our seats sloped at a precarious angle down to the front of the balcony. A man sitting in the centre of the balcony controlled two very large arc lights that crackled and sizzled when lit; he shined the spotlight on the performing stars. Fixed all along the balcony were large brass rails, to stop children, and adults if they had been to the theatre bar, from falling over to the circle below.

The pantomime plots had no surprises, at least for the adults, as the same shows, *Cinderella, Humpty Dumpty, Jack and the Beanstalk* and so on, are performed again and again. The characters are pleasingly familiar. Each production had an attractive girl (played by a girl), a principal boy (usually played by a girl) and at least one dame (always played by a man). There are the good or bad fairies, the comic sidekick and the 'straight guy' to bounce jokes off. To a young and gullible five year old this was all too much, and it was some time before I began to understand the absurdities of all this dressing up.

The second time I went to the Alhambra was again with my mum. Lawrence was none too keen on pantomimes and my dad was in Normandy, so it was left to me, aged six, to escort my mum. Or was it the other way round? This time I really took notice of the show. It was, I remember, *Humpty Dumpty*, with lots of audience participation. Sweets were thrown out to the children, but most landed in the stalls while others went to children seated in the lower family boxes on each side of the stage. I envied them, not only because they got the sweets, but also because they were sitting in a family box.

It was at *Humpty Dumpty* that I first saw one of pantomime's most popular dames, Norman Evans. Perhaps his best-known sketch was 'Over the Garden Wall', in which he created Fanny Fairbottom, the nosey neighbour complete with ample bosom and deficient in teeth. Constantly in mid-gossip, she leaned on the wall, then slipped off – denting her ample bosom. 'That's twice on the same brick this week,' she would exclaim. Fanny gossiped to an imaginary neighbour about everything that went on in her street. 'That coalman's at it again. Don't tell me it takes thirty-five minutes to deliver two bags of nuts!' This was a character I saw on stage that night, although I didn't understand the repartee too well, and it was a long time before I believed she was a man!

Two years later I saw Norman Evans again, in the pantomime *Mother Goose*. He did the entire sketch I had seen before, and while I enjoyed it just as much I was still convinced he was a woman.

The next pantomime I saw, the following year, was *Cinderella*, this time with Wilfred Pickles playing Buttons. Later, aged ten and sitting in our usual place in the balcony, the pantomime was *Humpty Dumpty* again, but this time with Bradford's own Albert Modley. Albert wore his cap throughout the pantomime and brought delight and rapturous applause from his hometown people when he mentioned Forster Square station, where he had worked in the parcel department many years earlier. His famous catchphrase was 'It's grand to be daft'.

Among the most famous juvenile dancing troupes was the Francis Laidler Sunbeams. One of the best-known personalities connected with British stage, his pantomimes were legendary. His chorus of little girls was initially recruited from local schoolchildren, and their welfare was always paramount to him. Months before the opening of a pantomime, mothers and their young girls could be seen queuing down Morley Street hoping for selection. The chosen few stayed in comfortable hostel accommodation and received education from qualified teachers throughout the pantomime season. Some time earlier my cousin Kathleen had come over from Middlesbrough to audition for the forthcoming pantomime, but she failed. Like many girls, she and her mother, Auntie Cassie, were disappointed.

All of a sudden I was a teenager, and pantomimes began to seem childish, especially as I now realised that Norman Evans was indeed a man. It was perhaps right that the last pantomime I saw was *Humpty Dumpty* with a favourite like Albert Modley.

Variety

From a very early age I had complemented the pantomimes with some of the many variety shows that the Alhambra staged out of the pantomime season.

From 1943 onwards, just as at the pantomimes, my mum and I sat in the balcony, observing the many stars who performed there throughout the 1940s.

There were usually six or eight acts in the evening shows. They came on stage in order of popularity, and the number of each act was illuminated at each side of the stage, matching the programme. The acts generally commenced with two or three dancing girls with shapely legs who gyrated to the melodies of the 1940s. Next there came the second spot comic. Many a future big name started off his career here, but others never progressed from this position in the programme. Over a period of many years they honed their acts to perfection, but received very little appreciation from a Monday night audience. The first house audience was made up of theatrical landladies and the owners of corner shops who displayed bills advertising the show; they were admitted free for this performance.

The comic was usually followed by a speciality act. There were many of these, including acrobats, jugglers, strongmen (and women), contortionists, quick-change artists, roller-skaters, magicians and ventriloquists. Sometimes these assorted variety acts were remembered better than the popular actors, actresses and singers who appeared on the same bill. The second top of the bill closed the first half of the show. This was usually a well-known singer.

The interval was the time to buy an ice-cream, and sit back and listen to the theatre orchestra playing a selection of popular music.

The second half started with the same dancing girls. Next came a well-established comic, who finished his act with a sentimental song. The act that occupied the top of the bill was either a top comedian such as Derek Roy, Max Miller, Arthur Askey or Vic Oliver, or a popular singer, for example David Whitfield, Issy Bonn or 'Hutch' (Leslie Hutchinson).

The last act brought everything to a climax before we realised it. The performers trooped down a wooden staircase on to the stage to take their final bows to the audience's applause. The curtain fell for the last time and the orchestra played God save the King, with everyone standing to attention. When the lights came up we went down the narrow stairs from the balcony that we had ascended so eagerly, and went out into a wartime world as drab as it was when we went in. Outside a queue for the second house was already forming. 'Is it good?' someone shouted. 'Yes,' we replied. It always was.

By now it was pitch black, but we were accustomed to going home in the blackout. We groped our way across Thornton Road and rode home on a dimly lit Lidget Green bus with its headlights hooded and dipped. Our faces glowed from the pleasure we had just experienced, and we chatted excitedly.

Among the many comedians we saw were Jimmy Jewel and Ben Warris, who were very popular on the radio, Sandy Powell, another popular comedian with the catchphrase 'Can you hear me mother?', and Tessie O'Shea, a large lady who joked and played the ukulele and was generally billed as 'Two Ton' Tessie

O'Shea. There was also the popular Rob Wilton, one of my favourites. He always exclaimed, with his finger in his mouth, 'The day the war broke out my missus said to me . . .' Audiences knew where they were with catchphrases like these, and they were a signal to fall about laughing. The popular musical duo Albert and Les Ward appeared many times at the Alhambra, playing an assortment of musical instruments that included bicycle pumps, washboards and virtually any other kitchen or garden implement to accompany their Country and Western songs.

My favourite was the supporting act of Wilson, Keppel and Betty. Wearing ancient Egyptian costumes and adopting postures like those painted on the walls of the pyramids, they performed a unique and never-changing Egyptian sand dance, in which they sprinkled sand on the stage and shuffled about to Middle Eastern music.

Many other names spring to mind, such as Reg Dixon (not the Blackpool Winter Garden organist). His catchphrase was 'I've been proper poorly', and he was always dressed in a very loud black and yellow striped blazer with a little hat on his head. But to me, as a youngster, he was not particularly funny. I also didn't have much time for Ronnie Ronalde, who whistled and did bird impressions – singing, for example, 'In a Monastery Garden' and bringing his bird impressions into it. Bob and Alf Pearson were a singing duo with the signature tune 'We Bring You Melody From Out Of the Sky, My Brother and I'. My mate Terry Moran and I could mimic them perfectly.

Two of the lesser-known comedians who were generally down the list of credits were the great character actors Nat 'Rubber Neck' Jackley and Ted Lune. Nat's character always wore a large coat, which kept slipping off his shoulders. His routines included eccentric dancing, with a neck jerk and a funny walk, and he played the part in pantomime many times. As a tall, thin, angular dame he was guaranteed a huge laugh whenever he entered the stage in a 'tube dress' that emphasised his skeletal frame. Of similar ilk and build was the popular Ted Lune, known for the distinctive goggle-eyed expression that became his signature gimmick.

One of the greatest British comedians of all time was Frank Randle. I only saw him once, when he had achieved his greatest popularity and notoriety as a comedian whose wild and manic temperament introduced a fresh note of invention into popular entertainment. His show was called Randle's Scandals, and during and after the war he also made a number of 'shoe-string' movies, which were very popular and endeared him to the British public. Frank was particularly inspired playing the part of a drunk, some would say a part that required no acting ability whatsoever. All our family loved him, and for years he was my dad's favourite comedian. My grandmother always went to Blackpool for her holidays when he was appearing at the resort's summer season show, and went to the theatre to see him every night. Quite a fan! Frank also had his catchphrases, including 'Get off me foot', and as the owner of a seaside pleasure boat, advertising a trip around the bay, 'Back in time for tea'.

Among the popular singers of the time that I was taken to see was a Jewish singer called Issy Bonn, with his popular rendition of 'Let Bygones be Bygones'. The Derry-born singer Joseph Locke was immensely popular in the 1940s. After singing favourites like 'Hear My Song Violetta' he always concluded with his most famous song, 'Goodbye'. When repeating the word 'Goodbye' the audience responded by waving their handkerchiefs at him. The famous singing duo Ann Ziegler and Webster Booth came, but they were not my favourites. I sat there listening, but didn't take much interest. Most of the time I was looking down from our balcony into the family boxes below, sighing and wishing it was me and my mum sitting there.

Leslie Hutchinson was a singer and a brilliant pianist who always wore a proper dress suit and had a red carnation in his lapel. One of his number ones was 'When You Begin the Beguine'. He carried a silk handkerchief and in between songs mopped his brow as part of the act. To everyone he was known as Hutch. I saw him twice at the Alhambra and once during the war at the Bradford Mechanics' Institute, which sometimes had concert party-type shows in its small theatre. They were called The Mechanics' Hall of Varieties, and were produced from 1941 until 1947 by Eric Martin. My mum thought Hutch was lovely. It was only midway through the war that she had become one of his fans, for up until 1941 her favourite singer and crooner had been Al Bowlly.

When we first saw Hutch at the Alhambra you could have heard a pin drop, thanks to his mastery of the keyboard and his soft velvet voice that rose to the Gods, where we sat as usual. Unfortunately I fell asleep, and fell off my seat, which sprang back with a resounding bang! According to my mum Hutch peered up into the balcony, but kept on singing. People around were concerned that I had hurt myself, and the attendants ushered us out of the exit doors and downstairs to the manager's office. The manager and a lady looked me over, discovering that I had a large lump on my head where I had hit the seat in front. A few minutes later a doctor appeared and examined me, my mum chuntering on that she was missing Hutch. To calm us both, she was given some tea and I an ice-cream. Later a tall, well-built man came in and spoke to my mum, then came over to me and asked how I was feeling. He proceeded to look at the bump on my head, smiled, ruffled my hair, and said something to my mum. At that point he shook her hand, kissed her cheek and left. Mum was all smiles. I don't think she washed her face for a week; after all, she had just been kissed by Hutch. He had also given her two free tickets for Saturday's performance 'as long as you don't bring him'. She didn't take me; she went with my Auntie Margaret and sat in the orchestra stalls. I wasn't too bothered, and kept telling my dad she had gone to see her boyfriend, at which he laughed and called me a flat-cake. I was rather annoyed that Hutch had asked my mum not to bring me, and only realised later it was a joke.

In May 1951, as a thirteen year old, I went to the Alhambra to see another favourite of my mum's. Auntie Cassie made the journey from Middlesbrough especially to see the singer Steve Conway, who was on the same bill as Vic Oliver. It was during the austerity years after the Second World War that we were introduced to a singer with a voice as unique as Bing Crosby, Al Bowlly and Al Jolson. By 1950 Steve Conway had firmly established himself as a top-of-the-bill act, and all was going well with his career and idyllic family life. One of his records, 'At the End of the Day', was to be used for over thirty years as Radio Luxembourg's signing-off record after each night's transmission.

For once, we were sitting in the stalls, which was a marvellous innovation for me as I could actually make out the faces of the performers on the stage and of the people in the family boxes. The orchestra seemed much louder. After a few minutes on stage Steve was suddenly taken ill and didn't return; later that week his place was taken by the radio singer Doreen Harris. He had had heart problems for some time, but recovered and continued working during the following months until the following year, 19 April 1952, he died from complications during an operation. He was only thirty-one. For many years I used to ask myself if I was the only person to remember Steve Conway.

Another venue that staged pantomimes and variety shows was the Prince's Theatre, at the bottom of Little Horton Lane. This had been built in 1876 directly above the old Star Music Hall, opened the previous year. I only went once, in the early 1950s with my mate Vincent, for the recording of a radio game show that was broadcast each week on Radio Luxembourg called *Shilling a Second*. The compère was Paul Carpenter, a film star of sorts, mostly in British B pictures. It was a very successful show, but you had to tune into the 208 wavelength and have a good reception to hear it. Each contestant had to remain on stage for as long as possible answering general knowledge questions. Prize money was awarded at a rate of 1*s* a second – a good prize if you could last a few minutes. It took nearly three hours to record the half-hour programme.

I could whistle quite loudly, so my whistle screeched out clearly among the typically polite English applause – until Paul Carpenter searched me out and asked in his Canadian accent if I would desist from making that 'crappy' noise! I stopped, as the alternative was to be thrown out; but many of the audience didn't like the word 'crappy', and a few choice terms of endearment were offered to Mr Carpenter by members of the audience. There were even threats that the show would be cancelled. While all this went on I sat quietly in my seat.

The show was on the radio a couple of weeks later. I listened to it at Vincent's house with most of his family present, and kept saying 'That's me whistling'. I was pleased; I had been on the radio.

By the early 1950s my interests had definitely turned to other things, such as girls. My outings to sit in the Gods at the Alhambra with my mum were less frequent. I had enjoyed every moment I had spent peering down into a world of colour, music and laughter, shared with my lovely mother. It was a wonderful experience – although I never did sit in one of those family boxes.

Local Picture Houses

Bradford's place in the annals of cinema history is important. From the 1890s the city was a hotbed of cinematic activity. Cinema-going in the city reached its peak in 1940, when over forty cinemas, large and small, advertised in two columns of the *Telegraph and Argus*. These cinemas were a haven for youngsters such as me. Each area in Bradford had two, three or more cinemas, with most of them changing programmes three times a week.

'Picture houses', as we called them, were our main source of entertainment. Here we lived out our dreams and fantasies while a war was still in progress, and into the austere 1950s. I was lucky to have, in a 1 mile radius of my home, the Empress, Arcadian, Elysian, Grange, and Victoria picture houses. For occasional visits, out on the fringes were the Elite and Coliseum, side by side in Toller Lane, Heaton. I spent a lot of time at our local picture houses, despite being a member of the Saturday morning club at the New Vic.

The beautiful New Victoria Cinema, later renamed Gaumont/Odeon. A jewel in Bradford's crown! *(CU)*

Inside the palatial Crescent Lounge, with barriers for queues. *(CU)*

The vast, stylish and beautiful auditorium. *(CU)*

BIRTHDAY GREETINGS

The Legend of the White Knight
"I pass this way but ONCE
If there is any good I can do
let me do it NOW – for I
shall not pass this way again"

My Saturday morning Gaumont British Junior Club birthday card, for my eighth birthday in 1946. It entitled me to a free show, for which I could also invite a guest.
(Author's collection)

The Gaumont British Junior Club

It was in October 1945, when I was seven, that Vincent, who was now my best pal, suggested we join the Gaumont British Junior Club at the New Victoria cinema (later to become the Odeon) in the town centre. Both he and I had heard from existing members how great it was, with both boys and girls being entertained for two hours. Apart from the films there were competitions, fancy dress or talent contests, and local artists who tried to entertain above the din. We got hold of membership forms, which on completion had to be signed by a parent. No membership card or club number was given, but our details were on record at the cinema and you could be challenged at any time for your name and address. It was much easier to join the club than gain entry as a non-member. Vincent and I were members within a week, and were advised that we could attend the next Saturday showing. A whole new world of two hours of entertainment was about to begin at the New Vic for the price of *6d*.

The New Victoria, known to all of us as the New Vic, was built on the site of the old William Whitaker brewery in Brewery Street, which had ceased brewing in 1928. This stunning red-brick theatre combined with cinema, ballroom, restaurant and café opened its doors on 22 September 1930. Costing a quarter of a million pounds to build, its Moorish citadel frontage contrasted with

The New Victoria celebrates its twenty-first birthday, 1951. The picture shows the Gaumont British Junior Club's 'Uncle Phil' (manager) and, cutting the cake, the attractive British film star Joan Rice. *(Graham Hall)*

the Alhambra Theatre next door. At the time of its construction it had the third largest cinema auditorium in England. The original cinema entrances were under the domed towers at each end of the building. Connecting the two entrances was the sweeping curve of the stalls, with polished brass barriers, potted palms, huge settees, mirrors and an ornate marble fireplace midway down its huge length. The panels between the pillars were covered in rich damask paper. Circle and balcony patrons had ornate mirrored and carpeted lounges for queuing. Lifts were provided in each lobby for speedy access to the top balcony. A three-manual ten-rank Wurlitzer pipe organ was installed at the rear of the huge curved orchestra pit (nearest the footlights). A motorised lift allowed the organ to rise above stage level and descend almost out of view. Afternoon teas were served in the Circle café above the entrance at the Great Horton Road end near the Alhambra. At the Thornton Road end, just right of the domed entrance, was a massive restaurant, flanked by square pillars supporting ornate lights and with windows that overlooked Thornton Road. This soon became a fashionable and elegant place to dine, with attentive waitresses resplendent in crisp black and white uniforms. The ballroom was situated above the restaurant; the entrance through double glass doors with canopy was situated midway between the two domed towers on New Victoria Street. This was the building that incorporated our much-loved Saturday morning club.

Saturday for us was the best day of the week: no school and Saturday morning pictures. A few hundred screaming children all gathered together in one place and not a teacher in sight! The queues were always orderly, entry being at the Great Horton Road end. The commissionaire, 'Old George', a middle-aged man with grey hair and moustache, was resplendent in uniform and white gloves; he was respected and well liked by us all. Once inside, Vincent and I soon became accustomed to the bedlam in the front stalls. Before long we were part of this mob of youngsters, shouting, ducking, climbing over seats and throwing missiles. There was always half an hour of pandemonium before the films started.

At ten o'clock the noise rose to a crescendo as Phil Ridler, the manager, known affectionately as 'Uncle Phil', walked from the rear stalls down the centre aisle to the stage, during which time missiles of all kinds were thrown at him and booing came from all quarters. Why we did this we had no idea, but Vincent and I added to the general mêlée. Once Uncle Phil was on the stage the noise subsided, although it still simmered. At this point the organ, played by local organist and broadcaster Arnold Loxham, rose from the depths of the orchestra pit, attracting another salvo of objects. Uncle Phil, using a microphone, then proceeded to list any club members' birthdays, and a slide was shown with the words of 'Happy Birthday'. The organ then commenced to play, and a bouncing ball on the screen followed the words to add encouragement as we sang 'Happy Birthday' in full voice, led by Uncle Phil. Other songs followed including 'The Lambeth Walk' and 'Ten Green Bottles'. After a few minutes it was time to sing

181

our club song, which always brought the house down as we knew that our pictures were about to begin. Again with Uncle Phil, the organ and the bouncing ball we sang:

> We come along on Saturday morning, greeting everybody with a smile,
> We come along on Saturday morning, knowing it's well worth while.
> As members of the G B Club we all intend to be, good citizens when we
>   grow up, and champions of the free.
> We come along on Saturday morning, greeting everybody with a smile,
>   smile, smile,
> Greeting everybody with a smile.

Uncle Phil then retreated back to the rear of the cinema, this time to cheers. The film started and, as if by magic, a silence fell over the cinema as our two hours of joy and wonder began. The format of the programme was always the same, starting with a cartoon, a short comedy film, next the serial, and finally the main film, which was nearly always a western B picture. The reason we were there was to see our favourite heroes, comedians, serials and cartoons. We didn't want any delay – and our very own Uncle Phil had to put up with our shouting, whistles and missile-throwing over many years. It wasn't personal. He loved it, and I'm sure we youngsters loved him.

When the picture drew to a close many children left their seats and moved to the rear of the picture house. As the hero and his sidekick rode off into the sunset to our cheers, the doors were thrown open and we all surged out into New Victoria Street. Buses and trams had to be caught, but others galloped home, smacking their hips (pretending to be on horseback) and shooting imaginary six-guns. The older boys and girls acted more dignified, but occasionally, when they thought nobody was looking, you saw them doing a 'fast draw' with a bent trigger finger around the imaginary six-gun.

On 2 May 1946, my eighth birthday, I received a birthday card from the Gaumont British Junior Club inviting me and a guest on the following Saturday morning. Vincent was my guest. On that morning I was one of around a dozen children to have our names read out on the vast stage by Uncle Phil. This time we had to go up on to the stage to receive a bar of chocolate: not one of us refused – as a free bar of chocolate when sweets were still rationed was indeed a birthday present not to miss. Uncle Phil shook our hands and gave each of us the chocolate. When I returned to my seat it lasted all of five minutes: Vincent and I had a couple of pieces each, and our other new friends the rest.

A few months later, on the morning of Friday 20 September 1946, we missed our Saturday morning club because of the floods. The front stalls of the New Vic, the orchestra pit and under-stage facilities were all below street level and were flooded. Quick thinking by a member of staff who raised the organ console to its full height saved the valuable instrument from any serious damage, but carpets, seating and items stored under the stage were destroyed. Films continued to be shown, with the audience in the circle and the balcony for several days until the front stalls had been cleaned up and dried out. There was no chance of hundreds of kids being allowed in the circle or the balcony, so when we returned we had to sit in the rear stalls. For weeks we could see a line high up along each wall in the front stalls showing the height of the flood waters, and there was a damp musty smell.

Across the city the Ritz cinema in Broadway was also affected on the same day; the entire stalls were flooded and the Compton organ console, which couldn't be raised in time, was totally destroyed and rendered beyond repair. Thereafter the New Vic remained the only city centre cinema with a working pipe organ.

As well as birthday call-outs, from time to time we had a magician, and on one occasion a lady with dogs that jumped through hoops. Even we could tell that they were amateurs who were probably using the venue as unpaid experience. These performers were subjected to boos that got louder when items were dropped or mistakes made: no-one escaped our wrath as we waited for the picture to begin. The only people who never suffered abuse or missiles were the two ice-cream ladies, who stood either side of the stage; an orderly queue always formed to each one.

Gangs from all parts of Bradford attended the club: the Canterbury Warriors gang, Longside Lane gang, White Abbey gang (most of whom I went to St Patrick's school with), Whetley Hill gang and many others. It was rare that any fights occurred: as it was the pictures we had come to see, all disputes and grievances were put to one side. Even after the show was over each gang went their own way shouting the youngster's parting, 'So long'.

Girls could be as bad as the boys, and there were a few you tended to avoid. One wrong look could fetch you a clout on the back of the head or, worse, chewing gum rubbed in your hair. One particular gang member, a good-looking but much-feared girl called Jean, was, as my mum would say, 'Sweet on me'. I was aged about twelve and she was around two years older. She was quite fancied by many of the older boys, but being only twelve I was not yet streetwise. She kept coming to sit next to me and physically moved anyone already sitting there, except Vincent, whom she knew was with me. Then she would try to kiss me, and I would become embarrassed as everyone around me looked, nudged each other and made remarks. This went on for a few weeks, and at one point I said to Vincent, 'If it doesn't stop I'm not going to the club again.' Vincent replied, 'I wish she fancied me.' As he was a little younger than me, I began to wonder if I should return the girl's affection: I suppose I thought of the prestige it would give me at the club and with many gang members. But the decision was taken out of my hands. As suddenly as it had begun it stopped. Her affections changed to some other dope, who unlike me fell for her charms and could be seen not only kissing her during the pictures but also holding hands on the way out. For quite some time I was pointed out as the dope who spurned Jean's affections, which in some way had some prestige.

Throughout the 1940s and early '50s the New Vic was our main entertainment venue. We went through the same trials and tribulations of all those attending: there was lots of laughter and a few tears. Those were the days when going to the pictures was more than watching one film and going home. The experience was full and wholesome, something you looked forward to all week and cherished as a memory for even longer. Vincent and I loved every minute of it and rarely missed our Saturday morning outing. New friends were made, both boys and girls, who came and sat with us week after week.

At the time of writing there are threats to demolish the New Vic, this unique landmark building. Bradford's hierarchy of councillors and outside consultants has still not learnt its lesson of the 1960s, and is still determined to demolish the city's heritage of beautiful buildings.

The Empress

My nearest and favourite cinema was the Empress in Legrams Lane, facing the allotments. It was situated close to Ira Ickringill & Co. Ltd (worsted yarn spinners) in a densely populated area of back-to-back and terraced houses. Built in the summer of 1914, it was a purpose-built stone picture house of simple design with a single-deck auditorium. The hall had a seating capacity of around 650 arranged in two blocks with two aisles and with two exits provided for each side.

From an early age until my teens I spent many happy hours here, enjoying all types of films from cartoons and comedy, to the serious and the classics of the time. In one evening I might watch Tom and Jerry, a short like Laurel and Hardy, and a classic like *The Maltese Falcon*.

It was my mum with her passion for westerns who introduced me to the pictures and the Empress. Sometimes we went as many as three times a week as the programmes changed three times: Monday–Wednesday, Thursday–Saturday, and Sunday evenings, with two performances from 6 to 8pm and 8.15 until 10.15pm. Winter and summer we always attended the first house, as it was known, 6–8pm.

My brother Lawrence had other interests and, being older, went to the pictures with his friends. Dad, on the other hand, was not really bothered, even before going into the army, unless it was to see Laurel and Hardy. So I was Mum's companion and excuse to spend a few hours at the pictures. We always had the same seats, on the back row of the front stalls, next to the wall and exit door, and set off early to make sure we secured them. Being small, I could sit on the arm of the seat to see over people's heads.

The Empress Cinema in Legrams Lane. This was my mum's favourite picture house. *(Author's collection)*

The music played before the start of the films was always the same, Johann Strauss's *The Blue Danube* (even during the war), Rossini's *Barber of Seville* overture and music from Tchaikovsky's *Swan Lake*. I knew to the exact second when it would finish, to be followed by the trailers, announcing the forthcoming attractions for the rest of the week. Advertisements were few; one always seemed to be for Carter's Little Liver Pills. The newsreels of Gaumont British ('the eyes and ears of the world'), Pathé News (with the crowing cockerel) and Movietone followed. During the war these showed what was happening to our troops at the front, and the picture house was always quiet and subdued as everyone thought about their own loved ones away in the forces. When the newsreel showed the British Tommies, the commentator nearly always said in a cheery voice, 'and still they're smiling'. At the end of the war the newsreels showed thee horrific atrocities of Belsen and other German concentration camps. There was no X certificate on these news films, so children saw them at all the cinemas for what seemed like many weeks. The reality of these scenes didn't disturb me, I think I was too young, but they left a lasting impression.

After the newsreel a short comedy was shown, to bring everyone back to life. Sometimes there was a travelogue, all of which seemed to end with a phrase like '. . . as the golden sun sinks slowly over this tropical island paradise, we bid farewell to a land of enchantment and mystery'. Then we had the big picture, or main feature, the reason for being there.

My mother, smoking a Woodbine, was soon engrossed in the film, especially if it was a western, and got great pleasure if there was a 'bust up' (her words) in the saloon. I enjoyed the films just as much, although when a love scene came on the screen I headed for the toilet at the rear by climbing over the back seat, returning the same way. I always noticed that the toilets seemed to fill up with youngsters who disappeared for a few minutes while these sloppy love scenes took place!

Once the lights had gone down and the film had started, my mum was intolerant of those sitting around her. God help them if they spoke, coughed or even whispered! At the top of her voice she would shout, 'Do you mind? We've come to watch the picture, not listen to you!' If some foolish patron said 'shush!', my mum's wrath was brought down on them, with 'Who do you think you are shushing?' Usually the fracas calmed down after the first altercation, but other times it went on and other voices joined in from all parts of the picture house. Sometimes a patron was ejected and all was quiet again. My mother would once again be engrossed in the film and I would come out from under the seat where, during these confrontations, I tried to make myself as small as possible.

At the end of the film, in wartime, we always sang the National Anthem. In the summer evenings the bright sunshine made you blink when you left, and people in the queue waiting for the second house always asked, 'What's the picture like?' In the winter, with the blackout, the entrance to the Empress was all in darkness, with small red lights at the box office, and on leaving it was really pitch black. That's when my mum would link my arm and frogmarch me home.

When we got home my dad would often ask, 'Has your mother had a do at the pictures?' I nearly always answered 'Yes'. As I grew older I began to realise why it was that my mum and I went to the pictures without dad.

Sometimes I went go to the Empress with my grandfather. I walked up from school to Fenton Street, Princeville, to my grandparents, had some tea, then off we went. Sometimes we stopped at Lister's sweet shop in the row of shops in Princeville, so he could buy an ounce of tobacco for his pipe. Grandfather always sat in the front of the back stalls. Quite often I left him to join one or two of my friends. This was all right if the film was a U certificate, but if it was an A certificate children had to be accompanied by an adult, and I had to stay with my grandfather. Children, both boys and girls, could be seen at the entrance to most cinemas asking adults to take them in if the film was an A certificate. Vincent and I did this a few times and never encountered any problems.

It was in the early 1950s that the Empress went modern with its music, and a few top twenty records began to amuse the patrons. The move was so sudden that it was a talking point in the area for many weeks. 'Music, Music, Music' by Teresa Brewer, 'Oh Mein Papa' by Eddie Calvert, 'Answer Me' by David Whitfield, the 'Harry Lime Theme' (Anton Karas) and many others made life at the Empress a little happier.

In 1954 my dad was working at Stroud Riley (worsted spinners) on Canal Road. To make a little extra money he took a job at the Empress as a part-time commissionaire (minus uniform). My mother had also tried working part time as an usherette at the Empress, but she had lasted only a fortnight. Tickets were not being torn and practically no one was being shown to their seats. There had been chaos on a Saturday night, with patrons standing, talking and even shouting in the aisles as they looked for seats. Arthur Maynell, the proprietor, politely told my mum that she wasn't up to it, and not to return the next night. Her problem was she had been too busy watching the film, which happened to be a Western. In contrast, my dad enjoyed his time as part-time commissionaire, and was well liked by most of the patrons. His highlight was on one summer Sunday evening. A group of five young lads aged around sixteen were making quite a noise in the front stalls. My dad shone his torch on the culprits and asked them to leave. Not one of them said anything as they trooped out of the Empress, shamefaced. They crossed the road and sat in the sun on the wall of the allotments opposite the picture house. The culprits were George Stockley, Terence Moran, Michael Farrell, Martin Monaghan and Derek Lister! I had been ejected from the Empress by my own father. When I returned home he just laughed. Mum said, 'It's a good job I wasn't there.' I agreed.

I think I was aged about three the first time I went to the Empress, in 1941, and continued to visit regularly until we moved to Wyke in 1955. I missed it because of the memories and the many happy times I spent there. The Empress closed in July 1956.

The Arcadian

The Arcadian was situated on the corner of Legrams Lane and Ingleby Road. A wooden building called the Arcadian Pavilion was built here in 1908, and was a popular venue for top quality concert parties. It was badly damaged by fire in 1931 and remained in ruins for eight years, until it was demolished and the site was cleared for a cinema, the Arcadian. Late 1939 saw the erection of this steel-framed building, ultra-modern with a hint of art deco. It seated a thousand people, with 680 in the stalls and 320 in the balcony in luxurious tip-up chairs. The cinema opened in March 1940.

As this was the start of the Second World War, with a blackout in force, ultra-violet lighting in the vestibule gave the effect of luminous paint – which gave sufficient illumination without contravening the blackout regulations. Like the Empress there was no external lighting, neon signs or display panels, and all street lighting was switched off.

My first visit to the Arcadian was in 1943. It was my grandfather who took me, to see *King Kong*. I didn't realise how scary the film would be and, aged five, spent most of the time holding my grandfather's hand over my eyes, adjusting his fingers so I could see! Walking out into the blackout didn't help, and I hung on to him all the way home. By the time we reached home I had forgotten King Kong, as my grandfather held my attention with his tales of 'When I was your age'.

The Arcadian, on the corner of Legrams Lane and Ingleby Road. This cinema was noted as the most updated and plush cinema in my area. The Saturday afternoons for children were wonderful entertainment. *(CU)*

It was after the war that I began to attend the Arcadian more frequently, in between my forays to the Empress with my mum. Aged seven, going on eight, I was old enough to go on my own or with my friends to the New Vic Saturday morning club, so there was no reason why I couldn't attend the Arcadian with my friends, in particular Vincent.

It was towards the end of the 1940s that the Arcadian started a Saturday afternoon children's matinée, from 2pm until 4pm, cost *6d*. The usual films for children were shown, starting with a cartoon, then a short comedy and a feature, which was always a B picture western with lots of action or a pirate film with lots of fencing. These films had the desired effect, for the cinema was always full – with over six hundred youngsters in the stalls. We could sit anywhere. Ice cream was on sale, and there was also a sweet kiosk, but with sweet rationing still in force and coupons scarce we gave this a miss. So it was an ice cream or a packet of crisps (with the salt in a little blue twist of paper) that made it a pleasant afternoon. A long queue formed well before the cinema opened at 1.30. The commissionaire in his uniform, whom no one liked, was very officious, always gruff, never smiled, and kept popping out to keep the queue orderly. Once we were in our seats he took great delight in walking up and down the aisle with a brass canister from which he sprayed air freshener. Cries of 'What a pong!' erupted from six hundred mouths, which only made him repeat the spraying, with even more gusto.

It was in 1943 that my grandfather took me to see *King Kong* at the Arcadian. I missed most of it by holding my grandfather's hand over my eyes. *(Kobal)*

On one occasion, unusually for the Arcadian, the film broke down during a western and at a most dramatic part. Numbers came up on the screen: 5–4–3–2–1. Most of us knowledgeable youngsters knew that the projectionist hadn't changed to the next reel. We tipped up our seats, sat on the edge of them, and six hundred pairs of feet clattered the wood base – the usual procedure at this time in the event of a breakdown. The noise was deafening. Our narky commissionaire didn't like this, and for once he couldn't control us. He shouted at the top of his voice but couldn't be heard. Suddenly the film resumed, the noise abated and he walked out of the rear door muttering to himself. He had an individual scowl for everyone when we left.

We were at an age to emulate our heroes in the western and pirate films, and most of those attending were boys. Anyone in the vicinity of the cinema on a Saturday afternoon at about 4pm in the winter would be astounded at the mayhem caused when the exits opened and the energy of hundreds of youngsters was unleashed. When winter set in we took our raincoats to the cinema, but when we came out we didn't use these as a protection against the cold or rain. Hundreds of boys emerged with their raincoats fastened by the top button and flowing like a cloak. Off at a gallop they went, holding a make-believe rein in the left hand and slapping their behinds with the other, as if on a horse. Woe betide anyone who got in the way of hundreds of boys moving at breakneck speed down Legrams Lane and Ingelby Road, adrenalin high and hearts pounding! Someone wrote to the *Telegraph and Argus* complaining of these Saturday afternoon vandals (aged seven to fourteen). Every week the cinema put up a slide on the screen asking us to walk out, but to no avail. Our commissionaire never stood in our way!

Sometimes I was at the New Vic in the morning, the Arcadian in the afternoon and another picture house in the evening; but the time came when I was getting too old for cowboys and Indians, and even pirates. It was time to lose some of my childhood habits and move on. The Arcadian had certainly played a major part in my enjoyment, even though it had been so different from the Empress.

I was working soon, so if I went to the Arcadian it was in the evening. Sometimes I sat in the balcony. I began to notice that the double seats at the rear of the stalls and on the balcony were usually full of courting couples. Once when I was there with Vincent and the cinema was quite full, I saw an empty double seat on the back row. I called him and began to edge along the row when about half a dozen voices told us in no uncertain terms to 'Bugger off', which we did. Perhaps one day!

The Arcadian 'super-cinema' lived up to its name and continued to be the premier cinema in the district. It completely outshone the nearby and much older Empress and Elysian picture houses, eventually outliving them. The Arcadian closed in February 1964.

The Elysian

The Elysian picture house was a single-storey, rather squat stone building, purpose-designed as a picture hall and opened in 1912. It was on Wheater Road, Lidget Green. The area was mainly through terraced houses. Originally the cinema had 535 seats, but this was later reduced to a more comfortable 400. The small and simple entrance in Wheater Road was only a few yards from the busy Beckside Road. Next door was the very popular Ida's sweet shop. She sold her own ice cream here, as well as from her home and business on

The Elysian cinema at Lidget Green was probably the smallest and the poorest of our local picture houses. But it had a certain charm and it was well worth fighting to stay on one of the two benches at the front – always a challenge! *(CU)*

The Elysian's Saturday afternoon children's matinee: a sea of young eager faces look forward in anticipation to the entertainment. *(CU)*

Horton Park Avenue.

We could go to the Elysian for *6d*, catching the trolleybus to Lidget Green and home for *1d* each way, and paying *4d* for a ticket. The *4d* seats were two long benches at the front, so it was pushing-up time when someone else arrived and sat on the end. As we moved up it was inevitable that someone would fall off the other end. One fearsome lad called Roy always made people fall off. This turmoil allowed the fallen to sneak back a couple of rows to the proper seats, which cost *6d* – until the manager walked down to the front and moved everyone back to the benches. Vincent and I worked out that a maximum of fifteen youngsters to a bench was comfortable, but it was not unusual for there to be over twenty, which caused a lot of pushing, shoving, elbowing, punching, kicking and the odd fight. All this while trying to watch the picture! We were only a few yards from the screen and as we were viewing at an angle we often had stiff and aching necks on the way home.

Although the Elysian was not as modern as the Arcadian, we had a certain affection for it. It played its part, especially when money was tight: even in the summer we could walk there and back and have two hours of good fun for *4d*, whether watching the film or roughing it on the bench! In the 1950s the Elysian became increasingly unable to compete with the Grange cinema or the nearby Arcadian. It closed in March 1955.

The Grange

The Grange picture house was situated in the busy Great Horton Road, a mile from the city centre just above the junction of Horton Grange Road. The surrounding district was densely populated with streets of terraced housing. The cinema was purpose built of stone in 1922. Adjoining its central entrance was Ivy Jowett's sweet, ice cream and tobacco shop. There was seating for 1100 people, in three blocks with two aisles. Although the Grange was just within a mile of my home, it was on another gang's territory, namely the dreaded Canterbury Warriors – one of the most feared gangs in the district. It was with trepidation we went to the Grange, and it had to be a really special film for us to make the trip. Most of the film was spent looking over our shoulders, although it wasn't so much that there was trouble inside the cinema: it was who was waiting for you outside. If you were with an adult there was no problem.

I first went to the Grange just after the war with my dad: as I've said, he liked Laurel and Hardy, and the film was *Way out West*. The last time was in 1956 with a girlfriend, Alma Beatty. Although I was much older, and with a nice young lady, I was still looking over my shoulder, more out of habit than anything else. The Grange closed in July 1961.

Victoria Cinema, Girlington. Known to all as 'The Little Vic', it became Morrison's first supermarket in 1962. *(Wm Morrison archives)*

The Victoria

Known to us as the Little Vic, the Victoria was built in 1914 in a prime position on Thornton Road close to the busy crossroads of Whetley Lane and Ingelby Road. The Girlington district was densely populated with streets of back-to-back and terrace housing. A purpose-built stone construction with a central entrance, the little Vic had 1000 seats in three blocks with two aisles, and two corresponding access doors to both stalls and circle with its fronted balcony.

As there were other picture houses much closer, our visits to the Little Vic were few and far between, but a pleasant option. After a serious fire in 1955 the cinema was refurbished; it reopened the same year, finally closing in December 1961. It was then purchased by William Morrison's, and became the very first Morrison's supermarket in November 1962.

Chapter 14
Our Favourite Films and Stars

The Western

The 1940s and '50s were great days for the western. Every Hollywood studio turned out hundreds of these great films. Cowboy B pictures (now known as second features) were our favourites, and we were usually more interested in these than in the 'big' picture. At our Saturday morning club and at other picture houses we watched all those cowboy heroes that helped form our childhood ideas of the 'Code of the West'. What great screen heroes they were, and what flashy outfits they wore! On screen they rarely missed a shot from the hip, and they were faster with a six-gun than the meanest gunslinger.

There were two types of cowboys, Good Guys and Bad Guys. Good Guys were good shots and Bad Guys were bad shots. The Bad Guys got killed and the Good Guys did the killing. The good thing about this was that the same Bad Guy got killed every week. Apart from his black hat, you could always tell a Bad Guy because he rarely shaved, had a moustache and was always smarmy. You knew as soon as the film started who was good and who was bad: the rules were set. In all these films there were 'Doc', 'Smithy', 'Bar Tender' and the 'Saloon Girl', who makes good in the end. All of them were probably killed, saving the Good Guy. Most cowboys liked their horse better than they liked girls, and some cowboys even sung to their horses. In my tender years I wasn't impressed with this!

The plots of these low budget pictures were slight variations on a theme. The hero and his sidekick drift into town and very quickly get involved in rescuing a pretty damsel from the clutches of a villain called Jake. Jake is part of a gang organised by the man who owns most of the town, and is leader of the baddies. It later transpires that the goodies are Texas rangers or US marshals, or are working undercover for the railroad company, Wells Fargo (a courier service

Gene Autry. It was notable that in fight scenes his clothes never got dirty. *(Kobal)*

The popular Roy Rogers. It was always an excuse to visit the toilet when he began to sing to a girl or his horse Trigger. *(Kobal)*

The dependable Hopalong Cassidy (William Boyd) with his popular side-kick George 'Gabby' Hayes. *(Kobal)*

Randolph Scott – probably the best of the best. *(Kobal)*

that transported money) or the Cattlemen's Association. The baddies are usually trying to steal all or part of the local land from the 'nesters', so they can somehow make a fortune. The picture climaxes with the posse, led by the goodies, trapping the baddies at their hideout. A shooting war breaks out and both sides use the famous western six-gun, which never needs reloading. As the baddies show signs of losing their leader sneaks away on his horse. Our hero spots him and goes after him. After a furious chase he jumps from his horse and pulls the baddie to the ground. In a short scuffle he knocks out the baddie with a single punch. A cheer rises from us all, and we all go home happy!

We didn't miss much in the westerns, be it mistakes, a film reel out of sequence, or repeated film footage. But like my friends I never noticed that there were no toilets in the saloon, jailhouse, baddies' hideout or the rich man's ranch; in fact we never remarked that our hero never went to the toilet – as indeed no one in our films did.

Some of our Heroes

Each of us had our own favourite cowboys. Among them was Johnny MacBrown, a good athlete and a good horseman, who was one of the better riders and among the best of the 'screen brawlers'. He was reputed to be the most proficient in the twirling and spinning of a six-shooter, and he did this often in his films. I tried to copy this when I finally got my own cap-gun six-shooter. I also liked Tex Ritter, who was also a popular western folk singer, famous for the soundtrack version of the film song 'High Noon'.

Gene Autry's films took place in a world precariously balanced between the Old West and the Modern World, featuring (often in the same movie) runaway stagecoaches, bar room brawls, high-powered cars, army tanks and aeroplanes. But he exuded a knightly demeanour that we as youngsters loved. When there was trouble on the range he urged everyone to stick together, no matter what the bank or the landowner threatened. I thought that he dressed up too much, and even after a scuffle there wasn't a mark on his clothes, but I still liked him – even though it slowed the plot down when he began to sing. He always wore gloves, some say because he had small hands.

Roy Rogers, 'King of the Cowboys', had flair and style. His films co-starred his horse Trigger and benefited from the comedy relief of sidekick George 'Gabby' Hayes. They usually took place in the Old West and featured plenty of action. Some of his later films became structured around musical routines, and we lost interest when he started to sing, especially to Trigger. It was time to go to the toilet!

William Boyd as Hopalong Cassidy was one of our favourites. His westerns established a formula where the pace began slowly and then gradually increased until it was time for a huge shootout, often involving several posses who joined together and rode to the rescue. He didn't waste time singing or being involved with women: 'Hoppy' was straight to the point. He looked older than his years with his premature grey hair, and dressed in black with pearl-handled six-shooters and his horse Topper, he looked to us like the archetypal cowboy. He was often accompanied by sidekicks, generally called 'Lucky', often the popular 'Gabby' Hayes as 'Windy'.

Charles Starrett, considered the most handsome western star with his white Stetson, black shirt and long flowing silk scarf (not a neckerchief), featured as the Durango Kid, a mysterious, masked Robin Hood-type hero – a Secret Service man working in the West.

Lash La Rue was another cowboy who wore an all-black outfit, with his Stetson cocked slightly to one side. He projected quite a different screen image from his contemporaries. His main weapon was an 18-foot bullwhip coiled at his holster, and he had a black horse to go with his outfit, a steed named Black Diamond. Again, any cowboy who dressed up in this sort of outfit we liked.

Jock Mahoney, ace stuntman and actor, was famous for his exploits as the Range Rider, an honest, principled and tough goodie, with the boyish sidekick Dick West. Dressed in fringed buckskin and a white Stetson, the Range Rider didn't wear boots, just moccasins. His horse was called Rawhide. Dick, sporting a dark military styled shirt and a black hat, rode a steed named Lucky. After many westerns he went on to play in films as one of the many Tarzans.

Randolph Scott, on his palomino Stardust, was remembered long after the days of matinées as one of the most widely known and successful heroes in western film history. His handsome, rugged, six-foot-four good looks, his straight-arrow authority, his respect for women and his superb good-guy image made him the ultimate cowboy hero. He was the only cowboy we went out of our way to see, even to picture houses in outlying districts. Of all cowboys he was our favourite.

There were many other cowboy film stars whom we liked: Rod Cameron, Bill Elliot, Tim Holt, George O'Brien, Tom Tyler, Bob Steel, Bill Williams, Cesar Romero, and many others. All played their part in keeping us enthralled from week to week.

Western Sidekicks
Cowboy films were often serious fare. There were Bad Guys to chase and capture and women to save from themselves, or from the Bad Guys. What could be done to lighten the picture and add some comedy? Enter the sidekick! All good cowboys had a sidekick who always seemed to get the good cowboy into trouble. These partners were often more of a liability than a help, but they all made good in the end. Sidekicks were usually scruffy, with mismatched clothes, unshaven or with a grey beard, and sometimes no teeth. They whined or they mumbled and tended to use phrases like 'Dag nad it!' They were given the funniest lines in the film, and sometimes even got a peck on the cheek from the leading lady.

**The good guy's 'side-kick',
Andy Devine, whose
trademark was his raspy
squeaky-toned voice.
(Kobal)**

There were many actors who filled these roles, but the most beloved tended
to move from star to star. Virtually the prototype of all grizzled old-codger
western sidekicks was George 'Gabby' Hayes, who spent his early years with
Hopalong Cassidy and later career with Roy Rogers. Among the well-known
ones were Andy Devine, the rotund comic character actor with his trademark
raspy, squeaky tones, who played Cookie Bullfincher in many films with Roy
Rogers; Smiley Burnette, who was well known for his turned-up Stetson and his
white horse with a black circle around one eye; Fuzzy Knight; Raymond Hatton;
Dub 'Cannonball' Taylor; Ken Curtis; and Al 'Fuzzy' St John.

Serials

One of the good things about our Saturday morning club was the serial: the
super heroes, who could fly faster than a speeding bullet, leap buildings and do
all manner of wonderful things. Even with these powers they still ended up in a
life-or-death situation at the end, frequently knocked out and placed in dire peril
by a car speeding towards a cliff, a burning warehouse or a conveyor belt headed
towards a saw. Every time the solution to the cliff-hanger had the hero simply
wake up and roll out of the way. Seventeen minutes later he fell into another
deadly trap – and we spent a week of agony waiting to find out how he escaped.
And so on for twelve to fifteen weeks, twelve to fifteen chapters, before the bad
guys got their comeuppance.

Perhaps the best serial was *Flash Gordon*. The original serials were our
introduction to space. Even though *Flash Gordon* (1936), *Flash Gordon: Space Soldiers*
(1936), *Flash Gordon's Trip to Mars* (1938), and *Flash Gordon Conquers the Universe*
(1940) were old by the time they were showing on our screens, there was nothing to
compare with them. They were packed with action-orientated episodes, filled with
fantastic spaceships, futuristic scenes, monsters and other imaginative creations. The
star was Larry 'Buster' Crabbe as the title character Flash Gordon, with blonde Jean
Rogers as Dale Arden, his girlfriend, and the villainous ruler of planet Mongo, Ming
the Merciless, portrayed by Charles Middleton. They made these serials such a
compulsive draw for us on those Saturday mornings.

Flash Gordon, Emperor Ming's adversary, played by 'Buster' Crabbe. *(Kobal)*

Charles Middleton's wonderful portrayal of Emperor Ming the Merciless. *(Kobal)*

Flash Gordon took place in a wide variety of settings, including a flying city, a city on the ocean bottom and underground caverns haunted by monsters. No one will ever forget the stubby silvery spaceships, spitting puffs of smoke and sparks while emitting a sound like a small motorboat. There were even some very wobbly flying saucers, piloted by the Lion Men. Monsters, such as the Clay Men, Monkey Men, Hawk Men, Shark Men, Mechanical Men and the Forest People tried to hinder Flash on his travels. Many of the extras playing these and other parts were also to be seen in western serials and B pictures.

Perhaps the villain we liked most was Emperor Ming. Living in Mingo, named in his honour, he was not a man of his word. On one occasion he offered Flash his freedom if he could kill a large ape-like creature called an Orangapoid. The serial ended with this monster just about to kill Flash. The following week the film has rolled back a few feet, reversing the position – and Flash kills the Orangapoid. Ming says, 'You have won', and Flash, thinking he is about to be freed, sighs with relief. But Ming continues, 'You have won the right to fight', and names another monster and the same conditions. Such a change from the code of the cowboys! It certainly kept us on our seats.

Many other serials abounded, and although they were exciting they didn't have the same impact as *Flash Gordon*. Some of them were *Zorro's Fighting Legion, Adventures of Captain Marvel, The Masked Marvel, The Monster and the Ape, The Scarlet Horsemen*. In this latter, the Scarlet Horseman wore a scarlet hood: because the film was in black and white we took this for granted! Kirk Alyn played Superman in two serials between 1948 and 1950.

Tarzan

Johnny Weissmuller (who won Five Olympic gold swimming medals) was always the real Tarzan to me. We saw all his films at the Saturday club, and then went home to practise our Tarzan yells and swing from ropes on the lampposts. He was a giant of a man whose great strength allowed him almost to leap out of the water as he swam. He performed many of his own stunts with apparent ease,

Johnny Weissmuller as Tarzan. He was always the real Tarzan to me. *(Kobal)*

lifting men over his head, riding on elephants and swinging on vines with grace and style. There was always a fight with a crocodile. If it was to save someone he dived into the water the knife blade in his mouth, fight the crocodile, rolling over and over until he sinks the blade in. We all knew it was a dummy, but we didn't care. Tarzan's favourite word was 'umgawa', which was meaningless yet meant everything, and could be heard in the streets and playgrounds of the land. Vincent and I were not too keen on his pet monkey, Cheeta. The films generally ended with the monkey's antics, upon which everyone in the scene would laugh, but not us. Johnny Weissmuller didn't waste any time in finding a new film role after his final Tarzan film. Jungle Jim was an ideal role for him. What the films lacked in storytelling they more than made up for with all-out action and over-the-top heroics. Vincent and I became fans of Jungle Jim.

Comedy
Many other comedy stars were around at this time, but the following were among our favourites.

There was nothing subtle about the comedy of Arthur Lucan and his wife Kitty McShane who found nationwide fame as Mother Riley and her daughter Kitty, the romantic lead (Vincent and I said she was older than our mothers!). Old Mother Riley was a washerwoman, and her humour relied wholly on slapstick, puns and the sight of a wiry fifty-something man in Victorian widow's clothes. This proved very popular with younger audiences. We saw all the films, fifteen in all. The best, we thought, was *Old Mother Riley meets the Vampire*, with the famous horror star Bela Lugosi.

Laurel and Hardy were always popular and the duo could do no wrong. Everything they did was funny and all the seven- to fourteen-year-olds at the Gaumont Saturday morning club shouted with laughter at the pair's antics. They gave twenty minutes of sheer joy at any picture house in Bradford.

From 1937 to 1958 the Bowery Boys, a troupe of lovable New York street kids, entertained us with many films and serials. Starring Leo Gorcey, Huntz

A favourite of ours: Old Mother Riley played by Arthur Lucan. *(Kobal)*

Leo Gorcey as Slip Mahoney, the brains behind the Bowery Boys. *(Kobal)*

Horace Debussy Jones, affectionately known as 'Sach' and played by Huntz Hall, a great favourite of Bowery Boys fans. *(Kobal)*

The inimitable Three Stooges: 1940s and '50s comedies wouldn't have been the same without Larry, Moe and Curly. *(Kobal)*

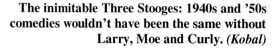

Hall and Bobby Jordan, the stories centred on a gang of street kids who turned away from a life of crime towards positive alternatives, including boxing, friendship and family ties. The great mix of comedy, hardboiled action and positive messages made these classics to be remembered. Through the years they changed their name from the Dead End Kids to the East Side Kids and then to the Bowery Boys. The final winning formula starred Leo Gorcey as Slip Mahoney (the Chief), who wore his hat turned up at the front, and Huntz Hall as Horace Debussy 'Sach' Jones (our favourite), wearing a baseball cap. They and the rest of the boys churned out forty-eight hilarious Bowery Boys films: I think Vincent and I saw them all.

The Three Stooges, commonly known by their first names of Larry, Moe and Curley, became famous for their many short features, which consisted of masterful showcases of their extremely physical brand of slapstick comedy. The opening credit used the tune 'Three Blind Mice'. The use of clever sound effects was important to the overall effect of the action. A good example is Moe whacking one of his fellow Stooges on the head with a hammer. Typically the sound of a hammer striking an anvil or a block of wood was used, suggesting that the characters were hard-headed in more ways than one. A blow to a kettledrum accompanied blows to the stomach, and for pokes in the eye a plucked violin string or a high-pitched piano note was used. Well, they made us laugh!

Cartoons
Most cartoons were funny. Their theme was always good against evil, with good almost always winning in the end. No one really got hurt. There were many, featuring Bugs Bunny, Tom and Jerry, Daffy Duck, Donald Duck and Porky Pig – with his 'That's all, folks!' at the end of the cartoon. Our favourite was Popeye. Although short, balding and downright ugly by anyone's standards, countless numbers of us grew up admiring and identifying with this unpretentious hero.

He was an underdog with a long fuse and a keen sense of fair play, until he finally said, 'Tha's all I can stands, and I can't stand no more!' It seems fitting that our most unlikely hero fell for the least likely of sex symbols, Olive Oyl. (Most of us have known one!). Flat as a board, with a pickle-shaped nose and a fickle heart to match, Popeye's 'goil' puts him through his paces. Her only real competition is spinach. The highlight of Popeye films is a fight with Bluto, the hairy 'heavy' with the glass jaw, who is always trying to take Olive away from him. Bluto always gets the upper hand until Popeye finds his tin of spinach, and with a squeeze, pops the contents down his throat. From then on Bluto has seven bells knocked out of him. Olive shouts 'My Hero' to Popeye and Popeye fades out singing 'I'm Popeye the Sailor Man', with smoke coming out of his pipe and two hoots like those from a ship's horn.

Chapter 15
Gangs and Games

Boyhood Friends

Most streets had gangs. These were made up of friends with whom you spent most of your time outside school – during evenings and school holidays – playing games, going on adventures and outings or the pictures, or sometimes making mischief.

My best pal from my schooldays was Vincent Davey. Vincent lived on Great Russell Street at no. 47, a back-to-back house like ours, although they had an attic, which was necessary because of the large family of five brothers and four sisters.

Vincent's father was a First World War veteran and his mother was a nice lady who was proud of being born in the same year as the Queen Mother, 1900. Gerard was the eldest son, who lived with his wife on Lower Great Russell Street. He had been in the Tank Corps during the Second World War and took great pleasure in showing us a German Luger 9mm pistol. We were always impressed! Another brother, Wilfred, also lived on Great Russell Street with his wife. Vincent and I used to babysit for them. One time at their house I went to drink from a lemonade bottle under the sink, but before I put it to my lips I smelt the top. It was ammonia! The sudden smell made me convulse and my eyes water, and I had difficulty in breathing for ten minutes. I was lucky. Vincent's other two brothers, Leo and Edmund, lived with an aunt in Scotchman Road in Manningham, because of the family's small house. His three older sisters were Eileen, Stella and Evelyn, and it was Eileen, who used to take Vincent and me to school, that I liked best. I was always wary of Stella, as she always seemed to be assertive – especially when I was buttoned up to the neck and Vincent had his shirt neck open. However, one day I proved a point. Maureen, the youngest of the family, was a late arrival, and when most of the family had grown up

Maureen was still playing with dolls and prams. Vincent once told me there had been two other brothers called Maurice and Austin, both of whom had died in infancy.

Trevor Clarkson lived with parents at 84 Great Russell Street. He was really the boss, or cock, of our gang. I don't think this was ever disputed, not because he was tough but because we never really fell out and it was never put to the test. Trevor's father died suddenly in about 1949, a shock to the neighbourhood.

Jack Robinson, perhaps the most likeable lad in the area, lived at 61 Great Russell Street with his parents and sister Valerie. Jack was born with his kneecaps reversed and had had an operation in infancy to correct them. The operation was a success but left a large scar down each leg. He couldn't run too well as his legs splayed out, but as he got older he always kept up with us, and later, when we were wearing long trousers, no one was aware of his disability. We never heard him complain. The name Jack Robinson, although not unusual, could cause a laugh, as it did at a church concert our gang attended at the Methodist church on Shearbridge Road. We were in the second row, and during one of the scenes an actor said, 'Before you can say Jack Robinson'. We shouted with gusto, 'He's here!' The actor forgot his lines and it was a while before he resumed his oration. In the meantime we had been ejected!

Barry Widdop, another Great Russell Street resident (at no. 74), lived with his parents and sister. Barry was a little more street-wise than us but was considered a good member of our gang. It was with these four friends that I spent most of my early life, although there were many others living in the streets who joined us or I mixed with from time to time.

For example, still on Great Russell Street, there were Barry Slater and David Gamwell. Barry's house, no. 56, was decorated with flags and bunting in 1945, making a colourful sight to welcome his father home from war. David was a little younger, but spent many hours at my house, swapping comics. His father Wilfred, a spare time watchmaker, mended everyone's watches for half town prices.

At 31 Legrams Street (my street) was Geoffrey Peel, whose father Harry had the only car in the area, which he parked on the street. Geoffrey always seemed to have new indoor games before anyone else, but he always invited us to take part. These games included Subbuteo, a miniature football game played by flicking small figures on hemispherical bases and an oversized ball, and Totopoly, a board game loosely based around horse racing. The horses were semi-flat die-cast metal, painted with stick-on numbers. A throw of the dice moved the horse around the board, with many obstacles – similar to Monopoly. Another popular horse-racing game was Escalado. A cloth was stretched across the table and you made this vibrate by turning a handle that sent five metal horses down the course. Nobody seemed to worry that it might encourage children to gamble. There was also the popular blow football, in which everyone used the same blowpipes over and over again. The trouble was that after four or five minutes you were covered in your opponent's spit or dizzy from the lack of oxygen! And the tablecloth was wet! Geoffrey was also a good chum with me on Plot Nights.

Tony Gilfoyle, a St Patrick's schoolboy like me, lived at no. 29 next to Geoffrey Peel. Tony's father Joe, who had been in the navy during the war, was a good singer, especially around the bonfires at Guy Fawkes – and also during the Coronation celebrations in 1953. His rendering of 'A Golden Coach' went on all through the night and into the next morning.

Geoffrey's good friend Brian Rigby lived with his family on the corner of Legrams Street and Edinburgh Street. Brian was to be the envy of us all in 1951 when he went to the Festival of Britain in London. On his return he showed us the festival's commemoration 5s coin in a plastic wallet.

John Harrison, a little older than us, lived with his one-armed father Fred at no. 21, up a passage in the centre of the street. John was always issuing threats or a thump, and was more than a little feared by all of us. He was also cheeky to grown ups and my mum had lots of run-ins with him, as he climbed on the middens and generally gave back-chat. My mother's favourite weapon for these occasions was a bucket of water. Out of the house she flew, to deposit the contents of the bucket on the middens. shouting 'I'll drown the lot of you' and 'you bold articles', and sometimes catching the odd culprit – although John always seemed to escape her wrath. John went to Princeville School, leaving at the age of fifteen in 1952. He joined the GPO as a telegram boy on foot working round the town centre. At seventeen, still with telegrams, he progressed to making deliveries on the well-known small red-painted GPO 125 James motorcycle. After he started work he became a different person: everyone liked him, in particular my mum. His manners were now impeccable; he was always smiling, and was a tribute to his father who had brought him up. In 1954, while I was working at Brown, Muff's, he was killed on his GPO bike in a collision with a West Yorkshire single-decker bus in Baildon. A dark cloud hung over the streets for many weeks.

Other boys on the street around my age were Dennis Richardson, John Padgett and brothers Dennis and Keith Jones, both excellent footballers. When teams were being picked in John Willie North's field for a kick-around, these two were eagerly sought after. Keith, when only sixteen, was taken on to the books of a famous London football club; but he failed the medical, and it was a case of 'what might have been'.

The next street, Legrams Terrace, also had a sprinkling of friends who joined us in games or misdeeds. Bobby Johnson lived in this street and was a good pal. He lived with his mother, sister Rhona and their grandmother at no. 30. Bobby's father had been killed in action in North Africa in 1942. His grandmother's favourite wireless programme was the repeat at 4.15 in the afternoon of 'Mrs

Dale's Diary'. She sat close to the wireless, and when we were playing indoors she shushed us to be quiet for the next fifteen minutes. Next door to Bobby lived the brothers Michael and Terence Steele, who also attended St Patrick's School. Another friend, Michael Ingleson, lived at no. 77 but attended St Williams School.

The top street was Fieldhead Street. At no. 47 lived Terry Bland – no mean footballer – and his cousin Barry Thomas, a prolific comic swapper. Tony Conley also lived on this street. My mother and Mrs Conley once had a confrontation, when she accused me of throwing Tony's cap in a puddle on Thornton Road on the way home from school; it was actually Michael Farrell. Peace was made and everyone remained friends. Tony's father Jim was with the famous Chindits in Burma during the war. When he came home he wore the slouched hat of the Chindits and was very dark skinned thanks to the sun of Burma and India, and probably the fatigue of the campaign.

At the top of Archibald Street lived the boys Joe, Billy and Alf Hannon. Their sisters Cathryn and Margaret lived at 29 Legrams Lane. Cathryn was a really bonny girl whom I used to fancy, but didn't have the courage to even say hello. All the Hannon family attended St Patrick's School.

These were just a few of my many friends who lived and played around these streets, and it was with them I spent most of my childhood around Legrams Street.

Boys and Girls Come Out to Play

As a child, and into my early teens, a knock at the house door could be one of my many friends asking 'Is Derek playing out?', or if I answered the door, 'Are ya playing out?' Playing out at any time was a ritual that didn't require any particular qualifications, and there were numerous games that we amused ourselves with. There could be no better exercise for mind or body, as most streets were ideal places to play – without the fear of being run over or chased by the police. The only problem was that there never seemed to be enough hours in the day! Meals were bolted down, the only thought being to get back outside again. Playing out in the school holidays started in the early morning and ended late in the evening: an average of twelve hours a day wasn't unusual. Every evening mothers shouted their children's names, each call being unique to each mother. If the child didn't hear there was always someone who would say, 'I've heard your mother calling for you' – as it was unusual for any child to be lost: someone somewhere knew where everyone was and who they were with. Summoned home, unkempt, dishevelled and tired children finally arrived back, physically and mentally exhausted, for a quick scrub down before bed. The following morning, batteries recharged, we were out again.

With our footwear of black pumps, sandals, boots or wellingtons, in short trousers, shirts with open necks or lumber jackets and windjammers, all seasons

A rest on a wall in Legrams Street. Left to right: Stewart Brooke, Derek Lister, Bobby Johnson, Norma Sherry. *(Author's collection)*

of play were the same. With grubby hands, chapped legs and dirty faces, we revelled in our games and fantasies for days on end. There was always the sound of laughter echoing around the streets.

Marbles

There were certain times of the year when many of our games were played. In spring the coming of the fine weather was marked by marbles (also known as taws) rattling in our pockets as we huddled around preparing for a game. A great deal of time was spent collecting, swapping and admiring marbles. Certain types were much prized, like 'glass alleys' and 'blood alleys', which could be worth several ordinary marbles. 'Bollys' (large steel bearings) were also sought after, particularly for their devastating effect on ordinary glass marbles when fired with any force. They were banned by mutual agreement in our group if any particularly valued marbles were being played with. An influx of clay marbles came on the scene in the late 1940s but were not considered particularly popular. My favourite bolly could disintegrate them with ease.

For a couple of months our causeway gutters were crowded with children of all ages playing marbles. Some went home with empty marble bags, while others stored away their new assets until the next spring.

Hopscotch, Rounders and Piggy

Hopscotch was played on the large Yorkshire paving stones which covered each street. Not all neighbours approved, though, especially if the playing area numbered 1 to 8 was marked in chalk outside their home. This generally resulted in the irate occupier washing away all traces of the chalk with a mop and bucket. We just moved on, re-chalking the numbers elsewhere.

Rounders was popular. With four borrowed dustbins formed into a square it was ideal for the centre of the street. We only played with a soft tennis ball, so when a window was hit it generally didn't break. There were many accidents as we slid into the dustbins. If empty, these rolled down the street, but cuts and bruises resulted if they were full of rubbish. Most of the players lived in the street in which we played, so there weren't complaints from adults as long as we put the bins back.

A 'piggy' was a piece of wood 2 to 3 inches long, whittled to a point at each end. The player hit one end of it with a stick, causing it to be 'tipped' up in the air. Then you hit it again, to make it travel as far as possible. This game was played on your own or in teams, the winner being the child or team who moved the piggy the furthest with the smallest number of 'tips'. Piggy could be dangerous!

Skipping Rope Games
In my young days skipping was mainly considered to be a girls' game; boys caught playing skipping were cissies. This didn't bother me, and from time to time I used to enjoy joining the girls at skipping. I was originally taught by the girl next door, Jean Glossop. Salt, Mustard, Vinegar, Pepper was one of the most popular games. Two players turned the rope while the others jumped over it, chanting repeatedly 'salt, mustard, vinegar, pepper'. Each time someone said 'pepper' the rope was turned faster. If you failed to jump the rope you were out; the last one left was the winner. The prize was to hold the rope! It was not unusual for as many as six boys and girls to be jumping in the centre of the skipping rope singing the rhymes until the rope, probably some mother's washing line, had to be returned.

Pollywash
During the hot summers, on no particular date but almost without fail for a few days, children from all streets would start to bounce the sun off mirrors, referring to this as Pollywash. Using hand mirrors both large and small, and even broken mirrors, they jumped and bounced the sun's reflection along the streets. The strong light would penetrate darkened front rooms until the householder came out to scold the perpetrator! Unsuspecting people caught in the beam could be temporarily blinded from long distances, resulting in a thump or a clip round the ear if you were caught. Where the name Pollywash originated no-one seemed to know. As suddenly as it had begun it would stop, until a few sunny days the following summer.

A related occupation on really hot days was focusing the sun through a magnifying glass on to asphalt between the cobbles, to see who could get the largest bubble before it burst. We also had silly moments in which we saw who could have the magnifying glass focused on his wrist the longest. It was never long!

Whip and Top

This was popular when I was a young boy. There was a knack to get the top spinning. The string from the whip was placed into the groove of the top and wound round it. With a sudden jerk, by pulling the string back, you sent the top whirling across the ground. We used to draw patterns in chalk on the top, so when it spun round the colours intertwined. Some tops were shaped like a mushroom, although the best were little and fat. The narrow ones were known as jumping jacks. If you worked them properly they could leave the ground and fly up into the air. There was no shortage of red marks on legs from those who were not very proficient with the whip. When I reached the age of ten, together with my other boyhood friends, I left this game behind as being too childish. The girls carried on with it until much later.

Tiggy and Hide and Seek

We always had boundless energy and rarely seemed to sit still for more than a few seconds at a time. Certain games were tailor made to use up some of our vigour. Chasing, running and racing always provided great excitement. One such simple but energetic game was Tiggy. There was no limit on how many could play. Someone 'had it' and had to chase everyone else. Whoever was caught was tapped on the shoulder or arm and the chaser said, 'You have it'. That person then chased another. The game went on until exhaustion took over. In our area the game could spread over four or five streets.

Another game that was played through the alleyways and passages, on middens and the street was Hide and Seek. Whoever was picked as 'it' remained at 'base' and counted, eyes closed, while the other players hid. Then 'it' said, 'Ready or Not, Here I Come', and rushed off to find everyone. The other players tried to get to the base without getting tagged, for then they were 'it'. This, again, was a game that could go on for hours.

Sword Play

This was another energetic game in which we tried to emulate the films of knights in armour carrying large swords and shields, foot soldiers carrying pikes, and all the rest who made up armies of the past, pillaging and generally causing mayhem. We gathered on the streets like a vast army and formed into two separate groups. Each faced the other with an assortment of weapons – dustbin lids for shields, swords made of wood in all shapes and sizes, brush handles for the pikemen, and clothes props as lances for the knights. Some wore soldiers' steel helmets from the last war, and one lad from Talbot Street wore a German helmet, a Second World War souvenir. Anyone who wore a helmet was a knight – including me, in my black air-raid warden's hat. Catapults and bows and arrows were barred, as all the battles were close combat. At a given signal we charged directly at each other, yelling at the top of our voices: the two solid groups met in the centre with an impact similar to that of two railway engines colliding. From the mass of bodies cries of pain and 'Yield!' came forth, as some of us fared better than others in the mêlée. Pairs broke away from the main battle to fight individual contests. Then, as suddenly as it had begun, everything ceased, either because everyone had had enough or to rest, regroup and start again some minutes later. Parents were ready at home with Dettol and lint for the various wounds that occurred. We were never chastised, probably because no-one got killed: it was quite a toughening up exercise.

For much lighter sword play (fencing) we used a thin bamboo cane, around 4 feet long, which replicated both foil and rapier. This was a much more gentlemanly occupation, and films such as *The Three Musketeers* or *Scaramouche* were played out simply, without the wounds of a furious battle. We all acquired the agility of a ballerina, so it was no wonder we weren't fat.

Cowboys and Indians
In the early days of my boyhood Cowboys and Indians took pride of place in our everyday games. These were mostly played in the cobbled streets that were a far cry from the plains of Arizona. Pistols or guns were generally wooden, until the model guns that fired caps became available. Caps came in two types: single, confetti-sized pieces with a centrally enclosed bang, and in rolls – red paper strips that supported a dotted black line of successive bangs. Initially these guns were scarce and expensive and it was some time before I acquired one, a second-hand gun with a white handled grip from Trevor Clarkson, whose father had bought him a new one. Most of us, who didn't have cap guns, made the noise of a gun ourselves – and of course we never ran out of ammunition! Some of our cowboys could also make the sound of a ricochet very realistically. We ran round the streets slapping our backsides as if whipping a horse and holding make-believe reins.

The Indians had bows and arrows. These were made quite cheaply by using a garden bamboo stick 4 feet long. The string was catgut, and the arrows were again garden bamboos, about 18 inches long. To give the arrow leverage and direction we wrapped thick adhesive electrical tape to the end. These were very accurate even at long range, and those who were cowboys often ended up with body bruises and lumps on the head. We didn't fire at too close a range because of the damage the arrow could do. Using the name 'Geronimo', I practised with my bow and arrows frequently, and was known among the other Indians to be a good shot. On one occasion I fired an arrow from the corner of Durran's

Confectioners on Legrams Street at one of the cowboys on the corner of Talbot Street, a distance of around 300 yards. I took aim and hit him between the shoulder blades. He was not happy, and was also a dead cowboy! It wasn't until I went into long trousers that I finally hung up my bow and arrows.

Guiders

These were a self-made plaything that gave us great joy. Vincent and I built a couple over the years, but construction was always dependent on the materials being available. Four wheels were essential but always scarce: they were mainly old pram wheels of all sizes, and matching pairs were desirable. The largest guider we built had two large pram wheels at the rear and smaller ones at the front. Once the wheels had been obtained, small and thick planks of wood were needed for the body. The wheels at the front were screwed to a small plank that was connected to the front by a large nut and bolt, a red hot poker having been used to burn the hole for the bolt through the body and the plank. Once the wheels were secured a rope was fixed to each end of the front axle to steer the guider. An old cushion to sit on was nailed to the rear. In all, a guider took a couple of weeks to complete, most of which was spent finding the materials.

On a quiet summer afternoon our guider was ready for its trials. A large crowd of boys and girls gathered around it in the centre of Archibald Street, where our test run was to begin. I sat on the cushion to guide our machine, while Vincent was to push; as it gathered speed he would hop on the back. The distance of the run was about 500 yards, from the tarmac of Archibald Street to the cobbles of Talbot Street. I wore my old tin hat and Vincent had borrowed an old leather flying helmet. With a last-minute check and adjustments, our journey was about to begin. We had thought of making a braking system of some kind but this really was beyond our ability, so we depended on our feet. To a rousing cheer off we went, with Vincent pushing. As planned he jumped on the back, holding on to me as I struggled to keep the guider straight. We were soon whizzing along. We were laughing and really enjoying the moment when disaster struck. At the end of the tarmac road our wheels came into contact with the cobbles. The front wheels spun sideways, locked, and the guider, Vincent and I were thrown into the air. We both collided with the pavement, while the guider hit a lamppost side-on and disintegrated into an assortment of wood splinters and buckled wheels. I grazed my arm and badly bruised my hip and leg, while Vincent had similar injuries. From time to time it was suggested that we build another guider, but after only a minute's thought our answer was always the same. 'No, I don't think we'll bother.'

Snowball Fights and Sledging

While the long, mostly hot, summers were ideal for most adventures, the coming of winter was a complete contrast. Winter seemed to be colder every year, with many days of snow and dark nights that limited our play-time, although it was not unusual still to be playing out at nine o'clock. Most of the usual games could be played until darkness set in, but when it snowed the situation changed dramatically and snowball fights erupted from nowhere. In a short time hundreds of hard packed snowballs were causing devastation to one and all. The sight of them coming down from the sky was reminiscent of the English archers' flights of arrows at Agincourt. To be caught in such a barrage was a never-to-be-forgotten experience. If you stumbled, slipped or fell, then all the snowballs were concentrated on you. Large snow castles were built, using the hard-packed snow formed into blocks. After dividing into two sides, one defending the castle and the other attacking, the game commenced. Sometimes as many as fifty boys and girls bombarded each other until exhausted or the castle was destroyed. Then all the children would melt away to their homes to dry off and nurse their injuries.

One of the worse things to happen was scooping up a handful of dog muck when you were making a snowball. There was no alternative but to return home to be cleaned up. This happened to me a few times, and I have never forgotten the smell and feeling of despair of having my fingerless gloves and hands covered in dog muck.

The other winter's game was sledging. Traffic was sparse, so Archibald Street down to Talbot Street was our bobsleigh slope. When covered with snow the road was soon like a glacier. After tea loads of children of all ages gathered to take the challenge. There was no queuing, as boys or girls pushed themselves their sledge, either lying or sitting on them. The few with really good sledges took a quick right-hand turn down Great Russell Street and continued the journey to Preston Street. Then you tramped back, and headed off again. I never had a really good sledge: mine was very heavy and the iron blades weren't turned up at the end, as on the best. I encountered every cobble or stone jutting up, and if I was moving at speed I would shoot off into the snow, hit someone on their way back or at worst hit a wall.

Later the road became a death trap for the many pensioners in the area. It was not uncommon when we arrived home from school to find that someone had thrown sand or ashes from their sand bin or fire grates on to our bobsleigh run. These were wonderful nights, and we all had rosy cheeks with permanent smiles. As it got late the voices of our mothers started to call us home. Within a short time the streets were silent once again and Archibald Street glistened in the lamplight with its thick covering of ice – until the next day.

Peashooters
I especially loved the tin ones purchased for sixpence. Using the correct ammunition, brown peas purchased at Mosley's shop, these weapons could cause havoc at ranges of up to 100 yards. The best way to obtain a good shot was to fill the mouth with peas and, with an almighty blow, spread devastation all around.

Our gang once joined in a peashooter battle at the Elysian cinema at Lidget Green. The cinema resounded with the tap-tap-tap of hundreds of peas hitting lamps, the odd person and even the screen. We were soon cleared out of the cinema together with the opposition, and the confrontation carried on into Arctic Parade until our ammunition was spent. Another type of shooter weapon was a thin glass phial, purchased from Rimmingtons the chemist for a few pence. These were about 6 inches long, and the ammunition was barley. Used mostly at school, these too were popular and accurate – but the humble peashooter had the edge.

Catapults and Knives

Catapults had always been a traditional toy for boys. I had one which I had carved out of a tree branch. They were used for harmless, skilful fun, the targets often being tin cans on walls. Later an aluminium catapult could be bought for just a few shillings, but there was something about making your own catapult from wood. Most boys had knives, which they used for wood-whittling and carving initials in wood. Like the rest of my pals, I used to throw my knife at trees hoping for it to stick and quiver as I had seen in the films. Some of us carried a knife in a belt sheath. In my few years of carrying a knife I never threatened anyone with it, or was threatened.

Conkers

During the months of September and October conkers from horse chestnut trees became available. The usual method to find a good one was to stand under the tree and throw sticks up into the branches, hoping this would dislodge the ripe fruit. Sometimes we climbed the trees, crawled along the branches and tried to shake them down. There was an element of danger to this, but it was all part of the fun and had its appeal. There were quite a few ways to make your conker harder, usually involving a week's soaking in vinegar and several hours of slow baking in the oven, then leaving them in the drying cupboard wrapped in a cloth bag for a year or two.

The game was simple to set up: all that was needed was a piece of cheap string threaded through your conker. There were many rules and many ways to cheat. As far as I was concerned, if I had a conker that had beaten others and was a champion, it wasn't long before it would be split into many pieces by a good accurate bash from my opponent. Well, there was always next year, and perhaps the conkers from the oven would be ready.

Only Joking

There was much harmless fun to be had from a range of intriguing items, tailor made for schoolboy misbehaviour. Stink bombs were always a favourite: they were small glass spheres that contained liquid with a putrid smell not unlike bad eggs. These were generally let off in public places, picture houses, department stores, shops and so on. Our speciality was to place one under the leg of a light chair. This booby trap worked when some unsuspecting person sat on the chair, by which time we were long gone! Itching powder could be obtained at the local joke shop, but we could make our own by cutting open a wild rosehip bud. Inside was a white hair substance, almost like cotton wool, that covered the seeds: it was devastating to friends and foe alike.

Many other jokes included black face soap, severed fingers, trick daggers, joke black eyes, sneezing powder and cigarette stinkeroos. In some cases a good clout or punch was given by those who thought our mischief were unfunny.

Songs

We sang constantly, but where these songs and chants came from no one seemed to know. From Clayton to Tyersal, Rooley Lane to Girlington, most boys and girls knew these particular Yorkshire chants. Some were rude, insulting or just childish lavatorial humour. Among them were:

> Old Mother Riley went to Bierley on the Bierley bus.
> The bus bumped, she trumped, on the Bierley bus.

Why Bierley and Old Mother Riley I never knew. Another example of this crude humour was:

> Ice cream, a penny a lump,
> The more you eat, the more you trump!

From Snow White and the Seven Dwarfs we sang:

> Hi Ho, Hi Ho,
> It's off to work we go.
> With a shovel and a pick and a rhubarb stick
> Hi Ho, Hi Ho

During the war we youngsters had other words for this ditty:

> Hi Ho, Hi Ho,
> It's off to work we go.
> We fight the Japs, the Dirty Rats,
> Hi Ho, Hi Ho.

Adolf Hitler was also included, and across the playground could be heard:

> Hitler, he only had one ball,
> The other is in the Leeds Town Hall.
> Himmler had something similar,
> But poor old Goebbels had no balls at all.

213

A good smack on the back of the head was forthcoming if a teacher heard you singing this wartime rendition. One obscure chant that was mostly sang by the girls was:

Eena meena mina mo,
Put a baby on the 'Po'.
When it's done, wipe its bum.
Eena meena mina mo.

There were also many rituals used to choose people to start games like tiggy, and many others. Again, where these ideas came from is lost in the past. One example is:

Dip dip, my blue ship,
sailing on the water like a cup and saucer,
and you do not have it, O, U, T spells out.

Another:

One two three four five,
Once I caught a fish alive.
Why did you let it go?
Because it bit my finger so.
One, two, three, four, five, Out!

There were many others, but perhaps the most popular was:

One potato, two potato, three potato, four.
Five potato, six potato, seven potato more.

This particular rhyme was chanted as clenched upturned fists tapped on the other player's fist.

If a game required volunteers, cries of 'ferry', this meaning first, and 'seccy', meaning second, were shouted out by the players.

Handstands
In between all these adventures of games and playing out, we took time to watch the girls doing handstands, usually in the passages, but also against the walls of the air-raid shelters and in the playgrounds of the schools. The public air-raid shelters on the streets were not demolished until well after the war and were a useful playground for adventurous children like ourselves. They had a murky interior and were dank and evil-smelling (mostly of urine) and spongy with

mildew. They put their hands on the ground, about a foot away from the wall, and kicked their legs backwards and upwards. Their dresses or skirts were tucked into their navy blue knickers legs before performing this exercise. Once the performance had been completed the knickers were on full view, much to the amusement of the onlookers (mostly gawping lads). I don't think some parents approved, but I never heard any of the boys complaining.

Cycling

It was little wonder that most girls and boys of that time were extremely fit. Almost all of us had thin wiry bodies and could run everywhere like whippets without the slightest hint of being out of breath. If that was not enough, there were bicycles – which for a while took over our young lives.

For my twelfth birthday my parents bought me a new 'sit up and beg'-style Hercules bicycle. I was never a good cyclist, and my furthest journeys were back and forth to my grandparents in Princeville. Vincent had a drop-handlebar cycle and was much more adventurous than me, going off for the day with some of the other lads. A common question for cyclists was 'Have you done Hollins Hill'? The challenge was to cycle up the long 1½ miles of the hill between Baildon and Guiseley to the top without stopping. It could be done, but not by me. For one thing my bike didn't have a three speed gear; most of the others, including Vincent's, had Sturmey-Archer or derailleur gears, which made the climb up the Hollins Hill gradient much easier.

My weekly journeys only covered about 2 miles, but like my friends I kept the bike clean, oiling it, keeping the chain tight and changing the brake blocks. I could even mend a puncture with the tools and materials that I kept in a small leather bag attached to the rear of the seat. The bag, my pump and sometimes my front and rear lamps were always left on the bike, with no thought that they would be stolen. I knew as time went on that I would be no Reg Harris (of international cycle fame).

One Sunday morning I decided to cycle to church. It was wet and damp as I cycled down Preston Street towards Thornton Road. When I applied the rear brakes the bicycle just carried on over the wet cobbles. As I slid across Thornton Road I just missed being hit by a large black Wolseley police car that was proceeding up towards Girlington, with its bell ringing. It swerved and mounted the pavement on the opposite side of the road, and hit the corner of a building with a loud smash. In the meantime I had slid to the other side of the road and hit the pavement. My front wheel buckled and I was thrown off into the gutter, which was full of water and dirt. Two policemen were soon at my side, asking if I was injured. I wasn't even bruised, just dirty and wet from the water in the gutter. When they saw this they had a right go at me, including the foulest language my young ears had ever heard. When they calmed down they picked up my bike and took me to their car, which was still on the pavement minus one

The *Bradford Telegraph and Argus* **Nignog** **badge.** *(By kind permission of the Bradford Telegraph and Argus)*

large headlamp and a bumper. One of the policemen used the car radio to report what had happened, with the sound of the emergency bell on the police car still ringing out. Whatever emergency they were going to it had definitely been curtailed by this lad. They bundled my bike into the boot and drove me the few hundred yards to my home, where two very annoyed policemen and one scruffy wet boy arrived five minutes later. Both policemen were very polite to my mum, of course, but said I could do with some lessons on how to ride a bike safely! They had to make a report out, more for the damaged police vehicle than me. It was only when I was older that I could imagine the shock they must have had when they just missed killing or injuring a thirteen year old. My mum chastised me when they had gone, but there was a hint of relief in her voice; for once her temper was subdued. Later the Chief Constable of Bradford sent a letter to my parents enquiring how I was, and telling me to be more careful in the future. He even suggested that I join the Nignog Cycle Club.

The Nignogs had nothing to do with race. I always thought that the character on the badge was an elf or an imp, but it turns out that Nig and Nog were moonbeams. It was the use of this word in the ITV sitcom *Love thy Neighbour* that hijacked an innocent word. Since then it has been out of bounds!

The Nignog Club was organised by the *Telegraph and Argus* in the 1930s. Over the years the club had grown to have over 40,000 members. There were sports, cycling and rambling groups, and even one for would-be actors and singers who performed each year at the Alhambra Theatre in the annual Nignog Revue. I had almost decided to pack in the cycling lark when we received the Chief Constable's letter. I thought I would give it a go, and joined the Nignog cycle club, receiving the Nignog brass enamelled badge with the letters B,T and A (*Bradford Telegraph and Argus* Nignog Club). In the centre of this was the moonbeam. My membership number was 3019.

A boy and his bike. I never went far. As John Harrison, a little older than me, said,
'You should keep your bike in a bloody glass case!' My dad ended up using the bike
to and from work. *(Author's collection)*

I went along on a few Saturday afternoons. The cycle journeys were to outlying districts, and once I went as far as Poole in Wharfedale, a long way for me. The adult leader went on with the pack, while another adult dealt with the stragglers, and punctures at the rear. After only a few weeks and a few outings I decided I had had enough; it was not for me. My Hercules bicycle was used by my dad to get to work at Stroud, Riley in Frizinghall: he had been a keen cyclist in his younger days, but his younger son didn't take after him. I didn't miss the bike as I preferred to walk or get the bus, and I think my reservations dated back to that confrontation with the police car on Thornton Road. My mother was also glad I was no longer interested. Although the bike was still kept in the scullery it was my dad who now got the blame for it. 'There's oil all over that floor again from that damn bike!'

Chumping

With the cold winter months in October rolling in, it was dark well before six o'clock in the evening. The streets were wet and damp, and a cold east wind blew down the streets and through the passages. Inside our house the coal fire in the hearth flickered and glowed from the back draught of wind blowing down the chimney. But for me, Vincent and the rest of my mates it was a happy time, as it was the lead-up to an exciting few weeks of chumping, Mischief Night and Bonfire Night on 5 November. Until 1959 it was illegal in England not to celebrate the date of Guy Fawkes's arrest. As youngsters we all knew the story of Guy Fawkes, although to us it was just a time to let off fireworks, have a big street fire and generally have a good time. Guy Fawkes was a Catholic, so was I and so were many neighbours, but although the Catholic Church in England frowned upon the burning of an effigy of Guy Fawkes no one seemed to take it personally.

Chumping, as we called it in Listerhills (although in some other parts of Bradford it was called progging), was the collecting of old wood and furniture weeks before Bonfire Night. My first real involvement in this was when I was nine in 1947, when Bonfire Night was officially restored. Throughout the Second World War there had been no plot nights, the main reasons being the black-out and the lack of fireworks in the shops.

Although chumping had no set date, we started collecting around the beginning of October. Most streets in our area had bonfires, which meant much fuel had to be collected. First a storage place had to be found: ours was down most passages in Legrams Street which, being under cover, kept everything dry. Parents and neighbours never seemed to object, and the passages soon filled up from end to end as Bonfire Night approached.

Most of my friends lived in other streets, so – for example – Vincent Davey, Jacky Robinson and Trevor Clarkson who lived in Great Russell Street chumped together, while I chumped with Geoffrey Peel, Brian Rigby, John Harrison and others who lived on Legrams Street. It was a good arrangement, and codes of conduct were established so that on Plot Night we could visit and take part in other streets' fires. It was also agreed that we wouldn't raid and pinch each others' chumps – although raiding other streets' precious piles out of area was considered fair game. For weeks up to Plot Night gangs of boys and youths were to be seen marauding up and down roads and streets intent on wrecking, setting light to or, the main objective, pinching the piles of chumps. Our non-pinching pact was rarely broken, so our main rivals were the Longside Lane gang. The Canterbury Warriors, thank goodness, were some distance away, and we wouldn't have dared approach their area! There was hell played with the Longside Lane gang on some nights, as running battles took place. It was all right pinching chumps, but once they had been pinched they had to be carried over long distances, with rival gangs having a go at us all the way home. Some large items were suddenly dropped and left, as we exhausted thieves scurried back to our area. I went on a few of these raids over the years, but was always scared stiff. I don't really know why, as I can't remember anyone really getting hurt. The next day rival gang members who attended the same schools were good pals; it was only for a few weeks that when night fell war was declared. Many times I sat on our midden on guard, as we called it, watching over the ever-growing pile, as similar scenes took place on other middens; we communicated with each other with torches. Sometimes when it was cold I thought of sneaking back into the house, but I would have lost face, and would have been missed if no reply had come from my torch. I was lucky: at the side of our toilets overlooking the midden was a large gas lamp, which gave ample light over the chumps. Sometimes my mum came out and asked if I was warm enough, or said 'You should be in bed'. But she knew this was a ritual and, in a way, was proud of me. At about nine o'clock we all went indoors, a few shouts of 'So long' echoing down the streets and passages. Then everything fell silent.

Even a youngster I was amazed at the amount of chumps that we collected each year. There were always upright pianos, settees, three piece suites, sofas, old chairs, sideboards, wardrobes, doors, buffets, carpets, lino and mattresses. It was a time to clear out all unwanted household rubbish, as long as it would burn. One time four of us went down to the coaly, the railway goods yard depot, and procured a railway sleeper. It took us all day to drag it up from the depot through John Willie North's Field and into Legrams Street. Not surprisingly we had to get a couple of adults to help us. The large wicker baskets called 'skeps', which were used for moving bobbins around the mills, in particular John Smith's in Preston Street where my dad worked, were always at a premium and much prized, not only for burning but for sitting on round the fire. They were always the last item to be put on the fire.

Mischief Night

Only one other date had to be observed before Plot Night, and that was Mischief Night on 4 November. I used to look forward to this, and Vincent and I made our presence felt. Like chumping, Mischief Night in our area also had set rules, the most important one being that we didn't upset old people and the infirm; we also didn't do anything to upset pets, and didn't use any fireworks (especially bangers). Our disguise on these nights was the good old balaclava, although constant use and sweating under it in the cold always caused chapped noses and chins. It kept us from being identified, though. Most adults turned off their lights to give the impression that no-one was home, but if you put your ear to the letter-box you could sometimes hear the wireless, a dead giveaway. We used to target the people we didn't like, or who had caused us problems during the year. One such person was Fanny Hardaker, who had the shop at the corner of our street. Although she was good to me, with under-the-counter cigarettes for my mum, each winter when it snowed she put hot ashes from her fire on the surface of Archibald Street where we had our sledging runs; just as we had got a good sledging surface, out she came with the ashes. She was always on our list. Nothing too drastic: tapping on her windows, tying tin cans to her doorknob and then knocking on the door, which made a loud noise when she opened the door to our knock – all repeated a few times. There were many things we did on that night of lawlessness, although some were a little bizarre. Householders' front doors were repeatedly assaulted with bogus calls, gates were removed, dustbin lids were hoisted up lampposts, windows were daubed with paint, doorknobs coated with treacle, evening newspapers (projecting from letterboxes) exchanged, house numbers unscrewed and fixed on to other houses, and backyards were turned upside down and ransacked. Perhaps a little more dangerous, we stuffed paper up the old iron drainpipes and set it alight. What could be more fun than Mischievous Night!

Plot Night

The finale of the previous few weeks was 5 November. My first full-blown Plot Night in 1947 was the only time that Legrams Street combined with top Great Russell Street: fuel was short that year, so the streets were brought together. Great Russell Street still had a long air-raid shelter down its centre, and the top of it was a good vantage point to observe the fire. I had purchased a small half crown box of Standard fireworks, but was annoyed as most were let off by adults – although I enjoyed sitting on top of the air-raid shelter with Vincent and his older sisters, Eileen, Stella and Evelyn. For the next few years, though, my Plot Night was different – as I made plans each year, saving my money for my own fireworks. Most shops had them on display, and there was no age restriction. You could buy as many as you could afford. I wasn't interested in boxes of fireworks as you were paying for the packaging, so I went for loose bangers. Little Demons cost only ½*d* each: for half a crown I could buy sixty. I supplemented these with other bangers, little imps, mighty atoms, cannons, squibs and, my favourite for dropping near girls, the rip-rap, which exploded and jumped around five or six times, causing havoc.

Legrams Street Bonfire Night was always an occasion, All the usual suspects took part: Brian Rigby, Geoffrey Peel, John Harrison and the Creswells, Padgetts, Guilfoyles, Stewarts, Richardsons, Newells, Hodgsons, Glossops, and many other neighbours. The building of the bonfire started after a quick tea when we got home from school at about 4.30pm. All the chumps were dragged out of the passages and piled high on the pavements. Old chairs, settees, sofas and the skips were strategically placed so people could sit close to the fire. As soon as everything was in place an adult lit the bonfire and, accompanied by a big cheer, the whole street lit up as flames and sparks rose high into the dark sky. Then the fireworks began, with lots of individual displays: catherine wheels impaled on gateposts, Roman candles popping like mortars in the air, and rockets of all sizes whooshing and disappearing from milk bottles with a few starbursts of many colours. All this was supplemented by bangs and louder bangs as the bangers were let off among the girls and women, causing screams more of delight than annoyance. As time went on Mr Padgett brought out his accordion, and as there was always a piano in the chumps someone played it before it departed into the fire. When the music started everyone sang the hit songs of the time, and oldies like 'Roll out the Barrel'. Pies and peas, gingerbread and potatoes were made available to everyone, as well as parkin pigs, plot toffee and jugs of beer from North's off-licence shop on Archibald Street. If you wished you could roast your own potatoes in the fire, though this was not for the faint-hearted. Putting the potato into the fire was easy, with a quick throw, but to retrieve it you had to rush forward and use a long stick to scoop it out, all the while with heat as from a blast furnace on your face and clothing. Sometimes the burning wood collapsed on to the potato and it was lost. Time to try again. Those potatoes were always worth the effort and the near burning to death: with a dash of salt they tasted so nice in the cold November air.

Once the fire had been lit I went back into the house to dress myself for the occasion. As it was winter I had to wrap up, and in the early days I still had short trousers so it was cold. With old pullovers, an old jacket, raincoat and my balaclava, I was soon wrapped up and ready for anything. I had already laid my fireworks (all bangers) out at the top of the cellar steps for safety. I never took them all, probably about twenty, in my trouser pockets to start with: I had heard the joke about 'The Boy stood on the Burning Deck'. Dressed and armed like a Royal Marine commando, I waited for the knock on the door. When it came it was Vincent, dressed the same and ready for action. Two other pieces of equipment were needed. One was mill-band, which my dad brought from work. It was old rope that had been in contact with oil in the mill over many years, which was ideal for lighting fireworks because it just smouldered, and when you blew it a red glow emerged. It was also good to swing around in the dark and make patterns with. The other essential item of equipment was a jam jar with a lit candle inside, held by a string handle. This was needed in dark passages to see how many bangers we had left. Out we went to mix with the revellers, pausing here and there to light and drop a couple of bangers in a skep that girls were sitting on, or throw a rip-rap into a group of girls and watch as it appeared to chase them around; it always seemed that rip-raps followed the victim. We saw no danger in lighting fireworks in our hands with the mill-band, watching the fuse fizz and then throwing it, but it was always at people's feet, never at their bodies or faces. Injuries were few, although from time to time someone could be hurt as some idiots put lighted bangers in jam jars with devastating effect. The only accident that I had was when I threw a banger. I had lit the blue touchpaper and waited for it to fizz before I threw it, but it exploded in my hand first and the fuse went sailing, fizzing, through the air. Own goal! My hand was jarred and numb for about an hour. Luckily I had been wearing a old pair of my dad's leather gloves, otherwise I would have had a problem. It was a Brocks firework, which rather put me off them. From then on I stuck with Lion or Standard Fireworks.

From time to time we went to our respective houses to replenish stocks, until we had none left. Then we sat around the fire, unless it was windy in which case you were forever moving away from the sparks, dodging from one side of the fire to the other. It was nice to sit with the older people and listen to their stories; it had always been better in their day. Some were a little worse for wear with the beer, but everybody was so nice that it seemed tranquil, and no one swore or fought. Even my mum came out to sit with our neighbour Lucy, outside their house facing the fire, drinking a small whisky and having the odd Woodbine. My dad sometimes popped out to see how my mum was, but not for too long, as he said 'I've heard enough bangs', referring to his wartime experiences.

One old character Mr Sugden always joined everyone at the fire at nine o'clock or so. There was always a seat made for him, and the ladies fussed around, giving him pie and peas and keeping the old drinking tankard he carried filled with beer. He was in his nineties and lived alone at the corner house in our street. We used to try to sit near him, as through the crackle of the fire he told us of the time he was a soldier with Lord Kitchener's army at Khartoum fighting the fuzzie-wuzzies, the name given by Rudyard Kipling to the Sudanese tribe who fought back in the face of superior British Army firepower in the Sudan, especially at Omdurman in 1898. We boys had seen films like *The Four Feathers*, so he was a hero to us. After about an hour he departed, his way of saying goodnight being to sing two verses of 'We're Soldiers of the Queen'. This always left a few people, both young and old, in tears, including my mum.

As it got late people started to drift home, laughing and singing. The settees, chairs and skeps had all gone, which meant there was nowhere to sit except the walls outside the front houses. Vincent headed off across the street to his home and I did the same. With bloodshot eyes, blackened faces and clothes that reeked of fire and mill-band, we said our 'so-longs, see you tomorrow', and another Bonfire Night was over for another year.

The mornings after were always the same: cold, damp, sometimes raining and misty, and with a smell of fire and pyrotechnics in the air. The first thing I looked for on the way to school was our fire, which was always still smouldering, ash filled with springs from chairs and settees, nuts and bolts from wood parts and pianos. All around the streets were spent fireworks, and even some that had not gone off – which we put in our pockets and tried to set off later. A trail of debris led through the streets all the way to school.

On our return from school it was a different story: the street was clean, with no signs of spent fireworks, and where the fire had been there were just black marks on the cobbles, the marker for the next year's bonfire. All our mothers had swept and cleaned the street while husbands were at work and the children were at school. Such was the pride in our street.

Pocket Money Jobs

Fortunately small boys no longer had to crawl up inside blackened chimneys to earn extra coppers, so their families could spread dripping on a stale slice of bread. We were not poor, but pocket money jobs were common with most youngsters of the time. To supplement my 1s 6d spending money, earning an extra copper was a priority. While 1s 6d wasn't a lot of money I was grateful for it, and I was further subsidised by my parents with other treats.

One of my first jobs was recycling glass. At this time glass bottles were mostly recycled: milk bottles were returned via the doorstep to the milkman; lemonade and other soft-drink bottles were returned to the shop from which they had been bought; and beer bottles went back to the pub, sometimes encouraged by a refundable deposit. My pal Vincent and I decided that jam jars were being overlooked because they were thought not to be worth the ½d return, but we thought differently. Night calls were always the best, as most people were in. Off we went with a large sack, to knock on the house doors and shout 'Any old jam jars, please.' We knew that most shops wouldn't accept them if they were chipped, cracked, or dirty, and although most householders did wash them out in some cases they were too dirty. Even if they couldn't be cleaned we still accepted them, and disposed of them later. If we refused we would have been thought to be too particular, and it would have been difficult to call back on a later occasion. It was quite a lucrative job, although it was hard work trudging around the streets, especially in winter with snow flurries and the wind howling through the gas lamps. We must have looked like two Dickensian characters, carrying a large sack, with the sound of

Lower Archibald Street. At the house to bottom left lived Miss Carter, whose father had been killed in the Crimean War (1854–56). *(Author's collection)*

glass on glass echoing along the dim streets into the night. It was a very large sack, so we had to place our jars in it very carefully so we didn't break them. We took turns carrying the sack, which got heavier as the night went on, although sometimes we lost several jars in a confrontation with stone paving slabs, resulting in a loss of earnings of 1 or 2*d* each. When the sack got too heavy we took the sack home and placed it in the air-raid shelter, to sort out and clean all the jars for disposal the next day. This took time. Many shops had to be visited, because not all stocked the jam jars we had on offer. 'That's not ours, and neither is that one,' shopkeepers exclaimed before we finally emptied the sack. It was no secret what we wanted the jars for, and people had been very generous in giving them to us. But all good things come to an end – and when we had been going for some months it became obvious that other lads had cottoned on. Too many lads were chasing the same jam jars, which put an end to our enterprise. We had averaged about 3*s* a load, 1*s* 6*d* each. It was good while it lasted.

A little later, through a friend of my mum's, I was asked if I could do a weekly shop for an old lady on Friday when I had finished school. Miss Carter was a spinster who lived on her own in a front back-to-back house where Talbot Street joined Archibald Street. This was in 1948; I was aged ten, she was ninety-four. She still dressed in Victorian attire: her dress to the floor and buttoned at the top in a choker round the neck, finished off with a large gold brooch in which her mother's hair was plaited. She had been a child, teenager and an adult before the end of the nineteenth century! Her house was cold, with drapes and thick curtains to limit the draughts. Like our house it had a Yorkshire range, where something always seemed to be on the boil. The house was dark, the only light coming from a lone gaslight set in the ceiling. It should have been converted to electricity, but she didn't like it – calling it 'the devil's torch'. I was always reminded of Pip in Charles Dickens's *Great Expectations*, and Miss Havisham's house – although Miss Carter's was smaller and on a less grand scale. But I had no need to worry. She was a lovely lady, and for the short time that I did her shopping she told me many things of her past. Aged ten, I was very receptive. Even today I can remember most of our conversations.

Miss Carter's father had been killed in the Crimean War (1854–56). Her mother was pregnant with her when he died. She had also had a brother and sister, whom she never knew as they died before she was born. Her mother had come to Bradford from Lincolnshire with her husband, who at that time was a recruiting sergeant with a local regiment. After his death her mother went back to Lincolnshire with her daughter. When her mother died Miss Carter came back to the Bradford area, working in domestic service and rising to be head housekeeper for one of Yorkshire's wool magnates. On retirement she was given a small annuity from the family, and the house where she now lived was purchased for her. She told me when she was young and naughty her mother would say that Spring-Heeled Jack, a character from Victorian folklore, would come for her if she didn't behave. (Later, in my grandmother Lily's childhood, the threat was Charley Peace – a prolific burglar and disguise artist, hanged in Armley gaol for the murder of two policemen.)

Miss Carter was not infirm but really quite agile, although she never went out much and didn't like callers. The only time she went out was in the evenings (in all weathers), wearing a large shawl and carrying a small jug. She walked two streets to John Willie North's off-licence on the corner of Archibald Street and Legrams Terrace, and came away with the jug filled with ale, a cover discreetly placed over the top. Every night the same scene took place all around the streets, with many old ladies scurrying to and from off-licences carrying their jugs of ale.

On my return with her shopping she always said, 'Here's a florin for you.' This, *2s*, was a lot of money for such an easy task: I never came back with more than one bag full of groceries.

In 1949 my links with mid-Victorian England closed when Miss Carter passed away. I remember being upset, for she had made such an impression on me. She always said my blue eyes reminded her of someone close when she was a young girl. I never knew her Christian name and often wondered what it was, and what she was like at my age – when they still had public hanging and transportation. Miss Carter was ten in 1864, and public hanging and transportation were abolished in 1868.

Probably one of the best paid jobs for a youngster in Listerhills was collecting pig swill for a farm in Allerton. This was run by Lilly and Fred Hurst, who also had the local milk round which covered most households in our area and other districts towards Allerton. Lilly was a lovely bubbly lady who called every morning at our house, rain or shine, to supply the milk; this was served in the old-fashioned way, from a large pail with two ladles measuring a gill and a pint hanging from the side. The churns she used to refill the ladles were kept in a yard in Archibald Street. Lilly was well known for her remedies for many childhood ailments that were prevalent, one of her many talents being the use of poultices – the effectiveness of which I can vouch for.

The farm had a lot of pigs, and the best and cheapest way to feed them was with swill – which was anything edible: food scraps, leftovers, potato peelings, cabbage, carrots; in fact any edible food, new or mouldy. The pigs were not fussy! Swill was collected from local households, the best times being Saturday and Sunday mornings, when meals were being prepared for the weekend. Most people left any unwanted food wrapped in newspaper on the outside scullery windowsill, but if nothing was there a shout of 'Any swill please' was still made, just in case the householder had forgotten or was still preparing the Saturday or Sunday lunch.

Trevor Clarkson, my pal who lived on Great Russell Street, had the franchise for this sought-after job. I believe that Lilly and Fred had had a son who died quite young, and it was probably this that made them close and attentive to most of the lads round our area, especially Trevor, who earlier had lost his father to a heart attack. When Trevor couldn't take the swill I was asked. I never thought of saying no, even though it meant missing the Gaumont British Junior Club on Saturday and going to an early Mass on Sunday morning. Ten o'clock was the time to start, as I had a large area to cover of over two over hundred houses. Beginning at the top of Shearbridge Road, I went down all the streets to Talbot Street, over to Preston Street, up Edinburgh Street, and then St Andrews Villas. The call was, 'Any swill please!' The journey took at least two and half hours. Each time a sack was full, or was too heavy, I had to go back to collect a new one. If it was raining the sack not only got wet but heavier, and each time I swung it on my back I could feel the soggy mess penetrating my coat down to my shirt. And then there was beetroot! I hated beetroot! If it was a wet day this marked through down to my skin, and I went home looking as if I had been in an accident. Sometimes the bath had to come out, and it wasn't even Friday! But there the problems ended, as Lilly always paid 10s, quite a sum for two mornings' work. I was rich! I always gave my mum 2s 6d, which she accepted with the smile of a mother who sees her son about to grow up.

Collecting

When I was young all boys were fascinated by collecting. My first collection, thanks to my interest in history, was coins, which in those days could be expensive. Our shillings and pence contained portraits of monarchs from Queen Victoria up to our present king, George VI: although many years old and much worn, they were all still legal tender. I had often wondered when fingering an old Victorian coin who, famous or infamous, might have had that same coin in their hands. I was about eight when I started collecting Victorian 'bun pennies'. This name refers to the new bronze coins circulated from 1860 to 1894, which used a new portrait of Queen Victoria wearing her hair in a bun. My friends and I didn't consider collecting silver coins, as we needed them to spend. After a while I had built up quite a collection, mostly from everyday change, totalling about fifty pennies: in monetary terms these were worth 5s; to a collector they were worth about 5s – not much progress!

I read a few books on coin collecting that showed different conditions and grades, but it all seemed a bit complicated – although like all new boy collectors I would have liked to have found the rare 1933 penny. (This is one of the great rarities. None were issued for general circulation, but seven were made: three proofs to place in foundation stones laid by King George V and four currency issues.) Having read all these books I lost interest and spent the 5s! I was about to give up coin collecting altogether when I passed a small antique shop with dirty windows as I walked home from school along City Road. I had a look through the window, and caught sight of a small copper bowl containing some old coins. On impulse I went in, and a large bell on the door rang out to let the proprietor know he had a customer. He was a Dickensian character with a large hooked nose, unshaven, wearing a top hat and smoking a clay pipe. Being eight years old and used to seeing such characters I wasn't perturbed, although the last person I had seen smoking a clay pipe was a woman! When I asked to see the coins he sniffed, reluctantly took the bowl with the coins from the window and pushed it under my nose. Among the many 'bun pennies' and foreign coins one particular coin stood out, it was a large heavy copper coin. I picked it out, and saw the head of what I thought was a Roman emperor. 'How much is the Roman coin, please?' I asked. The clay pipe-smoking character suddenly came to life and almost shouted, 'Roman coin? Roman coin? That's a cartwheel penny and your Roman emperor is George III.' He went on to explain what a cartwheel penny was, and explained its name had come about because of its size and weight. I listened and found it really interesting; and then he gave me an old book on coin collecting for beginners. My cartwheel penny cost me 6d. After I had read the book from end to end and progressed to other more detailed books, I gained quite a reputation for coin collecting over the next few years. I also gained a nice coin collection.

All this came about on a chance visit to that shop and meeting the man with the clay pipe. Each week I'd call in, to be greeted with 'Hello, Mr Cartwheel Penny'. Over that time I bought many coins from him, including more cartwheel pennies. Sadly he passed away not long after I had left school. He was a character and also a friend, to whom I was always grateful for reviving my interest in coins.

It was my interest in history that was probably the reason I became interested in stamp collecting as well. Those tiny pieces of gummed paper always had a bit of history to them.

Stamp collecting was an ideal hobby when we were young. Our curiosity was aroused by the very nature of the images depicted, for example sport, animals, flowers, ships, planes and, of course, the heads of monarchs, presidents, prime ministers and dictators. The unusual words, giving the currency value of the stamp and country of issue were also fascinating. Stamps taught us about culture, language, history and so much more, without us even realising that we were learning. Another benefit was that like coins they took up little space.

I started a stamp collection when I was collecting coins. After collecting general world stamps for a while I decided to focus on British stamps, and soon acquired a good collection of early Victorian examples, including penny blacks, penny reds and twopenny blues, some even valued at 10s or £1.

The stamp shop C. Clark's, close to Sykes and Sutcliffe's at the bottom of Westgate, was where we called for stamp-hinges, tweezers and loose pages for our stamp albums. It was dark inside the shop and we were always served (reluctantly, or so it seemed) by an elderly gentleman who was the proprietor. He didn't seem to have much time for us, considering that lots of boys like me spent our pocket money at his shop.

We seem to have taught ourselves the value of the stamps we collected. I learnt quite a lot from a pre-war (1935) Stanley Gibbon's catalogue that I had been given, even though it was a few years out of date. It was recognised as the Bible of stamp collectors, and even my old copy was scarce. All the time I was collecting I never had, or even saw, an up-to-date Stanley Gibbon's catalogue, only the pre-war issues. The hobby was quite complicated, with all the myriad differences that could exist regarding paper, watermarks, method of printing, printers, shade and type of ink, perforation, gumming, usage, franking marks and, of course, rarity and value.

It was Mr Barren (known to us as 'Hooky' Barren) at his pawn and antique shop near the old Theatre Royal on Manningham Lane who put me on to British Victorian stamps. I usually called in to look for stamps and coins. One day he showed me an old album with page upon page of many different types of these early stamps. Having the collector's bug I asked him how much the album was. To be fair he didn't say I couldn't afford it, but offered it to me at £4 10s, a large sum for a boy of twelve in 1950. Cheekily I asked if he would hold on to it for a couple of days so I could work out what I could afford, and also consult my parents. He said he would. At this time I was on the swill round on Saturdays and Sundays, and was earning 10s each week. I had £3 saved up for the holidays, and other things I could probably do without. My parents, as usual, said it was my money to do what I wanted with, and no objection was given, although I'm sure my dad called me a flat-cake as usual. They loaned me £1 10s to make up the amount I needed, and I paid them back with my swill money.

In 1950, when I was on holiday with St Patrick's Choir at Staithes, we paid a visit to Runswick Bay. Like Staithes it was not commercialised, and epitomised villages that hadn't changed for hundreds of years. On a hill in the small harbour was a beacon filled with wood, to be lit if ships came too close to the shore in bad weather and also in winter when the fishing boats returned to the harbour. On exploring this beacon I noticed, among the newspapers and other paper used to light it, hundreds of old Victorian letters in envelopes with beautiful copperplate handwriting. But what caught my eye were the stamps on the envelopes, mostly Victorian: penny blacks, twopenny blues and many penny reds, a real Aladdin's cave for a stamp collector like me. I started to collect as many as I could, and must have gathered about two hundred, all dry, in good condition and looking as if they hadn't been outside for long. But as I started to pack them away in my haversack Leo Muff, the choirmaster, came along and told me to put them back as they could be full of germs. I took some asking before I reluctantly replaced them. From that day on I never liked him, and I think the feeling was mutual. In those days such stamps on original envelopes could be quite valuable.

Stamp collectors had the stamp equivalent to the rare 1933 penny, which we boys could dream of finding. This was the British Guiana rarity found by a twelve-year-old boy in 1873, the only one in existence: in 1950 it was in a private collection and worth thousands of pounds. A tale was told to gullible young collectors like us that another British Guiana stamp had been found later, and the collector who had the original bought it and burnt it, so as to keep the rarity of his original stamp. Suffice it to say I never found one. Not many years later, when I finally finished with stamp collecting, I sold the album that I had invested £4 10s in and made a large profit, thanks to my parents and, of course, 'Hooky' Barren.

There were many other collecting fads at this time, some of which I dabbled in and some I left alone, like matchbox labels, cigarette packets and taking down car registration numbers – which never interested me. Standing on the roadside writing car numbers in a book was soon boring: I tried just once. Although trainspotting was perhaps more interesting than car numbers, our nearest railway was the city goods yard depot, with mostly shunting engines – so there wasn't much chance of seeing the *Flying Scotsman* down there.

A 'must' for all trainspotters was Ian Allan's ABC: a handy pocket-size book containing a complete listing of all locomotive numbers and their classes. Ian

Allan eventually brought out an ABC range for buses, coaches, cars, planes and just about anything that moved. The volume I became interested in was for British Road Services (BRS) lorries, which went the length and breadth of the country delivering all kinds of goods to industry. At the top of Archibald Street, around the corner in Legrams Lane, was a BRS depot (formerly Holdsworth and Burrill's Transport). Because of this depot and another on Water Lane, off Thornton Road, I ticked off many numbers in my Ian Allan *ABC for British Road Services*. One of the first numbers I collected was a lorry with 'A6 Bermondsey' on the side. I didn't know where Bermondsey was, but soon found out: another learning curve, and all down to the wonderful hobby of collecting!

Girls
We were all aware that boys and girls were different, and the fact that our parents took great care to try and conceal those differences guaranteed that they were well known to all of us. Most of us had only the vaguest idea why those differences existed, as most parents were not forthcoming in developing our understanding. What information I had was acquired informally from my peers at school; for parents or teachers to discuss such issues was unusual. I cannot remember any boy saying that he had received any instruction on this matter from his parents, and certainly neither of my parents had any meaningful conversation with me regarding procreation or the problems associated with romance and sex. It was my mum who suggested a book relating to the 'birds and the bees', and when I replied that I had been taught the facts of life at school I saw the look of relief on her face.

I can't have been that shy of girls as I tried to kiss my first love, Teresa Doherty, in the famous demarcation-line confrontation at St Patrick's Infants' School when I was five. I had slept and bathed with my cousin Kathleen when I was a baby on visits to Auntie Cassie and Uncle Stan in Middlesbrough during and after the war, but this stopped suddenly when we were aged about six. Being completely innocent we both complained, but to no avail; the reason given was that we were too big to be bathed together.

In the infants' school there were girls that I fancied, but when I went to the boys' school, aged seven, I was in a street gang – and all members, like William Brown, took a dislike to girls, especially little girls. This was not only because we considered them silly, but also because they could cause trouble and dissent, as William experienced with the awful lisping Violet Elizabeth Bott. We tended, therefore, to look at them from afar. I think it was probably that girls were more advanced than us, and we, being dopes, didn't wish to admit it.

I fell by the wayside a few times with Jean Glossop, our next door neighbour's girl. Jean was a year younger, a pretty girl, with the hairstyle of the time, a bob, always with a coloured ribbon. Her friend was another nice-looking girl, Joan Ainsworth, who lived at no. 14. Jean always wanted to play House. She

I always fancied Sandra Sherry, but that's as far as it got. Even so, we look a charming couple on holiday in Cleethorpes. *(Author's collection)*

was the wife and I the husband; it was all purely innocent, and played to a back drop of an air-raid shelter, middens and toilets. She would say, 'I'm just going to the shops,' and would disappear along the passage with her doll's pram, returning five minutes later to scold me, shouting and pointing her finger, for not cleaning up our make-believe house in the yard. Then I had to disappear for ten minutes, come back from make-believe work and say 'Is my tea ready?' It always was, and I would eat my non-existent meal with relish. There was no kissing or cuddling (it was one of those households)! When it came to bedtime we lay side by side on a blanket facing the air-raid shelter with the doll in the middle of us. The night passed in five minutes and then it was time for me to go to work again, for the baby to be fed, and for another day similar to every other. We went through a week in an hour. Once she even put a pinny and headscarf on, and folded her arms again to let loose a tirade of remarks. I was beginning to wish she was not my wife, especially when she put her mother's curlers in her hair to make things more realistic.

We also played Doctors and Nurses. I only played the doctor once: it seems that I was struck off for a misdemeanour, and had to spend the rest of the game in the make-believe ambulance. True to form Jean played both roles, bandaging me up and telling me to go to sleep, with blankets wrapped round me and the air-raid shelter wall for a pillow. Why I went along with this play-acting I can't say: my mum treated it with indifference and my dad uttered his usual comment:

**Fellas looking for lasses and lasses looking for fellas. It was another unsuccessful talent-
spotting day for Vincent and me in Scarborough. The quiff is still in evidence!**
(Author's collection)

'flat-cake'. It all came to an end one summer's day when Trevor and Vincent called
for me and saw me pushing a pram with a doll inside. The worst part was that Jean
was wearing a turban and had linked arms with me. Suffice to say the games stopped,
but they weren't forgotten by my fellow gang members for quite some time.

In Lower Westgrove Street off Sunbridge Road lived a girl called Brenda
Dutton. I used to pass the rear of her house through a long snicket, which
divided the houses from the log yard that belonged to the local bobbin mill. I
never knew which school she went to, but each morning I looked to see if she
was coming out of the back door. Sometimes she said hello, and when she did I
always wished she was my girlfriend. I was around ten or eleven years old, and
never got beyond the greeting.

At about the same time I kept being stopped by two girls from St Patrick's
Girls' School. I was embarrassed when one of them said, of her mate, Pat
Jackson, 'She goes with you.' That innocent expression reverberated around
streets and schools at the time. This was embarrassing, for I was still not
'streetwise', and it happened a few times. On one occasion they followed me
home. As I turned to go into the house I looked back, and they were halfway
down the passage behind me. I fled into the house. My mmum asked, 'What is
it?' and of course Don Juan said, 'Two girls have followed me home from
school.' Mum replied, 'You what?' and before I could repeat it, she had grabbed

the broom from the scullery and was running up the passage, chasing my admirers along Legrams Street.

Miss Edith Gallimore, a refined lady, lived at 64 Great Russell Street and was well known as a dressmaker. Her niece, named Angela, visited her on Sundays. She was, I thought, beautiful and dressed in expensive clothes. So I fell in love with her and tried to catch her eye or say hello, but received no response. I was always treated with indifference, as Pip was by Estella in *Great Expectations*.

Rita Wilford was a really attractive girl who lived on my street and went to Grange Grammar School, but I don't think she ever looked at me twice. The nearest I ever got to being with her was on Princeville Working Men's Club trip for children to Scarborough. I saw her arrive when I was already seated on the bus, and hoped she would come and sit next to me as I was on my own. Alas, no such luck: she sat with some suave dope in front, with his hair swept back with Brylcreem; my hair was in a quiff, so I had no chance against Rudolph Valentino.

I also liked Sandra Sherry, who lived with her parents and younger sister Norma on Legrams Terrace. I saw her many times when I was playing games in the street with my friend Bobby Johnson. In 1950 my parents, brother and I had a week's holiday in Cleethorpes with Sandra's family. I was close to Sandra then, but only as friends.

I had crushes on many girls at this time, but was never courageous or lucky enough to turn longing into reality. Although I had held hands with many girls in the infants' school and later even played Postman's Knock at parties, I had never had a real girlfriend. When I left school to work for Brown, Muff's, I began to take more notice of girls – as I was now in the company of young women who no longer wore a liberty bodice. The female staff wore dresses or suits with pencil skirts, high heels or flat shoes, and nylon stockings with suspender belts. Their hairstyles were permed and styled to suit their age and times. Gone was the schoolgirl look. There were many such beauties at Brown, Muff's, whom I admired from afar. I was still shy, small, and my hairstyle was still a quiff. At staff parties I made no inroads, and like the rest of the young juniors I stood against the wall, where we dared each other to ask some girl to dance. I always admired those who could do this as if it was second nature. In fact some of the ugliest male juniors seemed to have the most success.

Philip Holdsworth, the son of Bill Holdsworth the undertaker, had a sister whom I really fancied. Like me, Philip was a member of St Patrick's Choir – and I asked him about swapping some coins, so I could visit his house and see his sister, who was a little older than me. On this pretext I visited their house in Lillicroft Road a few times, and I tried to talk to her, as only an inexperienced dope of sixteen could. I even walked her to the bus stop one evening when she was going to meet her boyfriend! In the end I gave up, as even I could tell that she had no eyes for me. My mum said what I already knew, that I was a dope and that I would have plenty of time for girls later.

Later, when we had moved to Wyke and I was seventeen, I had my first date. I had seen the girl while attending Mass at St Winifred's Church on St Paul's Avenue, Wibsey, and one day I saw her in town. Surprising myself, I asked her if she would like to go to the pictures. She said yes, and we went to *The Tender Trap* at the New Vic. I don't remember if I held her hand, kissed her or made a good impression, but it seems unlikely: I never saw her again.

A little confidence had now been gained. Shortly afterwards, when I was working at Burton's one Saturday, Vincent was due to call for me as usual when I finished at six o'clock, so we could go to the pictures. At about 5.50pm I noticed a rather attractive girl waiting close to the shop entrance. Things were quiet and almost ready for closing, so I went outside and started chatting to her. She was waiting for her boyfriend. Come six o'clock Vincent arrived – but the young lady was still there. Her boyfriend hadn't turned up. I asked if she would like to come along with us to the Elite Picture House on Toller Lane, and she agreed. At the Elite she sat between me and Vincent: he watched the film intently, but I didn't see any of it as the girl and I were kissing and cuddling all the way through. As we left I asked her for a date, but she politely declined, saying that her boyfriend wouldn't like it. Full of confidence, I replied, 'That doesn't bother me;' but when she went on to tell me her boyfriend was one of the Lowthers I made an excuse and left, followed by Vincent.

As my life drifted towards National Service I went out with quite a few girls. Among them was Ann Mahoney. She lived with her family at Low Moor: her father, Jack, was a world-famous professional boxing referee. Ann was more of a mate than a girlfriend. She attended St Winifred's Church with her family and it was there that we used to meet. She also accompanied me to the Young Christian Workers' Society at St Joseph's Church on Packington Street. However, nothing developed and we were just good friends.

Another girl I had the odd date with was Alma Beatty. As well as visits to the cinema, she invited me to tea a couple of times at her house in Shearbridge. With my National Service looming, I made an incredible statement to her parents, telling them that when I was in the forces I would be an officer. I often wonder what Mr Beatty thought of this ridiculous statement, as he had been a soldier in the last war.

My problem was that I wore my heart on my sleeve: I fell in love with every girl I went out with. My mum, when asked by friends if I was courting, replied, 'No, not really – he loves them and leaves them.' I don't think she realised how her answer could be misinterpreted: it sounded as if I was insincere, and to be avoided like the plague.

Even on holidays I fell in love. When I went with Vincent for a week to Bridlington in 1955, it was a case of fellas looking for girls and girls looking for fellas. We met two girls from Hull and spent some time together, even going to a dance on the pier. Vincent's attitude was that he could take them or leave them, but I was completely the opposite. I fell in love with Miss Jean Atkinson of 656

Spring Bank West, Hull, but the dream ended like all the others. When the holiday was over our promises to write to each other were not kept, and I never saw her again.

A few months before I joined the army I met Collette Blessington, who lived on Haworth Avenue, Five Lane Ends. Collette and her family attended St Clare's Roman Catholic Church. We got on very well together and had quite a few dates, so for once I had a steady girlfriend. I went to tea at her house a few times and she visited my home. Her brother was a little older than me, and had just come out of the army after completion of his military service in the Royal Engineers. With the Suez Crisis looming, he was called back in late 1956. The night before he returned to his regiment the three of us went to the Alhambra to see Dickie Valentine (who was top of the bill), along with Morecambe and Wise. The show was excellent.

Collette was a nice girl, although one time she put me in my place. We were looking in a shop on North Parade as I wanted to buy something for my mum before going into the army. For years, even as a child, I had bought her a small bottle of Californian Poppy at 2s 6d. I thought she deserved something much nicer and a little more expensive, and when I saw a large bottle in the shop window I said to Collette, 'That scent looks nice.' She replied, 'It's not scent, it's perfume.' From that moment I knew I could also fall out of love.

A few weeks later, now in the army, I received a 'Dear John' letter from Collette. I pinned this up on the dartboard with many other similar letters sent to my new comrades, from girlfriends who couldn't wait for them to finish National Service. The dartboard reverberated from the many darts thrown at the accumulated 'Dear John' letters over the next few weeks.

I had been no Don Juan with the looks of the silver screen stars in my early and teenage life. On completion of my army service, and back in Civvy Street, I was determined to make up for lost time.

Chapter 16
Playing Fields and Open Spaces

The Rec

Just past the Arcadian cinema on Legrams Lane was a football pitch that was really a general-purpose recreation ground – the Rec. With old disjointed goalposts, this field served as a football ground for the local football teams in the Bradford Sunday League, although it was rumoured that it had been condemned for many years. There was no grass left on the surface: it was just rock-hard clay, full of holes, uneven and sloping. But as it vaguely resembled a football pitch we used it with enthusiasm. As the goalposts on the pitch were high and wide for our small frames we sometimes used our coats as goalposts.

A small crowd of us lads from the nearby streets often made our way to the Rec in an assortment of dress, most not even resembling football players. Leather football boots were scarce, and if anyone had a pair it had usually been handed down from older members of the family; judging from the styles, some were from before the First World War, with large toecaps and studs missing. Sometimes only one boot was available and it was not unknown to see a player with a shoe on one foot and a football boot on the other. Football jerseys were also at a premium. If anyone did have one he was looked at with envy, so it was usual to play in your everyday attire. Old leather footballs were used and it was essential to make sure the ball was hard. We blew it up with a special pump, but if this wasn't available we used a bicycle pump – with difficulty. The hardest part was lacing up the ball, making sure that the end of the lace was secure under the lace. If it wasn't, accidents could happen, as an insecure lace end could inflict serious damage when the ball was headed. Once the ball was ready, teams were picked from our group, with additions, as sometimes others (in some cases strangers whom we didn't know) asked for a game. Rarely did we say no. These strangers always seemed to be good football players, and were always included if they were around when we played again. I wasn't a particular good player, and tended to play in goal. The goals scored against me were always in double figures, and inevitably I was almost last to be picked. Groups of weary lads proceeded home with cuts, bruises, twisted ankles, and legs and thighs with bruises unmistakably caused by the ball. It certainly wasn't the type of football ground that attracted talent scouts.

When the cricket season arrived the same formidable group of enthusiasts proceeded to the Rec, this time to use the football ground as a cricket pitch! Dress again was limited: footwear was an assortment of pumps, sandals, baseball boots, and in one case Wellingtons. Our cricket equipment left a lot to be desired, although we did have a set of wickets, which were hammered into the hard ground with the flat of the bat rather than the usual bat handle. We had no bails, as these always got lost. We did have a bat or two, though these were old, with electrical adhesive tape on the handles and bat to strengthen them and cover cracks. The bottom of the bat was usually two inches short, from years of digging it into the crease. Importantly we had to make sure that the bat was a 'three spring' – with three rubber strips through the handle. This was the shock absorber when the hard ball hit the bat. The cricket ball, if one was available, was the 'corky'. A corky ball was a cheap imitation of the original leather ball: hard cork sprayed with red paint, mass-produced for such as us. They looked good when new, but after ten minutes on a pitch like ours the paint was gone. Bowled from young strong arms it had the effect of a cannon ball: once it hit the clay surface it could shoot in any direction, and casualties were heavy. For leg protection we had the odd cricket pad, another hand-me-down and very large, covering the waist as well as a leg. When running between the wickets it was a disadvantage, often causing the batsman to fall. As the stumper didn't have gloves, wicket-keeping was dangerous and often resulted in many byes. When a corky ball wasn't available we used a tennis ball, which always resulted in many sixes and high scores. If a dispute arose over whether a batsman was out, the batsman was asked to take three bat handles – to defend his wicket three times holding the bat upside down and using the bat handle to defend his wicket. If the wicket wasn't hit then the batsman was not out. I have no idea where this rule came from: it's not in the Lord's rule book. But it always worked for us and the batsman accepted the verdict. Another piece of equipment that one of the lads brought was a cricket box – to protect the batsman's private parts. It was unusual, and we thought it quite an occasion, although we had no thought of borrowing it. It was not a success, however, as it kept dropping out of his short trousers: we were all about twelve at the time.

What we lacked in equipment we made up for our enthusiasm to learn the rudiments of cricket, field places and sporting words like 'good shot', 'hard lines', 'slog it' and 'catch it'. We didn't bother with the lbw call as we had different ideas about how this should be interpreted, especially on our pitch. Being keen cricket and football fans we were brought down to earth on visits to Park Avenue cricket ground to watch Yorkshire play on its beautiful pitch, and also to watch football at the Bradford City and Park Avenue football grounds with their lush turf. Maybe someday we could play on similar grounds and pitches, but in the meantime we made do with our football ground and cricket pitch. After all it was our Rec.

Clayton Fields

Where we lived in Listerhills, playing fields for children were non-existent. Horton Park was the closest place with open spaces and grass areas that could be played on without the risk of grazing hands and knees, the usual results of playing in the street. As our mothers had a multitude of jobs to be done without us under their feet, we disappeared for hours on end to amuse ourselves. One of the places that gave us hours of pleasure was Clayton Fields. Off we went, not expected home until teatime. A trolleybus ride to the Clayton terminus by the Bull Inn was all that we needed to bring us to an area that was surrounded by green fields, and the feeling of being well away from our industrial environment – even though we had travelled only 3 miles. From the terminus we went across the roundabout to Low Lane, passing the eighteenth-century cottages with dates above the doors and also the house where Tom Pierrepoint, who was a farmer but also the public hangman, lived. He was a nice man who sometimes chatted to us. We were aware of his other job, but the subject was never broached and a pat on our heads sent us on our way. Returning home I would say to my mum, 'I've had a chat with Mr Pierrepoint the hangman.' Then we continued past a row of small cottages on the right, to a gap about 100 yards further along the dry stone wall. From here you could make out Drummond Road Mills in Lumb Lane, Bradford, in the distance: the word Drummond was painted in large letters on the roof. From here we walked down to a small valley, swishing through the long grass surrounded by clouds of small white butterflies. Over the other side was the path winding up to Thornton Road and Thornton Grammar School, and Leaventhorpe Lane on the right. In our small valley there was a stream, the start of the Bradford Beck – or Mucky Beck as it was known. We used to paddle in it with no adverse effects, and in the summer it was cool and refreshing to our hot sweaty feet.

In the school holidays we spent many happy hours here on sunny days, armed with bread and jam sandwiches and a couple of Tizer bottles filled with Spanish water. That was the name we gave to a bottle of water that was shaken up with a stick of liquorice. Although it resembled muddy water it was quite refreshing, and saved money. With the sandwiches and our Spanish water the cost of our day out would be only 2*d*: 1*d* each way on the trolleybus.

On the edge of a nearby field was a ditch with a small trickle of water in it.

The hangman Tom Pierrepoint, who lived in Clayton, often chatted to us and sent us on our way with a smile and a pat on the head. *(Syd Dearnley)*

Frogs and grasshoppers startled the unwary, and in the water there was frogspawn and lots of frogs which we caught. If you tickled the bottom of a frog's back it jumped – more out of fright than because of the tickle. We never took the frogs home but always left them in their environment. In the hedges were blackberries and bilberries, which we picked with grubby hands and ate unwashed to our heart's content without ever feeling sick. Nettles were everywhere and stings were many, but the stings were always soothed by collecting and spitting on dock leaves, then rubbing them on the nettle rash. Many wild flowers, yarrow, toadflax, sweet-scented clovers, could be picked to be taken home, sometimes with bluebells that grew on one side of the beck; at times these were a peace offering to our mothers if we were home later than usual. Dandelions we avoided, as they were rumoured to make us wet the bed. There was always a variety of birds in our Clayton fields, and we could identify most, such was our knowledge derived from our many visits. In the sky, hedges and woods were swallows, jays, song thrushes, skylarks, jackdaws, wrens and the odd kestrel, each one with its own song that provided a background to our play.

Cows were sometimes in the fields, giving us the odd scare. When we were younger it took a while before some streetwise member of the gang explained how to see they were not all bulls! It was inevitable that someone would tread in a cowpat, sometimes known locally as cowflap. It was said by one of the lad's great aunts that cowpat placed on an open wound could stop it becoming infected, and helped it to heal quicker. We knew the time would come when we would have to put this to the test, and it did. Climbing over a fence, Barry Widdop slipped and caught his leg on some rusty barbed wire, which ripped through his stocking and cut a deep wound in his calf. We gathered round, put some cowpat on the wound, then tied on our dirty old hankies, and took him home on the bus – wondering why other passengers were keeping their distance. Barry had to go to the hospital and have a few stitches and a jab, and nothing was said about the cowpat bandage. The wound healed quickly, or so we thought, and we put it down to the cowpat bandage.

In these fields we played games, ran and chased, made dens and played out our fantasies, be they Flash Gordon or Cowboys and Indians. At the bottom of our valley there was a small wooden footbridge over the beck. The water wasn't really deep but the stones were thick with moss and slippery. Many were the soakings we got, whether feet or all our clothes. On hot summer days an arrangement of wet clothes was laid out on the banks of the beck, dried, and later, wet again after another half an hour messing about in the beck, laid out again for further drying. Eventually, having eaten our jam sandwiches earlier and finished off the Spanish water, our stomachs told us it was nearly teatime.

We sometimes spent all day at our Clayton Fields and I cannot remember being bored. Vincent, Trevor, Jackie, Barry and I must have been about seven years old when we first went there on our own, and continued to visit until we left school. Sometimes we went home by scrambling along the edges of the Beck as far as Cemetery Road, then walking the rest of the way. We always returned home dirty, sweaty, sunburnt and tired, but above all happy.

Horton Park
Our visits to Clayton Fields were always a delight, but there were other open spaces to which Vincent, the gang and I could disappear all day. Only twenty minutes away was one such, Horton Park. Situated on Horton Park Avenue, it was predominantly residential and adjoined Yorkshire County Cricket Ground and the Bradford Park Avenue Football Club. I often left home at about ten o'clock, saying to my mum, 'I'm going to Horton Park with the lads and should be home about five o'clock.' She would reply 'All right', followed by her usual remark, 'And don't speak to any strange men.' I never did, although one old man once asked me and Vincent if we wanted to go to his house and see some newly born puppies. A good kick on his shin sent him hobbling away.

Horton Park was always a favourite playground. Here we could play both cricket (no 'corkys' allowed) and football on nicely grassed and level surfaces. The gardens were always well maintained, and the park had its own keeper who lived in the lodge situated by the Horton Park Avenue entrance. We also went fishing with our small bamboo *6d* fishing nets in the boating lake, catching mostly minnows and sticklebacks that we took home in a jam-jar. The next morning the jam-jar would smell, the water would be green and the fish would be dead. The fish were placed in a matchbox and ceremoniously buried in my front garden between the dustbins and the air-raid shelter – an area that after many years resembled a small Undercliffe 'Fish' Cemetery.

On the lakes there were small two-person paddle boats. One sat in the centre and turned the handles to propel the boat, while the other sat at the end and guided the boat with a tiller. As with the fairground dodgems we all smashed into each other when out of sight of the attendant. He wasn't averse to giving us a clip round the ears for our misbehaving. There were the usual comments: 'I'll tell my dad over you when I get home', to which the boatman's reply was, 'Tell him. I'll give him a clip as well if he comes down here.' A few minutes later we would have left the boating lake, forgotten the fracas and be looking around for the next adventure.

On sunny days the heat and running about made us very thirsty. If we had already drunk our pop or Spanish water there was a drinking fountain close to the glasshouses and conservatory where plants were on show. This fountain was set into the wall with the donor's name engraved on the stone. The water was always cool and so refreshing.

There were the usual swings and roundabouts. We sat on the large roundabout, pushed it round with our feet, jumped on and kept up the momentum. As we went at such great speeds you were in trouble if you let go. We were always careful not to go the 'sick way round', which was clockwise: the correct way was supposedly anti-clockwise. But at the speeds we used to spin we always came off staggering about and feeling dizzy.

The park was enemy territory – the domain of the Canterbury Warriors – so we were vigilant from the moment we set foot in Horton Park Avenue. Only once did we encounter them. Vincent, Trevor, Jacky and I had just got off the boats at the boating lake when we were surrounded by a dozen Warriors. Trevor and Vincent made a break for it and got away, leaving me and Jacky to await our fate. Just as things were looking bad, a voice from the rear of the Warriors shouted, 'Hello, Derek.' It was John Tindall – one of the gang's leaders, who was in the next bed to me when I had been in St Luke's Hospital two years before, when we were eleven. He asked if I remembered the Canterbury Warriors anthem he had taught me while in the hospital, and I recited it:

We are the Canterbury Warriors,
We stay out late at night.
If anyone dare comes near us,
There's sure to be a fight.
Last night we were in trouble,
Tonight we are in jail.
All because of pulling, pulling a donkey's tail.
So . . . way back, way back,
Come and get your money back,
Peas and pies for supper,
Our old lass has plenty of brass,
And we don't care a bugger.

John was dead chuffed! He went on to tell his gang that I was a good friend of his and that from then on I was an honorary member of the Canterbury Warriors. He said that if I was involved in any future confrontations with the Warriors or any other local gangs I was just to mention his name.

We met Vincent and Trevor on the way home. There were no recriminations about their running away: we had just been too slow, and Jacky would have had a problem with his disability. Soon word got around that I was an honorary member of the Canterbury Warriors, and I gained much respect from my friendship with John Tindall – although in some quarters it was said that I was a traitor. Other than this confrontation with the Canterbury Warriors we never had any other trouble.

Outside the park was Horton Park station on the Thornton–Queensbury line, a small Victorian station with a large stone entrance, on the top of which was carved a cricket bat across wickets and above a football. This represented Yorkshire County Cricket Ground and Bradford Park Avenue Football Club across the road. To finish off wonderful days we sometimes got the train into Bradford, which cost 1*d*.

Brackenhill Park
Brackenhill Park was situated in Hollingwood Lane, a residential area. Although a nice park and just a fifteen minute bus ride away it didn't seem to have the openness of Horton Park, although it had a good selection of roundabouts and swings. As it didn't offer the same appeal as our other open spaces, our visits were infrequent.

Peel Park
From Listerhills Peel Park seemed to be a great distance, involving a journey on two trolleybuses. The few times that I visited I was with my dad for the famous Bradford Whit Walks: we used to watch the finish with thousands of others: it was probably one of Bradford's premier athletic events. After many gruelling miles the walkers arrived, most of them thin, with bottoms wiggling and many bow-legged; but none seemed to be out of breath. My dad commented on our visits that I had the legs for the walk, which I found a bit insulting having seen the walkers' legs!

Lister Park
This was the park I visited most when I was younger, with my parents and later with the gang. It was two bus rides away but was well worth it, as it had all the amenities you could wish for. A beautiful lake was the centrepiece, with large family rowing boats. If you were quick-thinking you stopped the boat at the far end of the lake, out of earshot of the boat attendant who shouted your number and told you your time was up. There was also a large motorboat that took all the family.

Cartwright Hall in Lister Park at a time when most boys wore short trousers. The museum inside the hall catered for boys like us with a world of treasures and discoveries. *(Graham Hall)*

A tranquil picture of the boating lake in Lister Park.
(Graham Hall)

Three boys in a boat at Lister Park: me, Vincent and David Briggs. David is wearing a St Bede's Grammar School blazer. *(Author's collection)*

The Lido swimming pool was always crowded when the summer came. I didn't like swimming so this wasn't of much interest to me. Aged just two I had fallen into a small paddling pool situated above the Lido, and had never forgotten it. When asked why I didn't like swimming I used to blame this event, but as I got older I changed the original truthful excuse to having been pushed off the top diving board of the Lido aged seven. I had lots of sympathy for this.

Works bands and bands from county regiments played almost every weekend at the Victorian bandstand. During the summer crowds of families, young and old, sat on the seats provided or on the grass banking listening to operatic overtures, classical favourites and military marches. I couldn't help but be impressed by the professional musicians and the attentive audience, who gave generous applause especially to cornet players or trumpeters when they played their solos.

Set in the centre of all this activity was the beautiful Cartwright Hall. Each time we visited the park we went into the hall to see the popular glass-fronted beehive and the bees flying in and out through an aperture in the wall. There were mahogany boxes each side that we stood on when we were small, to have a better view. The nature exhibition also included rows of glass showcases full of moths, butterflies, stuffed animals and birds. In an adjoining room were beautiful scale models of Bradford trams, buses, trolleybuses and industrial machines used in the mills. Most were working models, and could be set in motion by turning a handle set in the front of the display case. These were always favourites, but I used to spend most of my time in the basement gallery that was dedicated to archaeology, in particular Roman history – thanks to the curator, Sydney Jackson. On the first and second floors were many sculptures and wonderful paintings, some by famous local artists such as Ernest Leopold Sichel and William Rothenstein. Portraits of Bradford wool barons adorned one gallery, looking down on the visitors, some of whom were still employed in their vast woollen empires.

On certain occasions there was a miniature railway outside the hall, with steam engines running on tracks, pulling small seats set on open carriages. The track was about 100 yards long, which gave the passengers a marvellous experience, resulting in shouts of glee from the children.

Bolling Hall

Tucked away in a leafy garden less than a mile from the city centre is the medieval mansion Bolling Hall, which was visited frequently by our gang. Inside the hall it was always the same, full of old highly polished furniture that gave off a scent of beeswax and turpentine, peculiar to historical buildings, and an array of Cromwellian armour, swords and lobster pot helmets, the favourite headwear of Cromwell's army. A copy of Cromwell's deathmask adorned one panelled wall. We had heard that someone had been pushed from the landing that overlooked the great hall to the floor below, and that where the victim fell blood marks appeared at certain times: we believed everything we were told. Sometimes we went cautiously into the bedroom where the Earl of Newcastle had spent the night during the Civil War. It was rumoured that he was visited by a ghost (a white lady), who had said, 'Pity poor Bradford!' We all shuffled out of the bedroom together, not wishing to be left alone in its eerie atmosphere. The oak panels throughout the hall were always tested by us with a quick tap, in the hope that we would discover a secret passage. We never did! Even after many visits we went through the same ritual, as there was something special about Bolling Hall. Its wealth of historical drama educated our young minds – but above all we enjoyed every visit.

Shipley Glen

One of the most popular places to visit for a day out, this beauty spot and pleasure gardens became the playground of many generations of the working classes, mostly mill workers. The journey to the Glen (other than through Baildon) was by way of the Shipley Glen Railway, which had been constructed in 1895. A tram (originally steam, later electric) transported hundreds of visitors a day in two open cable-hauled trucks: cables between each rail hoisted one tram up the hill while the other tram was gradually lowered. The quarter-of-a-mile

A ride on the Glen Railway was a must on visits to Shipley Glen. Walking down was much easier. *(Graham Hall)*

journey to the top was a pleasant ride compared with the long walk up the steep bridlepath. The price for the return journeys was reduced, thus persuading people to take the tram. Probably the most popular times were bank holidays and Whitsuntide, when families dressed in their Sunday best and paraded along the road that ran behind the moor edge. At the same time hundreds more people sat in large and small groups, having picnics or just lying in the sun. Away from factories' smoke and grime they had views across the valley to Bradford. To the north behind the Glen was Baildon Moor, and a few miles further on was Ilkley Moor. If all this was not enough, close to the top railway station was the wonderful pleasure garden. This was also a big attraction and home of the longest surviving amusement park ride in the country, the Aerial Glide, which was surrounded by an array of children's rides and amusement arcades. On the perimeter of this amusement park were ice-cream vans and a tea-room. Visiting the Glen was a day's holiday for Bradfordians and people of the surrounding areas.

I visited the Glen on many occasions, with my parents, our gang and older friends, sometimes even the odd visit with a girlfriend on a beautiful sunny day. There was nothing to compare with this idyllic setting – just a few miles from the cobbled streets and back-to-back houses of Listerhills.

Baildon Moor
In 1954 Sydney Jackson, curator of the Cartwright Hall Museum, started a local archaeological group. Vincent, Donald Swaine and I joined. Donald and I joined because of our love of archaeology; Vincent's interest was more limited. We went

on many of Mr Jackson's walks. These were educational, as he was always interesting and attentive to our queries, and we also got lots of fresh air! Most of these walks were centred on Baildon Moor, which seemed to be Mr Jackson's favourite place – as it had been for the famous archaeologist Sir Mortimer Wheeler who, as a child living in Saltaire, had spent many hours collecting Roman pottery and making a study of the local cup and ring marks; so we were in good company. Come rain or shine we were on the moors between lectures looking for flint arrowheads, flint chippings, pottery and spent Victorian rifle bullets close to the Victorian army rifle butts. Like Sir Mortimer Wheeler we saw remains of primeval dwellings, earthworks, burial mounds, upright stones, trenches and stone circles almost as perfect as the day they were made.

One day near the rifle butts I found a spent rifle bullet. I told Mr Jackson who proclaimed how wonderful I was to all the walkers (about sixty of them). Vincent and Donald wandered off shaking their heads, not wanting to be part of the embarrassing façade: after all, I didn't even have to dig for it as it was just lying on the ground. Later I got to know Mr Jackson very well and asked him if the bullet I had found had been planted by him. 'Certainly not,' he replied, with a wry smile on his face and a twinkle in his eye. But just before I went into the forces he asked me to go and see him at his home; he was living in Lidget Green. To my surprise he gave me a large and very heavy carton containing many fossils of all descriptions. Travelling to Wyke with this heavy box was a long and sweaty journey with this large heavy carton. When I arrived home I emptied out the contents to discover a treasure trove of history: Mr Jackson had been collecting since he came out of the forces in 1946. At the very bottom of the carton was a rather heavy tin cigarette box. As I smoked at the time I thought how nice, but when I opened the box inside were about fifty spent bullets similar to the one I had found that day on Baildon Moor. Mr Jackson may not have been famous, but he influenced many young lives with his enthusiasm for nature and the past.

Sunny Vale

Perhaps not as famous as Blackpool, Scarborough or even Lister Park was Sunny Vale, a small amusement park situated in Waterclough valley east of the village of Hipperholme. It was built by Joseph Bunce in 1883 and originally called the Pleasure Gardens, to cater for Sunday walkers passing his farm. My first visits to Sunny Vale were with my parents just after the war. It was a long journey by bus, but train journeys to Hipperholme were always quicker and much more interesting. The railway station was unusual in that the long Beacon Hill Tunnel, 1105 yards long, started almost from the edge of the platform. On arrival, there was a short walk from the station along Station Road to the Sunny Vale entrance, where a lane took you down to the valley bottom and the Pleasure Gardens.

Over the years these gardens had proved to be a great attraction. They included a miniature railway, two boating lakes, swings, maze and amusement arcades within a 40 acre site. The location was ideal, and the gardens attracted crowds of over 10,000 people in their heyday. Sunny Vale was very popular during the war, especially for local West Riding people, as visits to the coast during wartime were quite a ritual.

When we first started visiting, parts of the site were already in decline: the open air dancing and rollerskating facilities were no more. Even so, it was still quite an adventure. At the famous Sunnyvale Tea Room a thousand people could be seated. If it was a nice day you could pay a deposit of 2s 6d for a pot of tea – refundable when the tea-pot and cups were returned – and sit outside in the pleasant gardens or on the well-tended grassy banks overlooking the lake.

Tickets for the rides and boats were sold in books. Each ride cost 3d, but you could buy five rides for just 1s, meaning one ride was free. If it wasn't busy you could stay on the rowing boats for as long as you wished. One visit with St Patrick's Choir, Michael Farrell, Terry Moran and I, with a few others, were on the boats for three hours playing at roman galleys, throwing the heavy green weeds from the lake at each other's boats; the mêlée finally ended when one boat overturned – Romans one, Greeks nil. It wasn't deep, only wet, but the attendant made the survivors pull the overturned boat to the shore. We, the victors, returned to the grassy knoll and had our Roman victory meal – jam sandwiches, washed down with Tizer.

My last visit to Sunny Vale was with the school in 1953. It was only partially open: lots of the amusements were broken and needed repair, and the buildings were dilapidated. In 1953 Hipperholme station closed, leaving a travel problem for visitors. More and more people were going to the coast for daytrips and holidays, and in the mid-1950s Sunny Vale closed. After a few months nothing remained of its former glory.

Chapter 17
All the Fun of the Fair

Perhaps one of the most popular days out for both young and old was a visit to one of the many fairs that came to Bradford. (Although the name fair was generally used, they were also known locally as the 'Tides', a referral to the Bowling Tide holiday.)

Many fairs took place from Easter until September in areas including Wibsey, Peel Park, Great Horton and West Bowling. Not far from my home in Legrams Street there was a piece of spare ground in between Summerville Road and Rothesay Terrace that was visited by a fair at least twice a year. It was handy for me as I could pop home to borrow more pennies!

Perhaps the largest and best fair to visit Bradford was Marshall's, which took over Lister Park for a fortnight (not including Sundays). Every amusement, game and side-show imaginable was there, and it was worth at least two or three visits depending on how much money I had – but even without much loose change the experience was worth it. For the tiny tots and youngsters there were the usual kiddie-rides with fire engines, police cars, motorbikes, stagecoaches, trains and a bus (with an upstairs). There was always a fight among the children to ride on the fire engine as it had a large brass bell, which would be clanged repeatedly. You could win (or usually lose) your pennies on many stalls when gambling fever took over, the best outcome being to spend a couple of shillings and win something worth pence. Even if we won first time the showman still profited, as the value of the prize was less than the cost of the game. Most of the entertainment was games of strength or skill. At the coconut shy, in which you threw a (very light) wooden ball at the coconut, deeply set in a basin of sand and balanced on posts, the prize if you dislodged the coconut was a coconut! A children's favourite was hooking plastic ducks from a water trough. Every player was expected to win, so prizes (related to the number on the bottom of each duck), were not over-expensive! Ring and blocks was a game where the player threw a wooden hoop over the prizes, which were placed on wooden blocks; to win, the hoop had to go round the base of the block – and as the hoops were only slightly larger than the square blocks it always seemed that the hoop got caught on a corner of the block. Shooting included archery, darts and air rifles, with targets ranging from playing cards to ping-pong balls and bull's-eye targets. Most of us thought the airgun sights were misaligned and the flights on the darts worn and twisted.

Typical prizes included goldfish in small plastic bags and cuddly toys. When you were with a girlfriend it was part of the ritual to show off your skill at shooting to win her a cuddly toy. Needless to say none of my girlfriends received this coveted gift: I always explained that the sights were definitely crooked – but eyebrows would be raised: the girl always thought I was a rotten shot.

On the 2.2 rifle range no prizes were given: you just let loose your four shots at the many metal targets moving backwards and forwards. As live ammunition was used the rifle was chained to the counter; it could only point forwards, for obvious reasons. The sound of a bullet hitting metal and the smell of cordite in the air had a certain fascination for many males who wished to prove a point.

Every fairground had a roll-a-penny stall, where the penny was rolled from a wooden slide on to a large area marked with many small boxes, each marked with the appropriate winnings, in some cases as much as a shilling. If the penny fell on to a box, not touching any lines, you won. In another game of skill you had to throw ping-pong balls in the air and try to land them in a small goldfish bowl (minus a goldfish). A course of physics was required to show you how to get the ball into the bowl!

I liked the slot machines, where I believed I had some chance of making a small profit. I proved this many times, coming away with more money than I had started with. In the game you had to flick a ball-bearing round the circular frame, hoping it would enter one of the prize-bearing holes; obstructions were strategically placed to prevent you winning. The trick was in how you flicked the ball. As each machine was different I lost a few pence until I had mastered my flick, then went on to make a profit. I became so good that on one occasion I was winning so much on a machine in an arcade in Scarborough that I was thrown out for cheating!

Also popular were the automatic cranes with large claws that delved into a sea of prizes. If picked up, the prize would often slip off. A similar game involved steel hands that could be manipulated to pick up desirable objects, usually with little success – but when a 10s note was one of the prizes everyone had a go. I only ever saw one winner of a 10s note, in the late 1940s. The winner went berserk as that would probably have been half a week's wage for him.

Pinball machines never interested me, with their flashing lights and the ding-dong of large ball-bearings making contact with electrical mechanisms.

High scores were usually rewarded by extra playing time. A popular novelty machine on which two could play was two metal boxers in a glass case. To make the boxers spar you manoeuvred pistol grips on their sides and pulled the trigger. I wasn't ever sure how you won, but one of the steel men always ended up on his back.

In many corners of these arcades were the 'What the Butler Saw' machines, which cost 1*d* to view. Above these machines there was always a notice reading 'over 18s only', but I saw children aged about seven being lifted up by an older brother to view the scenes. I had a look a few times purely out of curiosity, and to be like the rest of the lads, but always got the feeling my mum was around. I saw lots of slaps dished out by irate parents who had caught their offspring looking into the machine. All I remember were women prancing about at great speed like a Charlie Chaplin film. I believe some of the machines dated from the early 1900s.

Other stalls sold refreshments – candyfloss stalls, toffee apples and a caravan selling chips. These chips were a bit different from today's: potatoes cut in half and fried, always the same, and always tasting so nice. Over this was a cacophony of music and noise – noise from the crowds of people and the many different rides and machines, as well as the gentle hum of generators which illuminated this small village of flashing lights and powered the side-shows. Everything was linked by miles of heavy duty black cables that snaked across the fairground, often tripping up the unwary.

The side-shows and amusement arcades were insignificant compared with the large rides. Bumper cars or dodgems were found at most fairs, with small electric cars drawing power from an overhead grid, with sparks flying, bumping their way around a large rectangular or oval track. If you were experienced you could make the car go backwards, sometimes necessary in the many pile-ups that occurred: no one took any notice of the signs saying 'This way round' and 'No bumping'. At every fair, without exception, there were show-off attendants who jumped from one car to another to obtain the fares, usually after the ride had started. These show-offs made a bee-line for two girls together in one car, and the girls loved it. If I was in another dodgem, or watching I always hoped the show-off would fall off. Sometimes they did, resulting in a large cheer from bystanders who had the same thought as me.

The swing carousel, with its chairs suspended on chains from the floating top, was not for the faint hearted. When the carousel was in full swing and the chairs were thrown outwards, it attracted lads who looked up at girls' underwear as they tried to hold their skirts down. Another carousel or merry-go-round was the traditional rotating platform with beautifully painted wooden horses or animals for the passengers to sit on. This moved up and down to simulate galloping, while lots of fairy lights, barleytwist poles and music from a large percussion organ and clashing cymbals in the centre made this an exciting ride.

251

The most spectacular and thrilling show was the Wall of Death. This was a 20 foot high wooden cylindrical wall, around the top of which was a viewing platform built for spectators to watch motorcycle riders tackle the vertical wall around the inside on vintage motorcycles. It was always worth a shilling to watch these stunt riders and I would always leave with the smell of methanol in my nostrils.

Dive bomber was a fearful ride, with twin cars mounted on a vertical rotating arm and each car spinning on its own axis. The trick was that the rider was never turned upside down; but I never put it to the test! Other rides included the waltzer, steamboat, shamrock, caterpillar and octopus, all designed to excite, shock or frighten us, or just to give us a good time: 'all the fun of the fair'!

Chapter 18
Daytrips and Family Holidays

Redcar

I suppose I was lucky as I spent some of the war years at the seaside, at Redcar. We stayed at Grangetown near Middlesbrough with my mum's sister Auntie Cassie, Uncle Stan and cousin Kathleen. Many nights were spent in the air-raid shelter while the docks were being bombed, but we had daytrips to Redcar.

Rows and rows of coiled barbed wire were strung along the beach, there were no road signs and the sand dunes near the golf club had been strewn with landmines. There were servicemen and women in abundance, and the shops and amusement arcades were full of them. They would hang around a very large juke-box, which had a selection of only eight records. Here it was that I heard many of the wartime pop tunes. Among these were the Andrews Sisters singing 'Don't Sit under the Apple Tree'. Other popular American songs of the time were 'Mairzy Doats' and 'Paper Doll'. The American servicemen seemed much taller than our forces and much better dressed. Every Yank (as we called them) chewed gum, sticks of which they dished out to the children as a new phrase entered our English language: 'Any gum, chum?' I received many packets of chewing gum, which were always given with a smile and an accent that I had only heard in films.

I spent many hours sitting on the promenade watching the Hudson bombers of RAF Coastal Command flying low over Redcar as they winged their way out to sea from the aerodrome at Thornaby on Tees. Sometimes I visited the old lifeboat house and gazed in wonder at the new and old lifeboats. As well as having a fairly modern lifeboat Redcar also displayed the *Zetland*, the oldest lifeboat in the world, built in 1802.

Auntie Cassie sometimes worked as a waitress in Redcar in one of the many cafés during and after the war. We always had a meal there, and received a bill of

Mum (left) and my favourite auntie, Cassie, walking along the seafront at Redcar.
(Author's collection)

sorts – but I don't remember the bill being paid. My auntie was beautiful, I thought, with lovely long blonde hair and an infectious laugh. Auntie Cassie looked and sang like Patti Andrews of the Andrews Sisters. Best of all, she always stuck up for me. In the late 1920s, as a teenager, she was in domestic service in London to the Hollywood star Anna May Wong, who was in England to make films.

It was at about noon on 3 August 1942 that my auntie was slightly injured when a single low-flying Dornier bomber dropped bombs on the LNER railway station in Middlesbrough. Eight people were killed and fifty-eight injured.

Travel during the war was always a problem, especially on the railways. With troop movements, workers, the general public, the risk of bombing and being

Mum, Dad and me on our caravan holiday in Redcar, 1953. The holiday was spoilt by an army of earwigs that was also on holiday in the caravan, but we all looked relaxed for the camera. *(Author's collection)*

**My cousin Kathleen and me
on the sands at Redcar,
1946.** *(Author's collection)*

asked 'if your journey was really necessary', it was no picnic. The trains were always full and people were packed in like sardines in every space available. Even the corridors filled up end to end, and the toilets were almost inaccessible.

It was the summer of 1943, and the school holidays. My brother Lawrence was already in Grangetown, staying at Auntie Cassie's. Mum and I followed later, after my dad had returned to his camp. For the journey to Redcar from Bradford Forster Square station, we had managed to get seats in a compartment full of soldiers who made space for us. They all smelled the same as my dad, a mixture of battledress and Blanco – a smell I'll never forget. I was standing by the door daydreaming that soon I would be walking along Redcar front eating an ice cream when the guard came along and slammed our door closed. A cry pierced the air, which I realised was from me: my thumb had been caught in the door. Then the pain came, and how it hurt! All of a sudden my mum and ten burly soldiers were around me. One of them released my thumb, jumped on to the platform and disappeared. He arrived back a minute later with the guard. The soldier picked me up and, with the guard and my mum following, carried me along to the stationmaster's office. An army doctor arrived very quickly and said my thumb wasn't broken, just badly bruised. A large bandage was wrapped around it and I was carried back to the waiting train. A cheer went up from the soldiers in our compartment, a whistle sounded and the train started on its journey. All this had taken place in ten minutes. It was wartime and the train had been held up for me! The soldiers were great and continued to make a fuss. One of them even let me hold his rifle, which had been stored with the others above in the luggage rack. They plied me with chocolate bars, all Fry's, and my mum was given two tins of cigarettes. I, for the moment, forgot the pain. At York, when we departed from the train, the soldiers all waved us goodbye, shouting to me that they hoped my thumb would soon heal. I never forgot this episode, and always hoped that these gallant soldiers all returned safely from the war to their loved ones.

By the late 1940s most mines had been cleared and the debris of war had been removed. Redcar was again fully functional as a holiday resort, predominantly for the working class from the north east.

Our last holiday in Redcar was in 1953. We stayed with my parents in a very small caravan just off the Stray. My mum didn't really enjoy it as she said we were all on top of each other, and I seem to remember that was an understatement. The grass under the caravan hadn't been cut, and the inside was infested with earwigs. I don't remember having much sleep as my mum spent most nights on 'hunt and destroy' missions. Some friends from Bradford, Mr and Mrs Calpin and their son Lawrence, were staying nearby in a caravan. Lawrence was a little younger than I but we got on well together over the holiday, spending most of our time in the amusement arcades and looking for crabs on the beach. Probably the best night we all had, particularly my mum, was *High Noon* showing at the Central Picture House. My mum was in her element, with two hours of sheer bliss away from those dreadful earwigs.

Blackpool

I remember a few holidays and daytrips during the war to Blackpool, with my mum and Lawrence. We stayed at a Mrs Rutter's boarding house. She had a parrot that could recite its name and address: I wasn't impressed as it smelt! Mrs Rutter was a small woman completely wrapped in a flowery pinny, with her greying hair scragged back behind into a bun, full of grips that needed to be continually pushed in. There was a Mr Rutter, too, although I have no mental picture of him: I think his wife used to keep him out of the way of the lodgers. The three of us were crammed in a small bedroom, where I slept with my mum and Lawrence slept on a small mattress on the floor. The lodgings were close to the railway station in the centre of town, but closer still was the gasworks in Princess Street. Between the smell of the parrot and the gas works there wasn't much fresh air. Even at a young age I was beginning to become intolerant.

These smells were overcome by the many amusements on offer. There was the wonderful Pleasure Beach, with a rich variety of rides, stalls and arcades. On arrival there the first thing you saw was the large Fun House Noah's Ark, which was set at an uneven angle and had moving walkways. One particular walkway blew a blast of air, which made girls' skirts rise in the air, showing stocking tops. Loud screams from those caught in the blast rent the air, while crowds of leering men looked on. The scene was almost identical to a saucy Bamforth postcard. Then there was that awful Laughing Sailor in a glass case, which for the sum of 1*d* roared with laughter and rolled from side to side. While it made adults laugh, I and many of my generation didn't find him funny, as his guffawing seemed designed to give us nightmares. He was also wearing a pair of pumps, which didn't seem to be appropriate and gave him a sinister look. Every day screams could be heard above all the fun of the fair from those on the famous Big Dipper. All this, then a tram ride back along the front to the centre of town, in time for tea at Mrs Rutter's. Food was still rationed, so our ration books had to be handed in to Mrs Rutter.

We had to leave the boarding house at 9am after breakfast and couldn't return until half past four for our tea at five o'clock. Trudging around all day wasn't too bad if the weather was sunny, as we could go to the beach and sit on the sand. The beach was always packed from one end to the other. It was here that I had my first introduction to the Punch and Judy show, which took place every day on the sands. A large 8 foot tall, 4 foot by 4 foot tent, almost like a telephone box with a small stage set at the top, was home to Punch and Judy. At the stage was so high the show could be viewed by crowds of children of all ages sitting on the sands. On the face of it the story of Punch and Judy is quite scary and gruesome, dealing as it does with murder and mayhem, love and death, ghosts and ghouls, a hangman and a sausage-eating crocodile. But we knew it was a story – that if we came back the next day everything would be back to normal and the baby and Judy would be alive. The show, which always lasted about twenty-five minutes, was great fun and I was hooked. During the week I would see it many times, and would always willingly put my 3*d* in the wooden coin box that was passed among the audience. For days after my visits I would still be shouting in the squeaky voice of Mr Punch, 'That's the way to do it!'

Taking donkey rides on the beach was also a first for me. At last I could emulate a trooper of the US Seventh Cavalry! I always wanted to gallop off on my own, but this was impossible as there was always an attendant holding the reins to guide you the hundred yards there and back. Some children older than I, and probably used to riding, had no one holding the reins and could canter along. How I envied them prancing along with bells jangling, while I was with the also-rans. No: I'd stick with Punch and Judy.

Blackpool also had a zoo of sorts, a small affair in the Blackpool Tower building. My dad used to tell me that one of the lions had eaten a kid called Albert when he poked it with a stick. It wasn't until much later that I found out it was a classic monologue by Stanley Holloway, called 'The Lion and Albert'.

If it rained we went to the pictures or sat in the Winter Gardens and listened

Me and Lawrence at Blackpool Pleasure Beach, 1940. The war and Mrs Rutter's parrot didn't affect our smiles. *(Author's collection)*

to the radio organist Reginald Dixon. There were hundreds of other people inside, some dancing but mostly standing around, all with the same intention – to get out of the rain. On every visit to Blackpool, come rain or shine, Mum dragged me and Lawrence along the promenade to Gypsy Rose, the famous fortune teller. She had a velvet curtained booth close to the Pleasure Beach. On the large display outside were photographs of her wearing a headband with coins hanging from it and large hoop earrings, taken with stars like George Formby, Rob Wilton and Vera Lynn. Mum rummaged through her purse, counted her money and then disappeared into the beckoning booth while we waited outside. We never learnt what Gypsy Rose had told her, but she always came out with a smile so it must have been worth the 2s 6d. Every seaside resort seemed to have a Gypsy Rose, and later I cottoned on that there had to be more than one!

For lunch or a cup of tea we had to join long queues. Sometimes, when we were close to the end of the queue, a notice went up saying 'Sold Out'. At Mrs Rutter's our tea was always a guessing game: sometimes I never knew what we were eating! The food was always served and cleared by an old and rather sinister hunchbacked lady. At six o'clock we had to go out again and stay out until exactly ten o'clock, or we would be locked out.

After the war, when my dad came out of the forces, we had a couple of holidays as a family, but we never learnt. We still went to Mrs Rutter's, to the same small bedroom, where the same rules applied and the parrot and the gasworks still smelt.

Eire

Probably the best family holiday we ever had was in Eire, which we visited for a fortnight in 1947. It was summer, Lawrence was home from college, and after such an awful winter my parents decided we should all go on holiday. My Auntie Margaret, and mum's friend Nancy, accompanied us to the place where they were both born, a village close to the sea in County Wicklow called Rathnew.

The trip was long and tiring but uneventful. We took the train in the afternoon from the Exchange station, changed twice and arrived at the port of Holyhead in the evening. Customs were very strict and we spent a couple of hours queuing in a large hangar before we could embark on the ship, which was still painted in wartime camouflage colours of dull grey and brown. On boarding, we found seats in a large lounge that soon filled up, after which people began to sit on the floor and along the gangways.

The ship set sail in the early hours of the morning. My mum's fear of water was obvious as she sat there, me on one side and Lawrence on the other. Our hands were held in a vice-like grip, and she was probably saying many Hail Marys. Despite her fears the trip was uneventful. The colour came back to my mum's face as soon as we disembarked at Dun Laoghaire. Trains were already waiting to take us to the main station in Dublin. After queuing for some time

Our lovely holiday in Eire. Kathleen, a local girl, taught me how to swing a pail of water over my head without spilling any of the water. *(Author's collection*

my parents and brother boarded the train – but I didn't, as I missed the step to the carriage and slipped down the gap between the platform and the train, ending up underneath the carriage. Mum screamed, and as I looked up hands were already reaching down for me. I was pulled up by some men who put me into my mum's outstretched arms! 'Oh God,' she said. 'I thought I'd lost him.' I felt all right until I noticed that my chest and the top of my legs were all scraped and bruised. I was uncomfortable for some time, but the fuss from my mum, Auntie Margaret and Nancy soon helped me to forget it. Referring to the incident some time later, Auntie Cassie said, 'Who but Gandhi could have slipped in between a train and a platform?'

After another train ride we arrived at the lovely village of Rathnew, shaded by the Wicklow Mountains, 3 miles from Wicklow Town. South of the town were the beautiful Silver Strand and Mahermore Beach. Our family was to stay in a bungalow with Nancy's relations. This was set close to a small meadow in which there was a well that provided us with water. At the bottom of the garden there was a large chicken coop, which held lots of hens and just as many small yellow baby chicks.

Almost every day we made our way to the beach with its beautiful golden sand, the like of which I had never seen before. The beaches was not as commercialised as at British holiday resorts; there were few people about. It was much quieter, as there were no amusement arcades or fairgrounds. We had wonderful days: the sea was blue, and the company of our new friends was complemented by clear skies and warm sunshine. It was the first time I had spent so much time jumping into the sea and playing in the sand. Grains of sand became lodged everywhere, until removed by my mum's rigorous towelling, but eight hours' sun exposure hours was only eased by slapping on Nivea cream. We had rides in a donkey cart, which I didn't enjoy much as my mum was very frightened, which made me apprehensive. Sometimes I rode on the family's donkey on my own – when I got it to move.

As the light and temperature changed, pullovers and cardigans were put on and sandals and socks were emptied of sand. With damp and tangled hair and sand between our toes, it seemed that the journey home always took longer. 'You'll sleep tonight,' my mum would say.

In Nancy's family there was a girl of my age to whom I grew quite attached. Her name was Kathleen. She was more of a country girl, and unlike Jean Glossop, the girl next door back home, didn't want to play House. I used to fetch water with her from the well, and on our return she showed me how to swing a pail of water over my head without spilling a drop. After many soakings I finally mastered this, and had to show everyone many times how easy it was.

Everything seemed so different, and I had never seen my mum look so well or laugh so much, especially after looking so ill a few months earlier at the end of that awful winter. There was still rationing in England, and – as Eire had not had rationing at all – it was a new and exciting experience to go into shops and buy as many sweets and chocolate as I wanted. We had eggs, bacon and meat almost every day, and we could eat as much as we wished. There was only one moment of sadness – when I stood on a small chick and killed it. I couldn't help it as there were hundreds of them in the field and garden. No one else seemed bothered, just me, so Kathleen and I took it away and buried it in a far corner of the field.

The holiday went very quickly, and it was soon time to take leave of old and new friends. They were just as sad on parting as we were. I said goodbye to Kathleen with a kiss – not our first, as we had been holding hands and kissing in the lower meadow. If my mum had only known! We were really quite shy, but had enjoyed each other's company, me with my boyish Yorkshire accent and her soft Irish lilt.

We were all very silent on the way home. At Dun Laoghaire the same camouflaged ship loomed up in the dark, and my mum was petrified again. Once on board the ship her tan was replaced with an ashen look, and again she held on to Lawrence and me as she looked out on to the deck at the nearest lifeboat. My dad was fast asleep!

The Irish customs were fine, but at Holyhead the English customs officers ruthlessly searched for items that were impossible to obtain in England. My mother had bought a Catholic statue of the Little Infant of Prague, and it was wrapped up in tissue paper. When a customs officer spotted this in my mum's case he didn't open the tissue paper, as he thought it was a bottle – and proceeded to screw off the statue's head. My mum, back on dry land again, suddenly came back to life. Her tan reappeared as the customs shed reverberated with her voice, bringing down the wrath of God on the miserable customs officer who had desecrated her statue. He apologised profusely and offered compensation of £2. The statue had cost *2s 6d*, and my mum accepted the money with grace.

Back home it was sunny, and we continued to have a good summer. I had enjoyed the holiday so much, but after a few weeks it was as if it had been a dream, especially as we had come back to rationing. I was also conscience-stricken because I had promised Kathleen that I would marry her, and thought I should tell my mum. Discretion being the better part of valour, however, I decided to live alone with my memories.

Scarborough
The seaside is a special place, with its own distinctive sounds, tastes and sights, the air filled with the smell of fish and chips mingled with the sharp salty fragrance of a fresh breeze. Sometimes, mainly in the late 1940s, we spent a holiday at the East Yorkshire costal resort of Scarborough. It always seemed cold, no matter when in the summer we went. A cold north-east wind always blew

My dad paddles in the sea on a lovely summer's day in Scarborough. The temperature could be over 100°F and he would still be wearing his collar and tie on the beach. *(Author's collection)*

down the coast; sometimes even a sea 'fret' covered us. Meanwhile a few miles inland the sun shone in a clear blue sky.

We stayed in far nicer accommodation here than we did in Blackpool. Our boarding house, was in a red-brick terrace on Tennyson Avenue, close to Peasholm Park and the county cricket ground. Mr and Mrs Spencer, who ran the house, were originally from Bradford. Rigid times to stay away and return weren't imposed, and we could come and go as we pleased. Mr Spencer had worked in the mills in Bradford, so he and my dad had a lot in common. Mrs Spencer was quite motherly to me; her only son George had been killed at Arnhem in 1944, so I was quite a favourite; she told me her son had had blue eyes just like mine. We always returned to the Spencers' for our Scarborough holidays, and also visited them if we were there only on a daytrip. My mum always said, in an affectionate way, 'They're a very nice couple.'

Down along Foreshaw Road there were many of my favourite amusement arcades, which were a cauldron of noise, colour and excitement. Also around the harbour were seafood stalls, where mum bought small white triangular paper bags containing winkles and I bought shrimps. I loved those salted shrimps sprinkled with vinegar – but the winkles were something else! I could never understand why my mum liked them, but it was probably because of her

Charles Laughton. The famous film star's advice to me in Scarborough was to always address adults as Mr or Sir. *(Kobal)*

childhood days in Redcar. I thought they were disgusting, especially when she withdrew them with a small pin, and I always associated them with something from the nose!

Sometimes we took a trip on the pleasure steamers, the *Regal Lady* and the *Coronia*, from Scarborough's old harbour. The *Coronia* had helped evacuate troops from Dunkirk in 1940; she was reported to have rescued over 900 troops. The *Regal Lady* had also assisted in the Dunkirk evacuation. This had taken place just a few years earlier, and I always felt proud being a passenger on these wonderful historic boats for a couple of hours.

The sandy beach was small, and on the few sunny days I remember it was wall to wall with people. We hired deckchairs, and my parents relaxed to the music drifting over from the nearby amusement arcades, or the Salvation Army singing hymns accompanied by a portable harmonium. During the day I would be sent to one of the many foreshore cafés for a jug of tea and cups. It cost 2*s* for the tea and 2*s* 6*d* deposit, for return of the jug and cups. My dad always fell asleep with his mouth open and a hankie with a knot on each corner on his head. He took his shoes and socks off, but never his tie, and he snoozed there, oblivious of the rest of the world – an icon of fashion! I was always fascinated to watch the many female sunbathers who struggled to change into a bathing costume concealed only by a very small towel and hoping not to expose any naked flesh. Many males, both young and old, would glance across, but were brought back to reality by a clip on the head from their irate girlfriend or wife.

At the end of the day, if we were tired, we took the wonderful funicular railway that was set in the side of the cliff, rather than walking up into the town centre. This took us right to the top, close to the Grand Hotel.

Once we took our holiday at the same time as Vincent, his parents and sister Maureen. It was the end of August, and they had come to attend the annual Yorkshire County Cricket Festival. Vincent and I spent a lot of time together; it was almost home from home, without the cobbled streets and back-to-back houses. We visited Scarborough Castle on the hill and the Roman signal station overlooking the bay, but perhaps the greatest treat was to visit Peasholm Park to watch the Battle of Peasholm Park, in which large-scale electrically powered Second World War battleships re-enacted a battle from England's naval heritage. When we were there it was the famous Battle of the River Plate, including HMS *Ajax*, HMS *Achilles* and HMS *Exeter*, and of course the famous German battleship *Graf von Spee*. The battle was re-enacted with great authenticity, and a tremendous noise from all the ships' naval guns. Everyone was thrilled, and we made more than one visit to see the Battle of the River Plate that week.

Both Vincent and I were keen cricketers, although our cricket pitch was generally the 'old Rec' in Legrams Lane. During the Yorkshire County Cricket Festival who should we see walking along Marine Drive but our cricketing hero, Freddy Trueman, with his wife. We got some scraps of paper and a pencil, and asked him politely for his autograph. 'F— off', he said. 'I'm on holiday.' And with that he walked off. With these words he lost two young fans, and from then on our allegiance changed. When he played for

England in the future we supported the other England fast bowler, Lancashire's Brian Statham.

One of my favourite films when I was young was *The Hunchback of Notre Dame*, starring Charles Laughton in the title role. During one holiday in Scarborough I had been down to the beach on my own to paddle. When I came back to the foreshore I sat on a bench to dry my feet in the sun. A gentleman, his hands clasped on a large ornate walking cane, sat next to me, peering out to sea. Recognising him as I put my socks on, I said, 'Are you Charles Laughton?' He sat up straight, looked up and said, with a smile, 'It's Mr Laughton!' He then struck up a conversation, telling me he was on a visit to see his brother in Scarborough. We didn't talk about films, and I really didn't know what to ask him. He was very interested in Bradford, and said that the film star Michael Rennie was Bradford-born and a very dear friend of his. I always remember his departure: he stood up, reached into his waistcoat pocket and gave me half a crown, saying, 'Always remember, never call elderly gentlemen by their Christian names. It's always Mr or, if you don't know their name, sir.' I always remembered his advice.

'What a tale!' my mum said. She was unimpressed, and advised me against taking money from and talking to strange men – but she thought differently when his photo appeared in the local newspaper, with a report that said he had been in Scarborough for a couple of days to visit his brother Tom.

Lobby Lud was a name to conjure with. The *Daily Mail* was promoted during the summer with a stunt involving a character named Lobby Lud. His silhouette appeared in the paper the day before his visit to a seaside town. The idea was that you had to try to spot him. If you thought you had, you had to approach him, with a copy of the *Daily Mail* under your arm, and issue a challenge, in these words: 'You are Lobby Lud and I claim the *Daily Mail* £5 prize.' One day Lobby Lud was due to visit Scarborough. Three times on that day my dad was approached and challenged. Each time he politely said he wasn't Lobby Lud, and called the inquirer a flat-cake. Others, who were more vulgar, would respond, 'Bugger off' when approached.

Cameras at this time were fairly large and cumbersome, so seaside photographers did a brisk business. They would hail you, raise an arm and adopt a semi-crouched position. Camera in hand, this total stranger, entirely unsolicited, would appear to take a photograph of you or your group and offer to sell it to you. If you agreed, it was almost essential a second photograph was taken; in most cases the first one was pretence. A numbered receipt was given, and you were told that the photographs would be ready for collection the next day, usually from a nearby kiosk. This is why thousands of homes in Britain had drawers full of photographs of people walking on a seaside promenade. We certainly had many.

Of all the local resorts I believe it was Scarborough that we liked best. Although flatter, Bridlington seemed to be brasher and not very clean. It too had a pleasure boat, the *Yorkshire Belle*, which like its sister boats in Scarborough had taken part in the evacuation of Dunkirk. Filey was too reserved and quiet, and sandwiched between Filey and Bridlington was Butlin's holiday camp. Butlin's, my dad said, was not for us, as he he'd had enough of camps and cookhouses to last him a lifetime when he was in the army. The picturesque fishing port of Whitby was worth a daytrip, but not a holiday. The town was very much based around the harbour, which was busy with boats of all kinds, including fishing cobbles, cargo vessels and pleasure craft. Smells of vinegar and beer, amusement arcades and shops selling gifts and postcards were all part of the bustle and atmosphere. The harbour was overlooked by the sinister-looking Whitby Abbey. Once we had a meal at the Royal Hotel on the western cliff top, close to the large whale bones that form an arch. It was at this hotel that Bram Stoker stayed many times while writing his famous novel *Dracula*. As well as the coastal towns, the beautiful villages of Runswick Bay, Robin Hood's Bay and Staithes were all accessible by train along the old cliff top Scarborough to Saltburn line.

We had many daytrips and holidays, each one more memorable than the last, in what seemed to be truly a tranquil age. They were wonderful and happy times.

Chapter 19
Memories of Wireless and Television

Early Wireless

Apart from newspapers, we relied on the wireless, as it was commonly known, for news and entertainment. It told us what was happening in the country and worldwide, although during the war, for obvious reasons, news was sparse – unless it was of a victory. There were only two BBC wave-bands: the Home Service, which was the serious stuff, and the General Forces Programme, which was lighter entertainment. After the war this became the Light Programme. I have many early recollections of some of the favourite wartime wireless programmes, although because of my age I was generally in bed before seven in the evening.

Our wireless sat on a table in the corner of the room. It was a large pre-war model, made of walnut. It had a 6 inch transparent dial and in the centre a knob to twirl to find the stations. Another knob was at each side, one for on and off, the other to change between long, medium and short wave. Above this was woven fabric with an art-deco design, covering the speaker. The names of many European radio stations were written on the dial next to their transmitting frequencies; rather a waste of time as we were unable to receive most of them! Most I had never heard of, although I did recognise Berlin. Over the years I began recognise some of the names, as my head was always only a few inches away from the set. The aerial wire ran through a small hole in the bottom of the window, and was connected outside to a spike in the wall we fixed the washing line to. Reception was good.

We were lucky to have electricity, as some of the houses nearby were still supplied by gas only. My grandparents up in Fenton Street, Princeville, still used gas, but had a wireless powered by a battery known as an accumulator. This had to be frequently recharged, which meant disconnecting it and taking it to a garage or cycle shop and exchanging it for a freshly charged one. As I got older it was one of my jobs to do this. It was a heavy job carting the battery up and down to Merrick's electrical and auto shop on Legrams Lane, so I used to borrow a small handcart. Every so often my mum said, 'Your grandma's accumulator wants recharging when you have a minute' – and I always knew she wanted it done quickly as she liked her special programmes. It was worth it: she was always grateful, and gave me 6*d*.

My mum always said that my grandmother's favourite programme during the war was Lord Haw Haw's propaganda broadcasts from Germany. I know that every time I visited the house he always seemed to be on her wireless, and she asked me, aged five or six, not to interrupt. I sat on a stool, my head cupped in my hands, and listened too. I had no idea who he was, but I have never forgotten his nasal voice and the words 'Garmany calling, Garmany calling'. My grandmother always seemed to be nodding, whether in approval or disgust it was hard for me to know.

We listened to the news avidly, both good and bad. In 1939 the BBC started to name the newsreaders, who had hitherto been anonymous. So we had new friends, who were less impersonal – like John Snagge, Alvar Liddell, Bruce Belfrage, Stuart Hibberd and, my favourite, Frank Phillips. As well as the news, announcements were given out appealing for witnesses to an accident or similar to ring Whitehall 1212; while out-of-touch relations were asked to contact hospitals if a relative was dangerously ill.

We also listened to the shipping forecast with places like Rockall, Malin, Bailey, Viking, Forties and Dogger Bank. One of our neighbours, an old sailor, said, 'We think we have it tough but the fishermen have to contend with the dangers of the sea as well as German U-boats up their arses.' Vincent and I thought this was funny and laughed, especially because of the swearword. My mother told me off for repeating it. But he was right.

I graduated to the wireless like many other children with *Children's Hour* and the voice of Uncle Mac (Derek McCulloch), with his greeting 'Hello children everywhere'. I didn't think much of Toytown, and could never understand that daft sheep with the trembling voice, Larry the Lamb. He doesn't make any sense, I thought. Surprisingly it was Uncle Mac who played the part of Larry the Lamb! 'Norman and Henry Bones, Boy Detectives', 'Bunkle', another boy detective and 'Wandering with Nomad', a walk introducing the joys of the countryside, all enlightened me and didn't seem childish.

Another wireless entertainment was the endless supply of cinema organists pounding away incessantly on the mighty wurlitzer. The most popular organists were Sandy McPherson, the soft-spoken Canadian with his programme *Chapel in the Valley*, Reginald Foort and Reginald Dixon, who played at the Tower Ballroom in Blackpool. My mum liked the Radio Doctor, Dr Charles Hill, who had many health tips – most of which seemed to be designed to keep your bowels open and regular. During the war he advised us about the use and care of gasmasks, and ways in which we should implement the blackout. My mum said he had the most soothing voice on the wireless, and it was a tonic just listening to him. I agreed, and often asked why he wasn't our doctor. One of my mum's other favourite programmes was *Music While you Work*, each morning and afternoon, with a non-stop medley of popular tunes, broadcast to keep the workers happy. Many times I heard my mum joining in the singing. We children had our own rendition of the signature tune:

Whistle while you work
Snow White made a shirt
Dopey wore it and he tore it
Wasn't he a twerp?

There was also *Workers' Playtime*, a lunchtime roadshow three times a week that went out live from factory canteens and shop floors up and down the country. The audience was made up of as many workers as could jam themselves into the venue. This and *Music While You Work* were a British institution, especially during the war years.

There was a lot of comedy on the wireless. The big show was Tommy Handley's *It's That Man Again* (*ITMA*), which had a colossal following. It was so popular (16 million listeners) that if the Germans had invaded at 8.30 on any Thursday evening resistance wouldn't have been up to much! *ITMA* was a series of sketches held together by a very thin plot, the purpose being to introduce a host of well-known and well-loved characters and their catchphrases: characters like Funf, 'This is Funf speaking', Mrs Mopp, 'Can I do you now, Sir?' and Colonel Chinstrap, 'I don't mind if I do' – an innocent inebriated reply to the offer of a drink. I knew most of the catchphrases, but the sketches were a little too adult for me.

There were also drama and plays, but it was one of the most famous and popular horror series that I stopped up for and listened to with my mum, sitting on the stairs with the light out! *Appointment with Fear* was presented by the sinister Valentine Dyall. In a sepulchral voice he introduced the story, later making comments and sometimes providing short narrative links. The stories were all riveting but the one I thought the scariest was 'The Monkey's Paw'. Later, in a similar format, he introduced 'The Man in Black', and again we sat on the stairs and scared ourselves to death. Meanwhile my dad sat in the room with the light on, reading the newspaper and shaking his head. When I went to bed later my mum had to leave the landing light on.

One of the best detective wireless series was *Paul Temple*: it was full of action and suspense, but without the horror of *Appointment with Fear*. It originally starred Kim Peacock as Paul Temple (1945–54) and Marjorie Westbury as his wife Steve. In the Temples' world of car bombs, poisoned cocktails, gentlemen and rogues, the villain was always caught and handed over to Chief Inspector Sir Graham Forbes. I always imagined that Steve looked like the Queen! The music for the original series was Rimsky Korsakov's *Scheherazade*, which give the series suspense and also introduced me to this kind of classical music. The music changed in later series to *Coronation Scot*.

It seems that I began to listen to the wireless with my mum, but this changed when my dad came back from the war. On winter evenings in front of the fire we all laughed together at comedy shows such as *Much Binding in the Marsh*, *Take it from Here*, *Happidrome*, *Garrison Theatre*, and the many comedians like Tommy Trinder, Arthur Askey, Richard Murdoch, and Elsie and Doris Waters (known to all as 'Gert and Daisy'). Then there was Max Miller ('the Cheeky Chappie'). When he came on, my parents were both eager to turn the wireless off: it wasn't until I was much older that I knew why! We also enjoyed the chat shows such as *Have a Go*, with Wilfred Pickles, his wife Mabel at the table and Violet Carson at the piano, 'presenting the people to the people'. The original trials of this popular programme were made by BBC Northern Region in Bradford, and the first edition to be broadcast was recorded on 16 February 1946 in Bingley.

Of interest to all the family on a lighter note was *In Town Tonight*, a programme of outside and studio broadcasting where interviews were carried out with well-known personalities on a variety of subjects, and also ordinary people who had done something particularly interesting. Richard Dimbleby going *Down Your Way* was of particular interest when his programmes were broadcast from a town or village in Yorkshire that we could identify with.

Desert Island Discs with Roy Plomley (even at a young age I loved his signature tune 'By the Sleepy Lagoon'), which introduced me to all kinds of people and their choice of eight records. Aged ten I compiled my eight favourite records in a notebook just in case I was asked to appear on the programme! My choice was constantly changed, but two always on the list were 'The Laughing Policeman' by Charles Penrose and Khachaturian's 'Sabre Dance'.

Programmes of light music were an interlude between the comedy and the drama. Among them was *Henry Hall's Guest Night*, on Sunday evenings at nine o'clock from the Grand Hotel, with the music of the Palm Court Orchestra led by Albert Sandler playing his Stradivarius violin, accompanied most weeks by the popular singers Ann Ziegler and Webster Booth.

During the day, if my mum was not busy, she listened to *Housewives' Choice*. On one occasion she sent a request to this programme for the record of Joan Hammond singing *O My Beloved Father*. When the presenter, popular George Elrick, played it she was out shopping – but most of Listerhills and Bradford heard it, and she was quite popular for a few days with friends, neighbours and people she didn't think she knew saying, 'Heard your record request on the wireless, Vida.' Sometimes my mum listened to *Woman's Hour*, but never *Mrs Dale's Diary*, for reasons she never disclosed!

There was a British male type who was held up as a hero to us all. His jaw was firm and clean-shaven, his smile whimsical and his hair short and well-trimmed, with a dash of Brylcreem. He usually wore a blazer or casual clothing of the most elegant cut, and always wore a tasteful and properly knotted tie. This was Dick Barton! In the mid-1940s the BBC's first radio serial, featuring private investigator and sometime special agent Dick Barton was born, with his two best mates Jock Anderson and Snowy White by his side. Former Captain Richard Barton of the Royal Marine Commandos managed to get into (and out of) some pretty tight spots, much to the delight of thousands of youngsters like me, and, it has to be said, quite a few adults. In the beginning our hero had all the vices: he smoked a pipe, enjoyed a drink and had a girlfriend. Very soon the BBC realised that many young people listened to the programme, so it was decided that the tone had to be watered down. There was to be no sex, no drinking, no bad language and all violence was to be limited to 'clean socks to the jaw'. Dick's girlfriend Jean Hunter always got in the way (so we thought), so when she no longer appeared she wasn't missed.

On the Light Programme at 6.45pm after the news, every Monday to Friday evening for the next five years, the announcer Hamilton Douglas rapped out '*Dick Barton Special Agent*' to the music 'The Devil's Gallop'. We never needed a watch when we were out playing; at 6.45 pm the streets were suddenly deserted as children ran indoors to listen to their hero. It was perhaps the only time that most parents knew where their children were. If we missed a programme we were always brought up to date the following day. In post-war Britain the fast-paced, tongue-in-cheek adventures were exactly what the doctor ordered. At its peak over 15 million listeners tuned in to his adventures, so much so that *Dick Barton Special Agent* was the programme we best remember.

Throughout the war the BBC General Forces Programme helped to keep the British sane. In the 1940s it helped keep our mind off rationing, bombs dropping and the general bleakness of life.

The programmes were simple and unsophisticated, and the fact that we had very little in the shops was often turned into comedy routines. Our ability to laugh at ourselves and to acknowledge that everybody was in the same boat made life a little more bearable, particularly for our parents. On 28 July 1945 it closed down, to be replaced the next day by the Light Programme.

Building a Crystal Set
With the advent of the 1950s I was now a teenager and my radio taste had become different to that of my parents. I had begun to call the wireless a radio, although my parents and older people continued to call it a wireless for many years.

I never had my own radio in my bedroom, as small wireless sets were very expensive. I read in comics that clever young lads like me could build their own radios, so with my small savings I bought the components for a crystal set from Merricks in Listerhills Road, and set out to build it. It was really quite easy with the help of Mr Glossop next door, who was an electrician, of sorts. When it was complete I placed the set in a small cardboard box held together with plasticine, glue and bits of wood. It looked presentable and was quite sturdy. I was very pleased with the finish.

With my dad's help I hung a long piece of wire out of the bedroom window and connected it to the outside drainpipe. This was my antenna. I couldn't really afford a pair of earphones, but was given a single earphone which was better than nothing. A crystal set didn't have to have a battery, as science told us that it ran off the radio waves it picked up in the air. It was absolutely free to use! Imagine my surprise and delight when, after fiddling with the cat's whisker coil, a radio station came through. I was impressed, as were my parents. The only problem was that the slightest movement could knock the cat's whisker off the crystal; but it was great fun, especially if I picked up a foreign station, which I did many times. Even so, it was mostly the Home Service and the Light Programme that I listened to. All this from a small cardboard box held together with plasticine and glue! My crystal set lasted for a few months until one night I went to sleep with the set in the bed. I woke up the next morning covered with bits of wood and plasticine around me and the crystal inside my pyjamas. Well, I had built a crystal set and it had worked for a while.

Favourite Radio Shows
By now I had finished with children's programmes and listened to comedy shows like *Ray's a Laugh* with Ted Ray. The programme was a domestic comedy, with Kitty Bluett playing Ted's wife and Kenneth Connor as a seedy character called Sidney Mincing. A catchphrase was developed by Bob and Alf Pearson who provided the musical interlude. It was Bob who provided the voice of the little girl, whose catchphrase was 'My name's Jennifer'. Two other catchphrases from this popular show were, 'He's lovely, Mrs Hodgkin, he's lovely!' and 'It was agony, Ivy!' Young and old thought these were hysterical, and everyone had their way of interpreting and mimicking them. God help you if your name was Jennifer, Mrs Hodgkin or Ivy. I didn't think it was that funny, but I was a fan of Kenneth Connor's character.

Another popular programme was *Much Binding in the Marsh*, with Kenneth Horne and Richard 'Stinker' Murdoch. The show always closed with a comic song. Dick Bentley and Jimmy Edwards were very funny in *Take it From Here*, which was still running from the 1940s. Later, in the 1950s, they introduced 'The Glums'. Mr Glum was a loud-mouthed bore (played by Jimmy Edwards) who presided over a household consisting of his ever-absent wife and his son

Ron, who was one degree removed from utter idiocy and was played with sublime incoherence by Dick Bentley. Ron's fiancé Eth, whose famous catchphrase was 'Oh Ron!' was played by a young June Whitfield. Each week Eth was foiled in her attempts to rise to a richer and happier life by the utter opacity of Ron, whose catchphrase was 'Give us a kiss, Eth!'

On many Sunday mornings the BBC always featured a religious service, which was followed at noon by *Two Way Family Favourites*. The alternative close to Christmas was *Forces Favourites*, a programme where people who were serving in the forces overseas could send loving messages to their families. Then there was *Billy Cotton's Band Show*, with his famous 'Wakey Wakey!', which had contributions from Doreen Stephens and Kathy Kay, as well as the singing of Alan Breeze – which was guaranteed to keep the listeners awake. Listened to by millions, it became a national institution.

A most ridiculous show followed, a radio programme starring a ventriloquist! *Educating Archie* had arrived. Archie Andrews was a grinning dummy with manic eyes, elegantly clad in a broad striped blazer. It was his master Peter Brough who threw his voice, and we all seemed to be taken in by this. Did he have the dummy up to the microphone as he did in publicity shots? The question was who was kidding whom? I only listened to the show because an up-and-coming comedian on the programme was, for a time, Tony Hancock.

Charlie Chester was another comedian who had his own show. It was called *Stand Easy*, and was very popular after the war and well into the 1950s. He, like other comedians, had catchphrases. Some, more statements than catchphrases, became very popular – with different connotations each week: an example is 'Down in the Jungle living in a tent, better than a prefab, no rent!'

Just Fancy was a character comedy show that starred a great comedian, Eric Barker. He said the famous words 'Steady Barker' when under stress.

Victor Silvester's overseas request programmes were very popular with what was termed the shiny shoe club. Housewives could practise the step of 'quick, quick, quick quick, slow' on the lino; I know as I sometimes partnered my mum as she spun around the scullery floor. I thought, like many other listeners, that he made up the request names, with places like British West Hartlepool – and who was listening in Lhasa, the capital of Tibet?

A break from all this frivolity came to this island every Saturday afternoon at 5pm. Fathers were poised with pen or pencil to check the football results on the programme *Sports Report*. It was most people's dream to win the football pools, and woe and betide any member of the household who made a sound or uttered a word during the broadcast. If Dad had eight draws, which gave him twenty-four points, he would at last be able to finish work, and buy a car and a new house. If there was a single person that week with this result then £75,000 would be theirs; if not, there was always next week.

The radio parlour game *Twenty Questions*, a hangover from the 1940s, was still very popular. Household names like Gilbert Harding, Anona Winn, Joy Adamson, Daphne Padel and Jack Train were regular panel guests. The idea was to identify objects by asking only twenty questions. Almost a catchphrase in its own right was 'And the next object is . . .' whispered close to the microphone by a mystery voice, informing the audience of the next object.

BBC plays and stories were excellent at that time, notably *The Lost World*, based on the book by Sir Arthur Conan Doyle. This serial was set deep within the Amazon jungle where no human being has ever set foot, an untamed region of mystery and wonder. This wilderness hid an ancient and dangerous prehistoric world, and a small band of explorers discovered marvels beyond imagination and terrors beyond belief! With the introduction supported by the wonderful music of Gustav Holst's 'Mars, the Bringer of War', I was scared stiff listening to each episode. The programme faded out, leaving me with the hairs on the back of my neck standing on end. Radio was definitely the theatre of the mind!

The Goon Show

Radio still dominated, but young and old were increasingly listening to different programmes: older people continued to enjoy traditional fare, while we listened to pop music. Just as divisive was the *Goon Show*, which outshone all other radio comedy of the time. It introduced a new form of manic humour which was almost incomprehensible to our parents. It was to change the face of British comedy. The Goons were Spike Milligan, Peter Sellers, Harry Secombe and Michael Bentine, who left the show in 1952. The storylines were surreal, including absurd logic, puns, catchphrases and ground-breaking sound effects. Characters such as Neddie Seagoon, Eccles, Bluebottle, Major Denis Bloodnok, Count Jim Moriarty, Hercules Grytpype-Thynne, Miss Minnie Bannister and Henry Crun all savaged the airwaves, helping to create an alternative and ludicrous view of the world. It was not until 1954 that each show began to have a single plot, its well-known format. I, like many others of my age, drove my parents to despair by mimicking the voices and playing the 'Ying Tong Song' and 'I'm walking backwards for Christmas' on the radio in the kitchen while my parents were in the front room watching the new television. My dad, listening to the racket of the Goons coming through the wall, would shake his head and utter his favourite word, flat-cake. The Goons were truly remarkable, and I will never forget them.

Watching the Coronation

Like many others I saw the Queen's coronation on a neighbour's television in 1953. Mr and Mrs McNamara, who lived on Naisby Street, off Shearbridge Road, were friends of my parents and invited them and me, together with what seemed like a hundred others, to watch the coronation. We were all crammed into the living room of a back-to-back house. I didn't really see much, as all around me was a hive of activity, with people sitting, standing, moving and being noisy. The front door open and closed every few minutes as young and old paraded down to the outside toilet, where a queue had formed. One old lady complained of feeling faint, which brought about shouts of 'Give her some air' – and everyone then proceeded to fall over each other to make some room for the distraught woman. Over the noise I heard a much older lady exclaim to the victim, 'I think your corsets are too tight.' As everyone moved I had the opportunity to view the screen in the distance, but only for a fleeting moment – as the picture started rolling. It came back just as the crowd surged back to their viewing positions, and again I was lost in a sea of bodies. I was distracted once more, this time when by a mouse close to the scullery door. I didn't know if I should say anything, but mentioned it to Mrs McNamara. 'A mouse!' she exclaimed, causing a sudden upheaval as the women, and some men, headed for the open front door. By then the mouse had disappeared. A drunken, loud-mouthed father of a 'dopey lass', who I didn't like, said that I should have more sense and deserved a clip around the earhole for causing the disturbance. Rescue was at hand, as my mum was sitting at the far side of the room with our neighbour Lucy. She stood up and shouted, 'You touch him and there'll be trouble!' He muttered something to my mum, which was a big mistake, but before she could intervene further Mr McNamara had forcibly picked up the drunken parent and hoisted him through the open door into the small garden. A cheer went up from the toilet queue, and things in the house returned to normal.

A moment or two later not a sound could be heard, only a few 'oohs' and 'aahs' from the women, and one of them, sitting on the arm of a settee, started crying and said, 'The Queen is crowned!' I didn't see it but I can always remember where I was on Coronation Day.

Our First Television
It was not until early in 1955 that we had our first television set, a Pye. It was rented from Scurrah's of Bankfoot. Televisions at that time, although a wonderful invention, were prone to problems that could be expensive to repair. There was always talk of the tube going, which was a frequent problem for many households; a rental set, although expensive, made sense as it was covered for call-outs and repairs. There was a 12 inch screen set in a floor-standing cabinet about 4 feet high. As the screen was quite small, we had to sit close to it. A large H-shaped aerial was fixed to the chimney and pointed to the transmitter at Holme Moss, joining many others that were now dominating the skyline.

Television programmes were only shown at certain times of the day, and ended quite early: the National Anthem was played, an announcer said 'goodnight' and reminded us to turn the television off. There seemed to be endless breakdowns in transmission, and interludes were used to fill in the time.

Sergeant Ernie Bilko (Phil Silvers). My hero! *(CU)*

No one seemed to complain as there was at least something to watch – either the potter's wheel or a white kitten playing with a ball of wool. If the screen was too small for comfort, a large magnifying glass could be purchased and strapped on to enlarge the picture. One problem with this was that if you sat to one side the picture became distorted, almost like looking through the bottom of a milk bottle. Other problems with the picture were ghosting, rolling scanning lines, white spots, interference from traffic and domestic appliances. However, when all was working free it was a joy to watch. Alas, TV sounded the death knell of many of Bradford's smaller picture houses.

Up until September 1955 there had only been one TV channel – BBC Television. With the advent of commercial television a new phrase came into the language of television viewers, 'Shall we see what's on the other side?'

I think my parents enjoyed the programmes more, as quite a high proportion were made to entertain older people. An example of a popular programme that they, especially my mum, enjoyed was *The Grove Family*, Britain's first soap for adults. The stories were centred on a lower middle-class family that was just beginning to be comfortably off after years of hardship. I watched it a few times but old granny Grove used to get on my nerves. My mum, unsurprisingly, was also enthralled by a host of imported cowboy films from America.

The panel game *What's My Line?* was avidly watched by us all. It was chaired by an Irish ex-boxer and former sports commentator, Eamonn Andrews. There were four celebrity panellists, the usual ones being the bespectacled and ruddy-faced Gilbert Harding, the TV illusionist supreme, David Nixon, a beautiful lady doctor turned broadcaster, Lady Isobel Barnett, and the dynamic Canadian comedienne and wife of Bernard Braden, actress Barbara Kelly. Again, this TV show was particularly enjoyed by my parents, although aged seventeen I thought that Lady Isobel Barnett was rather dishy!

Sunday Night at the London Palladium was another popular programme. Tommy Trinder was the host of the very first show, a regular at the Palladium since 1941. He was a well-liked comedian with his good-natured catchphrase, 'You lucky people'. Although the compère was crucial to the success of the show, the format rarely altered. The high-kicking Tiller Girls were followed by a warm welcome from the host, a couple of acts and then the fun game 'Beat the Clock'. Two more acts followed before the famous set-piece finale where the stars of the show waved goodbye from the celebrated revolving stage. The show was a topic of conversation for millions in factories, offices and on shop floors on Monday mornings. Sunday evening services in some churches started early so that the parishioners could be home in time to watch some of the world's most spectacular stars and the best of home-grown talent in their living rooms.

I enjoyed some television entertainment (if my parents weren't watching anything in particular), in between work, girlfriends, hitchhiking and holidays, but didn't let it dominate my life. *Robin Hood* was a particular favourite of mine, starring Richard Greene with Patricia Driscoll as Maid Marian. I thought she was lovely, and I sometimes stopped following the plot when she appeared. The Sheriff of Nottingham was played by the suave Alan Wheatley. I was also a fan of *Highway Patrol*, which starred Broderick Crawford as Chief Dan Matthews. It was one of the first TV cop shows, and its all-action storylines involved the pursuit of murderers and bank robbers by car, bike or helicopter along the highways and byways of the western United States. Surprisingly, it starred no other regulars apart from the star himself. 'Ten-four', meaning message received and understood, was a catchphrase from this series.

I also watched and enjoyed *Quatermass* and *The Quatermass Experiment*, two science fiction series. The sets were bland but the acting was superb, forcing you to watch each and every episode. Then along came George Orwell's *1984*, which had the power to shock and galvanise the entire nation. The programme went out live and was repeated live three days later! It was really top class dramatic television with the wonderful Peter Cushing in the lead. I cannot say at the time that I understood it, but I enjoyed it.

William George Bunter, the oversized school boy who attended Greyfriars School and got involved in a number of comic misadventures, graduated from children's comics to television. The lead was played by the incomparable Gerald Campion. As Basil Rathbone epitomised Sherlock, so Gerald Campion epitomised Billy Bunter. The series gave rise to two catchphrases, 'Yaroo' and 'Oh crikey'. Well, it was the 1950s!

In the Laurel and Hardy mould was the double act *Mick and Montmorency* (Charlie Drake and Jack Edwards). This programme starred the first children's comedy double-act, with Charlie Drake taking most of the pratfalls in fifteen minutes of fun-filled and disastrous adventures, in which the stars played a variety of roles, from removal men to scientists. It was funny and, for once, home-grown.

Whacko was British comedy at its best. It starred Jimmy Edwards as the corrupt, crafty and cane-swishing headmaster of Chiselbury School. His bullying wasn't confined to his students, for members of his staff were given a particularly rough ride, especially his weedy right-hand man, Mr Pettigrew (played by Arthur Howard, brother of the movie star Leslie Howard).

Of all the television stars of the fifties the one I most admired was Bilko, the part made for Phil Silvers. Corporals Barbella and Henshaw and his company of men ably assisted Bilko in his doomed-to-failure schemes, but it was the quick-thinking and smooth-talking Sergeant Bilko who provided the highlights of the show as he managed to extricate himself from many a tight corner. Love interest was provided by WAC Sergeant Joan Hogan, a secretary in the camp commander's office, who gave Bilko another advantage over the rest of the camp as she forewarned him of any new schemes. He then used this knowledge to dupe his victims, most frequently Mess Sergeant Rupert Ritzik. The bewildered Colonel Hall always tried to catch Bilko out, but never succeeded. Quintessential slob Private Duane Doberman, who thought he was a fat Cary Grant, was adored by the public. The show had an excellent supporting cast, and Phil ('Bilko') Silvers was a truly remarkable comedian, my favourite of all time.

There were many other television programmes that my family and I enjoyed in the 1950s, always introduced by impeccably dressed announcers who seemingly spoke to you direct. They were more like friends visiting your living room for the evening, and among their number were MacDonald Hobley, Peter Hague and the attractive Sylvia Peters and Mary Malcolm. At the end of the evening they signed off with a smile and wished you a peaceful night. 'This television programme is now closing down. . . .'

Chapter 20
From Rupert Bear to Julius Caesar

My mum was an avid reader, and I took after her, having got interested when she took me along to the local library. This was in Listerhills, but there was also a smaller library in a row of shops at Lidget Green. Mum only read fiction, sometimes borrowing what I called 'love books' – but it was her addiction to cowboy books that was remarkable: she read as many as four of these a week. It was a wonder that publishers could keep up with her insatiable need. To make sure she didn't borrow the same book twice she put a very small x in one corner of the last page of the book. She hoped that no one else was using the same code!

Comics

I was hooked on reading from a very early age. My first reading interest, aged three, was a comic strip called *Rupert Bear*, which was featured in the *Daily Express*. I didn't understand the small stories too well, but had quite a liking for this bear with his pals Bill Badger, Edward Trunk, Podgy Pig and Algy Pug. *Rupert Bear* was my first Christmas annual, and by the time I was four I was reading the strips quite fluently – and could also follow the stories. After Rupert other characters came along, but this time in comics that cost between 1*d* and 2*d*. My favourite early comics were the *Beano*, *Dandy* and *Knockout*. In these the characters actually spoke – with a speech balloon! It was much easier to understand for me, as each character had his own individuality.

Many characters and families, all getting into ridiculous scrapes in recognisable backgrounds, evolved from the *Beano* alone. There was Big Eggo, a not too attractive ostrich with scaly legs and feet, a scabby bald head, Mickey Mouse-style hands on the end of his wings, and unpleasant crescent moon eyes. Ugly! I thought he was great. It was Big Eggo who dominated the front cover of the Beano for many years – and sometimes I saw people who resembled him. Pansy Potter (the strong man's daughter) was a really strong girl who caused havoc with her strength. There were one or two Pansy Potters in Listerhills. Perhaps everybody's favourite strip featured Lord Snooty and his pals. Lord Marmaduke of Bunkerton, known to his friends as Snooty, was a very ordinary boy who happened to be an Earl. Rather than play with the friends who visited him at Bunkerton Castle, Snooty preferred to play with his real pals from Ash Can Alley. As well as Aunt Matilda, Snooty's guardian, the cartoon featured Joe, very fat and greedy (Big Fat Joe); Scrapper, who loved to fight; Liz, a very tall girl (Swanky, or Lanky Liz); Thomas, an indecisive boy whose hair was shaped like a question mark (Doubting Thomas); Rosie, a short blonde girl; Polly, a black girl; Snitch and Snatch, identical twin babies who were always bouncing about in their romper suits; and the Gasworks Gang, sworn enemies of Snooty and his pals. What a wonderful gang name this was. If only we had lived by the gasworks!

Later came Dennis the Menace and Jimmy and his magic patch. Dennis, wearing his striped jumper, used to get away with his mischief for a while, before ending up getting a spanking with a slipper from his father. Dennis's best defence was sticking a thick book down his shorts: his dad never noticed. Dennis's grandma also had a slipper, made of elephant skin and called the 'Demon Whacker'. There was a little of Dennis in most of us. Jimmy, on the other hand, had a life we could only dream of. Thanks to the magic patch on his shorts he was whisked back in time to have adventures with famous people in history. How I would have liked to have had a magic patch!

The *Dandy*, similar to the *Beano*, had many favourites who were just as popular and funny. Korky the Cat had the front page for many years. The inside pages bristled with household names, such as Keyhole Kate and Hungry Horace, names we sometimes used to refer unkindly to a girl with a long nose or a boy who was greedy. As Lord Snooty was in the *Beano* it was Desperate Dan in the *Dandy*. He was a Wild West character, and apparently the world's strongest man, able to lift a cow with one hand. His beard was so tough he had to shave with a blowtorch. His favourite food was cow pie, which had horns sticking out of the top: it was assumed this contained the meat from an entire cow. He was a desperado and on the wrong side of the law, hence the sobriquet 'Desperate'.

The *Knockout* was also popular. One character was 'Our Ernie', Ernie Entwhistle, a northern lad with a pet caterpillar, lived on Wigan Pier. His dad, an old-fashioned Northern working man, sat in an armchair reading the newspaper: his favourite remark was 'Daft, I call it!' Mother, a figure with apron and headscarf, was usually asked at the end of each episode, 'What's for tea, Ma'? Billy Bunter, another character, was very popular, with a host of room-mates including Jones Minor and Bob Cherry. The form-master, gimlet-eyed Mr Squelch, was always in attendance with his bamboo cane, ready to whack the overweight Bunter for any misdeeds. *Film Fun* was a comic in which the main characters were stars of films, among whom were Laurel and Hardy, Abbott and Costello, Red Skelton, George Formby and Terry-Thomas. In *Radio Fun* it was the stars of radio who were featured, like Arthur Askey, Sandy Powell and Flanagan and Allen.

None of us were rich enough to buy all the comics each week, but with a series of swaps most had been circulated by the time the next editions were on the market. My regulars for swapping comics were Terry Bland, Barry Thomas, Trevor Rhodes, David Gamwell and David Reynard. Almost every night one or the other of these friends called with his bundle of comics under his arm. Negotiations took place, 'this for that' and 'two for one', with the phrase 'Read it' often occurring. My dad smiled behind his newspaper as these exchanges took place, and once said, 'The government could learn something from your negotiating skills.'

Vincent and I had different tastes regarding comics; he read *Hotspur*, *Rover*, *Adventure* and *Wizard*, which were really stories in print rather than a comic strip. I could never become interested in a footballer called 'Baldy' Hogan, a left-back football player who was always scoring goals with his bald head and winning football matches. And then there was a strongman called Karga the Clutcher, who caused havoc with his metal hand. I wasn't impressed with these.

Nearly all comics issued a Christmas annual. I was lucky as I always received two, generally the *Dandy* and *Beano*.

But seriously . . .

I was lucky enough to have some rather more intelligent reading material, which I spent many happy hours with. Primarily this was a full set of Arthur Mee's children's encyclopaedias. These had been purchased (at so much a week) for my brother some years earlier, and were a wealth of information and learning. I also had five Harmsworth history books, which I had rescued from a skip containing items from the fire in 1950 that destroyed the old YMCA building in Forster Square. Like the encyclopaedias, these were a godsend to me with my overwhelming interest in history.

The Eagle

It was a month before my twelfth birthday, April 1950. I was sitting on the causeway edge in my street surrounded by our back-to-back houses. I was reading the first issue of the *Eagle*, which had just hit the shelves of Britain's newsagents. It was a wonderful comic, not only different in content, but the large glossy pages even smelt different, giving an air of high quality we had never seen before. It was an overnight success. There were twenty large pages, eight in colour, and on pages one and two in full colour was 'Dan Dare, pilot of the future'. Dan Dare, similar to our other hero Dick Barton, was a character closely modelled on the archetypal British war hero. He didn't drink or swear, he only fired in self defence and he always told the truth. There the similarity ended, as the iconic space adventurer Dan Dare, along with his dependable sidekick Digby and professor Jocelyn Peabody, who provided the love interest (we thought she was totally unnecessary), battled against all manner of intergalactic invaders. While Dick Barton fought the underworld of London, most of the Dan Dare stories featured the green-skinned Venusian Mekon as his arch-enemy. The comic's early humorous comic strips included 'Harris Tweed Extra Special Agent' and 'Captain Pugwash'. Many others followed, making it one of the best comics of the time.

American Comics
From America in the late 1940s came the DC comic books – featuring Batman, Superman, Captain Marvel and many others, including Hopalong Cassidy, Roy Rogers, Rod Cameron and most of the other popular western stars. These DC comics were very popular, although in Bradford the only outlets were Stringers and Dells in Kirkgate Market.

Listerhills Library
At the age of seven I joined our local public library in Listerhills, at 12 St Andrews Villas, a terraced house that had been decorated and slightly reconstructed in 1935 to form a downstairs lending department and a reading room. Originally several beautiful pictures from Cartwright Hall had adorned the reading room, but when I joined in 1945 the pictures were no more. Although the library was dark and gloomy I liked it, especially in the winter, as the darkness was offset by popping gaslights and the lovely warm glow of a gas fire in an old-fashioned fireplace.

The librarian was a very tall, thin gentleman who looked to me, as a young boy, like royalty. He was charming, polite and always wore a welcoming smile. After reading so many comics I had now become interested in reading books as well. It was the world of William Brown to which I was introduced by the helpful librarian, and within a short time I had read all the William books available and couldn't wait for the next titles to be issued. William Brown was very much like us: he had a gang and we had a gang. Although his family had a cook, a maid and a car I never once felt in any way envious of him. I also read Enid Blyton's Famous Five and Secret Seven books, all about children having adventures that I could only dream about – finding treasure, secret passages in old manor houses, uncles and aunts who had lots of money, had a car and had probably never been on a trolleybus.

The library also had a good history section, and it was here that my interest in the subject, especially Roman history, started. By the time I was eight I had read nearly all the books available about the Romans. These included a very large volume on Roman Britain and the life of Julius Caesar. It was so heavy that I had to carry it home in a very large bag.

I always returned my borrowed books on time, and never had to pay the 1*d* fine. Later, when a teenager, I was still using the library twice a week and reading four books each week. I loved this small library in St Andrews Villas, and years later would have loved to return to that world of musty books, the warmth from the gas fire and the slight smell of gas in the air.

Chapter 21
From 'The Teddy Bears' Picnic' to Rock 'n' Roll

Family Music

I can't say my family was really musical, but we enjoyed music of all kinds. We were not performers, although my dad had a certain flair for playing the piano. He said he was self-taught, and at family parties he sat at the upright piano and ran through his repertoire. To my young ears it sounded all right, as I had heard similar sounds coming from small pubs in the surrounding streets. Dad had also been quite a good drummer in the Boys' Brigade, which he reminded us of around the dinner table by drumming on the dinner plates with the table knives – much to my mum's consternation.

We had a beautiful upright piano in the front room of our house in Legrams Street. Where it had come from I never knew, since to me it had always been there. The piano was a well-known make, Welmar, with a highly polished non-burr walnut finish and a music rest in the centre. Even if the piano was not played it was still a beautiful piece of furniture, which more than matched the pianos in every other household in the street. Lawrence took piano lessons and could play quite well, but when he went to college the lessons stopped. I was asked many times by my parents if I wished to take piano lessons, and my mum said I had the long tapered fingers of a pianist. I always refused because I preferred to be 'playing out'. For many years I regretted my decision.

My grandparents in Fenton Street had a large pedal organ in their house. My grandfather played hymns mostly, and solemnly entertained us on our family visits. He told me that he had played the organ at Eastbrook Hall in Leeds Road, which he attended, and had also played at my church, St Patrick's in Westgate.

From quite a young age, between 'potty and puberty', I enjoyed music. I soon had my favourites, which I had heard on the wireless. These included

287

'Nellie the Elephant' (Mandy Miller), 'Runaway Train' (Vernon Delhar), 'The Laughing Policeman' (Charles Penrose), 'I tawt I taw a puddy cat' (Mel Blanc), 'The Teddy Bears' Picnic' (Henry Hall), 'Parade of the Tin Soldiers' (New Light Symphony Orchestra) and many others. I could mimic Al Jolson singing 'My Mammy', and performed this while standing in the kitchen sink in the house in Listerhills, being washed down by my dad. On one occasion this took place with my grandfather sitting there, smoking his pipe and looking on in approval. Well, I thought he was!

When I was a little older the wireless also gave me an introduction to classical music which now made me forget my childhood favourites. Although not ten years old I had built up quite a repertoire of classical music. These were played on an old wind-up gramophone we had been given so at least I had something to play my 78s on. Most of my records I had been given and the first one I bought for myself was Khachaturian's 'Sabre Dance' and 'Dance of the Young Maidens'. This was followed by Gustav Holst's suite *The Planets*, with 'Mars, the God of War' my favourite. A beautiful piano piece now joined my collection, Rachmaninov's Prelude in C sharp minor. This was followed by music of the composers Beethoven and Elgar.

My mum had her own idiosyncratic choice of music, including Mozart's 'Ave Verum Corpus', 'Oh my beloved father' by Joan Hammond, 'A deck of cards' by Wink Martindale (a look through fifty-two playing cards, each with a religious connotation), 'Rose Marie' by Slim Whitman and, from the sublime to the ridiculous, Teresa Brewer's 'Music Music Music'.

My dad's two favourites were 'Happy Days are Here Again' and 'Don't Bring Lulu'. Beethoven's 'Moonlight' Sonata had a certain wartime memory for him. His commanding officer in the army played it on the piano in the NAAFI in Nuremberg. During the performance my dad sat next to the film actor, Richard Greene, later of Robin Hood fame.

My brother bought a plastic flute with a facsimile signature of 'Pee Wee' Hunt, the bandleader, on the side. Walter 'Pee Wee' Hunt was a famous American jazz musician who made famous the number 'Twelfth Street Rag'. We had the record and played it constantly, and Lawrence tried to emulate the flute playing – to no avail! On commandeering the flute when he went to college I tried to play 'Twelfth Street Rag' as well, but was also unsuccessful. I did manage a rendition of the famous 'Trumpet Voluntary': those who were hard of hearing missed this, so they were lucky.

One time I bought a jew's harp, a small musical instrument often used in westerns. It consisted of a two-pronged metal frame which was inserted between the teeth and a spring-like 'tongue' that was plucked with the finger. Changes in the shape of the mouth cavity varied the pitch to produce a melody. I never made much in the way of melody as my teeth generally got in the way of this tricky operation. In contrast I could play the mouth organ quite well, and gave a good rendition of 'Oh! Susanna', much to everyone's amazement – although cries of 'can't you play anything else?' usually followed.

My mum could sing, but it was always the same songs, those of her pin-up Al Bowlly; although I remember her singing 'Little man you've had a busy day' to me when I was small. My dad's singing voice I never heard, or if I did I've forgotten. He was a whistler, and could always be heard on his way home from work when still a few hundred yards away. One thing about the Lister household was that there was always music of some kind being sung, played or whistled to match the mood of the moment.

When I was with St Patrick's choir we went to see the competition – the world-famous Vienna Boys' Choir, which was performing at St George's Hall. Perhaps we could learn something. I was not particularly impressed by these relentlessly cheerful Austrian children who 'fal-da-reeled' their way through the 'Happy Wanderer', as they reminded me of the Hitler Youth I had seen on the cinema newsreels not so long ago.

Gramophone Records

In 1950 my parents purchased a radiogram, a sizeable and impressive piece of furniture. Its large wooden cabinet with a luxurious rich varnish contained a mains radio and a record player for 78rpm records. The auto-changer meant they didn't have to be changed individually: up to eight records could be played without a break.

There were a few shops in Bradford that sold gramophone records. The most popular was Wood's music shop at the bottom of Sunbridge Road, which sold everything musical from sheet music to a variety of musical instruments. This was one of the first shops in the area to adopt the American method of selling records via a record booth. After selecting a record you wished to hear you were sent to a numbered booth, a similar size to a telephone box. You then listened to the record from a speaker in the booth, as it was played on a turntable at the rear of the staff counter. Vincent and I were actually barred from the shop for a short while for asking for too many requests – ten in all. Following our banishment a notice was posted to the effect that only two requests were allowed per visit.

Shuttleworth's on Darley Street, while a much smaller shop, always had a good selection of records, although the sale of sheet music was their speciality. Inside nearby Kirkgate Market was the very successful music shop of Haydn Robinson, who in the evening ran a dance orchestra, the Dunedin Players. On Saturdays Haydn introduced the American innovation, unique in Yorkshire, of a girl singer who sang songs from sheet music. If you asked for the sheet music of a song, and Haydn wasn't available to play it on the piano, then Sandra Anstey obliged by singing the number. She was very popular, and her wonderful voice could be heard high above the noise and bustle of the market. Sometimes John

Sandra Anstey's beautiful voice could be heard high above the noise and bustle of Kirkgate Market as she performed songs from sheet music. *(Author's collection)*

Hockney and I, in our lunch hour from Burton's, bought a Lyons individual fruit pie from the Maypole shop and popped into the market, not to hear her voice but just to ogle her. She was beautiful. Both of us really fancied her, but she was out of our league – although sometimes she gave us a smile. Once she said hello to me when she passed me in Godwin Street. I was so chuffed that I didn't look where I was going and fell over a small child. The child's mother started shouting and bawling at me, and I went crimson. I only hoped that the beautiful singer hadn't seen or heard the fracas.

Teddy Boys
Teddy boy fashion was becoming increasingly popular, with drainpipe trousers, velvet collars, brightly coloured socks, 2 inch crepe-soled shoes, commonly known as 'brothel creepers' and a string tie. The hair was greased back in a DA (duck's arse) hairstyle. I didn't take the clothes fashion up, having to be well dressed and presentable in my position as a menswear salesman, although my quiff had gone. My trouser bottoms narrowed to 16 inches, although my dad didn't like this: less cloth being used in the garment industry could mean worker reductions in the mills.

Teddy boys were beginning to have a bad image, being associated with rebellion, gangs, knives, and violence. This was brought home to the people of Bradford when gangs of Teddy boys, some armed with knives, fought a running battle around Bert Shutt's dance hall at Bankfoot. My bus on its journey to Wyke was caught up in this riot, and it wasn't a pretty sight. I was glad I had decided to sit on the top deck.

Rock 'n' Roll
And then along came rock 'n' roll, emerging in 1954–55, and nothing would ever be the same. Like most of my generation I was hooked. I entered the rock 'n' roll era at the beginning, being one of those lucky ones to be just seventeen in the mid-1950s when Elvis's 'Blue Suede Shoes' and 'Hound Dog' were prominent in the hit parade. At the same time hooligans were ripping up cinema seats (for reasons best known to themselves) to the sound of Bill Haley's 'Rock around the Clock' from the film *The Blackboard Jungle*.

One of my first introductions to the world of rock 'n' roll was at the Queen's Dance Hall in Idle. It was rather a small place with subdued lighting and loud music from the speakers. There was no disc jockey. The room was wall-to-wall with people and it was hot, humid and sticky. The slow numbers, such as Sam Cooke's 'Ivory Tower', were ideal for a smooch and chatting up the girls. It was at the Queen's that I found out the fast numbers for jiving or bopping were not for me. Not only did I find that I had little sense of rhythm, but I was also sweating profusely. Within seconds I had to make an excuse, leave the floor, look for air and dry off. Try making conversation with a nice girl you fancy with sweat running off your chin and nose! So for the next few years I became one of the many lads who spent most evenings in dance halls sitting out these gyrating numbers.

For 1*s* admission plus bus fares it wasn't a bad night out. This was also the time of the dance bands, with such venues as Bert Shutt's, the Textile Hall, the Gaiety, the Gaumont and the Coop Hall. But these were still more or less for modern ballroom dancing. Rock 'n' roll was more my style, and I didn't want to join the 'shiny shoe club'.

Surprisingly some of our parents liked rock 'n' roll. My mum knew and could sing all the words of Gene Vincent's popular hit number 'Be-bop-a-lula'. My dad's usual comment was made: we were both flat-cakes.

Soon, our radiogram boomed to the sound of Chuck Berry ('Johnny B Goode'), Little Richard ('Good Golly, Miss Molly') and Carl Perkins ('Blue Suede Shoes'). But it was Elvis who was dominating the rock 'n' roll scene. My favourites of his were 'Mystery Train' and 'Honey Don't'. 'Rock Island Line' by Lonnie Donegan was a massive hit, one that most people could sing along to. Not strictly rock 'n' roll, Lonnie Donegan's music was more skiffle with lyrical content that appealed to young working-class people: his songs were about outlaws, cotton-pickers, railwaymen and workers.

What a time it was! The girls had powdered faces, crimson lipstick, tight blouses and flouncy skirts with layers of petticoats underneath. When the girls spun round their skirts flared out and show a mass of colour, and sometimes stocking tops and suspenders. I danced with a girl dressed in this style at the Queens in Idle. Later I walked her to her bus stop. It was a beautiful summer's evening as she held my hand, and I felt really proud of being with this lovely girl who had a beautiful figure. Old people stared and shook their heads, while young lads leered at her tight sweater. Later I was thankful that I had never had a proper date with her and fallen in love, as all I could think of was walking hand in hand up Ruffield Side towards my house to meet my mum!

What fantasies I had as a pimply adolescent, standing in front of a mirror with a comb in my hand, acting with a pretend microphone and singing along with Elvis or Gene Vincent. But my time in the forces was due, so I had to put away my coloured socks, string tie and 2 inch crepe shoes. My trousers with 16 inch bottoms were placed on a hanger and stored away, and my Tony Curtis hairstyle was soon to be transformed into the old short back and sides. It had been nice while it lasted, and I knew that whatever happened, rock 'n' roll was here to stay.

Chapter 22
Early Working Life

My First Job

Leaving school in 1953 aged fifteen, I suddenly found myself looking for a job. Having a secondary school education didn't bar me from anything much, other than a university education. I was among the many fifteen year olds looking for a job in a new world!

The Congress Stores manager, Mr Shepherd, in Legrams Lane, where my mum shopped, suggested I should apply for a position with another Congress branch in Thornton Road, Girlington. Congress Stores were general food shops established in Bradford by the Dunne family. In the early 1960s, like Morrison's, they were among the first in the area to have a self service system, albeit in corner shops.

I started on the Monday and finished on Wednesday lunchtime! The staff were all right, but as I was fifteen, naïve and vulnerable, two of the girls made me blush! Alas, I was not streetwise. Part of the job was to deliver some of the orders. The bike I used was one of those large delivery bicycles you see in Norman Wisdom films and in *Open All Hours*, complete with a large basket on the front to take boxes. I could ride a bike, but this one was too heavy and, being just over 5 foot tall, I couldn't reach the pedals. I was told that I would have to carry the boxes instead, which I did this for two days all around Girlington. As soon as I had delivered one box of groceries another was ready. Not only was I exhausted but my arms ached, especially with carrying one particular box, a very large egg box filled to the top with groceries. I remember the address was the Old White Abbey flats, up the stairs on the second floor, and not even a thank you!

Wednesday was half day closing. When I arrived home my mum knew all was not well; I had deep red marks on my upper arms, made by the boxes I had carried. 'You're not going back,' she said, much to my relief. The next day, unbeknown to me, she went to the store for my P45 and told the manager that

Brown, Muff's was one of the most prestigious stores in the North of England. The Gents' Tailoring Department was on the right on the second floor of the later façade, facing Fattorini's jewellers. *(Graham Hall)*

The toy department, where I helped Harry Corbett, of Sooty fame, to display his puppets for a children's matinée. I was rewarded with 2s 6d. *(House of Fraser)*

he should hire a carthorse. Thank goodness I wasn't there to hear my mum. So ended my illustrious career with the Congress Stores!

This episode was perhaps a blessing in disguise, as my next job taught me discipline, smartness and additional good manners.

Brown, Muff's

Brown, Muff's was a well-known department store situated in a beautiful purpose-built building (1870) in Tyrrell Street. In 1814 Elizabeth Brown established a small shop in Market Street selling underclothing, cloth and textiles. In 1824 her son Henry, who was now running the shop, married Betsy Muff, and in 1845 he took her brother Thomas Muff as a partner. In 1870 the store was demolished and a new building erected on the site.

Following an advert in the *Telegraph and Argus* for junior staff I applied. My interview was with a Miss Thomas, a middle-aged lady who could sum up applicants in seconds. I was informed later she had told one of her staff that I had potential, but for what she didn't say! I would be working in the gents' tailoring department as a junior, and my salary (remember this was Brown, Muff's: not wage, but salary) 35s per week with six month reviews.

I had not got a suit, my attire being grey flannel trousers, white shirt, tie and sports jacket. An inspection took place at home on the Sunday before my start the following day: my dad checked my shoe insteps, and yes, they were polished too. He used to say that people see any dirt under your instep when you walk upstairs – his discipline from the army. I still clean my insteps today.

So it was that in August 1953 I joined what was probably the North of England's most famous department store. Friendliness and courtesy is what you got at Brown, Muff's, and knowledge you were dealing with local people. The first thing I had to get used to was clocking in. This was in Tyrrell Street, at the store entrance opposite Fattorini's, the jewellers, at 8.30am. Two ex-army be-medalled commissionaire sergeants held court here: discipline was tight and bad time-keeping was not tolerated.

The gents' tailoring department was on the second floor, the rear windows overlooking Fattorini's. Harry Longfellow was the buyer (the name given to departmental managers). I liked him from the start, and it was he that gave me the nickname Pinocchio, as I was just over 5 feet tall. The staff consisted of First Sales, a Mr Williams, well into his sixties and rather patronising; he liked ordering me about. There was also Jimmy Lee, in his thirties, 6 foot plus, with the charisma and looks of a film star. My favourite was Colin Senior, a lovely man in his thirties always smiling and joking. He was one of the first British soldiers to arrive at Belsen concentration camp in 1945. Then there was Jack Duane, again in his thirties. Jack, or should I say Mr Duane as I was never allowed to use any of their Christian names, was still there when Brown, Muff's closed in 1978. At the rear of the floor was a large fitting room where Mr

Peel Square. Sir Robert Peel's statue stared down on me as I carried clothes for alterations to Brown, Muff's workshop at the bottom of Leeds Road. Sometimes I had to use a handcart, much to my indignation! *(John Stanley King)*

Colehan measured and fitted all the bespoke customers. He was well in his seventies then, but knew the ABC of tailoring; he was a craftsman. He used to have the odd conversation with me, but other than that I was generally ignored until his area had to be cleaned and dusted.

Next to our gents' tailoring department was the ladies' lingerie department, the rear of which joined ours. All their staff looked like models; in fact, I had to teach myself not to stare, and averted my eyes from the many types of lingerie on display. At fifteen I was seeing items of ladies' underwear that I didn't know existed.

As a junior I had to do all the menial tasks that went with the position, and there were many. The rear was partitioned off near the staff lift, and here we packed and unpacked parcels. I was working with another junior called Brian who was two years older than me; he was from Batley and really streetwise. I could never understand why he was allowed to wear large crepe-soled shoes, 'brothel creepers', with his brown 'Jack the lad' suit; after all, this was Brown, Muff's! Brian used to boss me about, and I was rather pleased when he was off work for some time, having gone to Blackpool on a trip, got drunk and then being knocked down by a tram near the Pleasure Beach; luckily he only sustained superficial injuries. Leslie, who was in his seventies, a veteran of the Boer War, also helped with the packing – and also ordered me about. In the Home Guard during the Second World War, he was mentioned in despatches while on searchlight duty; he had a German plane in the beam of the searchlight for some time before it was shot down. Or so he said.

As I had no experience of selling, the early days were made up of rather mundane tasks, but looking back they were all part of the discipline. On arrival every morning I had to 'sleeve' all the suits (that is, pull sleeves tight and tuck them in on the many suits displayed in the racks). Each rack had to look neat and tidy. I looked on with dismay and anger when customers or staff pulled the sleeve out to look at the price and size label, and inevitably fail to put it back. I was always called on to take the alterations to the workrooms on the fifth floor of a building at the bottom of Leeds Road, many times a week and in all weathers. Suits, coats and other items had to be altered. While some saw this as a nice break, I didn't: I was all dressed up and sometimes had to use a heavy handcart, which needed much guidance over Peel Square cobbles. Off I would go with this, while Sir Robert Peel's statue looked down on me with a smile as I struggled. Sometimes I went via the Swan Arcade, especially when the weather was bad, as it offered shelter and a chance to look at the televisions on sale; I wished we had a television at home. There were times when I got a lift on the small electric van that went back and forth to the warehouse all day, driven by a small and happy fellow called George.

After a few weeks Mr Longfellow offered me a suit at a greatly reduced price, as he wanted me to join in the selling, though only when no senior staff were available. The suit cost 6 guineas, reduced to 4 guineas for me, and the favour of 5s per week from my salary. For the first time I was the owner of a grown-up suit. This made me proud, and I could also sense the same from my mum and dad, but dressed up pushing my handcart I somehow didn't look the part, especially as I now had to collect very large parcels from C. & M. Sumries of Leeds at Forster Square station, marked 'to be called for'.

The store sent juniors to classes to teach them how to wrap parcels (a skill that you never forgot) and how to treat customers: the customer was always right. On the instigation of Mr Longfellow I went to night school at Barkerend Road School and Drewton Street during the day for the City and Guilds Retail Distribution Certificate, which I passed some eighteen months later.

Mr Frederick Maufe was the chairman at this time; his son Ambrose was also in the business. Ambrose was an impeccably dressed and handsome young man, whose beautiful green Lagonda would be parked outside the store. The managing director was Ernest Marriot, who had joined the store in the packing department some forty years previously. During the First World War he had been awarded the Military Medal and bar for gallantry. An astute man, he didn't suffer fools gladly but he was fair. When the word passed along the departments that Mr Marriott was on his way, it meant there was to be an inspection. On some occasions he wore a white cotton glove and ran a finger over surfaces. This was an old soldier's trick – and he inevitably found dust or dirt. The odd time our department was caught out, guess who took the blame. Mr Marriot had two sons, Geoffrey and Michael, who were both involved with the business. Twice weekly I had to go to the offices on the fifth floor to see Mr Geoffrey, so he could sign the order books for Mr Longfellow. He always had a word, enquired about my health, and whether I was enjoying being with Brown, Muff's. Sadly, while I was employed there he was killed in a car accident on his way home from his honeymoon; his wife survived. The whole store was in shock for some time. He was a true gentleman.

After what seemed ages I started making the odd sale, waistcoats, and pairs of trousers. It was Colin Senior who taught me how to measure an inside leg and waist, so everyone seemed confident I could 'go forward', which meant approach the customer. I was now enjoying speaking to and advising the customers, but sometimes had to call on senior staff to help me out!

When cash was taken, or a sale made, it was sent up to accounts via a vacuum phial. The cash was placed in a tube and whoosh! it was gone, to return a few moments later with a receipt and change.

One day when we were busy I noticed a small rotund man with the garb and collar of what I thought was a vicar. He asked me about the new-fangled pac-a-mac, which had just been introduced and was selling well. I showed it to him in its colours of grey and black. He liked the black and I helped him on with it, over his jacket, and took him to the fitting room mirror. He liked it, and said he would have one in black and one in grey: what a sale at 5s each. At this point he asked me how long I had been with the store, and I replied 'Just a few months.' Harry Longfellow then came up and addressed him as 'My Lord'; and I gave him his change and wished him good morning. He said thank you, turned to Harry and said, 'You have wonderful staff, Harry,' and with that made his way to the stairs. At this point I noticed he was wearing black gaiters with silver buttons on each side. Harry turned to me and said, 'Well done. You have just sold two pac-a-macs to Bishop Blunt! He it was who in 1936 had made a speech that had prompted King Edward VIII to abdicate because of his love for Mrs Simpson.

A strange character used to visit the store frequently, an old gentleman in his seventies with a disability in his legs and a speech impediment, wearing an old trilby and an old gabardine. I used to say, 'Good morning, sir,' and he used to reply, but I could never understand what he said. All the sales staff used to avoid him, despite the chance to earn commission. This went on for some time until one day, after the usual good mornings, he added the word 'raincoat'. Within five minutes I had sold him a new Burberry raincoat priced at 14 guineas. This was expensive – three months' salary for me. The other staff couldn't believe it. A few years later when I was speaking to Mr Marriott I discovered that this gentlemen was from one of Bradford's leading wool families and was a millionaire in his own right; but the family kept him and his name in the dark for business reasons. Sad!

The store provided entertainments and functions from time to time. I went to the juniors' dance where all the fifteen to sixteen year olds got together to drink soft drinks and the boys egged each other on to ask some girl to dance. I seem to remember an empty dance floor and wall-to-wall lads and lasses. At one of the events I was dared to ask Mrs Maufe, the chairman's wife, for a dance. I did, and she accepted! Having done a little dancing at St Patrick's teenage club I could just about manage a waltz. For many days it was the talk at Brown, Muff's! Incidentally, she was charming. Mr Maufe had looked on over his glasses, probably seeing no competition!

Brown, Muff's was a magnet for the sons and daughters of other family stores, who spent twelve months working in all departments to gain experience. Among them was Nigel Robinson of Mathias Robinson's of Leeds, who was very well spoken. He didn't return each day to the family estate but stayed in lodgings at Lidget Green – and sometimes he gave me a lift home in his red MG, dropping me off in Listerhills. Michael Ward of Ward's department store in Hastings was another trainee, well spoken, quiet and a practising Methodist. Even though he knew I was a Catholic we got on very well, with no religious arguments. I remember also Keith Briar of Briars Textiles of Forster Square, later of the Wool Exchange. Keith had just finished his National Service with the RAF, and seemed to get on well with everyone.

At times I helped out in the gents' hat department adjacent to gents' tailoring. I learnt a lot about sizes and types – including the homburg (Anthony Eden's favourite), the popular trilby, which seemed to adorn all the wool men who popped in from the famous Wool Exchange, and the flat caps that at the time were still just as popular. A sale was always concluded by asking if the customer would like his initials impressed on the inside: all part of the service!

Once I worked for a day in the toy department, and had to help a guest magician with a puppet to display his equipment for 10am and 2pm shows for children. I remember he was quite fussy and followed me around, moving, adjusting and generally getting on my nerves. I also had to help out at the show which was really not well attended, and was surprised later when he gave me 2s 6d. I liked him then – and still did when Harry Corbett and Sooty were at the top. Little did I know that years later I would write a biography of him in my second book, *Bradford's Own*.

While most customers were from the area, a large proportion seemed to be from the Heaton district of Bradford, at the time one of the most affluent areas. When a customer said 'Put it on my account', the address always seemed to be Heaton! If you had an account you could take the goods on approval, or 'appro' as it was called. Sometimes suits and trousers were returned as not acceptable with confetti in the trouser turn-ups, theatre tickets in pockets or drink stains on lapels. It was my job to sponge and press the suits, brush them down, clean turn-ups and press. They were sponged with Spotto. One whiff from the bottle was almost lethal: one time I had to sit by an open window to be revived. 'He'll be all right,' said the staff nurse, the voice from far away. The suits were then put back into stock until the next time – and the next whiff!

I played cricket for the store a few times, and one evening I remember in particular. It was in May 1954 at the cricket field off Cleckheaton Road, Odsal, and the same night on which the Rugby League Challenge Cup final replay match between Warrington and Halifax was taking place at Odsal Stadium. At the time I didn't realise the significance of the attending record-breaking crowd of 102,583 until much later!

Also in 1954 I went with Brown, Muff's to the Great Yorkshire Show for three days, to help to sell shooting sticks, hats and gloves from a marquee. The weather was beautiful and everyone seemed happy. I thought it was wonderful, and we did so well that on the second day we sold out of hats! On the way back home we stopped at the Black Bull Inn, Otley – an event for me as it was my first real visit to a pub.

The Day I Met Laurel and Hardy

The undoubted highlight of 1954 was when the popular duo of Laurel and Hardy made a visit to the Bradford Alhambra as part of their UK tour. I had been a fan since seeing them at the Grange cinema as a four year old in the film *Way Out West*. Aged sixteen, I wondered if I would be able to obtain their autograph during the week of their visit. So I took my autograph book with me to work.

Almost all prominent stars appearing locally at the time stayed at the Midland Hotel in Cheapside. I had a contact, Mr Freschini, the head waiter. Dressed in my suit and grasping my autograph book, I headed for the hotel. Luck was on my side and he was in. Five minutes later he came along dressed as you would imagine a head waiter to be, impeccable! I asked if Laurel and Hardy were staying at the hotel, and – looking over his shoulder – he guided me to a far corner of the reception area. 'Yes' he answered. 'They're stopping here.' I declared the reason for my visit, and he replied, 'No chance', following up with 101 reasons why not. I must have looked disappointed, for he suddenly said, 'Follow me.' He led the way up the wide stairs to a second-floor landing, along a corridor, and halfway along to a large oak door. Mr Frescini knocked on the door, turned to me and said 'Good luck.' Then he disappeared along the corridor. The next few seconds were an eternity. Was it all a joke at my expense? Then the door opened and a small man appeared. His face was lined and stern, and he was quite thin. A smile appeared and his voice broke the silence, a voice I had heard many times – but only in films. It was Stan Laurel! 'Hello, young man,' he said. I was suddenly brought back to reality when I heard my voice saying, 'Hello, Mr Laurel. Could I please have your autographs?' 'Come in,' he replied. I entered to behold a large suite with beautiful furniture, paintings on

I spent fifteen minutes in the company of Laurel and Hardy and their wives in their suite at the Midland Hotel in 1954. (*Kobal*)

the wall and a very large settee, on which were seated two elderly ladies, one blonde, the other brunette. Stan shook my hand then introduced me to the ladies, the duo's wives. A table was laid with an assortment of food and drink, and one of the ladies asked if I wanted anything to eat – but I just had a glass of orange juice. At that moment a door opened and a figure emerged, a large figure. It was Ollie! He looked across at me, turned to Stanley and said 'What is it, Stanley?' in another familiar voice. 'This young man wants our autographs,' he replied. A large grin spread across Ollie's face and another famous remark was uttered, 'Why, certainly.'

This large man seemed to float across the room. He shook my hand and all I could say was 'Hello, Mr Hardy.' I was asked to sit down in a large armchair, at which point they began to ask me questions. How old was I? Where did I work and what did I do? Both seemed genuinely interested as did their wives. My answers seemed not to make sense as I was in another world. I was bound to wake up and find it was all a dream! Stan told me how years earlier he had appeared at the Empire Theatre in Morley Street with the stage show Fred Karno's Army, and at the old Princess Theatre. He added that in those days he had stopped at a theatrical boarding house in Great Horton Road, not in posh hotels like this. Not once was I asked how I had got to their room; it was if I was an old friend. By now I was relaxed and smiling. They must have realised how nervous I was, but their charm had overcome it.

After a while it was time for the autograph. Ollie stuck one of their special character pictures in my autograph book, and they both signed the page. The whole episode had taken about fifteen minutes. It was time to go. Both wives kissed me on the cheek, which made me blush, and Ollie and Stan gave me that well-known smile and walked me to the door. Hands were shaken, door opened, and I was bid farewell with the word from many of their films, 'Goodbye!'

I walked down the corridor and looked back when I got to the end. Stan was still there and he gave me a wave. Then he was gone. Savour the moment! I couldn't believe what had just taken place. How I wish I had had a camera, asked more questions, taken more notice. But no one could take it away from me. For fifteen minutes I had been in the company of probably the world's greatest - ever comedy team.

On the Friday of that week I went with my mum to see the show at the Alhambra, seats in the balcony at *2s 6d*. The show was great. They had the last half hour of the bill, which had included Harry Worth. The comedy scene took place in a railway station, with the usual cutting of ties in half, mixing up of each other's bowler hats, the usual remarks, and tears from Stan. On the way out from the balcony there were advertising cards hanging from the gas lamps on the wall, which said 'Bernard Delfont presents Laurel and Hardy', alongside their portraits. I took one as a souvenir.

My mum said she would like to see them come out at the stage door, so off we went. I was surprised how few fans were outside, probably about a dozen, as most people were off for the last bus home. After we wiated ten minutes they emerged to meet the taxi that was waiting to take them to the hotel. Everyone stood back, but I went forward and opened the rear door of the taxi. In went Ollie with a nod, followed by Stan, who said, 'Thank you, young man.' Where had I heard that before? Did he remember me? And with that Stan and Ollie went out of my life. I looked at my mum, she smiled, linked my arm and we walked home, laughing all the way.

Moving On

I had been with the store some twenty months when, after an altercation with a member of the sales staff, I thought it was time to move on. That was in late March 1955. I was now a few inches taller, more mature and disciplined. Brown, Muff's had given me an opportunity which I was always grateful for. It was a more tranquil era, with standards and nice people. The end came in February 1978 when Brown, Muff's became Rackhams.

Wyke, Where They're All Alike!

This was the frequent response when you told someone you lived in Wyke! It was during my last few weeks at Brown, Muff's in early 1955 that my parents received the news that we had been allocated a council house at the new estate at Delph Hill, Wyke, having had their names on the list for some years. A change was taking place in Bradford: people were on the move and new housing estates were being built all over the city; the old back-to-back houses were being condemned and demolished. It was over twenty years before our house in Legrams Street was demolished, and our neighbours Arthur and Lucy still lived in the street until 1978.

Aged nearly seventeen, using the tin bath was now embarrassing for me, and also for my parents. As well as using the Farrell family's bathroom in Handel

Gilbert Harding served as a police constable in the Bradford City Police Force in the early 1930s. His beat was Wyke. *(CU)*

Street, my dad and I sometimes used the communal baths (slipper baths) in Morley Street, which were in the same building as the Windsor Baths. The cost was 1s. There were two rows of cubicles, ten at each side, each containing a bath. The water was controlled to each cubicle from the outside by hot and cold taps used by the attendant. It was a luxury to lie back in a huge bath filled with hot steaming water, and such a contrast from the tin bath. When it started to cool off and you required more hot water you banged on the door and shouted to the attendant, 'More hot water number two, please' or whatever your number happened to be, and likewise for cold water. Twenty minutes was allowed, including undressing and dressing. Soap and towels could be hired but I always brought my own towel and Fairy household soap. The baths were always clean, with an overpowering smell of bleach, disinfectant and carbolic soap.

The downside of moving was leaving our lovely neighbours and all my mates, especially my best friend Vincent. Everyone seemed to be crying. We had been together since the beginning of the war, through the good and bad times. And where was Wyke? I had never even been there before. I found out later that when Gilbert Harding was in the Bradford City Police Force Wyke had been his beat. Famed as Britain's rudest man, columnist, broadcaster and TV legend on *What's My Line?*, it was in 1933, while living with his mother (who was the matron at Bowling Park Institution), that he joined the police.

Our new home was 47 Ruffield Side, Delph Hill, Wyke. On the bus from outside the Odeon cinema, Manchester Road, it was a 4 mile ride to Wyke. The estate was set back off Woodside Road, and its entrance was from the centre of Woodside Road. The first right-hand road was Ruffield Side: at the top was a cul-de-sac and no. 47. The new house, with front and rear gardens, had three bedrooms and a separate bathroom and toilet. The kitchen was very large compared with our old scullery, with large worktops and plenty of cupboard space. We also had central heating, which ran from a coke-burning stove in the kitchen, and in the front room there was a gas miser fire. We could now have constant hot water and heating. I had a large bedroom at the back, which was three times the size of my old room in Listerhills. My parents had the large front bedroom, and there was another small front bedroom. The rear garden rose up to an old stone wall, which ran the length of the back of the houses on the cul-de-sac. Over the wall was a large field, and a five minute walk over to the left brought you to Judy Woods, a narrow band of beech woodland stretching from Wyke to Woodside and Shelf. To the right of the field, about half a mile away, was Royd's Hall and Royd's Hall Reservoir. Out of the estate across Woodside Road into Huddersfield Road was a cluster of shops: greengrocer, grocer, post office, small cake and sweet shops, and the inevitable fish and chip shop. We also had visits from a Low Moor grocer, Mr Marshall, and his grocery van. Although it was a mile from Wyke centre the estate was quite well provided for. There was also a good Bradford Corporation bus service at 4*d* to and from the city centre. Ledgard's Bus Company also ran buses through Wyke to Huddersfield from Bradford.

Life resumed, albeit at a different address and with different neighbours. Mr and Mrs Waterhouse, with son Lynton and daughter Linda, were a really nice family; other close neighbours were the Burlesons and Nicholls. We were lucky again. I made lots of new friends in Wyke, especially as I met the same people day after day on the bus to and from Bradford. One of these meetings led to a new friendship that I will never forget.

Ernest Raymond Jones, Ray as I was to call him, lived on Temperance Street in Wyke with his wife. It was during my weekly travels to work that I met him, forming a friendship on these bus journeys. Ray was aged thirty-five or thirty-six and was a general labourer. He was married, but I don't remember him saying if he had any children. He always wore an open neck shirt and his jacket, though smart, could have been used for working in. He had a ruddy complexion, dark wavy hair, and epitomised an Irishman than an Englishman. I used to enjoy his company and we would while the time away, conversing on many subjects. This went on for around eighteen months, until I told him that I had passed my medical and would be going in the army at the end of October 1956. 'Must celebrate,' he said. Up until this time I had only seen him on the bus, so I was rather surprised. I had always assumed, as he was older than me and had his mates whom he sometimes mentioned, that I was too young for his company. He had never mentioned whether he had been in the forces during the war or later, so his offer of celebration came out of the blue.

The week before I went into the army we met up at the County Hotel in Bradford after work on a Friday evening. We were joined by two of his mates, whom I had not met before, although I had heard him mention their names. I was not a heavy drinker and only had a couple of pints, but smoked lots of cigarettes and soon joined in with the laughs and jokes. After a couple of hours I left the pub, leaving him with his mates. He shook my hand and wished me well in the army. As a parting gesture he shoved a £1 note in my top pocket. I never saw him again. It wasn't until I came out of the army that I heard he had been hanged for murder in February 1959.

Ray had broken into the Co-operative store at Lepton, near Huddersfield, on 30 September 1958. The store manager, Richard Turner, returned to the store and Jones hit him once on the head, then making his escape. In court he maintained that he carried no weapon, and that he had only intended to render Turner unconscious. But the blow had fractured Turner's skull, and the crime was one of capital murder (in the furtherance of theft). An appeal was dismissed, and he was duly hanged at Armley Prison. It was a shock to find out that the person whom I used to sit and discuss life with had been hanged for murder.

Gone for a Burton

Rumour has it that the phrase that introduces this section relates to an RAF office over a Burton's shop, where men went to sit exams. Anyone failing the exam was said to have 'gone for a Burton'.

Moving on from Brown, Muff's with a good reference from Harry Longfellow, I became a junior sales assistant at Montague Burton, tailors, Branch 32, 44–48 Kirkgate, on Monday 3 April 1955. The Kirkgate branch of Burton's faced H. Samuel, jewellers, Finley's cigarette and sweet kiosk and to its left the tailors Weaver to Wearer. At the side was Albion Court with a passage that ran down to the rear of Fattorini's. In Albion Court was Laycock's tea rooms. This had originally been Laycock's Temperance Hotel, built in 1867 and later used for some of the first meetings of the Independent Labour Party, attended by Keir Hardy. In the late 1950s it became one of the first Chinese restaurants in Bradford, named The Dragon and Peacock.

Burton's was set back from the road. To the right was the bottom of Westgate with the large ladies' fashion shop Novello's and next door the bombed-out basement of Lingard's, which was being used as a car park. To the left of Burton's was Chapel Court. This cobbled street only ran a few yards up to

Montague Burton's, No. 32 Branch, 44–48 Kirkgate where I worked from 1955 to 1956.
(Bradford Libraries)

Malcolm from the Tyrrell Street branch of Burton's believed that I had met the chairman. Here Malcolm and I are on the Wyke bus, heading home for lunch.
(Author's collection)

John Hockney, brother of David Hockney. On Wednesday half-day closing we often spent our time at the cinema.
(*John Hockney*)

wooden steps, about 6 feet high, which gave access to James Street through a large cindered area, also being used as a car park. This was the site of Kirkgate Wesleyan Methodist Chapel, built in 1811, destroyed by German bombs in 1941 and later demolished. In Chapel Court at the Burton side there was an old small house that the Burton building had been built around, in the standard Burton design of the time. Between the house and Burton's was an entrance with steps leading down to the billiard hall. At the other side of Chapel Court was Kirkgate Market, which had escaped with only slight damage during the 1940 bombing raid on this congested area.

Burton's façade consisted of two large front windows and one at the corner, displaying the suits and cloths available. (At this time no accessories, including shirts or ties, were sold in any Burton shops.) The entrance gave way to a large open area with oak tables and parquet floors. The oak-panelled walls had shelves, again in an oak finish, on which were displayed neatly folded rolls of sample cloth. This was the bespoke department, where garments from sample swatches and cloth were chosen by the customer. He was then measured and the details were sent to the factory at Hudson Road Mills, Leeds, to be made up.

In a corner at the rear of the ground floor was a large office, and at the side a large double staircase led to the first floor. This was the ready-made department, which included suits, jackets, overcoats and raincoats, all neatly sleeved as at Brown, Muff's, and hanging on rails in large open wardrobes, finished in pine. At the end of the department were large windows overlooking Kirkgate. At the top of the stairs were the staff tea-room and toilets, overlooking the rear cindered area.

Jim Telford was the manager, a small bald-headed man with glasses (nicknamed the Mekon – Dan Dare's main protagonist from the *Eagle* comic) He was a hard taskmaster of the old school. Never once did he call me Derek; it was always Lister. He had seen service in the First World War and also in India on the North-West Frontier. Asians were now arriving in Bradford, and when any came into the shop he conversed with them in their own languages. The look on their faces was amazing: they had travelled thousands of miles to a foreign land and this small man was speaking in their mother tongue. It was quite impressive, and they always seemed to make a purchase.

Raymond Bairstow was First Sales and had been in Ceylon with the forces during the Second World War. He never spoke to me directly, and I got the feeling that I didn't impress him. Likewise! Another senior salesman was Percy Wigglesworth, a nice old man who looked like a picture book owl and was just as wise. 'Wiggy' was in his sixties and another veteran of the First World War, having served with the West Yorkshire Regiment. It was from him I heard the story about his regiment going into the forward trenches in France. The Germans in their trenches several hundred yards away started playing 'On Ilkley Moor 'baht 'at'!

Then, to use the army phrase, there were the 'other ranks'. Most had seen military service, either as regulars or on National Service. Colin Bannon looked and spoke like the actor Dale Robertson (Jim Hardy in the television series *Wells Fargo*). Colin, then in his mid-twenties, took me under his wing, made me streetwise, and gave me tips for the inevitable National Service. Later he joined the well-respected Fred Barnett Cleaners. Clifford Harrison was from Darlington. Cliff was ambitious, and it showed – but he could relax with me as I was no competition. Harry Bolton, a good friend and a little older, had seen service in the Canal Zone in Egypt. He was always considerate and helpful, and is the only one of my former colleagues from those times who is still working today in the gents' outfitters trade, now in his seventies. Maurice Thornton, another Canal Zone veteran, and Herbert Robinson were both married with beautiful wives. The other juniors and I gawped at these ladies when they waited outside for their husbands. If Jim Telford saw them, like a flash he called them in to wait, and we juniors were told to go upstairs and get sleeving! Jim's fussing over the women always made Wiggy mutter 'Silly bugger!' under his breath. There were two other junior sales assistants, Philip Conway and John Hockney. Philip dressed very smartly, although his suit was in the Teddy Boy style. Jim seemed to have a soft spot for Philip as he never said anything about this. I believe that Jim had no children and Philip's mother had died recently, so in a way Jim looked after Philip. When we had a visit from the area manager Captain Hargreaves (Military Cross, ex-prisoner of war), Jim kept Philip out of the way. John Hockney was the brother of the artist David Hockney, and joined just after me. Then there was the cleaner Ma Sowden. As the floors were the original parquet she took great pride in creating a highly polished finish – so much so that she didn't like anyone walking on it, including the customers, whom she would admonish with a scowl. The caretaker was Tom, a 6 foot tall, thin and stooping ex-First World War guardsman, a nice old man who lived with his wife in the small house in Chapel Court.   T h e office, which had large glass windows with a reception and paying-in window, was run by two women. The older of the two was Barbara; later she would marry our Clifford Harrison.

These were my friends and colleagues with whom I would be working for the foreseeable future, for the weekly sum of £3. I only hoped that staying in retail was the correct decision.

Starting time was 8.30am. As I was now living in Wyke, I caught the bus at 7.50 to arrive at Nelson Street in the city centre, just above Dalby's antique shop on the corner, at 8.10; a five minute walk brought me to Burton's. Everyone seemed to be wearing a raincoat, rain or shine, or carrying it over the arm with the lining showing. A well-known family remark at the time was 'Don't forget your mac, just in case.' I was always early, as were most of the other staff. Good time-keeping was quite normal in those days. We gathered round the shop entrance like a crowd of penguins waiting for the arrival of their leader! The chattering suddenly ceased when Jim arrived round the corner from Westgate in his two-tone 1938 Standard Ten. He parked the car in Chapel Court, the door opened, and he emerged resplendent, wearing an overcoat, a light blue Homburg hat and with an unlit pipe protruding from his mouth. Good mornings were noted, he unlocked the door and we all entered for 'morning prayers'. This was the unofficial title given to the gathering of all staff around one of the large tables at 8.45. Compliments were given, also threats, and we were told who was doing what wrong, and why. Morning prayers over, everyone set about their allotted task. In the juniors' case, this was generally 'whisking' – taking a whisk brush and dusting the readymade stock, then straightening and sleeving it; the same with the bolts of cloth: whisk, and return to fixtures.

It was a busy shop and we were encouraged to make sales, but as at Brown, Muff's the senior staff had to be all engaged before we were allowed to take part. Saturday was the busiest day, and a British Legion commissionaire was hired to stand at the entrance to open the doors and show the customers inside. Jim was a smart man, resplendent in a white peaked hat, dark uniform, polished brass buttons and a black polished shoulder belt over one shoulder, bulled shiny boots, and an array of campaign medal ribbons. His only problem was that he was bad on his feet – a legacy from time spent in the wet and mud of Flanders. Poor old Jim, he had to have constant breaks in the staff tea-room to rest. He was a smiling old soldier, but behind that smile what awful memories and pain. I found it was an honour to know such men.

On a Saturday tea and biscuits were served to all women who were accompanying their husbands or partners. It was not unknown to serve fifty or more customers and, although we didn't make the tea, it was down to Philip, John and me to serve and collect the leftovers; this was in between serving customers. We were on commission but the Burton Tea Party limited our success on Saturdays. To be fair, I think Jim realised this after a time and brought two ladies in to do the job. The commission was only 1 per cent, but it did help. I saw staff fall out over commissions, with comments like 'That should have been my customer!' It could get quite vicious, especially among the ones who were married. Needs must! One of the best sources for commission was 'spiffs'. Any suits, garments or even cloth bolts that had been in stock for some time and had been reduced in price were marked (on the tag alongside the price)

5s, 7s 6d or even 10s. If you sold that item this spiff was yours. It was surprising how much old stock that had been gathering dust was sold quickly once this lucrative incentive was marked.

John Hockney's brother David always impressed me when he visited our shop. I think he was at Bradford Art College at the time. He had many hairstyles and hair colours, one time black and white like a zebra, another with a tartan pattern. We all thought he was strange. David purchased many made-to-measure clothes that were outlandish at the time, and he chuckled all the time he was trying things on. John, on the other hand, was a smart young man with short cropped black hair, dark suit, white shirt and tie, a complete contrast to his brother.

Wednesday was half day closing. We could all disappear when the weekly delivery of stock from head office had been delivered at 12.20, but as everywhere else was closed as well, what to do? It was always a visit to the cinema. I frequently went with John, who was good company. John had a thing about French films. In a way so did I, but you had to put up with the English captions popping up at the bottom of the screen. We thought that one at the Gaumont cinema sounded quite risqué; it was called *Refifi*. It wasn't as exciting as we thought it would be: it was simply about a jewel heist!

John got hold of the risqué magazine *La Vie Parisien*. Where he got it from I never knew. It wasn't available at Stringers or Dells, the then popular book and magazine shops in Kirkgate Market. I know because I asked!

One of my party pieces was doing impressions. Some victims were hard; others like Jim were easy. One quiet day in the staff room I was remonstrating with John as Jimmy, saying, 'You'll have to go, laddie'. John was laughing and I was quite loud. Suddenly John's face came over serious, and I thought he was about to join in. But there was a tap on my shoulder: it was Jim. He had been down to the toilet along the passage at the rear of the staff room, and how long he had been behind me I didn't know. I waited for the onslaught but it didn't come. All he said was, 'Not a bit like me. Keep practising.' Needless to say I didn't.

With an hour for lunch I sometimes went home, but it was much more convenient to eat locally, especially in Kirkgate Market. Baxendall's and other places did nice home-cooked lunches with a sweet and tea for 2s. It was nice to sit in those Dickenson pews that abounded in the market, which hadn't changed since it had been built in 1872. Then there was time for a nice walk around town, or if it were Thursday up to the open air market off Westgate. For snacks we popped across the road to Finley's sweets and tobacconists for a Bounty bar, or the new biscuit, Wagon Wheels. For a treat I sometimes went for lunch at the Co-op department store (later Sunwin House) with Maurice and his wife Joan. Joan worked in Bradford and sometimes called for Maurice for lunch. Like the restaurants at Brown, Muff's, Busby's and the Gaumont, it was run very professionally. The waitresses wore black garments with spotless aprons, cuffs and headwear, and were very polite – greeting everybody as 'Sir' or 'Madam'. It was expensive for me, around 4s, but I enjoyed being waited on and being called Sir! Joan, Maurice's wife, always looked lovely.

Sometimes Herbert and his wife Mollie came along, and for a change we went to the Wee Café, in a building at the rear at the Town Hall in Norfolk Street. It was cheaper, a three course meal for 1s 3d.

Like Brown, Muff's, Burton's had its own workrooms. These were situated on the top floor of the Mechanics' Institute building, overlooking the roundabout at the bottom of Manchester Road. Two nice middle-aged ladies did all the repairs. One day they repaired the lining of my trousers while I sat in my underpants with a coat over my lower half. The repair was free of charge, and they gave me tea and a cream cake bought from Betty's Café in Darley Street. It was my seventeenth birthday, one birthday when I remember where I was.

In Bradford centre there were two other Burton's outlets, both on Tyrrell Street. The one at the corner of Aldermanbury was smaller than ours in Kirkgate, but it also had a billiard hall in the basement, with a small entrance next to the store's main entrance in Tyrrell Street. It is mostly remembered for the Gaiety Ballroom, which was above. In the evening the music of the dance bands could be heard even in Town Hall Square, as the windows of the dance hall were opened wide to disperse the oppressive heat generated by the many dancers. The sound of the music echoing through the streets on cold winter evenings could be quite comforting! The other Burton's shop was on the corner of Tyrrell Street.

I had a few trips to Hudson Road Mills in Leeds to collect 'specials' – but my first trip was nearly my last. The weather was bad, and it was after lunch when I finally arrived at Head Office. It was another hour before I tracked down where to pick up my parcel, and when I did it wasn't ready. Finally, with the parcel under my arm, I headed back to Bradford by bus and train. It was almost 4.30 before I arrived back at the shop. Jimmy's face was like thunder. 'Where have you been? It doesn't take that long;' and on he went. It had rained most of the day. and I was wet through and had had nothing to eat. I stood there with a soggy parcel under my arm listening to this abuse, with all the rest of the staff hovering about within earshot. Enough was enough. I flung my soggy parcel across the room, said 'Piss off', turned round, walked out of the door and went home. My mum was horrified, not because I had probably lost my job, but because of the language I had used (I rarely made remarks of this kind). My dad just called me the usual flatcake. The next day I arrived at work at the usual time, and on coming round the corner a small cheer went up from the other staff waiting in the doorway. I think it was sympathy really. Wiggy was laughing, so I asked him what he thought would happen. Without hesitation he said, 'Jimmy will sack you.' This took the wind out of my sails, as it only confirmed what I was thinking. At that moment Jimmy's car came round the corner and he parked in his usual place in Chapel Court. He came to the entrance with the usual good mornings, the door was unlocked and everyone went in, including me at the rear. As I ventured forward, he turned round and came towards me. 'A word, outside', he exclaimed. As we walked outside I began thinking that the *Telegraph and Argus* first edition would be out at 10.30 with pages of situations vacant, so I would soon have a job! We walked round the corner into Chapel Court towards his car. Again I thought, 'Is he going to sack me and run me home?' He leaned on his car and said, 'Laddie, don't ever speak to me like that again', and asked me if I had anything to say. I apologised. 'Back in you go, and we'll forget this matter' were his final words. I was shocked as I really thought I would get the sack. In those days there were no warnings: it was 'Here's your cards' (insurance) and out the door! Wiggy told me some time later that although Jimmy had been shocked at what I had said to him and my throwing the parcel half the length of the room, he had admired me for standing up for myself. He had also been impressed that I had the courage to return to work the following morning not knowing if I still had a job. My respect for Jimmy increased immensely from that day. The episode helped me grow up and be more respectful and sensible.

I made further trips to Hudson Road Mills: sometimes it took a long time, but nothing was said. On one occasion I was sitting in the large reception area waiting to collect a special delivery, filling in the time reading one of the many Second World War books then being published, when a smart elderly gentleman approached and asked what I was reading. I told him, and of my interest in military history. He seemed impressed with my knowledge of the subject, and asked me to follow him along an oak-panelled corridor and into a large oak-panelled room at the end – the board room. In the centre was a long table with many leather-backed chairs around it. The walls were adorned with large portraits and photographs. He turned to a large flat-topped display case, opened it and took out some very large photographs, placing them on the table. He explained that these were the original German aerial photographs taken of Hudson Road Mills during the Second World War. The details were sharp; one was actually in colour and had bombing target co-ordinates marked. The factory was a prime target during the war since it made uniforms, and supposedly housed a secret establishment. The old gentleman could see I was impressed, and went on to say that the photographs had been found after the war and donated to Burton's. He then returned with me to the reception where my parcel was waiting. He asked my name and which branch I was employed at, then shook my hand and disappeared. On the way out I asked the commissionaire on the door who he was. 'Only the chairman,' he replied.

Back at the shop I mentioned the meeting to Jimmy. I don't think he believed me, and he called Wiggy in to tell him my story. Wiggy's reply was, 'We had better be careful; he has friends in high places'. The news spread down to the Tyrrell Street branch, and on the bus home one evening I had to tell my story to

Malcolm, a friend of mine, who worked at the Tyrrell Street branch and lived off Abb Scott Lane. After some time it seems to have been accepted as the truth, as even Captain Hargreaves, MC, the area manager, started to say 'Good Morning' to me.

One day in June 1956 'No Other Love' sung by Ronnie Hilton, the popular singer of the 1950s, drifted from loudspeakers strategically positioned across the road at our competitor's premises. Weaver to Wearer had been refurbished and was due to reopen on that day. Ronnie was cutting the ribbon. The bunting was in place and the sun was warm, reflecting off their shop windows and making our side of the road look dull. We had a grandstand view from our first-floor windows; if only the customers would stop coming in to spoil our viewing! 'No Other Love' played continuously through those speakers, and at an ever-increasing volume. I've remembered every word to this day! Ronnie arrived at noon in a black Rolls-Royce. Getting out of the car, he stood back and waved to the many hundreds of women who wanted a glimpse of the good-looking crooner. The road was completely blocked and traffic had to be diverted. 'No Other Love' came through the speakers again, and much to the delight of the crowd Ronnie mimed his way through it. A cheer intermingled with screams went up, he turned round, cut a large yellow ribbon, waved again and disappeared into the shop. He had only been in the shop ten minutes when the waiting fans took up a chant, 'We want Ronnie'. He came to the entrance, waved and disappeared again. I looked over my shoulder and saw Wiggy shaking his head! Half an hour later Ronnie finally emerged, the crowd rushed forward, to be gently moved back by just three policemen (a lesson in crowd control). Ronnie saw the gap, waved, then ran to the waiting Rolls. The car edged through the crowd, gathered speed and moved away along Kirkgate, with a hand still waving through the rear window. The music stopped, the crowd dispersed, customers came in and we started serving again, with a certain tune still going through our heads.

Time began to pass very quickly. Philip was called up for his National Service in the Royal Artillery. It wasn't long after his training that he paid us a visit, looking resplendent in his uniform, to say his goodbyes. He had been posted to Germany. This was ominous for me, as I knew it would not be long before it was my turn to join the colours. In the meantime I carried on with my career of choice.

Smoking

By now I was growing up fast, and one of the ways in which this was expressed was by becoming a regular smoker. All our role models in magazines and on the cinema screen were regularly shown with a cigarette in their hands, and smoking was fashionable for teenagers; it was a grown-up activity and something to aspire to. Even as a child we could emulate grown-ups by buying a packet of Barratt's Gold Flake 'sweet' cigarettes – complete with ends coloured red to suggest a smoking effect.

I had my first cigarette at the age of fourteen on a visit to Clayton Fields during the school holidays. The brand was Craven A, because this was what my mum smoked. On the way I had purchased a packet of ten to share with my mate Vincent. He had more sense than me and said he wasn't really interested, so I lit one up. I wasn't impressed, especially when I inhaled the smoke or swallowed. With a green, sweating face, slurred speech and pounding heart I must have cut a strange figure to Vincent, who just rolled about laughing. On the way home I bought some chewing gum to take the taste and the smell of my breath away, hoping that my mum wouldn't notice. Nothing was said on my arrival, although I got a funny look when I said I didn't want any tea, and I'm sure I could still hear Vincent laughing in his house across the road

My dad had never smoked, even in the army, but Mum was what they called a light smoker, social occasions only, and only in the house when neighbours Nellie or Lucy came in for a gossip. After the war I obtained most of her cigarettes, especially if we were going to the pictures. 'Nip to Fanny's and see if she will let you have five Woodbines,' she would say. Fanny Hardaker's shop at the end of our street was our illicit supplier. The shop was converted from a house and sold odd items of groceries, sweets and cigarettes. Cigarettes were still scarce, and she kept under the counter stock for special customers. I must have been special as I was always successful, and came away with a packet of five Woodbines discreetly placed in a sweet bag, much to my mum's delight.

My grandfather smoked (as did my brother later), but his was a pipe which never seemed offensive. One of my joys as a youngster was to sit with him in the Empress Picture House, smell the pleasant aroma and hear his gentle puffing on his pipe.

A couple of years later, the Clayton Fields' incident forgotten, I decided to join my friends and started smoking. I was just seventeen and working at Burton's. I gradually overcame the swallow and was soon smoking around twenty cigarettes a week, still Craven A. I suppose I enjoyed it because it made me feel more grown up. When I first told my mum that I had started smoking (I think she already knew), she just said, 'As long as you buy your own.' Dad just called me a flat-cake, as usual. Like so many of my generation, I never smoked at home. I believe I was embarrassed.

With such a large percentage of the population smoking, I never really noticed the smell of cigarettes. Yet smoking was all around to see. At the cinemas, in the light-beam of the projector to the screen, clouds of cigarette smoke rose and never dispersed, from the hundreds of cigarettes lit up during the performances. In most cinemas there was a small brass ashtray on the rear of each seat, intended to be where cigarettes were stubbed out. Some patrons, intent on watching the film, missed the ashtrays – so after a few minutes the smell of smouldering clothing mingled with the cigarette smoke. Likewise, the smell of singed hair added to the atmosphere. An unsuspecting girl with long hair might flick her hair back into the ashtray, and if a smoker had only partially stubbed out his cigarette all hell would be let loose.

Smoking was permitted upstairs only on double-decker buses. On dark wet cold nights over thirty passengers might be seated upstairs, wrapped in damp or wet overcoats, raincoats, hats and scarves, and a large percentage lit up. As the bus trundled along the cigarette smoke rose to the nicotine-stained metal roof, curling round and round with nowhere to go. Sometimes I made a contribution to it.

Tobacconists' shops abounded in the city. Some had been there many years, such as Pollards on the corner of John Street and James Street. This and other shops catered for the smoker's every whim. Added to their number were small corner shops and newsagents, which helped to keep the many thousands of smokers in the city amply supplied. Many corner shops sold single cigarettes at 2*d* each to hard-up smokers – who were also not averse to having a drag on a friend's cigarette: the saying 'give us a drag' was the term generally used. Cigarette machines, which had been plentiful before the war, were back again, mostly stationed outside newsagents; they didn't seem to get vandalised. Many smokers rolled their own, as it was significantly cheaper and you couldn't really offer them around. Some rolled with their fingers, copying the cowboys in films, while others bought small machines with rollers for the tobacco and paper: press down, and a cigarette popped out. I tried both versions, but to no avail as I inevitably lost most of the tobacco. Smokers saved a cigarette for later by docking or nipping the end off. I had a friend who did this, and managed to smoke just one cigarette a day.

Cigarette brands were numerous: Craven A, Bar One, Players No. 6, Passing Cloud, Regal, Robin, Royal, Double Ace, Black Cat, Kensitas, Gold Flake, Three Castles, Piccadilly, Wills Woodbines, and many more. One brand that everyone seemed to know, or smell, was Pasha. Many were the shouts in the cinemas of 'Who's smoking Pasha?' They were made from Turkish tobacco and were not very popular because of their smell. A favourite saying of the time was:

The boy stood on the burning deck damping down the ashes.
The captain looked around and said, 'Who's been smoking Pashas?'

Turf cigarettes were popular with schoolchildren, not for smoking but because each packet contained a card with a picture of a popular sports personality. We all tried to make up a full set of fifty, something I only achieved once – with the help of Charlie, my barber in Preston Street. When Charlie sold packets to customers he asked for the card inside.

Capstan Full Strength were just that. I only tried them once, and required a fifteen-minute recovery sit down. There were also thin black cheroots. On our visits to the cinema John Hockney smoked them, as he said they made him feel and look suave. They did.

It was very much frowned on for a woman to be seen smoking in the street. It was more than a novelty, and names were called: common, slut, slag and others, most unprintable.

Choosing birthday or Christmas presents for a smoker wasn't difficult, as the shops were full of appropriate gifts. A cigarette lighter (Ronson and Zippos were popular), or a cigarette case with engraved initials could be purchased for a few pounds. For families of smokers there were table lighters or fancy onyx ashtrays for the home.

I had to admire Vincent as he had never smoked. The closest he got was taking snuff. One day we thought we would try it as it looked quite suave and elegant, especially when we thought of Stewart Granger in the film *Beau Brummel.* Like chewing tobacco it was a non-starter, and after sneezing possibly a hundred times we agreed it was not for us.

I was never really a heavy smoker and it was many years later that I was shocked into stopping. In the army I had begun to smoke Senior Service, and in the doctor's surgery one day I saw a notice on tar content that stated that one of my cigarettes was equal to ten tipped cigarettes. I stopped smoking.

Hitch-Hiking Days

Being indoors at work all day, in cinemas for relaxation on our half-day holiday, and then in the town's smoky atmosphere when I was outside gave me the gaunt appearance of Peter Cushing. Some kind of healthy weekend activity had to be found.

Most of my friends were working during the week, including Vincent who worked at Woolcombers. We decided that on Sundays, especially in the summer, we would go hitch-hiking to bring the colour back to our cheeks. We decided we would try to get to York. Although we set out many times we never actually reached our destination – but not for want of trying. Over the months we made many excuses: it was too hot, too cold, it was raining, we were tired, there were no lifts, and many others. There wasn't the volume of traffic that there is now and we knew that lifts would be few. We made a pact that nothing would stop us, come rain or shine, and off we went with thumbs at the ready. I dressed in a jacket, flannels, pullover, shirt, shoes and sometimes a tie! Vincent's outfit was almost identical, but without the tie. Over my shoulder I carried an ex-army gasmask bag in which were the sandwiches, my Brownie camera to record the adventures, and a pac-a-mac. This was to placate my dad who had told me I should take my raincoat over my arm, just in case!

Our first attempt was a disaster as we tried to set off from Manningham Lane. It was a mistake as there were too many routes from there, and no one was stopping. We needed to be out in the country on a main road heading for York. With a short walk on Pool Road out of town towards Pool Bridge, we thought we would be on our way. So for our second try we took the bus to Otley, but no

Me and Vincent on one of our hitch-hiking outings. One dope is even wearing a tie.
(Author's collection)

lifts were forthcoming as we walked the 2 miles from Otley to Pool Bridge. The day was warm, the sun was out and we were sweating. Vincent had borrowed a framed rucksack and we had put everything in it. Although it was heavy and cumbersome, at least we could take it in turns to carry it. We crossed the bridge over the river Wharfe and sat on the sloping river bank for our well-earned rest. The rucksack rolled down the bank, fell in the river and started to float away. We waded into the river, and managed to grab it before it moved to deeper water.

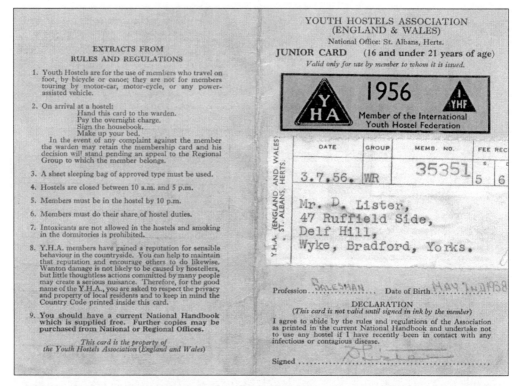

Inside the card image:

EXTRACTS FROM
RULES AND REGULATIONS

1. Youth Hostels are for the use of members who travel on foot, by bicycle or canoe; they are not for members touring by motor-car, motor-cycle, or any power-assisted vehicle.

2. On arrival at a hostel:
   Hand this card to the warden.
   Pay the overnight charge.
   Sign the housebook.
   Make up your bed.
   In the event of any complaint against the member the warden may retain the membership card and his decision will stand pending an appeal to the Regional Group to which the member belongs.

3. A sheet sleeping bag of approved type must be used.

4. Hostels are closed between 10 a.m. and 5 p.m.

5. Members must be in the hostel by 10 p.m.

6. Members must do their share of hostel duties.

7. Intoxicants are not allowed in the hostels and smoking in the dormitories is prohibited.

8. Y.H.A. members have gained a reputation for sensible behaviour in the countryside. You can help to maintain that reputation and encourage others to do likewise. Wanton damage is not likely to be caused by hostellers, but little thoughtless actions committed by many people may create a serious nuisance. Therefore, for the good name of the Y.H.A., you are asked to respect the privacy and property of local residents and to keep in mind the Country Code printed inside this card.

9. You should have a current National Handbook which is supplied free. Further copies may be purchased from National or Regional Offices.

This card is the property of the Youth Hostels Association (England and Wales)

YOUTH HOSTELS ASSOCIATION
(ENGLAND & WALES)
National Office: St. Albans, Herts.

JUNIOR CARD   (16 and under 21 years of age)
Valid only for use by member to whom it is issued.

Y H A 1956 YHF
Member of the International
Youth Hostel Federation

DATE	GROUP	MEMB. NO.	FEE REC
3.7.56.	WR	35351	5 6

Y.H.A. (ENGLAND AND WALES) ST. ALBANS, HERTS.

Mr. D. Lister,
47 Ruffield Side,
Delf Hill,
Wyke, Bradford, Yorks.

Profession...SALESMAN... Date of Birth...MAY 2nd 1938

DECLARATION
(This card is not valid until signed in ink by the member)
I agree to abide by the rules and regulations of the Association as printed in the current National Handbook and undertake not to use any hostel if I have recently been in contact with any infectious or contagious disease.

Signed ...D. Lister.........................

My Youth Hostel Association membership card, 1956. A strict rule was that members could only use youth hostels if they travelled on foot or by bicycle or canoe. Nobody questioned our journey from Bradford to Kent in half a day. *(Author's collection)*

We surveyed the damage. Everything inside was wet through: sandwiches, camera, cigarettes and maps (my dad had wondered if we were going to the other side of the world thanks to the number of maps we had included). But the worst part was that we were soaking from the thighs down and had no spare clothing. It didn't take long to decide we had better return home. Sitting on the bus, wet and dishevelled, we hardly spoke – only to say 'never again'. Our resolution didn't last, and the following weekend we were off again, destination York once more.

It was always the same: we could never quite make it to York. We always started at Otley: Otley to Huby, Otley to Follifoot, Otley to Goldsborough, Otley to Kirk Hamerton, and the farthest we ever achieved, Upper Poppleton. We knew them all. Sometimes villagers nodded to us, as old friends or so it seemed – scratching their heads and wondering who the two idiots were who passed through their village every Sunday.

We travelled in all kinds of transport: hay carts, tractors, pre-war cars, including a left-hand drive American Packard driven by a mad American serviceman who demonstrated how fast it went, especially on the wrong side of the road. The worst lift we had was in a large cattle wagon full of cattle. Every hundred yards the driver stopped, took a large stick and went to the rear to prod the cattle and wail in a loud voice. We thought this was rather cruel until he explained that he had to keep the cattle on the move and upright; if he didn't they would suffocate if they fell to the floor. As we were getting nowhere we made an excuse, got out and walked, but also to clear the smell from our nostrils and clothes: it had certainly brought the colour back to our cheeks! On one occasion we had a lift in a Wolseley police car, the kind with the square box police sign on the roof. It was raining. The two police officers said they felt sorry for us and took us a few miles. We thought later that the only reason they had pulled up was because they were suspicious of two soaking scruffs, one wearing a tie.

Although we had had no success in reaching our destination we decided to have one more try. This time, to be more adventurous, we headed for Durham! There was a reason for our madness. Lawrence was studying for the priesthood at Ushaw College, Durham. The church organised bus trips at holiday periods so students' families could visit the college, and my parents went on these. It was a bank holiday in August when Vincent and I decided to set off at the same time, hitch-hiking. The coach trip was on the Monday, so we set off on the Sunday, intending to make a grand entrance the next day. We were dressed in our usual attire, but had borrowed a small tent and two rucksacks; knowing our luck we envisaged an overnight stop. It was a beautiful weekend, hot, sunny, with lots of traffic, and for once our thumbs were not ignored. The trip was uneventful, and so good were the lifts that we were approaching Crook, County Durham, towards teatime. After our York efforts this was a dream. With no more lifts forthcoming it was getting late, and we were still a few miles from Ushaw, so we decided to camp down for the night. A small field in a valley looked to be just the site we needed. We pitched our tent, talked a while and retired. It was around 10pm and still light, but we were tired enough to be soon asleep. It was not to be! A couple of miles away at the end of the valley was a large steel mill complex. As it got dark the sky lit up with an enormous red and orange glow, and a large steel hammer made contact, steel on steel, every fifteen seconds. A resounding clang echoed along the valley. With no sleep possible, what could we talk about for the next few hours, especially as we had talked throughout the day? The night passed very slowly and we were up at 4am, tired, hungry and completely knackered. We had no stove as we had called at the odd café on the way up, but had a couple of tins of beans, which we ate cold, reflecting that they didn't taste like those seen on the cowboy films. Then we drank some water from a horse trough in a lane. It tasted nice, but an hour later we were sick, and back came the beans. Nothing was going right. We both felt so bad that we decided to concede defeat and head back home: the story of our life!

A few hours later we were going down a road when I saw a coach approaching. As it passed I said to Vincent, 'I'm sure that's my mum and dad's coach that's visiting Ushaw College.' I turned, and just as the coach disappeared round a bend I saw the sun reflecting off my dad's bald head as he sat on the back seat.

A little later, in mid-1956, summer was at its height. I had been living in Wyke for over a year and not just over the road from Vincent as I had been in Listerhills, but we were still meeting up during the week. Like most families we didn't have a phone at home, so our arrangements were made on parting. Where to? What day? Time and place? Rarely did we not keep to our commitments.

When Vincent, the originator of ideas, suggested joining the Youth Hostel Association, I replied that it sounded like a good idea, but where would we go and how would we get there? His reply was a single word: 'Hitchhiking'. I'd been here before. Even so, after some thought I was convinced, especially as I had now turned eighteen and knew that the army would soon be knocking at my door for my National Service. Perhaps it was time to have some kind of holiday while I could, before putting on a uniform and being sent to goodness knows where. The York and Durham hitchhiking fiascos behind us, we decided to take a week's holiday, hitch-hiking to London.

I wrote off to the YHA and for my 5s 6d duly received my membership card, No. 35351, dated 3 July 1956. On the card there was one rule particularly made for the likes of me and Vincent: youth hostels were for the use of members who travelled on foot, by bicycle or canoe; not for members who were touring by motor car, motor-cycle, or any power-assisted vehicle!

On past experience we would probably be back home in a day, but not put off we set a date and booked a week off work. We had two borrowed rucksacks, and I had a pair of the new American baseball boots with rubber soles, blue in colour with white edging, and white rubber circles over the ankle bone. These would turn the girls' heads!

On a Sunday morning in late July we set off. We met at the bottom of Bridge Street and caught the trolley bus up to Tong. From there we intended to start hitching along the Wakefield Road to reach the old A1, the main road north and south, some 12 miles away. Forty minutes later we were on our road and had started thumbing. We had only just started when a large black saloon car drew up alongside us. The driver, a young man, wound the window down and asked 'Where to?' 'A1,' I replied. 'Hop in,' he said. Vincent and I wasted no time. Within a few seconds Vincent was in the back seat with the rucksacks and I was in the front seat, and off we went. 'Where are you heading?' the driver asked, 'London,' I replied, and to our astonishment he said, 'I'm going to Kent. You're welcome to come all the way, or I'll drop you off in London.'

By now we had both recognised the driver, with his boyish good looks, wavy black hair, piercing blue eyes and well-known voice. He was immaculately dressed in a three piece suit with a flower in his buttonhole. He told us he had been appearing in a play at one of the local theatres for the week and was on his way to Rochester. Although he was star of many films, most people knew him for his role as Wing Commander Guy Gibson in the recent film *The Dambusters*, which had been released the previous year. He enthralled us on the journey

Best wishes.
Richard Todd. Derek

The signed photograph of Richard Todd, who was our chauffeur on our journey to Kent. *(Author's collection)*

talking about this, and his life in films and the theatre, and how he was with the Parachute Regiment on the D-Day landings on Pegasus Bridge in 1944; but he was just as interested in our lives and chosen careers.

We stopped twice on the journey for refreshments at transport cafés on the A1. The treat, he said, on both occasions was on him. I was surprised how small he was when he left the car, as he looked much taller when he was driving and in his films. In the cafés he was recognised, and people approached our table with scraps of paper for his autograph, which he always gave with a smile and a few words.

The journey to London took five hours. In the meantime we had changed our mind, and asked if we could go all the way to Rochester. As Vincent and I had never been to London, our driver made a detour: it was a revelation to see parts of the city, and he pointed out places of interest. Later, as we travelled through the beautiful Kent countryside, we consulted our map and discovered that the nearest youth hostel to Rochester was in a village called Kemsing. Half an hour later, as we approached the village, our friend turned to us and said, 'Not long now. I think I know where the youth hostel is; I'll drop you outside.' I looked at Vincent. He turned away and looked out of the window, leaving me to explain. 'We're supposed to walk, cycle, or even arrive by canoe, but not to travel by any type of motorised vehicle.' He grinned and said, 'Don't worry. I'll drop you about a mile away from the hostel. That should keep you safe from prying eyes.' A few minutes later we kept low when he pointed out the youth hostel as we passed. Still grinning, he came to a stop some distance away. Before we got out of the car we asked him for his autograph. 'Better than a scrap of paper,' he said, 'give me your addresses and I'll send you both a signed photograph.' We stretched ourselves and gathered up our rucksacks, shook hands and he wished us luck. We said our goodbyes, and Richard Todd drove away into the summer evening.

Vincent and I strode away trying to put some life into our bodies after sitting for over five hours. But the most important thing on our minds was how to convince them at the youth hostel that we had just walked 250 miles!

Epilogue

On becoming eighteen years of age on 2 May 1956, I knew it would be only a matter of time before I would be called up to do my National Service. I had seen and heard of older male friends who had gone to the four corners of the world, via the army, navy and air force, so I had no qualms about being conscripted. I knew every male between the ages of eighteen and twenty-one had to comply, so as it was not a lottery and was therefore much easier to accept. In fact, I was looking forward to playing my part.

My birthday had come and gone and it was in September that I was contacted to attend an X-ray and blood test at St Luke's Hospital, this being part of the medical. On 3 October 1956 I had to attend the full medical at the Mechanics' Institute on Tyrrell Street. The Mechanics' Institute had been used during the war years for forces medicals; in fact my dad had attended his medical there in 1942. It had also been used during the First World War for the same purpose. Some of our forbears who had passed through at that time were soldiers in the 'Bradford Pals' Battalion (16th–18th West Yorkshire Regiment), of whom a large number would not return. I thought it was something of an honour to be following in their footsteps.

I arrived at the prescribed time and was ushered into a large room with cubicles. In each cubicle was a local doctor, each of whom was examining a particular part of the anatomy. After filling in a form with the usual questions about my health, I was given a card with letters of the alphabet that designated each cubicle. An orderly queue was formed my dozen or so fellow conscripts. On looking round I didn't recognise any familiar faces. My card was checked by the doctor in each cubicle. Eyes, ears, nose, throat and other parts of the body were examined quickly and professionally. Even holding my testicles and coughing went well, as I had heard all the jokes about this ritual. I was surprised to find in

The impressive Bradford Mechanics' Institute, where generations of Bradford's young men had their Armed Forces medical. I was following in the footsteps of the famous Bradford Pals, 16th and 18th West Yorkshire Regiment. (J.W. Firth)

one cubicle my own doctor, Jack Howard, who had known me since 1945. He was a wonderful doctor, who actually came out of his surgery and into the waiting room. He was always resplendent in a well-cut suit and bow tie and looked cautiously over his spectacles to greet each patient. Dr Howard's speciality at this medical was the chest, and he gave me a thorough examination. On my way out he winked and said, 'You shouldn't have a problem passing the medical.'

When the examinations ended we were taken to a large room and were told to sit down and await our results. Names were called in alphabetical order (discipline had begun). I must admit, even after Dr Howard's confident signal, that I was still very nervous. I had had many ailments when young and had spent most of my life with my coat buttoned up and a scarf around my neck. If the wind blew on me I was ill. My mother, I know, also had reservations about me passing my medical and thought it was odds-on that I would fail.

When my name was called I was sent into an office and asked to sit down by a bespectacled elderly man who was seated at a large desk. He was looking at my notes and writing details on a card. He then stood up and gave me the card, saying, 'You have passed your medical A1.' I said 'Thank you' and took the card from him. I was totally in shock; the outsider had come in at a thousand to one. Nearly all the lads with me on that day passed. The few who had failed seemed happy, with looks of joy on their faces – passing remarks to the effect that we were all losers! No, they were the losers; I was so glad I had passed my medical and never ever changed my mind. Before we left the building we were paraded before a magistrate to swear allegiance to our sovereign, the Queen. No turning back!

I don't remember much about the journey home as I was so elated and couldn't wait to give my mum the good news. But I did a stupid thing. As I passed the kitchen window I could see my mum was ironing. She looked up, and when I opened the kitchen door she had already sat down. Looking at me she said, 'Well, how have you gone on?' 'I've failed, I have a weak heart,' I said. 'Oh no', she replied. 'Not your heart. Anything but that!' She had gone white and tears rolled down her cheeks. I suddenly realised what I had done and how utterly stupid I had been. Taking the card out of my pocket, I held it in the air and shouted, 'No, I've passed A1.' I didn't see my mum's hand move but I felt an enormous slap across my face; my head shook as it jolted back and bells began to ring in my ears. 'Don't you ever do anything like that again,' she said. I never did. A few moments later we were hugging each other, she was still crying and so was I, but my tears were from the good slap she had given me. I had deserved it.

Others were equally shocked at my passing the National Service medical. My best pal Vincent's sisters, Stella and Evelyn, who thought I was soft, especially as sometimes I called for Vincent dressed like Captain Scott of the Antarctic, while Vincent was wearing just a jacket with an open-necked shirt. I couldn't wait to call at their house and wave my A1 card around. As soon as I arrived the family gathered round and said 'Well?' I held the card aloft for all to see, exclaiming 'A1'. I saw the looks of utter shock on their faces – mostly from

NATIONAL SERVICE ACTS

GRADE CARD

Registration No. *BRF 66070*

Mr. *Derek Anthony Joseph Lister*

whose address on his registration card is

47 Ruffed Side

Deep Lane Wyke Bradford

was medically examined at *Bradford*

and placed in GRADE* *I (one)*

on *3 - 10 - 56*

Chairman of Board *R Chester*

Medical Board Stamp *BRADFORD MEDICAL BOARD No. 2*

Man's Signature *Lister*

* The roman numeral denoting the man's Grade
(with number also spelt out) will be entered in
RED ink by the Chairman himself, e.g., Grade I
(one), Grade II (two) (a) (Vision).

N.S.55.   **[P.T.O.**

My medical grade card, showing that I had passed Grade I.
(Author's collection)

Evelyn and Stella. I relished those few minutes. It was ironic that when Vincent attended his National Service medical some months later he failed, because of a perforated eardrum, I think. I was very sorry about this as he would have made a good soldier, but most of all because he was my best childhood mate.

Two weeks after the medical my papers arrived, containing a 1s postal order (this was my 'Queen's shilling'). Also included was a railway warrant to Portsmouth. My journey into the unknown was about to begin.

At 7.30am on a bleak cold morning, Tuesday 30 October 1956, I was standing on the platform of Bradford Exchange station, with a small suitcase and a packet of sandwiches that my mum had made for me. I'm sure I could still hear her crying, albeit only in my mind, for I had said my goodbyes to her earlier. 'Who would have thought', she had said, 'that my little Derek, who at one time as a baby I didn't think would live, is off to join the army!' With me was my dad, who I'm sure had tears in his eyes as he gave me some advice: 'Do as you're ordered,' and much more, concluding with, 'And never volunteer!' Well, he should know, I thought. Dotted around the station were a few fathers also with sons, no mothers or girlfriends – just fathers. Each conscripted son had a small suitcase, similar to mine.

The train was now at the platform, and when the ticket barriers opened a trickle of fathers and sons moved on to the platform. Fathers now began to talk to each other, probably reminiscing about their own departure to join the forces during the war. I got into conversation with the other lads as we all seemed to be making for the same carriage. I soon found out that two of the lads who boarded the train with me were Neil Sutcliffe, from Halifax, and fellow Bradfordian Ken Gee, who were also joining the same regiment as myself. Our goodbyes were said to our respective fathers on the platform with a firm handshake. We were men now, and there was to be no kissing similar to that which had taken place earlier in the morning with mothers and girlfriends. No doubt this scene was being re-enacted all over the United Kingdom.

As the whistle blew and the train moved slowly out of the station we gathered at the open windows and waved goodbye to our fathers. We were on our way, and within twenty-four hours I would be in Her Majesty's Army as 23349511 Private D.A.J. Lister. But that's another story!

I was away from home a long time, and it was a revelation to see how much Bradford had changed on my occasional leave. I knew then that when I finally returned to 'Civvy Street' that Bradford of the 1940s and '50s, and my life then, would just be memories.

**Aged eighteen, one month before National Service, my quiff had gone
and the smile shows a certain foreboding!**
(Author's collection)

School Friends, Playmates and Friends who have Passed Away
Rest In Peace

Paul Baines, Terry Bland, John Boyle, Terry Boyle, Denis Conroy,
Philip Conway, Peter Doherty, Teresa Doherty, Cathryn Hannon,
Joseph Hannon, John Harrison, Ernest Hetherington, Paul Hanson,
Harry Hodgson, Michael Ingleson, Dennis Jones, Malcolm McAllister,
Bernard McCann, Kevin McCusker, Paul McKee, Brian Moran, Terry Moran,
Terry Parry, Geoffrey Peel, Josh Ramsden, Brian Rigby, George Stockley,
Alan Sugden, Donald Swaine, Ken Taylor, John Timlin, John Tindall,
Freddie Vickers, John Walsh, Danny Webster.

Appendix
The Listers

We all have ancestors, direct or indirect. My ancestors cover seventeen generations from the year 1434, before, and through marriage beyond.

My ancestors the Listers (or Lysters) have been associated with the county of Yorkshire, in particular the area around Gisburn, and the Lister-Westby (Westbye) families. These Listers were descended from the Kings and Earls of Mercia on the female side of Isabel de Cliderow. The coronet on the top of the family crest depicts the royal descent for these monarchs of the Mercian kingdom, who were the royalty at that time. This connection also incorporates into my ancestry Hereward the Wake (1032–73; a legendary Saxon hero of the English resistance to the Normans in 1070, whose fate is unknown – but many legends have grown up around him).

Throughout history wealth, fame or destitution could be decided on the toss of a coin: by choosing the winning side in battle, having good friends when in need, being in the right place at the right time, being the first son and heir, or having the good luck not to be taken in early life by pox, plague or other disease. An unlucky example is Captain William Lister, a Parliamentarian officer who was killed at the Battle of Tadcaster in 1642, in the English Civil War.

From the late seventeenth century the Listers appear to have taken up an increasingly wide variety of positions, including innkeepers, church sextons, schoolmasters and farmers.

The Listers' Direct Line of Ancestors

In 1434, when the King of England was the Lancastrian Henry VI, a boy named Christopher Lister was born in Gisburn. He married Joan Calverley (b. 1438) in 1459. Joan of Arc had recently been burnt at the stake in Rouen in France. So begins the earliest we know of the Listers. After six hundred years of English history, with all its joys and pain, trials, tribulations, suffering and glory, the Listers are still here!

Christopher and Joan had a son, Thomas, born in 1464. By this time Edward VI, the Yorkist, was king and the Wars of the Roses were at their height. No doubt the Listers were involved. In 1485 Thomas married Isabel de Cliderow (b. 1465). Their son was another Thomas, who was born in 1487, just after the battle of Bosworth. He married Effamia (Lucy) de Westbye in 1516. Their son was another Thomas (b. 1516). The king by this time was Henry VIII and the battle of Flodden Field had just taken place. This Thomas married Anne King in 1534.

A change of Christian name heralded Anthony Lister, born in 1539, just as King Henry was dissolving the monasteries. Anthony married Margaret Wriglesworth in 1564. Elizabeth I was now Queen and the population of England had swollen to four million. Anthony and Margaret had a son, born in 1565, and reverted to the Christian name Thomas. At this time Elizabeth was having trouble with Mary Queen of Scots.

Thomas married Alice Houghten. They had a son, Anthony (b. 1582). Elizabeth was still queen and Francis Drake was sailing around the world. Anthony married Elizabeth Parker in 1615 and their son, also Anthony, was born in 1617. James I was king and the *Mayflower* was about to sail to the Americas.

Anthony married Eliza (Elizabeth) in 1661; her surname is not known. In 1662 they had a son, John. Charles II was king. John married Maybella in 1697 and they had a son in 1698, again called John. At this time William of Orange and Mary were ruling. John married Mary Swainson in 1723, by which time George I had come to the throne and Christopher Wren had recently died. John and Mary's son was William (b. 1729). George II was now king.

William married Margaret Whitaker (or Whitacer) in 1750, not long after the battle of Culloden. They had a son, also William, in 1756, who married Anne Moorby in 1777, when George III was king and the Americans had just declared independence.

William and Anne produced yet another William, who married Isabella Davy in 1798. The battle of the Nile had just taken place, with a victory for Nelson. William and Isabella returned to the name Thomas for their son who was born in 1807, just as the slave trade was being abolished.

Thomas married Mary Anne Metcalfe, a true daughter of the Dales, in 1837, when Victoria was queen and Samuel Morse had invented the telegraph. They had a son, Thomas, born in 1843. He married Jane Raper in 1867, at the time that England was at war with Abyssinia. They produced another Thomas in 1878. The Zulu Wars were about to begin, with the defeat of the British at Isandhlwana followed by the British victory at Rorke's Drift. Thomas married Lillian Thompson between the Boer War and First World War, in 1907.

APPENDIX

In 1909 Thomas and Lillian had a son Harold, who married Sophia Cooper in 1930. Their first son, Lawrence, was born in 1932, and in 1938, at the height of the Civil War in Spain, your author Derek Anthony Joseph Lister was born.

Derek married Diana Mary Winnard in 1966, and in 1968 a son was born to them, Alexander Viscount. A daughter was born in 1971: Angelique Victoria. Alexander married Michelle Jepson-Smith in 1995. In 1997 Maximillian was born; in 2000 another son, Sebastian, followed.

Derek Lister.
(Author's collection)

About the Author
Soldier, Author and Explorer of Kwa Zululand

Derek Lister was born on 2 May 1938 at Walden Drive, Heaton, Bradford. His life until 1956, when he was called up for National Service, is recounted in detail in this book.

After active service in Aden and Cyprus, Derek returned to Civvy Street, working for a while at Grattan's Warehouse, then Stenhouse Insurance Brokers in Wells Street. During this time he had a rock 'n' roll group called Dal Stevens and the Four Dukes. For five years from 1960 he also worked as a semi-professional disc jockey for Top Rank at the Gaumont and Majestic Ballrooms in Bradford (see his *Bradford's Rock 'n' Roll: The Golden Years 1959–1965*, Bradford Libraries, 1991).

In 1965 Derek embarked on a career in selling and sold insurance, advertising (for the well-known *Bradford Pictorial* magazine), trolls and prams, until 1969 when he joined Concord Lighting, working as a representative in Yorkshire and the North-East. After being made redundant in 1980 he joined the leisure industry, selling and later marketing equipment to sports and leisure centres. Derek retired in 2003. During his last two years of employment and into retirement he wrote the popular book *Bradford's Own*, published by Sutton Publishing in 2004.

Derek's hobbies include writing non-fiction, especially local history, training at the gym, metal detecting and collecting medals. He is a member of the Orders, Medals Research Society and an authority on British campaign medals. He visits South Africa annually, primarily Kwa Zululand, where he lives with the Zulu people and explores the areas involved in the Zulu Wars of 1877–9. He is an authority on the defence of Rorke's Drift and the battle of the Isandhlwana. Among the highlights of these trips was contracting tic fever, confrontation with one of the world's deadliest snakes, the black mamba, and in 2006 breaking his wrist while crossing the Buffalo River in flood.

Lightning Source UK Ltd.
Milton Keynes UK
UKOW041807281111

182846UK00007B/18/P